Microsoft® Office Word 2007

ILLUSTRATED

INTRODUCTORY

Jennifer Duffy

COURSE TECHNOLOGY
CENGAGE Learning·

Australia • Brazil • Japan • Korea • Mexico • Singapore • Spain • United Kingdom • United States

COURSE TECHNOLOGY
CENGAGE Learning™

Microsoft® Office Word® 2007—Illustrated Introductory
Jennifer Duffy

Senior Acquisitions Editor: Marjorie Hunt

Senior Product Manager: Christina Kling Garrett

Associate Product Manager: Rebecca Padrick

Editorial Assistant: Michelle Camisa

Senior Marketing Manager: Joy Stark

Marketing Coordinator: Jennifer Hankin

Contributing Author: Elizabeth Eisner Reding

Developmental Editor: Pamela Conrad

Production Editor: Daphne Barbas

Copy Editors: Harold Johnson, Gary Michael Spahl

QA Manuscript Reviewers: John Freitas,
 Serge Palladino, Jeff Schwartz, Danielle Shaw,
 Teresa Storch

Cover Designers: Elizabeth Paquin, Kathleen Fivel

Cover Artist: Mark Hunt

Composition: GEX Publishing Services

For product information and technology assistance, contact us at
Cengage Learning Customer & Sales Support, 1-800-354-9706

For permission to use material from this text or product, submit all requests online at **cengage.com/permissions**
Further permissions questions can be emailed to
permissionrequest@cengage.com

ISBN-13: 978-1-4239-0526-4

ISBN-10: 1-4239-0526-1

Course Technology
25 Thomson Place
Boston, Massachusetts 02210
USA

Cengage Learning is a leading provider of customized learning solutions with office locations around the globe, including Singapore, the United Kingdom, Australia, Mexico, Brazil, and Japan. Locate your local office at:
international.cengage.com/region

Cengage Learning products are represented in Canada by Nelson Education, Ltd.

For your lifelong learning solutions, visit **course.cengage.com**

Purchase any of our products at your local college store or at our preferred online store **www.ichapters.com**

Trademarks:
Some of the product names and company names used in this book have been used for identification purposes only and may be trademarks or registered trademarks of their respective manufacturers and sellers.

Microsoft and the Office logo are either registered trademarks or trademarks of Microsoft Corporation in the United States and/or other countries. Course Technology is an independent entity from Microsoft Corporation, and not affiliated with Microsoft in any manner. Microsoft product screen shot(s) reprinted with permission from Microsoft Corporation.

Printed in the United States of America
7 8 9 11 10

About This Book

Welcome to *Microsoft Office Word 2007—Illustrated Introductory!* Since the first book in the Illustrated Series was published in 1994, millions of students have used various Illustrated texts to master software skills and learn computer concepts. We are proud to bring you this new Illustrated book on the most exciting version of Microsoft Office ever to release.

As you probably have heard by now, Microsoft completely redesigned this latest version of Office from the ground up. No more menus! No more toolbars! The software changes Microsoft made were based on years of research during which they studied users' needs and work habits. The result is a phenomenal and powerful new version of the software that will make you and your students more productive and help you get better results faster.

Before we started working on this new edition, we also conducted our own research. We reached out to nearly 100 instructors like you who have used previous editions of this book and our Microsoft Office texts. Some of you responded to one of our surveys, others of you generously spent time with us on the phone, telling us your thoughts. Seven of you agreed to serve on our Advisory Board and guided our decisions.

As a result of all the feedback you gave us, we have preserved the features that you love, and made improvements that you suggested and requested. And of course we have covered all the key features of the new software. (For more details on what's new in this edition, please read the Preface.) We are confident that this book and all its available resources will help your students master Microsoft Office Word 2007.

Advisory Board

We thank our Advisory Board who enthusiastically gave us their opinions and guided our every decision on content and design from beginning to end. They are as follows:

Kristen Callahan, Mercer County Community College

Paulette Comet, Assistant Professor, Community College of Baltimore County

Barbara Comfort, J. Sargeant Reynolds Community College

Margaret Cooksey, Tallahassee Community College

Rachelle Hall, Glendale Community College

Hazel Kates, Miami Dade College

Charles Lupico, Thomas Nelson Community College

Author Acknowledgments

Jennifer Duffy Many talented people at Course Technology helped to shape this book — thank you all. I am especially indebted to Pam Conrad for her precision editing, sage encouragement, and endless good cheer throughout the many months of writing. On the home front, I am ever grateful to my husband and children for their patience and support.

Preface

Welcome to *Microsoft Office Word 2007—Illustrated Introductory*. If this is your first experience with the Illustrated series, you'll see that this book has a unique design: each skill is presented on two facing pages, with steps on the left and screens on the right. The layout makes it easy to digest a skill without having to read a lot of text and flip pages to see an illustration.

This book is an ideal learning tool for a wide range of learners—the rookies will find the clean design easy to follow and focused with only essential information presented, and the hotshots will appreciate being able to move quickly through the lessons to find the information they need without reading a lot of text. The design also makes this a great reference after the course is over! See the illustration on the right to learn more about the pedagogical and design elements of a typical lesson.

What's New in This Edition

We've made many changes and enhancements to this edition to make it the best ever. Here are some highlights of what's new:

- **New Getting Started with Microsoft® Office 2007 Unit**—This unit begins the book and gets students up to speed on features of Office 2007 that are common to all the applications, such as the Ribbon, the Office button, and the Quick Access toolbar.

- **Real Life Independent Challenge**—The new Real Life Independent Challenge exercises offer students the opportunity to create projects that are meaningful to their lives, such as a personal letterhead.

- **New Case Study**—A new case study featuring Quest Specialty Travel provides a practical and fun scenario that students can relate to as they learn skills. This fictional company offers a wide variety of tours around the world.

Each two-page spread focuses on a single skill.

Concise text introduces the basic principles in the lesson and integrates a real-world case study.

UNIT C
Word 2007

Working with Indents

When you **indent** a paragraph, you move its edge in from the left or right margin. You can indent the entire left or right edge of a paragraph, just the first line, or all lines except the first line. The **indent markers** on the horizontal ruler indicate the indent settings for the paragraph in which the insertion point is located. Dragging an indent marker to a new location on the ruler is one way to change the indentation of a paragraph; changing the indent settings in the Paragraph group on the Page Layout tab is another; and using the indent buttons in the Paragraph group on the Home tab is a third. Table C-2 describes different types of indents and some of the methods for creating each. You indent several paragraphs in the report.

STEPS

QUICK TIP
Press [Tab] at the beginning of a paragraph to indent the first line ½".

1. **Press [Ctrl][Home], place the insertion point in the italicized paragraph under the title, then click the Increase Indent button in the Paragraph group on the Home tab**
   The entire paragraph is indented ½" from the left margin, as shown in Figure C-15. The indent marker also moves to the ½" mark on the horizontal ruler. Each time you click the Increase Indent button, the left edge of a paragraph moves another ½" to the right.

2. **Click the Decrease Indent button in the Paragraph group**
   The left edge of the paragraph moves ½" to the left, and the indent marker moves back to the left margin.

TROUBLE
Take care to drag only the First Line Indent marker. If you make a mistake, click the Undo button, then try again.

3. **Drag the First Line Indent marker ▽ to the ¼" mark on the horizontal ruler**
   Figure C-16 shows the First Line Indent marker being dragged. The first line of the paragraph is indented ¼". Dragging the First Line Indent marker indents only the first line of a paragraph.

4. **Scroll to the bottom of page 1, place the insertion point in the quotation, click the Page Layout tab, click the Indent Left text box in the Paragraph group, type .5, click the Indent Right text box, type .5, then press [Enter]**
   The left and right edges of the paragraph are indented ½" from the margins, as shown in Figure C-17.

5. **Press [Ctrl][Home], place the insertion point in the italicized paragraph, then click the launcher in the Paragraph group**
   The Paragraph dialog box opens. You can use the Indents and Spacing tab to check or change the alignment, indentation, and paragraph and line spacing settings applied to a paragraph.

6. **Click the Special list arrow, click (none), click OK, then save your changes**
   The first line indent is removed from the paragraph.

TABLE C-2: Types of indents

indent type: description	to create
Left indent: The left edge of a paragraph is moved in from the left margin	Enter the position you want the left edge of the paragraph to align in the Indent Left text box in the Paragraph group on the Page Layout tab; or drag the Left Indent marker on the ruler right to the position where you want the left edge of the paragraph to align
Right indent: The right edge of a paragraph is moved in from the right margin	Enter the position you want the right edge of the paragraph to align in the Indent Right text box in the Paragraph group on the Page Layout tab; or drag the Right Indent marker on the ruler left to the position where you want the right edge of the paragraph to end
First line indent: The first line of a paragraph is indented more than the subsequent lines	Drag ▽ on the ruler right to the position where you want the first line of the paragraph to begin; or activate the First Line Indent marker in the tab indicator, and then click the ruler at the position where you want the first line of the paragraph to begin
Hanging indent: The subsequent lines of a paragraph are indented more than the first line	Drag the Hanging Indent marker on the ruler right to the position where you want the hanging indent to begin; or activate the Hanging Indent marker in the tab indicator, and then click the ruler at the position where you want the second and remaining lines of the paragraph to begin
Negative indent (or Outdent): The left edge of a paragraph is moved to the left of the left margin	Enter the negative position you want the left edge of the paragraph to align in the Indent Left text box in the Paragraph group on the Page Layout tab; or drag the Left Indent marker on the ruler left to the position where you want the negative indent to begin

Word 61   Formatting Text and Paragraphs

Hints as well as troubleshooting advice appear right where you need it—next to the step itself.

Tables are quickly accessible summaries of key terms, buttons, or keyboard alternatives connected with the lesson material. Students can refer easily to this information when working on their own projects at a later time.

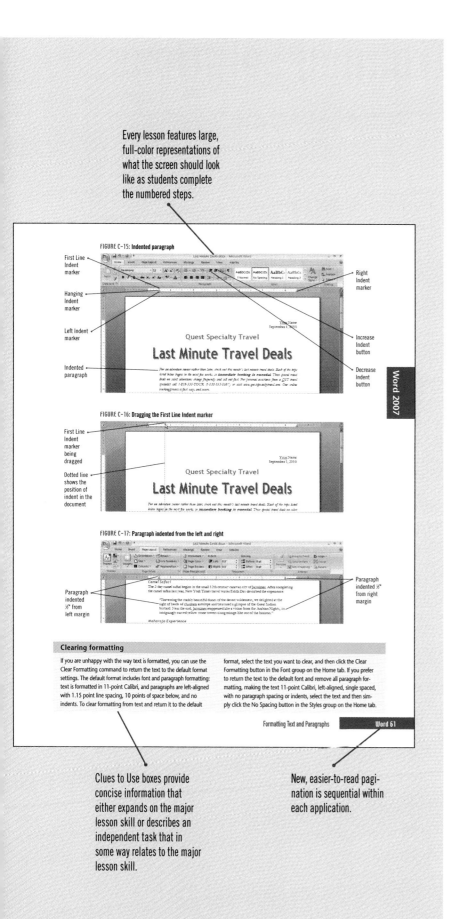

FIGURE C-15: Indented paragraph

First Line Indent marker

Hanging Indent marker

Left Indent marker

Indented paragraph

Right Indent marker

Increase Indent button

Decrease Indent button

Quest Specialty Travel
Last Minute Travel Deals

FIGURE C-16: Dragging the First Line Indent marker

First Line Indent marker being dragged

Dotted line shows the position of indent in the document

Quest Specialty Travel
Last Minute Travel Deals

FIGURE C-17: Paragraph indented from the left and right

Paragraph indented ½" from left margin

Paragraph indented ½" from right margin

Clearing formatting

If you are unhappy with the way text is formatted, you can use the Clear Formatting command to return the text to the default format settings. The default format includes font and paragraph formatting: text is formatted in 11-point Calibri, and paragraphs are left-aligned with 1.15 point line spacing, 10 points of space below, and no indents. To clear formatting from text and return it to the default format, select the text you want to clear, and then click the Clear Formatting button in the Font group on the Home tab. If you prefer to return the text to the default font and remove all paragraph formatting, making the text 11-point Calibri, left-aligned, single spaced, with no paragraph spacing or indents, select the text and then simply click the No Spacing button in the Styles group on the Home tab.

Formatting Text and Paragraphs   **Word 61**

Word 2007

- Content Improvements—All of the content in the book has been updated to cover Office 2007 and also to address instructor feedback. See the instructor resource CD for details on specific content changes for Word.

Assignments

The lessons use Quest Specialty Travel, a fictional adventure travel company, as the case study. The assignments on the light purple pages at the end of each unit increase in difficulty. Data files and case studies provide a variety of interesting and relevant business applications. Assignments include:

- **Concepts Reviews** consist of multiple choice, matching, and screen identification questions.

- **Skills Reviews** provide additional hands on, step-by-step reinforcement.

- **Independent Challenges** are case projects requiring critical thinking and application of the unit skills. The Independent Challenges increase in difficulty, with the first one in each unit being the easiest. Independent Challenges 2 and 3 become increasingly open-ended, requiring more independent problem solving.

- **Real Life Independent Challenges** are practical exercises in which students create documents to help them with their every day lives.

- **Advanced Challenge Exercises** set within the Independent Challenges provide optional steps for more advanced students.

- **Visual Workshops** are practical, self-graded capstone projects that require independent problem solving.

Assessment & Training Solutions

SAM 2007

SAM 2007 helps bridge the gap between the classroom and the real world by allowing students to train and test on important computer skills in an active, hands-on environment.

SAM 2007's easy-to-use system includes powerful interactive exams, training or projects on critical applications such as Word, Excel, Access, PowerPoint, Outlook, Windows, the Internet, and much more. SAM simulates the application environment, allowing students to demonstrate their knowledge and think through the skills by performing real-world tasks.

Designed to be used with the Illustrated series, SAM 2007 includes built-in page references so students can print helpful study guides that match the Illustrated textbooks used in class. Powerful administrative options allow instructors to schedule exams and assignments, secure tests, and run reports with almost limitless flexibility.

Student Edition Labs

Our Web-based interactive labs help students master hundreds of computer concepts, including input and output devices, file management and desktop applications, computer ethics, virus protection, and much more. Featuring up-to-the-minute content, eye-popping graphics, and rich animation, the highly interactive Student Edition Labs offer students an alternative way to learn through dynamic observation, step-by-step practice, and challenging review questions. Also available on CD at an additional cost.

Online Content   Blackboard

Blackboard is the leading distance learning solution provider and class-management platform today. Course Technology has partnered with Blackboard to bring you premium online content. Instructors: Content for use with *Microsoft Office Word 2007—Illustrated Introductory* is available in a Blackboard Course Cartridge and may include topic reviews, case projects, review questions, test banks, practice tests, custom syllabi, and more.

Course Technology also has solutions for several other learning management systems. Please visit *www.course.com* today to see what's available for this title.

Instructor Resources

The Instructor Resources CD is Course Technology's way of putting the resources and information needed to teach and learn effectively into your hands. With an integrated array of teaching and learning tools that offers you and your students a broad range of technology-based instructional options, we believe this CD represents the highest quality and most cutting edge resources available to instructors today. Many of these resources are available at *www.course.com*. The resources available with this book are:

- **Instructor's Manual**—Available as an electronic file, the Instructor's Manual includes detailed lecture topics with teaching tips for each unit.

- **Sample Syllabus**—Prepare and customize your course easily using this sample course outline.

- **PowerPoint Presentations**—Each unit has a corresponding PowerPoint presentation that you can use in lecture, distribute to your students, or customize to suit your course.

- **Figure Files**—The figures in the text are provided on the Instructor Resources CD to help you illustrate key topics or concepts. You can create traditional overhead transparencies by printing the figure files. Or you can create electronic slide shows by using the figures in a presentation program such as PowerPoint.

- **Solutions to Exercises**—Solutions to Exercises contains every file students are asked to create or modify in the lessons and end-of-unit material. Also provided in this section, there is a document outlining the solutions for the end-of-unit Concepts Review, Skills Review, and Independent Challenges. An Annotated Solution File and Grading Rubric accompany each file and can be used together for quick and easy grading.

- **Data Files for Students**—To complete most of the units in this book, your students will need Data Files. You can post the Data Files on a file server for students to copy. The Data Files are available on the Instructor Resources CD, the Review Pack, and can also be downloaded from www.course.com. In this edition, we have included a lesson on downloading the Data Files for this book, see page xvi.

Instruct students to use the Data Files List included on the Review Pack and the Instructor Resources CD. This list gives instructions on copying and organizing files.

- **ExamView**—ExamView is a powerful testing software package that allows you to create and administer printed, computer (LAN-based), and Internet exams. ExamView includes hundreds of questions that correspond to the topics covered in this text, enabling students to generate detailed study guides that include page references for further review. The computer-based and Internet testing components allow students to take exams at their computers, and also saves you time by grading each exam automatically.

CourseCasts—Learning on the Go. Always available...always relevant.

Want to keep up with the latest technology trends relevant to you? Visit our site to find a library of podcasts, CourseCasts, featuring a "CourseCast of the Week," and download them to your mp3 player at *http://coursecasts.course.com*.

Our fast-paced world is driven by technology. You know because you're an active participant—always on the go, always keeping up with technological trends, and always learning new ways to embrace technology to power your life.

Ken Baldauf, a faculty member of the Florida State University Computer Science Department, is responsible for teaching technology classes to thousands of FSU students each year. He knows what you know; he knows what you want to learn. He's also an expert in the latest technology and will sort through and aggregate the most pertinent news and information so you can spend your time enjoying technology, rather than trying to figure it out.

Visit us at *http://coursecasts.course.com* to learn on the go!

Brief Contents

Contents

WORD 2007

Unit E: Creating and Formatting Tables   105

WORD 2007

Unit F: Illustrating Documents with Graphics   129

WORD 2007 | **Unit G: Working with Themes and Building Blocks** | **153**

WORD 2007 | **Unit H: Merging Word Documents** | **177**

Read This Before You Begin

Frequently Asked Questions

What are Data Files?

A Data File is a partially completed Word document or another type of file that you use to complete the steps in the units and exercises to create the final document that you submit to your instructor. Each unit opener page lists the Data Files that you need for that unit.

Where are the Data Files?

Your instructor will provide the Data Files to you or direct you to a location on a network drive from which you can download them. Alternatively, you can follow the instructions on the next page to download the Data Files from this book's Web page.

What software was used to write and test this book?

This book was written and tested using a typical installation of Microsoft Office 2007 installed on a computer with a typical installation of Microsoft Windows Vista. The browser used for any steps that require a browser is Internet Explorer 7.

If you are using this book on Windows XP, please see the next page "Important notes for Windows XP users." If you are using this book on Windows Vista, please see the Appendix at the end of this book.

Do I need to be connected to the Internet to complete the steps and exercises in this book?

Some of the exercises in this book assume that your computer is connected to the Internet. If you are not connected to the Internet, see your instructor for information on how to complete the exercises.

What do I do if my screen is different from the figures shown in this book?

This book was written and tested on computers with monitors set at a resolution of 1024 × 768. If your screen shows more or less information than the figures in the book, your monitor is probably set at a higher or lower resolution. If you don't see something on your screen, you might have to scroll down or up to see the object identified in the figures.

The Ribbon—the blue area at the top of the screen—in Microsoft Office 2007 adapts to different resolutions. If your monitor is set at a lower resolution than 1024 × 768, you might not see all of the buttons shown in the figures. The groups of buttons will always appear, but the entire group might be condensed into a single button that you need to click to access the buttons described in the instructions. For example, the figures and steps in this book assume that the Editing group on the Home tab in Word looks like the following:

1024 × 768 Editing Group

Editing Group on the
Home Tab of the
Ribbon at 1024 × 768

If your resolution is set to 800 × 600, the Ribbon in Word will look like the following figure, and you will need to click the Editing button to access the buttons that are visible in the Editing group.

800 × 600 Editing Group

Editing Group
on the Home Tab of the
Ribbon at 800 × 600

800 × 600 Editing Group clicked

Editing Group on the Home Tab of the Ribbon at
800 × 600 is selected to show available buttons

Important Notes for Windows XP Users

The screenshots in this book show Microsoft Office 2007 running on Windows Vista. However, if you are using Microsoft Windows XP, you can still use this book because Office 2007 runs virtually the same on both platforms. There are a few differences that you will encounter if you are using Windows XP. Read this section to understand the differences.

Dialog boxes

If you are a Windows XP user, dialog boxes shown in this book will look slightly different than what you see on your screen. Dialog boxes for Windows XP have a blue title bar, instead of a gray title bar. However, beyond this superficial difference in appearance, the options in the dialog boxes across platforms are the same. For instance, the screen shots below show the Font dialog box running on Windows XP and the Font dialog box running on Windows Vista.

FIGURE 1: Dialog box in Windows XP

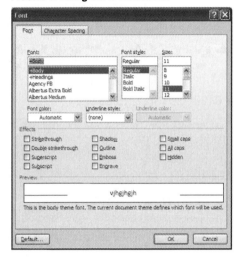

FIGURE 2: Dialog box in Windows Vista

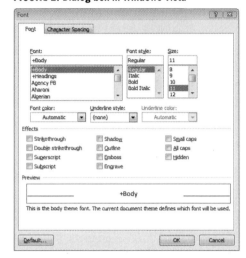

Alternate Steps for Windows XP Users

Nearly all of the steps in this book work exactly the same for Windows XP users. However, there are a few tasks that will require you to complete slightly different steps. This section provides alternate steps for a few specific skills.

Starting a program

1. Click the **Start button** on the taskbar
2. Point to **All Programs**, point to **Microsoft Office**, then click the application you want to use

FIGURE 3: Starting a program

Saving a file for the first time

1. Click the **Office button**, then click **Save As**
2. Type a name for your file in the File Name text box
3. Click the **Save in list arrow**, then navigate to the drive and folder where you store your Data Files
4. Click **Save**

Opening a file

1. Click the **Office button**, then click **Open**
2. Click the **Look in list arrow**, then navigate to the drive and folder where you store your Data Files
3. Click the file you want to open
4. Click **Open**

FIGURE 4: Save As dialog box

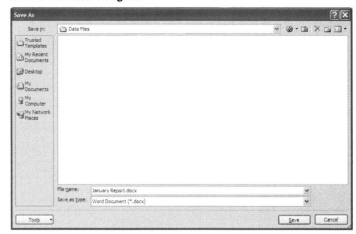

FIGURE 5: Open dialog box

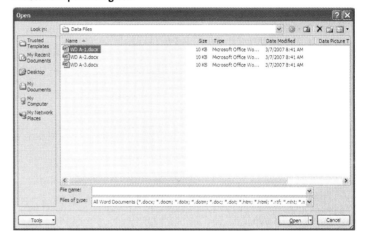

Downloading Data Files for This Book

In order to complete many of the lesson steps and exercises in this book, you are asked to open and save Data Files. A Data File is a partially completed Word document, Excel workbook, Access database, PowerPoint presentation, or another type of file that you use as a starting point to complete the steps in the units and exercises. The benefit of using a Data File is that it saves you the time and effort needed to create a file; you can simply open a Data File, save it with a new name (so the original file remains intact), then make changes to it to complete lesson steps or an exercise. Your instructor will provide the Data Files to you or direct you to a location on a network drive from which you can download them. Alternatively, you can follow the steps below to download the Data Files from this book's Web page.

1. Start Internet Explorer, type www.cengage.com/coursetechnology/ in the address bar, then press [Enter]

2. Click in the Enter ISBN Search text box, type 9781423905264, then click Search

3. When the page opens for this textbook, click the About this Product link for the Student, point to Student Downloads to expand the menu, and then click the Data Files for Students link

4. If the File Download – Security Warning dialog box opens, click Save. (If no dialog box appears, skip this step and go to Step 6)

5. If the Save As dialog box opens, click the Save in list arrow at the top of the dialog box, select a folder on your USB drive or hard disk to download the file to, then click Save

6. Close Internet Explorer and then open Computer and display the contents of the drive and folder to which you downloaded the file

7. Double-click the file 9781423905264.exe in the drive or folder, then, if the Open File – Security Warning dialog box opens, click Run

8. In the WinZip Self-Extractor window, navigate to the drive and folder where you want to unzip the files to, then click Unzip

9. When the WinZip Self-Extractor displays a dialog box listing the number of files that have unzipped successfully, click OK, click Close in the WinZip Self-Extractor dialog box, then close Computer

    The Data Files are now unzipped in the folder you specified in Step 8 and ready for you to open and use.

Getting Started with Microsoft Office 2007

Files You Will Need:

OFFICE A-1.xlsx

Microsoft Office 2007 is a group of software programs designed to help you create documents, collaborate with co-workers, and track and analyze information. Each program is designed so you can work quickly and efficiently to create professional-looking results. You use different Office programs to accomplish specific tasks, such as writing a letter or producing a sales presentation, yet all the programs have a similar look and feel. Once you become familiar with one program, you'll find it easy to transfer your knowledge to the others. This unit introduces you to the most frequently used programs in Office, as well as common features they all share.

OBJECTIVES

Understand the Office 2007 Suite

Start and exit an Office program

View the Office 2007 user interface

Create and save a file

Open a file and save it with a
new name

View and print your work

Get Help and close a file

UNIT
A
Office 2007

Understanding the Office 2007 Suite

Microsoft Office 2007 features an intuitive, context-sensitive user interface, so you can get up to speed faster and use advanced features with greater ease. The programs in Office are bundled together in a group called a **suite** (although you can also purchase them separately). The Office suite is available in several configurations, but all include Word and Excel. Other configurations include PowerPoint, Access, Outlook, Publisher, and/or others. Each program in Office is best suited for completing specific types of tasks, though there is some overlap in terms of their capabilities.

DETAILS

The Office programs covered in this book include:

- **Microsoft Office Word 2007**

  When you need to create any kind of text-based document, such as memos, newsletters, or multi-page reports, Word is the program to use. You can easily make your documents look great by inserting eye-catching graphics and using formatting tools such as themes. **Themes** are predesigned combinations of color and formatting attributes you can apply, and are available in most Office programs. The Word document shown in Figure A-1 was formatted with the Solstice theme.

- **Microsoft Office Excel 2007**

  Excel is the perfect solution when you need to work with numeric values and make calculations. It puts the power of formulas, functions, charts, and other analytical tools into the hands of every user, so you can analyze sales projections, figure out loan payments, and present your findings in style. The Excel worksheet shown in Figure A-1 tracks personal expenses. Because Excel automatically recalculates results whenever a value changes, the information is always up-to-date. A chart illustrates how the monthly expenses are broken down.

- **Microsoft Office PowerPoint 2007**

  Using PowerPoint, it's easy to create powerful presentations complete with graphics, transitions, and even a soundtrack. Using professionally designed themes and clip art, you can quickly and easily create dynamic slideshows such as the one shown in Figure A-1.

- **Microsoft Office Access 2007**

  Access helps you keep track of large amounts of quantitative data, such as product inventories or employee records. The form shown in Figure A-1 was created for a grocery store inventory database. Employees use the form to enter data about each item. Using Access enables employees to quickly find specific information such as price and quantity, without hunting through store shelves and stockrooms.

Microsoft Office has benefits beyond the power of each program, including:

- **Common user interface: Improving business processes**

  Because the Office suite programs have a similar **interface**, or look and feel, your experience using one program's tools makes it easy to learn those in the other programs. Office documents are **compatible** with one another, meaning that you can easily incorporate, or **integrate**, an Excel chart into a PowerPoint slide, or an Access table into a Word document.

- **Collaboration: Simplifying how people work together**

  Office recognizes the way people do business today, and supports the emphasis on communication and knowledge-sharing within companies and across the globe. All Office programs include the capability to incorporate feedback—called **online collaboration**—across the Internet or a company network.

FIGURE A-1: Microsoft Office 2007 documents

Word document

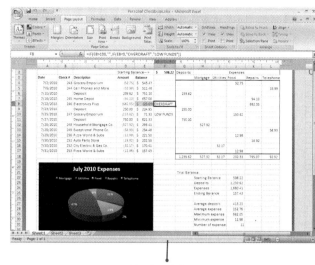

Excel worksheet

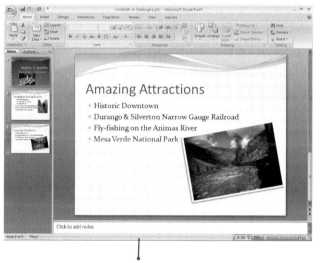

PowerPoint presentation

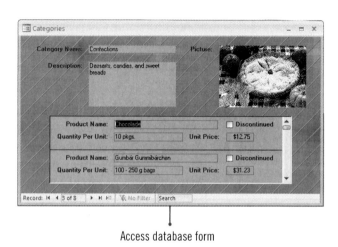

Access database form

Deciding which program to use

Every Office program includes tools that go far beyond what you might expect. For example, although Excel is primarily designed for making calculations, you can use it to create a database. So when you're planning a project, how do you decide which Office program to use? The general rule of thumb is to use the program best suited for your intended task, and make use of supporting tools in the program if you need them. Word is best for creating text-based documents, Excel is best for making mathematical calculations,

PowerPoint is best for preparing presentations, and Access is best for managing quantitative data. Although the capabilities of Office are so vast that you *could* create an inventory in Excel or a budget in Word, you'll find greater flexibility and efficiency by using the program designed for the task. And remember, you can always create a file in one program, and then insert it in a document in another program when you need to, such as including sales projections (Excel) in a memo (Word).

Starting and Exiting an Office Program

The first step in using an Office program is of course to open, or **launch**, it on your computer. You have a few choices for how to launch a program, but the easiest way is to click the Start button on the Windows taskbar, or to double-click an icon on your desktop. You can have multiple programs open on your computer simultaneously, and you can move between open programs by clicking the desired program or document button on the taskbar or by using the [Alt][Tab] keyboard shortcut combination. When working, you'll often want to open multiple programs in Office, and switch among them throughout the day. Begin by launching a few Office programs now.

STEPS

QUICK TIP
You can also launch a program by double-clicking a desktop icon or clicking an entry on the Recent Items menu.

QUICK TIP
It is not necessary to close one program before opening another.

QUICK TIP
If there isn't room on your taskbar to display the entire name of each button, you can point to any button to see the full name in a Screentip.

QUICK TIP
As you work in Windows, your computer adapts to your activities. You may notice that after clicking the Start button, the name of the program you want to open appears in the Start menu; if so, you can click it to start the program.

1. **Click the Start button 🔵 on the taskbar**
   The Start menu opens, as shown in Figure A-2. If the taskbar is hidden, you can display it by pointing to the bottom of the screen. Depending on your taskbar property settings, the taskbar may be displayed at all times, or only when you point to that area of the screen. For more information, or to change your taskbar properties, consult your instructor or technical support person.

2. **Point to All Programs, click Microsoft Office, then click Microsoft Office Word 2007**
   Microsoft Office Word 2007 starts and the program window opens on your screen.

3. **Click 🔵 on the taskbar, point to All Programs, click Microsoft Office, then click Microsoft Office Excel 2007**
   Microsoft Office Excel 2007 starts and the program window opens, as shown in Figure A-3. Word is no longer visible, but it remains open. The taskbar displays a button for each open program and document. Because this Excel document is **active**, or in front and available, the Microsoft Excel – Book1 button on the taskbar appears in a darker shade.

4. **Click Document1 – Microsoft Word on the taskbar**
   Clicking a button on the taskbar activates that program and document. The Word program window is now in front, and the Document1 – Microsoft Word taskbar button appears shaded.

5. **Click 🔵 on the taskbar, point to All Programs, click Microsoft Office, then click Microsoft Office PowerPoint 2007**
   Microsoft Office PowerPoint 2007 starts, and becomes the active program.

6. **Click Microsoft Excel – Book1 on the taskbar**
   Excel is now the active program.

7. **Click 🔵 on the taskbar, point to All Programs, click Microsoft Office, then click Microsoft Office Access 2007**
   Microsoft Office Access 2007 starts, and becomes the active program.

8. **Point to the taskbar to display it, if necessary**
   Four Office programs are open simultaneously.

9. **Click the Office button 🔵, then click Exit Access, as shown in Figure A-4**
   Access closes, leaving Excel active and Word and PowerPoint open.

FIGURE A-2: Start menu

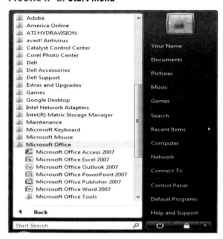

FIGURE A-3: Excel program window and Windows taskbar

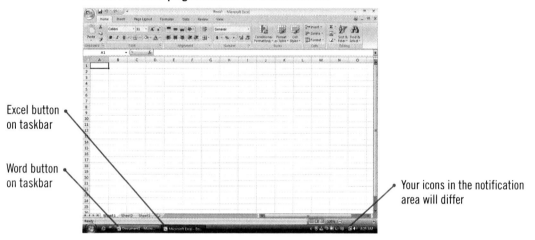

Excel button on taskbar

Word button on taskbar

Your icons in the notification area will differ

FIGURE A-4: Exiting Microsoft Office Access

Microsoft Office button

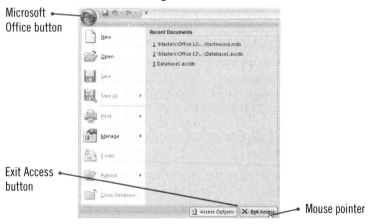

Exit Access button

Mouse pointer

Using shortcut keys to move between Office programs

As an alternative to the Windows taskbar, you can use a keyboard shortcut to move among open Office programs. The [Alt][Tab] keyboard combination lets you either switch quickly to the next open program, or choose one from a palette. To switch immediately to the next open program, press [Alt][Tab]. To choose from all open programs, press and hold [Alt], then press and release [Tab] without releasing [Alt]. A palette opens on screen, displaying the icon and filename of each open program and file. Each time you press [Tab] while holding [Alt], the selection cycles to the next open file. Release [Alt] when the program/file you want to activate is selected.

Viewing the Office 2007 User Interface

One of the benefits of using Office is that the programs have much in common, making them easy to learn and making it simple to move from one to another. Individual Office programs have always shared many features, but the innovations in the Office 2007 user interface mean even greater similarity among them all. That means you can also use your knowledge of one program to get up to speed in another. A **user interface** is a collective term for all the ways you interact with a software program. The user interface in Office 2007 includes a more intuitive way of choosing commands, working with files, and navigating in the program window. Familiarize yourself with some of the common interface elements in Office by examining the PowerPoint program window.

STEPS

1. **Click Microsoft PowerPoint – [Presentation1] on the taskbar**

   PowerPoint becomes the active program. Refer to Figure A-5 to identify common elements of the Office user interface. The **document window** occupies most of the screen. In PowerPoint, a blank slide appears in the document window, so you can build your slide show. At the top of every Office program window is a **title bar**, which displays the document and program name. Below the title bar is the **Ribbon**, which displays commands you're likely to need for the current task. Commands are organized into **tabs**. The tab names appear at the top of the Ribbon, and the active tab appears in front with its name highlighted. The Ribbon in every Office program includes tabs specific to the program, but all include a Home tab on the far left, for the most popular tasks in that program.

2. **Click the Office button**

   The Office menu opens. This menu contains commands common to most Office programs, such as opening a file, saving a file, and closing the current program. Next to the Office button is the **Quick Access toolbar**, which includes buttons for common Office commands.

3. **Click again to close it, then point to the Save button on the Quick Access toolbar, but do not click it**

   You can point to any button in Office to see a description; this is a good way to learn the available choices.

4. **Click the Design tab on the Ribbon**

   To display a different tab, you click its name on the Ribbon. Each tab arranges related commands into **groups** to make features easy to find. The Themes group displays available themes in a **gallery**, or palette of choices you can browse. Many groups contain a **dialog box launcher**, an icon you can click to open a dialog box or task pane for the current group, which offers an alternative way to choose commands.

5. **Move the mouse pointer over the Aspect theme in the Themes group as shown in Figure A-6, but do not click the mouse button**

   Because you have not clicked the theme, you have not actually made any changes to the slide. With the **Live Preview** feature, you can point to a choice, see the results right in the document, and then decide whether you want to make the change.

6. **Move away from the Ribbon and towards the slide**

   If you clicked the Aspect theme, it would be applied to this slide. Instead, the slide remains unchanged.

7. **Point to the Zoom slider on the status bar, then drag to the right until the Zoom percentage reads 166%**

   The slide display is enlarged. Zoom tools are located on the status bar. You can drag the slider or click the plus and minus buttons to zoom in/out on an area of interest. The percentage tells you the zoom effect.

8. **Drag the Zoom slider on the status bar to the left until the Zoom percentage reads 73%**

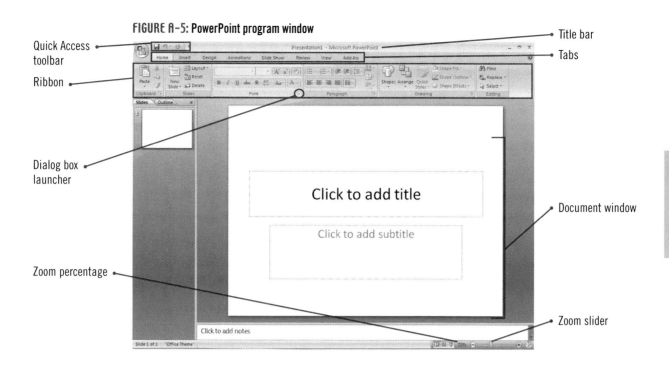

FIGURE A-5: PowerPoint program window

Quick Access toolbar

Ribbon

Dialog box launcher

Zoom percentage

Title bar

Tabs

Document window

Zoom slider

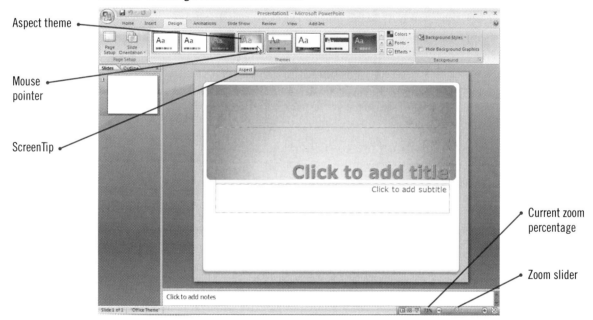

FIGURE A-6: Viewing a theme with Live Preview

Aspect theme

Mouse pointer

ScreenTip

Current zoom percentage

Zoom slider

Customizing the Quick Access toolbar

You can customize the Quick Access toolbar to display your favorite commands. To do so, click the Customize Quick Access Toolbar button in the title bar, then click the command you want to add. If you don't see the command in the list, click More Commands to open the Customize tab of the Options dialog box. In the Options dialog box, use the Choose commands from list to choose a category, click the desired command in the list on the left, click Add to add it to the Quick Access toolbar, then click OK. To remove a button from the toolbar, click the name in the list on the right, then click Remove. To add a command to the Quick Access toolbar on

the fly, simply right-click the button on the Ribbon, then click Add to Quick Access Toolbar on the shortcut menu. You can also use the Customize Quick Access Toolbar button to move the toolbar below the ribbon, by clicking Show Below the Ribbon, or to minimize the Ribbon so it takes up less space onscreen. If you click Minimize the Ribbon, the Ribbon is minimized to display only the tabs. When you click a tab, the Ribbon opens so you can choose a command; once you choose a command, the Ribbon closes again, and only the tabs are visible.

Creating and Saving a File

When working in a program, one of the first things you need to do is to create and save a file. A **file** is a stored collection of data. Saving a file enables you to work on a project now, then put it away and work on it again later. In some Office programs, including Word, Excel, and PowerPoint, a new file is automatically created when you start the program, so all you have to do is enter some data and save it. In Access, you must expressly create a file before you enter any data. You should give your files meaningful names and save them in an appropriate location, so they're easy to find. Use Microsoft Word to familiarize yourself with the process of creating and saving a document. First you'll type some notes about a possible location for a corporate meeting, then you'll save the information for later use.

STEPS

1. **Click** Document1 – Microsoft Word **on the taskbar**

2. **Type** Locations for Corporate Meeting, **then press** [Enter] **twice**
   The text appears in the document window, and a cursor blinks on a new blank line. The cursor indicates where the next typed text will appear.

3. **Type** Las Vegas, NV, **press** [Enter], **type** Orlando, FL, **press** [Enter], **type** Chicago, IL, **press** [Enter] **twice, then type your name**
   Compare your document to Figure A-7.

> **QUICK TIP**
> A filename can be up to 255 characters, including a file extension, and can include upper- or lowercase characters and spaces, but not ?, ", /, \, <, >, *, |, or :.

4. **Click the** Save button 🖫 **on the Quick Access toolbar**
   Because this is the first time you are saving this document, the Save As dialog box opens, as shown in Figure A-8. The Save As dialog box includes options for assigning a filename and storage location. Once you save a file for the first time, clicking 🖫 saves any changes to the file *without* opening the Save As dialog box, because no additional information is needed. In the Address bar, Office displays the default location for where to save the file, but you can change to any location. In the File name field, Office displays a suggested name for the document based on text in the file, but you can enter a different name.

5. **Type** Potential Corporate Meeting Locations
   The text you type replaces the highlighted text.

> **QUICK TIP**
> You can create a desktop icon that you can double-click to both launch a program and open a document, by saving it to the desktop.

6. **In the Save As dialog box, use the Address bar or Navigation pane to navigate to the drive and folder where you store your Data Files**
   Many students store files on a flash drive or Zip drive, but you can also store files on your computer, a network drive, or any storage device indicated by your instructor or technical support person.

> **QUICK TIP**
> To create a new blank file when a file is open, click the Office button, click New, then click Create.

7. **Click** Save
   The Save As dialog box closes, the new file is saved to the location you specified, then the name of the document appears in the title bar, as shown in Figure A-9. (You may or may not see a file extension.) See Table A-1 for a description of the different types of files you create in Office, and the file extensions associated with each. You can save a file in an earlier version of a program by choosing from the list of choices in the Save as type list arrow in the Save As dialog box.

TABLE A-1: Common filenames and default file extensions

File created in	is called a	and has the default extension
Excel	workbook	.xlsx
Word	document	.docx
Access	database	.accdb
PowerPoint	presentation	.pptx

FIGURE A-7: Creating a document in Word

Save button

Your name should appear here

Insertion point

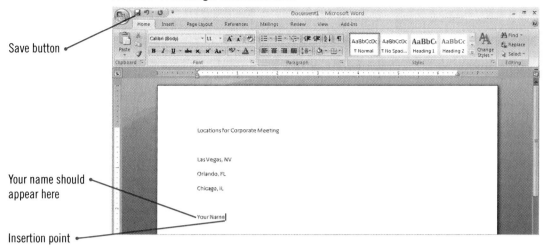

FIGURE A-8: Save As dialog box

Address bar

Navigation pane; your links and Folders setting may differ

File name field; your computer may not be set to display file extensions

Previous Locations list arrow

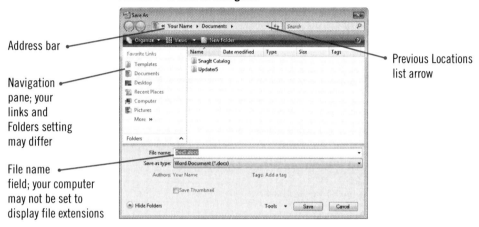

FIGURE A-9: Named Word document

Name appears in title bar

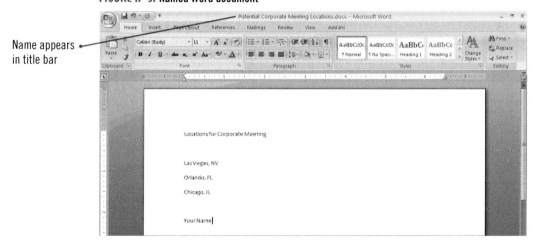

Using the Office Clipboard

You can use the Office Clipboard to cut and copy items from one Office program and paste them into others. The Clipboard can store a maximum of 24 items. To access it, open the Office Clipboard task pane by clicking the launcher in the Clipboard group in the Home tab. Each time you copy a selection, it is saved in the Office Clipboard. Each entry in the Office Clipboard includes an icon that tells you the program in which it was created. To paste an entry, click in the document where you want it to appear, then click the item in the Office Clipboard. To delete an item from the Office Clipboard, right-click the item, then click Delete.

Opening a File and Saving it with a New Name

In many cases as you work in Office, you start with a blank document, but often you need to use an existing file. It might be a file you or a co-worker created earlier as a work-in-progress, or it could be a complete document that you want to use as the basis for another. For example, you might want to create a budget for this year using the budget you created last year; you could type in all the categories and information from scratch, or you could open last year's budget, save it with a new name, and just make changes to update it for the current year. By opening the existing file and saving it with the Save As command, you create a duplicate that you can modify to your heart's content, while the original file remains intact. ▰▰▰▱ Use Excel to open an existing workbook file, and save it with a new name so the original remains unchanged.

STEPS

QUICK TIP

If you point to a command on the Office menu that is followed by an arrow, a submenu opens displaying additional, related commands.

1. **Click Microsoft Excel – Book1 on the taskbar, click the Office button 🔘, then click Open**

   The Open dialog box opens, where you can navigate to any drive or folder location accessible to your computer to locate a file.

2. **In the Open dialog box, navigate to the drive and folder where you store your Data Files**

   The files available in the current folder are listed, as shown in Figure A-10. This folder contains one file.

3. **Click OFFICE A-1.xlsx, then click Open**

   The dialog box closes and the file opens in Excel. An Excel file is an electronic spreadsheet, so it looks different from a Word document or a PowerPoint slide.

QUICK TIP

The Recent Items list on the Office menu displays recently opened documents; you can click any file to open it.

4. **Click 🔘, then click Save As**

   The Save As dialog box opens, and the current filename is highlighted in the File name text box. Using the Save As command enables you to create a copy of the current, existing file with a new name. This action preserves the original file, and creates a new file that you can modify.

QUICK TIP

The Save As command works identically in all Office programs, except Access; in Access, this command lets you save a copy of the current database object, such as a table or form, with a new name, but not a copy of the entire database.

5. **Navigate to the drive and folder where your Data Files are stored if necessary, type Budget for Corporate Meeting in the File name text box, as shown in Figure A-11, then click Save**

   A copy of the existing document is created with the new name. The original file, Office A-1.xlsx, closes automatically.

6. **Click cell A19, type your name, then press [Enter], as shown in Figure A-12**

   In Excel, you enter data in cells, which are formed by the intersection of a row and a column. Cell A19 is at the intersection of column A and row 19. When you press [Enter], the cell pointer moves to cell A20.

7. **Click the Save button 🔘 on the Quick Access toolbar**

   Your name appears in the worksheet, and your changes to the file are saved.

Exploring File Open options

You might have noticed that the Open button on the Open dialog box includes an arrow. In a dialog box, if a button includes an arrow you can click the button to invoke the command, or you can click the arrow to choose from a list of related commands. The Open button list arrow includes several related commands, including Open Read-Only and Open as Copy. Clicking Open Read-Only opens a file that you can only save by saving it with a new name; you cannot save changes to the original file. Clicking Open as Copy creates a copy of the file already saved and named with the word "Copy" in the title. Like the Save As command, these commands provide additional ways to use copies of existing files while ensuring that original files do not get inadvertently changed.

FIGURE A-10: Open dialog box

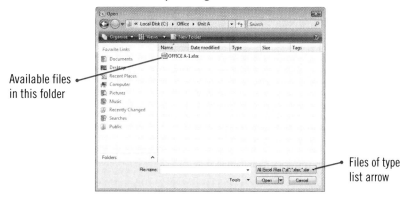

Available files in this folder

Files of type list arrow

FIGURE A-11: Save As dialog box

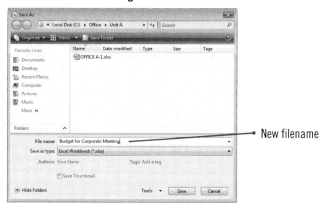

New filename

FIGURE A-12: Adding your name to the worksheet

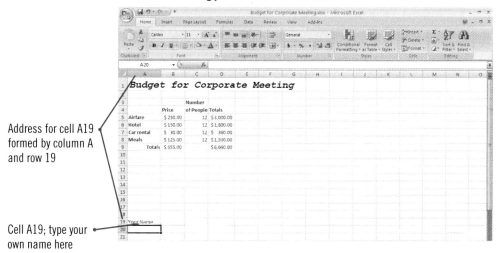

Address for cell A19 formed by column A and row 19

Cell A19; type your own name here

Working in Compatibility mode

Not everyone upgrades to the newest version of Office. As a general rule, new software versions are **backward-compatible**, meaning that documents saved by an older version can be read by newer software. The reverse is not always true, so Office 2007 includes a feature called Compatibility mode. When you open a file created in an earlier version of Office, "Compatibility Mode" appears in the title bar, letting you know the file was created in an earlier, but usable version of the program. If you are working with someone who may not be using the newest version of the software, you can avoid possible incompatibility problems by saving your file in

another, earlier format. To do this, click the Office button, point to the Save As command, then click a choice on the Save As submenu. For example, if you're working in Excel, click Excel 97-2003 Workbook format. When the Save As dialog box opens, you'll notice that the Save as type box reads "Excel 97-2003 Workbook" instead of the default "Excel Workbook." To see more file format choices, such as Excel 97-2003 Template or Microsoft Excel 5.0/95 Workbook, click Other Formats on the Save As submenu. In the Save As dialog box, click the Save as type button, click the choice you think matches what your co-worker is using, then click Save.

Viewing and Printing Your Work

If your computer is connected to a printer or a print server, you can easily print any Office document. Printing can be as simple as clicking a button, or as involved as customizing the print job by printing only selected pages or making other choices, and/or **previewing** the document to see exactly what a document will look like when it is printed. (In order for printing and previewing to work, a printer must be installed.) In addition to using Print Preview, each Microsoft Office program lets you switch among various **views** of the document window, to show more or fewer details or a different combination of elements that make it easier to complete certain tasks, such as formatting or reading text. You can also increase or decrease your view of a document, so you can see more or less of it on the screen at once. Changing your view of a document does not affect the file in any way, it affects only the way it looks on screen. ░░░░ Experiment with changing your view of a Word document, and then preview and print your work.

STEPS

1. **Click** Potential Corporate Meeting Locations – Microsoft Word **on the taskbar**

    Word becomes the active program, and the document fills the screen.

2. **Click the** View tab **on the Ribbon**

    In most Office programs, the View tab on the Ribbon includes groups and commands for changing your view of the current document. You can also change views using the View buttons on the status bar.

3. **Click** Web Layout button **in the Document Views group on the View tab**

    The view changes to Web Layout view, as shown in Figure A-13. This view shows how the document will look if you save it as a Web page.

QUICK TIP

You can also use the Zoom button in the Zoom group of the View tab to enlarge or reduce a document's appearance.

4. **Click the** Zoom in button ⊕ **on the status bar** eight times **until the zoom percentage reads** 180%

    Zooming in, or choosing a higher percentage, makes a document appear bigger on screen, but less of it fits on the screen at once; **zooming out**, or choosing a lower percentage, lets you see more of the document but at a reduced size.

5. **Drag the** Zoom slider ▽ **on the status bar to the** center mark

    The Zoom slider lets you zoom in and out without opening a dialog box or clicking buttons.

6. **Click the** Print Layout button **on the View tab**

    You return to Print Layout view, the default view in Microsoft Word.

7. **Click the** Office button ⊛, **point to** Print, **then click** Print Preview

    The Print Preview presents the most accurate view of how your document will look when printed, displaying the entire page on screen at once. Compare your screen to Figure A-14. The Ribbon in Print Preview contains a single tab, also known as a **program** tab, with commands specific to Print Preview. The commands on this tab facilitate viewing and changing overall settings such as margins and page size.

QUICK TIP

You can open the Print dialog box from any view by clicking the Office button, then clicking Print.

8. **Click the** Print button **on the Ribbon**

    The Print dialog box opens, as shown in Figure A-15. You can use this dialog box to change which pages to print, the number of printed copies, and even the number of pages you print on each page. If you have multiple printers from which to choose, you can change from one installed printer by clicking the Name list arrow, then clicking the name of the installed printer you want to use.

9. **Click** OK, **then click the** Close Print Preview button **on the Ribbon**

    A copy of the document prints, and Print Preview closes.

FIGURE A-13: Web Layout view

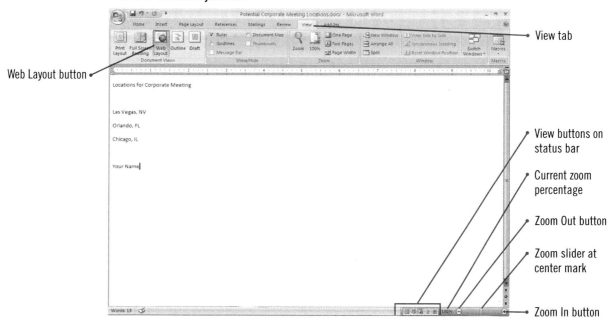

Web Layout button

View tab

View buttons on status bar

Current zoom percentage

Zoom Out button

Zoom slider at center mark

Zoom In button

FIGURE A-14: Print Preview screen

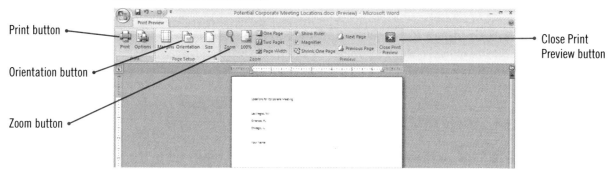

Print button

Orientation button

Zoom button

Close Print Preview button

FIGURE A-15: Print dialog box

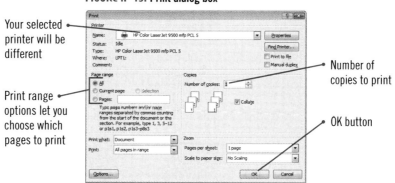

Your selected printer will be different

Print range options let you choose which pages to print

Number of copies to print

OK button

Using the Print Screen feature to create a screen capture

At some point you may want to create a screen capture. A **screen capture** is a snapshot of your screen, as if you took a picture of it with a camera. You might want to take a screen capture if an error message occurs and you want Technical Support to see exactly what's on the screen. Or perhaps your instructor wants to see what your screen looks like when you create a particular document. To create a screen capture, press [PrtScn]. (Keyboards differ, but you may find the [PrtScn] button on the Insert key in or near your keyboard's function keys. You may have to press the [F Lock] key to enable the Function keys.) Pressing this key places a digital image of your screen in the Windows temporary storage area known as the **Clipboard**. Open the document where you want the screen capture to appear, click the Home tab on the Ribbon (if necessary), then click Paste on the Home tab. The screen capture is pasted into the document.

Office 2007

Getting Help and Closing a File

You can get comprehensive help at any time by pressing [F1] in an Office program. You can also get help in the form of a ScreenTip by pointing to almost any icon in the program window. When you're finished working in an Office document, you have a few choices regarding ending your work session. You can close a file or exit a program by using the Office button or by clicking a button on the title bar. Closing a file leaves a program running, while exiting a program closes all the open files in that program as well as the program itself. In all cases, Office reminds you if you try to close a file or exit a program and your document contains unsaved changes. ▓▓▓▓ Explore the Help system in Microsoft Office, and then close your documents and exit any open programs.

STEPS

1. **Point to the Zoom button on the View tab of the Ribbon**

   A ScreenTip appears that describes how the Zoom button works.

2. **Press [F1]**

   The Word Help window opens, as shown in Figure A-16, displaying the home page for help in Word. Each entry is a hyperlink you can click to open a list of related topics. This window also includes a toolbar of useful Help commands and a Search field. The connection status at the bottom of the Help window indicates that the connection to Office Online is active. Office Online supplements the help content available on your computer with a wide variety of up-to-date topics, templates, and training.

3. **Click the Getting help link in the Table of Contents pane**

   The icon next to Getting help changes and its list of subtopics expands.

4. **Click the Work with the Help window link in the topics list in the left pane**

   The topic opens in the right pane, as shown in Figure A-17.

5. **Click the Hide Table of Contents button 📖 on the Help toolbar**

   The left pane closes, as shown in Figure A-18.

6. **Click the Show Table of Contents button 📖 on the Help toolbar, scroll to the bottom of the left pane, click the Accessibility link in the Table of Contents pane, click the Use the keyboard to work with Ribbon programs link, read the information in the right pane, then click the Help window Close button**

7. **Click the Office button 🔘, then click Close; if a dialog box opens asking whether you want to save your changes, click Yes**

   The Potential Corporate Meeting Locations document closes, leaving the Word program open.

8. **Click 🔘, then click Exit Word**

   Microsoft Office Word closes, and the Excel program window is active.

9. **Click 🔘, click Exit Excel, click the PowerPoint button on the taskbar if necessary, click 🔘, then click Exit PowerPoint**

   Microsoft Office Excel and Microsoft Office PowerPoint both close.

FIGURE A-16: Word Help window

Help toolbar

Search field

Hide Table of
Contents
button

The colors
of your links
may differ

Connection status

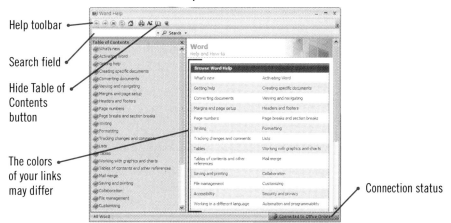

FIGURE A-17: Work with the Help window

Print button

Icon indicates
expanded topic

Work with
the Help
window link

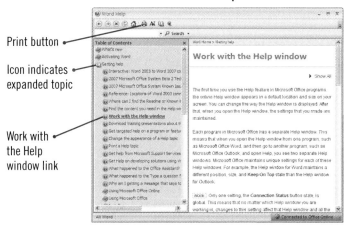

FIGURE A-18: Help window with Table of Contents closed

Show Table of
Contents button

Recovering a document

Sometimes while you are using Office, you may experience a power failure or your computer may "freeze," making it impossible to continue working. If this type of interruption occurs, each Office program has a built-in recovery feature that allows you to open and save files that were open at the time of the interruption. When you restart the program(s) after an interruption, the Document Recovery task pane opens on the left side of your screen displaying both original and recovered versions of the files that were open. If you're not sure which file to open (original or recovered), it's usually better to open the recovered file because it will contain the latest information. You can, however, open and review all versions of the file that were recovered and save the best one. Each file listed in the Document Recovery task pane displays a list arrow with options that allow you to open the file, save it as is, delete it, or show repairs made to it during recovery.

Practice

If you have a SAM user profile, you may have access to hands-on instruction, practice, and assessment of the skills covered in this unit. Log in to your SAM account (http://sam2007.course.com/) to launch any assigned training activities or exams that relate to the skills covered in this unit.

▼ CONCEPTS REVIEW

Label the elements of the program window shown in Figure A-19.

FIGURE A-19

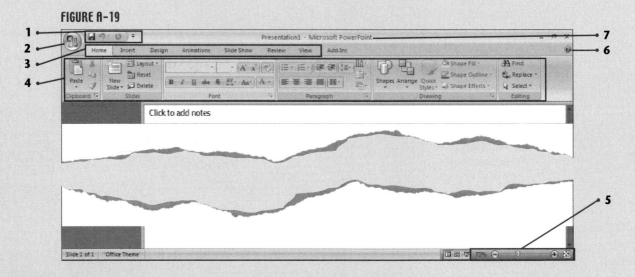

Match each project with the program for which it is best suited.

8. Microsoft Office PowerPoint	a. Corporate expansion budget with expense projections
9. Microsoft Office Excel	b. Business résumé for a job application
10. Microsoft Office Word	c. Auto parts store inventory
11. Microsoft Office Access	d. Presentation for Board of Directors meeting

▼ INDEPENDENT CHALLENGE 1

You just accepted an administrative position with a local car dealership that's recently invested in computers and is now considering purchasing Microsoft Office. You are asked to propose ways Office might help the dealership. You produce your proposal in Microsoft Word.

    a. Start Word, then save the document as Microsoft Office Proposal in the drive and folder where you store your Data Files.

    b. Type Microsoft Office Word, press [Enter] twice, type Microsoft Office Excel, press [Enter] twice, type Microsoft Office PowerPoint, press [Enter] twice, type Microsoft Office Access, press [Enter] twice, then type your name.

    c. Click the line beneath each program name, type at least two tasks suited to that program, then press [Enter].

    d. Save your work, then print one copy of this document.

Advanced Challenge Exercise

    ■ Press the [PrtScn] button to create a screen capture, then press [Ctrl][V].

    ■ Save and print the document.

    e. Exit Word.

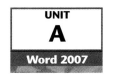

Creating Documents with Word 2007

Microsoft Office Word 2007 is a word processing program that makes it easy to create a variety of professional-looking documents, from simple letters and memos to newsletters, research papers, blog posts, business cards, résumés, financial reports, and other documents that include multiple pages of text and sophisticated formatting. In this unit, you will explore the editing and formatting features available in Word and create two documents. You have been hired to work in the Marketing Department at Quest Specialty Travel (QST), a tour company that specializes in cultural tourism and adventure travel. Shortly after reporting to your new office, Ron Dawson, the vice president of marketing, asks you to use Word to create a memo to the marketing staff and a fax to one of the tour developers.

OBJECTIVES

Understand word processing software

Explore the Word program window

Start a document

Save a document

Select text

Format text using the Mini toolbar

Create a document using a template

View and navigate a document

Understanding Word Processing Software

A **word processing program** is a software program that includes tools for entering, editing, and formatting text and graphics. Microsoft Word is a powerful word processing program that allows you to create and enhance a wide range of documents quickly and easily. Figure A-1 shows the first page of a report created using Word and illustrates some of the Word features you can use to enhance your documents. The electronic files you create using Word are called **documents**. One of the benefits of using Word is that document files can be stored on a hard disk, CD, flash drive, or other storage device, making them easy to transport, exchange, and revise. Before beginning your memo to the marketing staff, you explore the editing and formatting capabilities available in Word.

You can use Word to accomplish the following tasks:

- **Type and edit text**

  The Word editing tools make it simple to insert and delete text in a document. You can add text to the middle of an existing paragraph, replace text with other text, undo an editing change, and correct typing, spelling, and grammatical errors with ease.

- **Copy and move text from one location to another**

  Using the more advanced editing features of Word, you can copy or move text from one location and insert it in a different location in a document. You also can copy and move text between documents. Being able to copy and move text means you don't have to retype text that is already entered in a document.

- **Format text and paragraphs with fonts, colors, and other elements**

  The sophisticated formatting tools available in Word allow you to make the text in your documents come alive. You can change the size, style, and color of text, add lines and shading to paragraphs, and enhance lists with bullets and numbers. Formatting text creatively helps you highlight important ideas in your documents.

- **Format and design pages**

  The Word page-formatting features give you power to design attractive newsletters, create powerful résumés, and produce documents such as business cards, CD labels, and books. You can change the paper size and orientation of your documents, organize text in columns, and control the layout of text and graphics on each page of a document. For quick results, Word includes preformatted cover pages, pull quotes, and headers and footers, as well as galleries of coordinated text, table, and graphic styles that you can rely on to give documents a polished look.

- **Enhance documents with tables, charts, diagrams, and graphics**

  Using the powerful graphics tools available in Word, you can spice up your documents with pictures, photographs, lines, shapes, and diagrams. You also can illustrate your documents with tables and charts to help convey your message in a visually interesting way.

- **Use Mail Merge to create form letters and mailing labels**

  The Word Mail Merge feature allows you to send personalized form letters to many different people. You can also use Mail Merge to create mailing labels, directories, e-mail messages, and other types of documents.

- **Share documents securely**

  The Word Document Inspector feature makes it quick and easy to thoroughly remove comments, tracked changes, and unwanted personal information from your files before you share them with others. You can also add a digital signature to a document, convert a file to a format suitable for publishing on the Web, and easily recognize a document that might contain a potentially harmful macro.

FIGURE A-1: A report created using Word

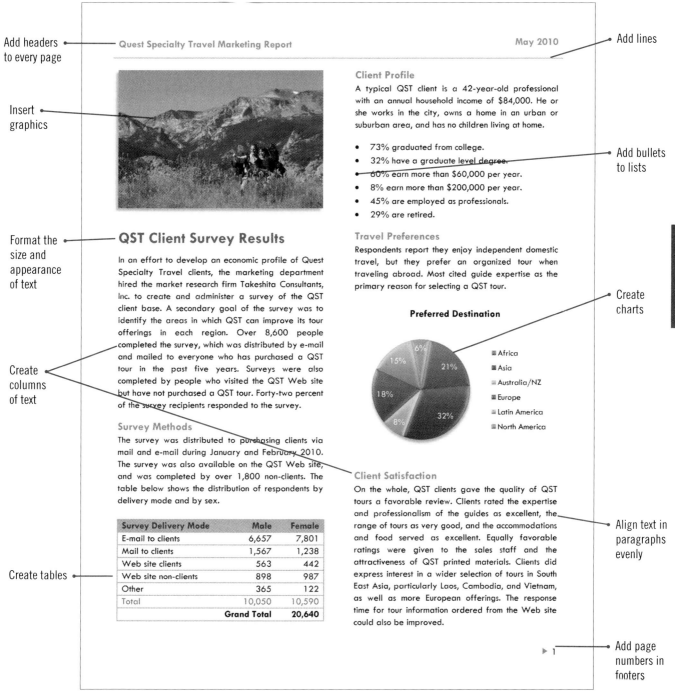

Add headers to every page

Insert graphics

Format the size and appearance of text

Create columns of text

Create tables

Add lines

Add bullets to lists

Create charts

Align text in paragraphs evenly

Add page numbers in footers

Planning a document

Before you create a new document, it's a good idea to spend time planning it. Identify the message you want to convey, the audience for your document, and the elements, such as tables or charts, you want to include. You should also think about the tone and look of your document—are you writing a business letter, which should be written in a pleasant, but serious tone and have a formal appearance, or are you creating a flyer that must be colorful, eye-catching, and fun to read? The purpose and audience for your document determines the appropriate design. Planning the layout and design of a document involves deciding how to organize the text, selecting the fonts to use, identifying the graphics to include, and selecting the formatting elements that will enhance the message and appeal of the document. For longer documents, such as newsletters, it can be useful to sketch the layout and design of each page before you begin.

Exploring the Word Program Window

When you start Word, a blank document appears in the document window. You examine the elements of the Word program window.

1. **Start** Word

   The **Word program window** opens, as shown in Figure A-2. The blinking vertical line in the document window is the **insertion point**. It indicates where text appears as you type. The blank document opens in Print Layout view. **Views** are different ways of displaying a document in the document window.

2. **Move the mouse pointer around the Word program window**

   The mouse pointer changes shape depending on where it is in the Word program window. You use pointers to move the insertion point or to select text to edit. Table A-1 describes common pointers in Word.

3. **Place the mouse pointer over a button on the Ribbon**

   When you place the mouse pointer over a button or some other elements of the Word program window, a ScreenTip appears. A **ScreenTip** is a label that identifies the name of the button or feature, briefly describes its function, conveys any keyboard shortcut for the command, and includes a link to associated help topics, if any.

   Using Figure A-2 as a guide, find the elements described below in your program window.

   - The **title bar** displays the name of the document and the name of the program. Until you give a new document a different name, its temporary name is Document1. The title bar also contains resizing buttons and the program Close button. These buttons are common to all Windows programs.
   - Clicking the **Office button** opens a menu of commands related to managing and sharing documents, including opening, printing, and saving a document, creating a new document, and preparing a document for distribution. The Office button also provides access to the Word Options dialog box, which is used to customize the way you use Word.
   - The **Quick Access toolbar** contains buttons for saving a document and for undoing, redoing, and repeating a change. You can modify the Quick Access toolbar to include the commands you use most frequently.
   - The **Ribbon** contains the names of the Word tabs. Each **tab** includes buttons for commands, which are organized in **groups**. For example, the Home tab includes the Clipboard, Font, Paragraph, Styles, and Editing groups, each containing buttons related to editing and formatting text. The Ribbon also includes the **Microsoft Office Word Help button**, which you use to access the Word Help system.
   - The **document window** displays the current document. You enter text and format your document in the document window.
   - The rulers appear in the document window in Print Layout view. The **horizontal ruler** displays left and right document margins as well as the tab settings and paragraph indents, if any, for the paragraph in which the insertion point is located. The **vertical ruler** displays the top and bottom document margins.
   - The **vertical scroll bar** and the **horizontal scroll bar** are used to display different parts of the document in the document window. The scroll bars include **scroll boxes** and **scroll arrows**, which you can use to move easily through a document.
   - The **status bar** displays the page number of the current page, the total number of pages and words in the document, and the status of spelling and grammar checking. It also includes the view buttons, the Zoom level button, and the Zoom slider. You can customize the status bar to display other information.
   - The **view buttons** on the status bar allow you to display the document in Print Layout, Full Screen Reading, Web Layout, Outline, or Draft view.
   - The **Zoom level** button and the **Zoom slider** provide quick ways to enlarge and decrease the size of the document in the document window, making it easy to zoom in on a detail of a document or to view the layout of the document as a whole.

QUICK TIP

To display a different tab, you simply click its name on the Ribbon.

TROUBLE

Click the View Ruler button at the top of the vertical scroll bar to display the rulers if they are not already displayed.

FIGURE A-2: Elements of the Word program window

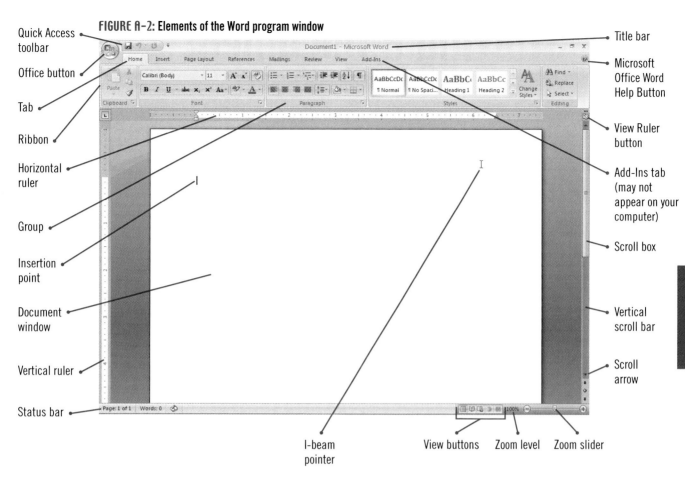

Quick Access toolbar

Office button

Tab

Ribbon

Horizontal ruler

Group

Insertion point

Document window

Vertical ruler

Status bar

I-beam pointer

View buttons   Zoom level   Zoom slider

Title bar

Microsoft Office Word Help Button

View Ruler button

Add-Ins tab (may not appear on your computer)

Scroll box

Vertical scroll bar

Scroll arrow

Word 2007

TABLE A-1: Common mouse pointers in Word

name	pointer	use to
I-beam pointer	I	Move the insertion point in a document or to select text
Click-and-type pointers: left-align click-and-type pointer; center-align click-and-type pointer	I≡ or I≡	Move the insertion point in a blank area of a document in Print Layout or Web Layout view; double-clicking with a Click and Type pointer automatically applies the paragraph formatting (alignment and indentation) required to position text or a graphic at that location in the document
Selection pointer	⬭	Click a button or other element of the Word program window; appears when you point to elements of the Word program window
Right-pointing arrow pointer	⬮	Select a line or lines of text; appears when you point to the left edge of a line of text in the document window
Hand pointer	👆	Open a hyperlink; appears when you point to a hyperlink in a task pane or when you press [Ctrl] and point to a hyperlink in a document
Hide white space pointer	⊞	Hide the white space in the top and bottom margins of a document in Print Layout view
Show white space pointer	⊞	Show the white space in the top and bottom margins of a document in Print Layout view

Starting a Document

You begin a new document by simply typing text in a blank document in the document window. Word includes a **word-wrap** feature so that as you type Word automatically moves the insertion point to the next line of the document when you reach the right margin. You only press [Enter] when you want to start a new paragraph or insert a blank line. ▄▄▄▟ You type a quick memo to the marketing staff.

STEPS

1. **Type Memorandum, then press [Enter] twice**

   Each time you press [Enter] the insertion point moves to the start of the next line.

2. **Type TO:, then press [Tab] twice**

   Pressing [Tab] moves the insertion point several spaces to the right. You can use the [Tab] key to align the text in a memo header or to indent the first line of a paragraph.

3. **Type QST Managers, then press [Enter]**

   The insertion point moves to the start of the next line.

4. **Type: FROM: [Tab] [Tab] Ron Dawson [Enter]**
   DATE: [Tab] [Tab] July 12, 2010 [Enter]
   RE: [Tab] [Tab] Marketing Meeting [Enter] [Enter]

   Red or green wavy lines may appear under the words you typed, indicating a possible spelling or grammar error. Spelling and grammar checking is one of the many automatic features you will encounter as you type. Table A-2 describes several of these automatic features. You can correct any typing errors you make later.

5. **Type The next marketing staff meeting will be held on the 16th of July at 1 p.m. in the conference room on the ground floor., then press [Spacebar]**

   As you type, notice that the insertion point moves automatically to the next line of the document. You also might notice that Word automatically changed "16th" to "16th" in the memo. This feature is called **AutoCorrect**. AutoCorrect automatically makes typographical adjustments and detects and adjusts typing errors, certain misspelled words (such as "taht" for "that"), and incorrect capitalization as you type.

6. **Type Heading the agenda will be the launch of our new Mai Chau Mountain Tribal Trek, a ten-day walking and rafting tour of the sultry rivers, hidden villages, and misty forests of northern Vietnam, scheduled for February 2012.**

   When you type the first few characters of "February," the Word AutoComplete feature displays the complete word in a ScreenTip. **AutoComplete** suggests text to insert quickly into your documents. You can ignore AutoComplete for now. Your memo should resemble Figure A-3.

7. **Press [Enter], then type Wim Hoppengarth is in Hanoi hammering out the details. A preliminary draft of the tour brochure is attached. Bring your creative ideas for launching this exciting new tour to the meeting.**

   When you press [Enter] and type the new paragraph, notice that Word adds more space between the paragraphs than it does between the lines within each individual paragraph. This is part of the default style for paragraphs in Word, called the Normal style.

8. **Position the I pointer after for (but before the space) in the last line of the first paragraph, then click**

   Clicking moves the insertion point after "for."

9. **Press [Backspace] three times, then type to depart in**

   Pressing [Backspace] removes the character before the insertion point.

10. **Move the insertion point before staff in the first sentence, then press [Delete] six times to remove the word staff and the space after it**

    Pressing [Delete] removes the character after the insertion point. Figure A-4 shows the revised memo.

FIGURE A-3: Memo text in the document window

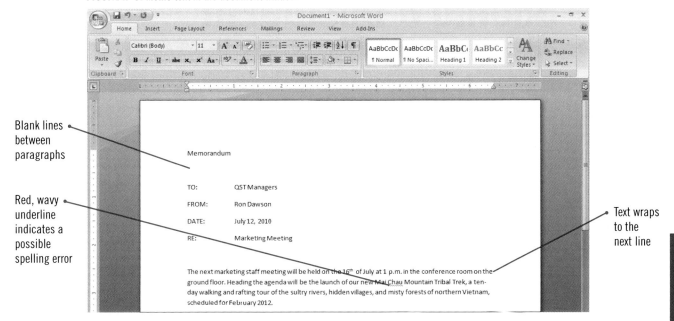

Blank lines between paragraphs

Red, wavy underline indicates a possible spelling error

Text wraps to the next line

FIGURE A-4: Edited memo text

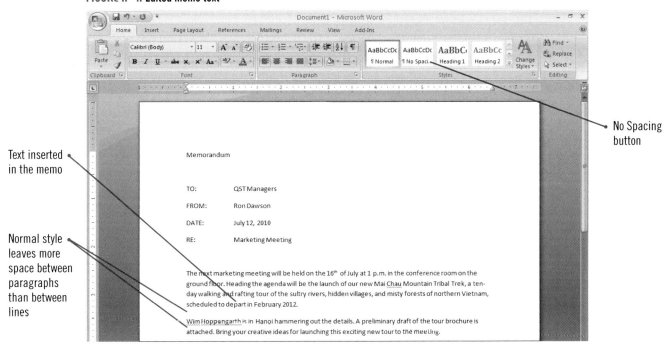

Text inserted in the memo

Normal style leaves more space between paragraphs than between lines

No Spacing button

TABLE A-2: Automatic features that appear as you type in Word

feature	what appears	to use
AutoComplete	A ScreenTip suggesting text to insert appears as you type	Press [Enter] to insert the text suggested by the ScreenTip; continue typing to reject the suggestion
AutoCorrect	A small blue box appears when you place the pointer over text corrected by AutoCorrect; an AutoCorrect Options button ⚡▾ appears when you point to the corrected text	Word automatically corrects typos, minor spelling errors, and capitalization, and adds typographical symbols (such as © and ™) as you type; to reverse an AutoCorrect adjustment, click the AutoCorrect Options list arrow, then click Undo or the option that will undo the action
Spelling and Grammar	A red wavy line under a word indicates a possible misspelling; a green wavy line under text indicates a possible grammar error	Right-click red- or green-underlined text to display a shortcut menu of correction options; click a correction to accept it and remove the wavy underline

Saving a Document

To store a document permanently so you can open it and edit it in the future, you must save it as a **file**. When you **save** a document you give it a name, called a **filename**, and indicate the location where you want to store the file. Files created in Word 2007 are automatically assigned the .docx file extension to distinguish them from files created in other software programs, including previous versions of Word. Files created in previous versions of Word carry the .doc file extension. You can save a document using the Save button on the Quick Access toolbar or the Save command on the Office menu. Once you have saved a document for the first time, you should save it again every few minutes and always before printing so that the saved file is updated to reflect your latest changes. ▰▰▰ You save your memo using a descriptive filename and the default file extension.

STEPS

TROUBLE

If you don't see the extension .docx as part of the filename, Windows is set not to display file extensions.

1. **Click the Save button 🖫 on the Quick Access toolbar**

   The first time you save a document, the Save As dialog box opens, as shown in Figure A-5. The default filename, Memorandum, appears in the File name text box. The default filename is based on the first few words of the document. The default file extension, .docx, appears in the Save as type list box. Table A-3 describes the functions of some of the buttons in the Save As dialog box.

2. **Type Vietnam Tour Memo in the File name text box**

   The new filename replaces the default filename. Giving your documents brief descriptive filenames makes it easier to locate and organize them later. You do not need to type .docx when you type a new filename.

TROUBLE

Click Browse Folders in the Save As dialog box to display the Navigation pane and folder window.

3. **Navigate to the drive and folder where you store your Data Files**

   You can navigate to a different drive or folder either by clicking a location in the Address bar to go directly to that location, or by clicking an arrow next to a location in the Address bar to open a list of subfolders, and then selecting a new location from the list. Click the double arrow in the Address bar to navigate to the next highest level in the folder hierarchy. You can also double-click a drive or folder in the Navigation pane or the folder window to change the active location. When you are finished, the drive or folder where you store your Data Files appears in the Address bar. Your Save As dialog box should resemble Figure A-6.

QUICK TIP

To save a document so it can be opened in a previous version of Word, click the Save as type list arrow, then click Word 97-2003 Document (*.doc).

4. **Click Save**

   The document is saved to the drive and folder you specified in the Save As dialog box, and the title bar displays the new filename, Vietnam Tour Memo.docx.

5. **Place the insertion point before ten-day in the second sentence, type rugged, then press [Spacebar]**

   You can continue to work on a document after you have saved it with a new filename.

6. **Click 🖫**

   Your change to the memo is saved. Saving a document after you give it a filename saves the changes you make to the document. You also can press [Ctrl][S] to save a document.

Working with XML and binary files

The default x suffix in the .docx file extension indicates a file is saved in the Office **XML format**, which is new to Word 2007. Earlier versions of Word employed a binary file format, signified by the familiar .doc file extension. To facilitate file sharing between the different versions of Office, Word 2007 allows you to open, edit, and save files in either XML or binary format. When you open a binary file in Word 2007, the words Compatibility Mode appear in the title bar next to the filename. You can also turn on Compatibility Mode by saving a copy of an XML file in Word 97-2003 format. When you are working in Compatibility Mode, some Word 2007 document features, including built-in document themes, margins, text boxes,

SmartArt, bibliographies, mail merge data, and certain theme colors, fonts, and effects will be permanently changed or behave differently.

Converting a binary file to XML format is simple: click the Office button, click Convert on the Office menu, and then click OK in the Microsoft Office Word dialog box that opens. This turns off Compatibility Mode. Once a file is converted to XML, you can save the converted file, which replaces the original .doc file with a .docx file of the same filename, by clicking the Save button, or you can use the Save As command on the Office menu to create a new .docx file, preserving the original binary .doc file.

FIGURE A-5: Save As dialog box

Click an arrow in the Address bar to change the active folder or drive

Address bar

Active folder

Search for an item in the active location

Navigation pane

Click Folders button to display expandable list of folders in the Navigation pane

Folder window displays the folders and files in the active folder or drive (yours will differ)

Default filename and file extension are selected

Click to change the file type

Click to hide the Navigation pane and folder window

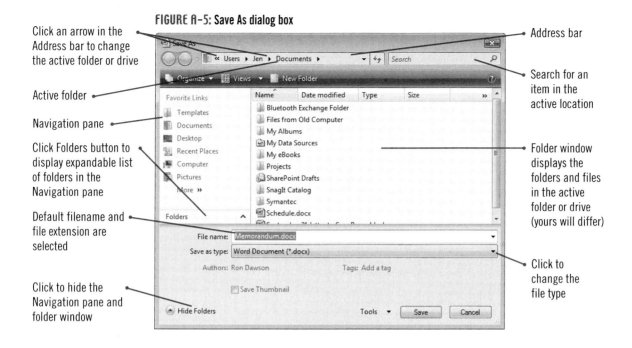

FIGURE A-6: File to be saved to the Unit A folder

Location of Data Files (yours might differ)

Your folder window might list the files and folders in the active location

New filename

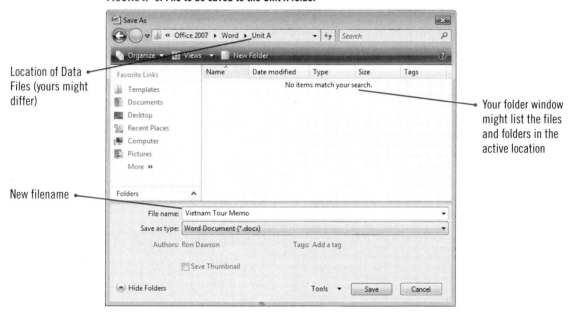

TABLE A-3: Save As dialog box buttons

button	use to
⬅ Back	Navigate back to the drive or folder that was previously active in the Address bar
➡ Forward	Navigate forward to the drive or folder that was previously active in the Address bar
Organize ▾ **Organize**	Open a menu of commands related to organizing the selected file or folder, including Cut, Copy, Delete, Rename, and Properties
Views ▾ **Views**	Change the way folder and file information is shown in the folder window in the Save As dialog box; click the Views list arrow to open a menu of options
New Folder **New Folder**	Create a new folder in the current folder or drive

Selecting Text

Before deleting, editing, or formatting text, you must **select** the text. Selecting text involves clicking and dragging the I-beam pointer across text to highlight it. You also can click with the ⅍ pointer in the blank area to the left of text to select lines or paragraphs. Table A-4 describes the many ways to select text. You revise the memo by selecting text and replacing it with new text.

STEPS

1. **Click the** Show/Hide ¶ button ¶ **in the Paragraph group**

   Formatting marks appear in the document window. **Formatting marks** are special characters that appear on your screen and do not print. Common formatting marks include the paragraph symbol (¶), which shows the end of a paragraph—wherever you press [Enter]; the dot symbol (•), which represents a space—wherever you press [Spacebar]; and the arrow symbol (→), which shows the location of a tab stop—wherever you press [Tab]. Working with formatting marks turned on can help you to select, edit, and format text with precision.

2. **Click before** QST Managers, **then drag the** I **pointer over the text to select it**

   The words are selected, as shown in Figure A-7. For now you can ignore the faint toolbar that appears over text when you first select it.

3. **Type** Marketing Staff

   The text you type replaces the selected text.

4. **Double-click** Ron, **type your first name, double-click** Dawson, **then type your last name**

   Double-clicking a word selects the entire word.

5. **Place the pointer in the margin to the left of the RE: line so that the pointer changes to** ⅍, **click to select the line, then type** RE: [Tab][Tab] Launch of new Vietnam trekking tour

   Clicking to the left of a line of text with the ⅍ pointer selects the entire line.

6. **Select** sultry **in the third line of the first paragraph, type** meandering, **select** misty forests, **then type** stunning limestone peaks

7. **Select the sentence** Wim Hoppengarth is in Hanoi hammering out the details., **then press** [Delete]

   Selecting text and pressing [Delete] removes the text from the document.

8. **Click** ¶ , **then click the** Save button 💾 **on the Quick Access toolbar**

   Formatting marks are turned off and your changes to the memo are saved. The Show/Hide ¶ button is a **toggle button**, which means you can use it to turn formatting marks on and off. The edited memo is shown in Figure A-8.

TABLE A-4: Methods for selecting text

to select	use the pointer to
Any amount of text	Drag over the text
A word	Double-click the word
A line of text	Click with the ⅍ pointer to the left of the line
A sentence	Press and hold [Ctrl], then click the sentence
A paragraph	Triple-click the paragraph or double-click with the ⅍ pointer to the left of the paragraph
A large block of text	Click at the beginning of the selection, press and hold [Shift], then click at the end of the selection
Multiple nonconsecutive selections	Select the first selection, then press and hold [Ctrl] as you select each additional selection
An entire document	Triple-click with the ⅍ pointer to the left of any text, press [Ctrl][A], or click the Select button in the Editing group on the Home tab, and then click Select All

FIGURE A-7: Text selected in the memo

Selected text

Left document margin

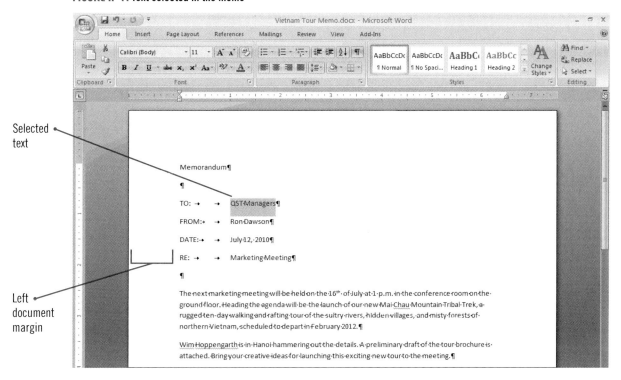

FIGURE A-8: Edited memo with replacement text

Replacement text

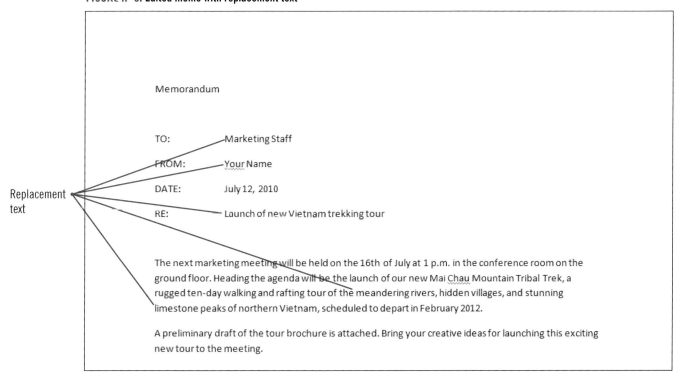

Formatting Text Using the Mini Toolbar

Changing the format of text is a fast and fun way to spruce up the appearance of a document and highlight important information. You can easily format text with fonts, colors, styles, borders, and other formatting options by selecting the text and clicking a command on the Home tab. The **Mini toolbar**, which appears faintly above text when you first select it, also includes the most commonly used text and paragraph formatting commands. Table A-5 describes the function of the buttons on the Mini toolbar. You enhance the appearance of the memo by formatting the text using the Mini toolbar. Before printing the finished memo, you preview it in Print Preview.

STEPS

1. **Double-click** Memorandum

   The Mini toolbar appears in ghosted fashion over the selected text. When you point to the Mini toolbar, it becomes solid, as shown in Figure A-9, and you can click a formatting option to apply it to the selected text.

2. **Click the** Center button **≡ on the Mini toolbar**

   The word Memorandum is centered between the left and right document margins.

3. **Click the** Grow Font button **Å on the Mini toolbar eight times, then click the** Bold **button B on the Mini toolbar**

   Each time you click the Grow Font button the selected text is enlarged. Applying **bold** to the text makes it thicker and darker.

4. **Select** TO:, **click** B, **select** FROM:, **click** B, **select** DATE:, **click** B, **select** RE:, **then click** B

   Bold is applied to the heading text.

5. **Click the blank line between the RE: line and the body text, then click the** Bottom Border **button ▦ in the Paragraph group**

   A single-line border is added between the heading and the body text in the memo.

6. **Click the** Office button **⬤, point to** Print, **then click** Print Preview

   The document appears in Print Preview. Before you print a document, it's a good habit to examine it carefully in **Print Preview** so you can identify and correct any problems before printing.

7. **Move the pointer over the memo text until it changes to ⬤, then click the word** Memorandum

   Clicking with the ⊕ pointer magnifies the document in the Print Preview window and changes the pointer to ⊖. The memo appears as it will look when printed, as shown in Figure A-10. Clicking with the ⊖ pointer reduces the size of the document in the Print Preview window.

8. **Click the** Magnifier check box **in the Preview group**

   Deselecting the Magnifier check box turns off the magnification feature and allows you to edit the document in Print Preview. In edit mode, the pointer changes to Ⅰ.

9. **Examine your memo carefully for errors, correct any mistakes, then click the** Close Print Preview button **in the Preview group**

   Print Preview closes and the memo appears in the document window.

10. **Save the document, click ⬤, click** Print, **click** OK **in the Print dialog box, click ⬤, then click** Close

    A copy of the memo prints using the default print settings. You can use the Print dialog box to change the current printer, change the number of copies to print, select what pages of a document to print, and modify other printing options. After printing, the document closes, but the Word program window remains open.

FIGURE A-9: Mini toolbar

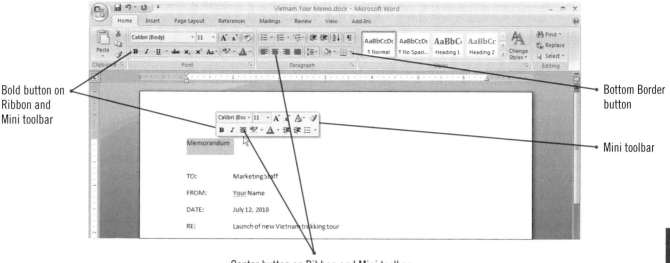

Bold button on Ribbon and Mini toolbar

Bottom Border button

Mini toolbar

Center button on Ribbon and Mini toolbar

FIGURE A-10: Completed memo in the Print Preview window

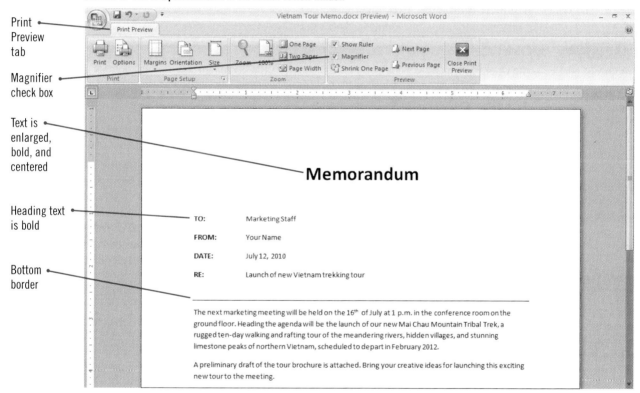

Print Preview tab

Magnifier check box

Text is enlarged, bold, and centered

Heading text is bold

Bottom border

TABLE A-5: Buttons on the Mini toolbar

button	use to	button	use to
Calibri (Boc ▾	Change the font of text	_I_	Italicize text
11 ▾	Change the font size of text	☰	Center text between the margins
A˄	Make text larger	aʙ̃ ▾	Apply colored highlighting to text
A˅	Make text smaller	A ▾	Change the color of text
A	Apply a style to text	⫶	Decrease the indent level of a paragraph
✍	Copy the formats applied to text to other text	⫶	Increase the indent level of a paragraph
B	Apply bold to text	☰ ▾	Format paragraphs as a bulleted list

Creating a Document Using a Template

Word includes many templates that you can use to quickly create memos, faxes, letters, reports, brochures, and other professionally designed documents. A **template** is a formatted document that contains place-holder text, generic text that you replace with text specific to your needs. You use the New command on the Office menu to open a file that is based on a template. You then replace the placeholder text with your own text, and save the document with a new filename. You want to fax a draft of the Vietnam tour brochure to Wim Hoppengarth, the tour developer for Asia. You use a template to create a fax cover sheet.

STEPS

1. **Click the** Office button 🗐, **then click** New

   The New Document dialog box opens, as shown in Figure A-11.

2. **Click** Installed Templates **in the Templates Categories pane, scroll down the list of Installed Templates, then click** Oriel Fax

   A preview of the Oriel Fax template appears in the New Document dialog box.

3. **Click** Create

   The Oriel Fax template opens as a new document in the document window. It contains placeholder text, which you can replace with your own information.

4. **Click** [Pick the date]

   The placeholder text is selected and appears inside a content control. A **content control** is an interactive object that you use to customize a document with your own information. A content control might include placeholder text, a drop-down list of choices, or a calendar. To deselect a content control, you click a blank area of the document.

5. **Click the** Pick the date list arrow

   A calendar opens below the content control. You use the calendar to select the date you want to appear on your document—simply click a date on the calendar to enter that date in the document. You can use the arrows to the left and right of the month and year to scroll the calendar and display a different month.

6. **Click the** Today button **in the calendar**

   The current date replaces the placeholder text.

7. **Click** [TYPE THE RECIPIENT NAME], **type** Wim Hoppengarth, Guest, **click** [Type the recipient fax number], **then type** 1-84-4-555-1510

   You do not need to drag to select the placeholder text in a content control, you can simply click it. The text you type replaces the placeholder text.

8. **Click** [Type the recipient phone number], **press** [Delete] **twice, press** [Backspace] **seven times, then type** HOTEL NIKKO HANOI, ROOM 1384

   The recipient phone number content control is removed from the document.

9. **If the text In the From line is not your name, drag to select the text, then type your name**

   When the document is created, Word automatically enters the user name identified in the Word Options dialog box in the From line. This text is not placeholder text, so you have to drag to select it.

10. **Replace the remaining heading placeholder text with the text shown in Figure A-12, click** 🗐, **click** Save As, **then save the document as** Wim Fax **to the drive and folder where you store your Data Files**

    The document is saved with the filename Wim Fax.

FIGURE A-11: New Document dialog box

Installed templates

Types of templates available with an active Internet connection

Select to create a blank document

Your list of recently used templates will differ or may not appear at all

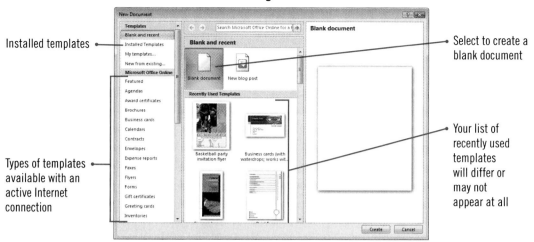

FIGURE A-12: Document created using the Oriel fax template

7/12/2010

TO: Wim Hoppengarth, Guest

FAX: 1-84-4-555-1510

HOTEL NIKKO HANOI, ROOM 1384

FROM: Your Name

FAX: 619-555-0937

PHONE: 619-555-1223

PAGES: 3, including cover sheet

RE: Mai Chau tour brochure

CC:

COMMENTS:
[Type comments]

FAX

[Type the sender company name] [Type the company address] [Type

Using the Undo, Redo, and Repeat commands

Word remembers the editing and formatting changes you make so that you can easily reverse or repeat them. You can reverse the last action you took by clicking the Undo button on the Quick Access toolbar, or you can undo a series of actions by clicking the Undo list arrow and selecting the action you want to reverse. When you undo an action using the Undo list arrow, you also undo all the actions above it in the list—that is, all actions that were performed after the action you selected. Similarly, you can keep the change you just reversed by using the Redo button on the

Quick Access toolbar. The Redo button appears only immediately after clicking the Undo button to undo a change.

If you want to repeat an action you just completed, you can use the Repeat button on the Quick Access toolbar. For example, if you just typed "thank you," clicking inserts "thank you" at the location of the insertion point. If you just applied bold, clicking applies bold to the currently selected text. You also can repeat the last action you took by pressing [F4].

Viewing and Navigating a Document

The Word Zoom feature lets you enlarge a document in the document window to get a close-up view of a detail, or reduce the size of the document in the document window for an overview of the layout as a whole. You zoom in and out on a document using the tools in the Zoom group on the View tab and the Zoom level button and Zoom slider on the status bar. You find it's helpful to zoom in and out on the document as you finalize the fax cover sheet.

STEPS

1. **Click the down scroll arrow at the bottom of the vertical scroll bar until COMMENTS: is at the top of your document window**

   The scroll arrows or scroll bars allow you to **scroll** through a document. You scroll through a document when you want to display different parts of the document in the document window. You can also scroll by clicking the scroll bar above and below the scroll box, or by dragging the scroll box up or down in the scroll bar. In longer documents, you can click the Previous Page button ⬆ or the Next Page button ⬇ on the scroll bar to display the document page by page.

2. **Click [Type comments], then type A draft copy of the Mai Chau tour brochure is attached. Please revise the text for accuracy. The photos are for placement only. Have you hired a photographer yet?**

   QUICK TIP
   You can also click the Zoom button in the Zoom group on the View tab to open the Zoom dialog box.

3. **Click the Zoom level button `100%` on the status bar**

   The Zoom dialog box opens. You use the Zoom dialog box to select a zoom level for displaying the document in the document window.

4. **Click the Whole page option button, then click OK**

   The entire document is displayed in the document window.

5. **Click the text at the bottom of the page to move the insertion point to the bottom of the page, click the View tab, then click the Page Width button in the Zoom group**

   The document is enlarged to the width of the document window. When you enlarge a document, the area where the insertion point is located appears in the document window.

6. **Click in the Urgent box, type x, then click the One Page button in the Zoom group**

   The entire document is displayed in the document window.

7. **Click Fax to move the insertion point to the upper-right corner of the page, then move the Zoom slider to the right until the Zoom percentage is 100%, as shown in Figure A-13**

   Moving the Zoom slider to the right enlarges the document in the document window. Moving the zoom slider to the left allows you to see more of the page at a reduced size. You can also move the Zoom slider by clicking a point on the Zoom slider, or by clicking the Zoom Out and Zoom In buttons.

8. **Click the Zoom In button ⊕ three times, click the vertical placeholder [Type the sender company name], press [Delete] twice, click [Type the company address], press [Delete] twice, click [Type the company phone number], then type Quest Specialty Travel, San Diego, CA**

   The text you type replaces the vertical placeholder text. You do not always need to replace the placeholder text with the type of information suggested in the content control.

9. **Preview the document in Print Preview, correct any errors, close Print Preview, click `130%`, click 100%, click OK, save the document, print it, close the file, then exit Word**

   The completed fax coversheet is shown in Figure A-14.

Creating Documents with Word 2007

FIGURE A-13: Zoom slider

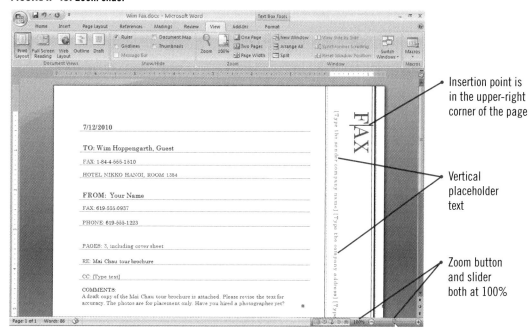

Insertion point is in the upper-right corner of the page

Vertical placeholder text

Zoom button and slider both at 100%

FIGURE A-14: Completed fax cover sheet

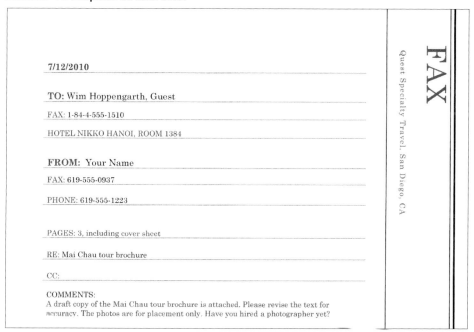

Using Word document views

Each Word view provides features that are useful for working on different types of documents. The default view, **Print Layout view**, displays a document as it will look on a printed page. Print Layout view is helpful for formatting text and pages, including adjusting document margins, creating columns of text, inserting graphics, and formatting headers and footers. Also useful is **Draft view**, which shows a simplified layout of a document, without margins, headers and footers, or graphics. When you want to quickly type, edit, and format text, it's often easiest to work in Draft view. Other Word views are helpful for performing specialized tasks. **Full Screen Reading view** displays document text so that it is easy to read and annotate. You can easily highlight content, add comments, and track and review changes in Full Screen Reading view. **Web Layout view** allows you to accurately format Web pages or documents that will be viewed on a computer screen. In Web Layout view, a document appears just as it will when viewed with a Web browser. Finally, **Outline view** is useful for editing and formatting longer documents that include multiple headings. Outline view allows you to reorganize text by moving the headings. You switch between views by clicking the view buttons on the status bar or by using the commands on the View tab. Changing views does not affect how the printed document will appear. It simply changes the way you view the document in the document window.

Practice

If you have a SAM user profile, you may have access to hands-on instruction, practice, and assessment of the skills covered in this unit. Log in to your SAM account (http://sam2007.course.com/) to launch any assigned training activities or exams that relate to the skills covered in this unit.

▼ CONCEPTS REVIEW

Label the elements of the Word program window shown in Figure A-15.

FIGURE A-15

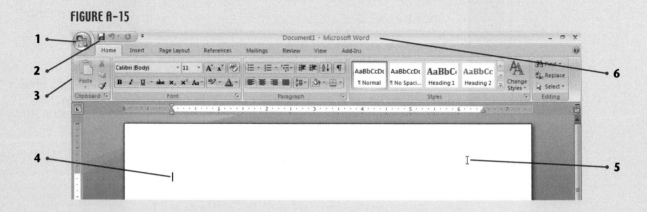

Match each term with the statement that best describes it.

7. Template
8. Formatting marks
9. Status bar
10. Ribbon
11. AutoComplete
12. Horizontal ruler
13. AutoCorrect
14. Zoom slider

a. Enlarges and reduces the document in the document window
b. Special characters that appear on screen but do not print
c. Provides access to Word commands
d. Displays tab settings and paragraph indents
e. A formatted document that contains placeholder text
f. Fixes certain errors as you type
g. Displays the number of pages in the current document
h. Suggests text to insert into a document

Select the best answer from the list of choices.

15. Which of the following does not contain commands?
a. The Mini toolbar
b. The status bar
c. The Ribbon
d. The Office menu

16. Which tab includes buttons for formatting text?
a. Home
b. Insert
c. Page Layout
d. View

17. Which of the following is not included in a ScreenTip for a command?
a. Keyboard shortcut for the command
b. Alternative location of the command
c. Description of the function of the command
d. Link to a help topic on the command

18. Which element of the Word program window shows the settings for the top and bottom document margins?
a. View tab
b. Status bar
c. Vertical scroll bar
d. Vertical ruler

19. What is the default file extension for a document created in Word 2007?

    a. .doc   **c.** .docx

    b. .dot   **d.** .dotx

20. Which view is best for annotating text with comments and highlighting?

    a. Draft view   **c.** Full Screen Reading view

    b. Outline view   **d.** Print Layout view

▼ SKILLS REVIEW

1. Explore the Word program window.

  a. Start Word.

  b. Identify as many elements of the Word program window as you can without referring to the unit material.

  c. Click the Office button, then drag the pointer through the menu commands, pointing to the arrow when commands include an arrow.

  d. Click each tab on the Ribbon, review the groups and buttons on each tab, then return to the Home tab.

  e. Point to each button on the Home tab and read the ScreenTips.

  f. Click the view buttons to view the blank document in each view, then return to Print Layout view.

  g. Use the Zoom slider to zoom all the way in and all the way out on the document, then return to 100%.

2. Start a document.

  a. In a new blank document, type FAX at the top of the page, then press [Enter] two times.

  b. Type the following, pressing [Tab] as indicated and pressing [Enter] at the end of each line:

    To: [Tab][Tab] Joanna Card

    From: [Tab] [Tab] Your Name

    Date: [Tab] [Tab] Today's date

    Re: [Tab] [Tab] Reservation confirmation

    Pages: [Tab] [Tab] 1

    Fax: [Tab] [Tab] (603) 555-5478

  c. Press [Enter] again, then type Thank you for your interest in our summer festival weekend package, which includes accommodations for three nights in downtown Montreal, continental breakfast, and a festival pass. Rooms are still available during the following festivals: International Jazz Festival, Just for Laughs Festival, Montreal Fringe Festival, and Le Festival des Arts du Village. Please see the attached schedule for festival dates and details.

  d. Press [Enter], then type To make a reservation, please call me at (514) 555-7482. I will need payment in full by the 3rd of June to hold a room. No one knows how to celebrate summer like Montrealers!

  e. Insert Grand Prix Festival, before International Jazz Festival.

  f. Using the [Backspace] key, delete 1 in the Pages: line, then type 2.

  g. Using the [Delete] key, delete festival in the last sentence of the first paragraph.

3. Save a document.

  a. Click the Save button on the Quick Access toolbar.

  b. Save the document as Card Fax with the default file extension to the drive and folder where you store your Data Files.

  c. After your name, type a comma, press [Spacebar], then type Global Montreal

  d. Save the document.

4. Select text.

  a. Turn on formatting marks.

  b. Select the Re: line, then type Re: [Tab] [Tab] Summer Festival Weekend Package

  c. Select three in the first sentence, then type two.

  d. Select 3rd of June in the second sentence of the last paragraph, type 15th of May, select room, then type reservation.

  e. Delete the sentence No one knows how to celebrate summer like Montrealers!

  f. Turn off the display of formatting marks, then save the document.

5. **Format text using the Mini toolbar.**
   a. Select FAX, then click the Grow Font button on the Mini toolbar 11 times.
   b. Apply bold to the word FAX, then center it on the page.
   c. Apply a bottom border under the word FAX.
   d. Apply bold to the following words in the fax heading: To:, From:, Date:, Re:, Pages:, and Fax:.
   e. View the document in Print Preview.
   f. Click the word FAX to zoom in on the document, then proofread the fax.
   g. Switch to edit mode, then correct any typing errors in your document.
   h. Close Print Preview, then save the document. Compare your document to Figure A-16.
   i. Print the fax using the default print settings, then close the document.

FIGURE A-16

FAX

To:	Joanna Card
From:	Your Name, Global Montreal
Date:	April 14, 2010
Re:	Summer Festival Weekend Package
Pages:	2
Fax:	(603) 555-5478

Thank you for your interest in our summer festival weekend package, which includes accommodations for two nights in downtown Montreal, continental breakfast, and a festival pass. Rooms are still available during the following festivals: Grand Prix Festival, International Jazz Festival, Just for Laughs Festival, Montreal Fringe Festival, and Le Festival des Arts du Village. Please see the attached schedule for dates and details.

To make a reservation, please call me at (514) 555-7482. I will need payment in full by the 15th of May to hold a reservation.

6. **Create a document using a template. This exercise requires an Internet connection.**
   a. Click the Office button, then click New to open the New Document dialog box.
   b. Scroll down the list of Microsoft Office Online templates in the Templates pane, click Memos, select the Memo (Professional design) template, click Download, then click Continue. (*Note:* You must be working with an active Internet connection to download a template from Microsoft Office Online. Select a different memo template if the Professional design memo is not available to you.)
   c. Type Louis Philippe Ouellette to replace the To placeholder text, type your name to replace the From placeholder text, then type Sold out summer festival packages to replace the Re placeholder text.
   d. Select the Cc line, then press [Delete]. The date in the document should be the current date.
   e. Click the Office button, click Convert, click OK, then save the document with the filename Sold Out Memo to the drive and folder where you store your Data Files.

7. **View and navigate a document.**
   a. Scroll down until How to Use This Memo Template is at the top of your document window.
   b. Delete the text How to Use This Memo Template.
   c. Select the remaining placeholder body text, type Packages for the following summer festivals are sold out: First Peoples' Festival, Chamber Music Festival, and Dragon Boat Race Festival. We had expected these packages to be less popular than those for the bigger festivals, but interest has been high. Next year, we will increase our bookings for these festivals by 30%.
   d. Use the Zoom dialog box to view the Whole Page.
   e. Click Company Name Here to move the insertion point to the upper-right corner of the page, then use the Zoom slider to set the Zoom percentage at approximately 200%.
   f. Replace Company Name Here with Global Montreal, then reduce the zoom percentage to 100%.
   g. Preview the document in Print Preview, correct any errors, close Print Preview, save the document, print it, close the file, then exit Word. Compare your document to Figure A-17.

FIGURE A-17

Global Montreal

Memo

To:	Louis Philippe Ouellette
From:	Your Name
Date:	6/1/10
Re:	Sold out summer festival packages

Packages for the following summer festivals are sold out: First Peoples' Festival, Chamber Music Festival, and Dragon Boat Race Festival. We had expected these packages to be less popular than those for the bigger festivals, but interest has been high. Next year, we will increase our bookings for these festivals by 30%.

▼ INDEPENDENT CHALLENGE 1

Yesterday you interviewed for a job as U.S. marketing director at Edo Design Services. You spoke with several people at Edo, including Mayumi Suzuki, chief executive officer, whose business card is shown in Figure A-18. You need to write a follow-up letter to Ms. Suzuki, thanking her for the interview and expressing your interest in the company and the position. She also asked you to send her some samples of your marketing work, which you will enclose with the letter.

a. Start Word and save a new blank document as **Edo Letter** to the drive and folder where you store your Data Files.

FIGURE A-18

Mayumi Suzuki
Chief Executive Officer

Edo Design Services

5-8, Edobori 4-chome
Minato-ku
Tokyo 108-0034
Japan

Phone: (03) 5555-3299
Fax: (03) 5555-7028
Email: msuzuki@edodesign.com.jp

b. Begin the letter by clicking the No Spacing button in the Styles group. You use this button to apply the No Spacing style to the document so that your document does not include extra space between paragraphs.

c. Type a personal letterhead for the letter that includes your name, address, telephone number, and e-mail address. If Word formats your e-mail address as a hyperlink, right-click your e-mail address, then click Remove Hyperlink. (*Note*: Format the letterhead after you finish typing the letter.)

d. Three lines below the bottom of the letterhead, type today's date.

e. Four lines below the date, type the inside address, referring to Figure A-18 for the address information. Be sure to include the recipient's title, company name, and full mailing address in the inside address. (*Hint*: When typing a foreign address, type the name of the country in capital letters by itself on the last line.)

f. Two lines below the inside address, type the salutation.

g. Two lines below the salutation, type the body of the letter according to the following guidelines:
  - In the first paragraph, thank her for the interview. Then restate your interest in the position and express your desire to work for the company. Add any specific details you think will enhance the power of your letter.
  - In the second paragraph, note that you are enclosing three samples of your work and explain something about the samples you are enclosing.
  - Type a short final paragraph.

h. Two lines below the last body paragraph, type a closing, then four lines below the closing, type the signature block. Be sure to include your name in the signature block.

i. Two lines below the signature block, type an enclosure notation. (*Hint*: An enclosure notation usually includes the word "Enclosures" or the abbreviation "Enc." followed by the number of enclosures in parentheses.)

j. Format the letterhead with bold, centering, and a bottom border.

k. Save your changes.

l. Preview and print the letter, then close the document and exit Word.

▼ INDEPENDENT CHALLENGE 2

Your company has recently installed Word 2007 on its company network. As the training manager, it's your responsibility to teach employees how to use the new software productively. Now that they have begun working with Word 2007, several employees have asked you about sharing Word 2007 documents with colleagues who are using an earlier version of Word. In response to their queries, you decide to write a memo to all employees explaining file compatibility issues between Word 2007 and previous versions of Word. Rather than write the memo from scratch, you revise a memo you wrote earlier on this topic to the department heads. That memo was written on your home office computer, which still has Word 2003 installed.

a. Start Word, open the file **WD A-1.doc** from the drive and folder where you store your Data Files, then read the memo to get a feel for its contents. The .doc file extension lets you know this file was created in a previous version of Word. Notice the words Compatibility Mode in the title bar. Compatibility Mode ensures that no new features in Word 2007 are available while you are working with the document so that the document will be fully accessible to people who use previous versions of Word.

b. Save the file in Word 97-2003 format as **XML Memo** to the drive and folder where you store your Data Files.

c. Replace the information in the memo header with the information shown in Figure A-19. Make sure to include your name in the From line and the current date in the Date line.

d. Apply bold to **To:**, **From:**, **Date:**, and **Re:**.

e. Increase the size of **WORD TRAINING MEMORANDUM** to match Figure A-19, center the text on the page, add a border below it, then save your changes.

FIGURE A-19

WORD TRAINING MEMORANDUM	
To:	All employees
From:	Your Name, Training Manager
Date:	Today's date
Re:	File compatibility in Word 2007

f. In order to save the memo in XML format, click the Office button, click Convert, read the text in the Microsoft Office Word dialog box, then click OK. Notice the phrase Compatibility Mode no longer appears in the title bar. Compatibility Mode is turned off.

g. Click the Save button. Notice the file extension in the title bar changes to .docx if Windows is set to display file extensions on your computer.

Advanced Challenge Exercise

■ Using the Font list on the Mini toolbar, apply a different font to **WORD TRAINING MEMORANDUM**. Make sure to select a font that is appropriate for a business memo.

■ Using the Font Color button on the Mini toolbar, change the color of **WORD TRAINING MEMORANDUM** to an appropriate color.

■ Save a copy of the memo in Word 97-2003 format as **XML Memo ACE** to the drive or folder where you store your Data Files. (*Hint*: Click the Office button, point to Save As, then click Word 97-2003 Document.)

h. Preview and print the memo, then close the document and exit Word.

▼ INDEPENDENT CHALLENGE 3

You are an expert on global warming. The president of the National Park Association, Jeremy Moynihan, has asked you to be the keynote speaker at an upcoming conference on the impact of climate change on the national parks, to be held in Glacier National Park. You use one of the Word letter templates to write a letter to Mr. Moynihan accepting the invitation and confirming the details. Your letter to Mr. Moynihan should reference the following information:

• The conference will be held June 4–6, 2010, at the Many Glacier Hotel in the park.

• You have been asked to speak for an hour on Saturday, June 5, followed by one half hour for questions.

• Mr. Moynihan suggested the lecture topic "Melting Glaciers, Changing Ecosystems."

• Your talk will include a 45-minute slide presentation.

• The National Park Association will make your travel arrangements.

• Your preference is to arrive at Glacier Park International Airport in Kalispell on the morning of Friday, June 4 and to depart on Monday, June 7. You would like to rent a car at the airport for the drive to the Many Glacier Hotel.

• You want to fly in and out of the airport closest to your home.

a. Start Word, open the New Document dialog box, click Installed Templates, and then select an appropriate letter template. Save the document as **Moynihan Letter** to the drive and folder where you store your Data Files.

b. Replace the placeholders in the letterhead with your personal information. Include your name, address, phone number, and e-mail address. Delete any placeholders that do not apply. (*Hints*: Depending on the template you choose, the letterhead might be located at the top or on the side of the document. You can press [Enter] when typing in a placeholder to add an additional line of text. You can also change the format of text typed in a placeholder.)

c. Use the Pick the date content control to select the current date.

d. Replace the placeholders in the inside address. Be sure to include Mr. Moynihan's title and the name of the organization. Make up a street address and zip code.

e. Type **Dear Mr. Moynihan:** for the salutation.

f. Using the information listed previously, type the body of the letter:

- In the first paragraph, accept the invitation to speak and confirm the important conference details.
- In the second paragraph, confirm your lecture topic and provide any relevant details.
- In the third paragraph, state your travel preferences.
- Type a short final paragraph.

g. Type **Sincerely,** for the closing, then include your name in the signature block.

h. Adjust the formatting of the letter as necessary. For example, remove bold formatting or change the font color of text to a more appropriate color.

Advanced Challenge Exercise

- ■ Zoom in and out on the document, looking for spelling, grammar, and formatting errors.
- ■ Correct your spelling and grammar errors, if any, by right-clicking any red- or green-underlined text and then choosing from the options on the shortcut menu.
- ■ View the letter in Full Screen Reading view, then click the Close button to return to Print Layout view.

i. Proofread your letter, make corrections as needed, then save your changes.

j. Preview the letter, print the letter, close the document, then exit Word.

▼ REAL LIFE INDEPENDENT CHALLENGE

This Independent Challenge requires an Internet connection.

The computer keyboard has become as essential an office tool as the pencil. The more adept you become at touch typing—the fastest and most accurate way to type—the more comfortable you will be working with computers and the more saleable your office skills to a potential employer. The World Wide Web is one source of information on touch typing, and many Web sites include free typing tests and online tutorials to help you practice and improve your typing skills. In this independent challenge, you will take an online typing test to check your typing skills. You will then research the fundamentals of touch typing and investigate some of the ergonomic factors important to becoming a productive keyboard typist.

a. Use your favorite search engine to search the Web for information on typing. Use the keywords **typing** and **typing ergonomics** to conduct your search.

b. Review the Web sites you find. Choose a site that offers a free online typing test, take the test, then print the Web page showing the results of your typing test.

c. Start Word and save a new blank document as **Touch Typing** to the drive and folder where you store your Data Files.

d. Type your name at the top of the document.

e. Type a brief report on the results of your research. Your report should answer the following questions:

- What are the URLs of the Web sites you visited to research touch typing and keyboard ergonomics? (*Hint*: A URL is a Web page's address. An example of a URL is www.course.com.)
- What are some of the benefits of using the touch typing method?
- In touch typing, on which keys should the fingers of the left and right hands rest?
- What ergonomic factors are important to keep in mind while typing?

f. Save your changes to the document, preview and print it, then close the document and exit Word.

▼ VISUAL WORKSHOP

Create the cover letter shown in Figure A-20. Before beginning to type, click the No Spacing button in the Styles group on the Home tab. Add the bottom border to the letterhead after typing the letter. Save the document as **Wong Cover Letter** to the drive and folder where you store your Data Files, print a copy of the letter, then close the document and exit Word.

FIGURE A-20

Your Name

345 West 11th Avenue, Anchorage, AK 99501
Tel: 907-555-7283; Fax: 907-555-1445

June 28, 2010

Ms. Sylvia Wong
Wong Associates
2286 East Northern Lights Blvd.
Suite 501
Anchorage, AK 99514

Dear Ms. Wong:

I read of the opening for a public information assistant in the June 27 edition of adn.com, and I would like to be considered for the position. I am a recent graduate of Greater Anchorage Community College (GACC), and I am interested in pursuing a career in public relations.

My interest in a public relations career springs from my publicly acknowledged writing and journalism abilities. For example, at GACC, I was a reporter for the student newspaper and frequently wrote press releases for campus and community events.

I have a wealth of experience using Microsoft Word in professional settings. Last summer, I worked as an office assistant for the architecture firm Coleman & Greenberg, where I used Word to create newsletters, brochures, and financial reports. During the school year, I also worked part-time in the GACC Office of Community Relations, where I used the Word mail merge feature to create form letters and mailing labels.

My enclosed resume details my skills and experience. I welcome the opportunity to discuss the position and my qualifications with you. I can be reached at 907-555-7283.

Sincerely,

Your Name

Enc.

Editing Documents

Files You Will Need:

WD B-1.docx

WD B-2.docx

WD B-3.docx

WD B-4.docx

WD B-5.docx

WD B-6.docx

WD B-7.docx

The sophisticated editing features in Word make it easy to revise and polish your documents. In this unit, you learn how to revise an existing file by opening it, copying and moving text, and then saving the document as a new file. You also learn how to perfect your documents using proofing tools and how to quickly prepare a document for distribution to the public. You have been asked to edit and finalize a press release for a QST promotional lecture series. The press release should provide information about the series so that newspapers, radio stations, and other media outlets can announce it to the public. QST press releases are disseminated by fax and by e-mail. Before distributing the file electronically to your lists of press contacts and local QST clients, you add several hyperlinks and then strip the file of private information.

OBJECTIVES

Cut and paste text

Copy and paste text

Use the Office Clipboard

Find and replace text

Check spelling and grammar

Research information

Add hyperlinks

Prepare a document for distribution

Cutting and Pasting Text

The editing features in Word allow you to move text from one location to another in a document. The operation of moving text is often called **cut and paste**. When you cut text, it is removed from the document and placed on the **Clipboard**, a temporary storage area for text and graphics that you cut or copy from a document. To cut text, you select it and then click the Cut button in the Clipboard group on the Home tab. To insert the text from the Clipboard into the document, you place the insertion point where you want to insert the text, and then click the Paste button in the Clipboard group. You also can move selected text by dragging it to a new location using the mouse. This operation is called **drag and drop**. You open the press release that was drafted by a colleague, save it with a new filename, and then reorganize the information in the press release using the cut-and-paste and drag-and-drop methods.

QUICK TIP
Use the Open button on the Quick Access toolbar if the toolbar has been customized to include this button.

1. **Start** Word, **click the** Office button, **click** Open, **navigate to the drive and folder where you store your Data Files, click** WD B-1.docx, **then click** Open

   The document opens. Once you have opened a file, you can edit it and use the Save or the Save As command to save your changes. You use the **Save** command when you want to save the changes you make to a file, overwriting the file that is stored on a disk. You use the **Save As** command when you want to leave the original file intact and create a duplicate file with a different filename, file extension, or location.

2. **Click**, **click** Save As, **type** Wanderlust PR **in the File name text box, then click** Save

   You can now make changes to the press release file without affecting the original file.

3. **Replace** Ron Dawson **with your name, scroll down until the headline Katherine Quoss to Speak... is at the top of your document window, then click the** Show/Hide ¶ button **in the Paragraph group on the Home tab to display formatting marks**

4. **Select** Alaskan guide Gilbert Coonan, **(including the comma and the space after it) in the third paragraph, then click the** Cut button **in the Clipboard group**

   The text is removed from the document and placed on the Clipboard. Word uses two different clipboards: the **system Clipboard** (the Clipboard), which holds just one item, and the **Office Clipboard**, which holds up to 24 items. The last item you cut or copy is always added to both clipboards. You'll learn more about the Office Clipboard in a later lesson.

QUICK TIP
You can also paste text by right-clicking where you want the text to be located, and then clicking Paste on the Edit menu.

5. **Place the insertion point before** Serengeti **(but after the space) in the first line of the third paragraph, then click the** Paste button **in the Clipboard group**

   The text is pasted at the location of the insertion point, as shown in Figure B-1. The Paste Options button appears below text when you first paste it in a document. You'll learn more about the Paste Options button in the next lesson. For now, you can ignore it.

6. **Press and hold** [Ctrl], **click the sentence** Ticket prices include lunch. **in the fourth paragraph, then release** [Ctrl]

   The entire sentence is selected.

TROUBLE
If you make a mistake, click the Undo button on the Quick Access toolbar, then try again.

7. **Press and hold the mouse button over the selected text until the pointer changes to**

   Notice the pointer's vertical line. You use this to indicate the location where you want the text to be inserted when you release the mouse button.

8. **Drag the pointer's vertical line to the end of the fifth paragraph (between the period and the paragraph mark) as shown in Figure B-2, then release the mouse button**

   The selected text is moved to the location of the insertion point. It is convenient to move text using the drag-and-drop method when the locations of origin and destination are both visible on the screen. Text is not placed on the Clipboard when you move it using drag-and-drop.

9. **Deselect the text, then click the** Save button **on the Quick Access toolbar**

FIGURE B-1: Moved text with Paste Options button

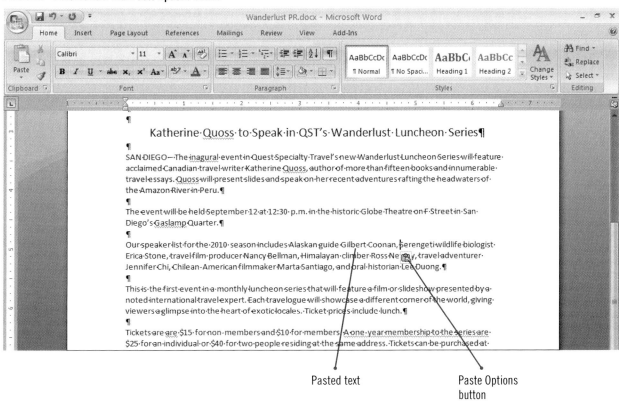

Pasted text

Paste Options
button

FIGURE B-2: Text being dragged to a new location

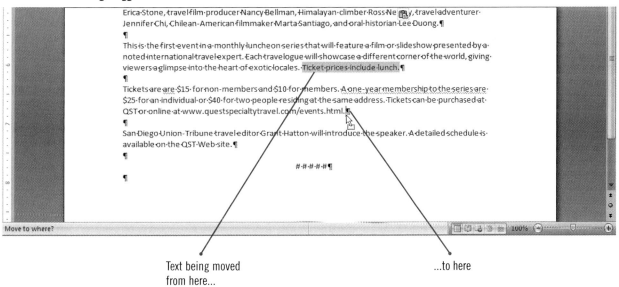

Text being moved
from here...

...to here

Using keyboard shortcuts

Instead of using the Cut, Copy, and Paste commands to edit text in Word, you can use the **keyboard shortcuts** [Ctrl][X] to cut text, [Ctrl][C] to copy text, and [Ctrl][V] to paste text. A **shortcut key** is a function key, such as [F1], or a combination of keys, such as [Ctrl][S], that you press to perform a command. For example, you can press [Ctrl][S] to save changes to a document instead of clicking the Save button on the Quick Access toolbar or clicking Save on the Office menu. Becoming skilled at using keyboard shortcuts can help you to quickly accomplish many of the tasks you perform frequently in Word. If a keyboard shortcut is available for a command, then it is listed in the ScreenTip for the command.

Copying and Pasting Text

Copying and pasting text is similar to cutting and pasting text, except that the text you copy is not removed from the document. Rather, a copy of the text is placed on the Clipboard, leaving the original text in place. You can copy text to the Clipboard using the Copy button in the Clipboard group on the Home tab, or you can copy text by pressing [Ctrl] as you drag the selected text from one location to another. You continue to edit the press release by copying text from one location to another.

STEPS

1. **Select Wanderlust Luncheon in the headline, then click the Copy button 🖹 in the Clipboard group**

   A copy of the text is placed on the Clipboard, leaving the text you copied in place.

2. **Place the insertion point before season in the third body paragraph, then click the Paste button in the Clipboard group**

   "Wanderlust Luncheon" is inserted before "season," as shown in Figure B-3. Notice that the pasted text is formatted differently than the paragraph in which it was inserted.

3. **Click the Paste Options button 🖹, then click Match Destination Formatting**

   The Paste Options button allows you to change the formatting of pasted text. The formatting of "Wanderlust Luncheon" is changed to match the rest of the paragraph. The options available on the Paste Options menu depend on the format of the text you are pasting and the format of the surrounding text.

4. **Select www.questspecialtytravel.com in the fifth paragraph, press and hold [Ctrl], press and hold the mouse button until the pointer changes to 🔖**

5. **Drag the pointer's vertical line to the end of the last paragraph, placing it between site and the period, release the mouse button, then release [Ctrl]**

   The text is copied to the last paragraph. Since the formatting of the text you copied is the same as the formatting of the paragraph in which you inserted it, you can ignore the Paste Options button. Text is not copied to the Clipboard when you copy it using the drag-and-drop method.

6. **Place the insertion point before www.questspecialtytravel.com in the last paragraph, type at followed by a space, then save the document**

   Compare your document with Figure B-4.

Splitting the document window to copy and move items in a long document

If you want to copy or move items between parts of a long document, it can be useful to split the document window into two panes so that the item you want to copy or move is displayed in one pane and the destination for the item is displayed in the other pane. To split a window, click the Split button in the Window group on the View tab, drag the horizontal split bar that appears to the location you want to split the window, and then click. Once the document window is split into two panes, you can drag the split bar to resize the panes and use the scroll bars in each pane to display different parts of the document. To copy or move an item from one pane to another, you can use the Cut, Copy, and Paste commands, or you can drag the item between the panes. When you are finished editing the document, double-click the split bar to restore the window to a single pane, or click the Remove Split button in the Window group on the View tab.

FIGURE B-3: Text pasted in document

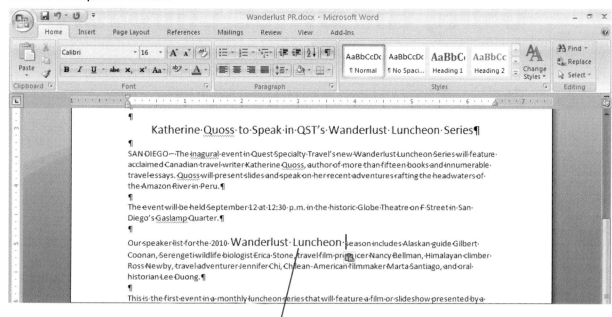

Formatting of the pasted
text matches the headline

FIGURE B-4: Copied text in document

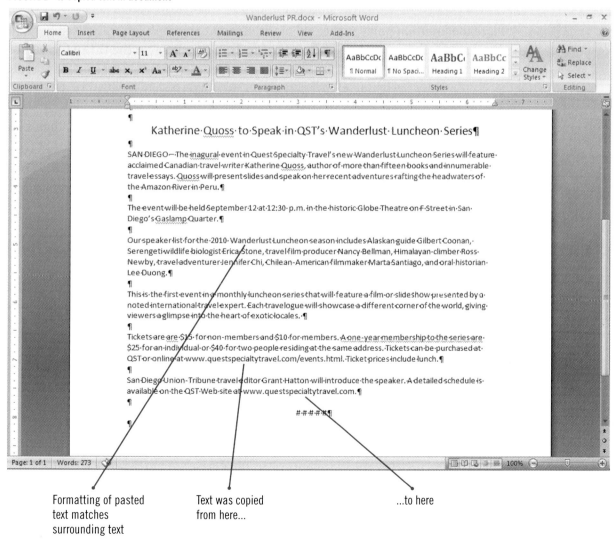

Formatting of pasted
text matches
surrounding text

Text was copied
from here...

...to here

Using the Office Clipboard

The Office Clipboard allows you to collect text and graphics from files created in any Office program and insert them into your Word documents. It holds up to 24 items and, unlike the system Clipboard, the items on the Office Clipboard can be viewed. To display the Office Clipboard, you simply click the launcher in the Clipboard group on the Home tab. You add items to the Office Clipboard using the Cut and Copy commands. The last item you collect is always added to both the system Clipboard and the Office Clipboard. You use the Office Clipboard to move several sentences in your press release.

STEPS

QUICK TIP

You can set the Office Clipboard to open automatically when you cut or copy two items consecutively by clicking Options in the Clipboard task pane, and then selecting Show Office Clipboard Automatically.

1. **Click the launcher in the Clipboard group**

   The Office Clipboard opens in the Clipboard task pane. It contains the Wanderlust Luncheon item you copied in the last lesson.

2. **Select the sentence San Diego Union-Tribune travel editor ... (including the space after the period) in the last paragraph, right-click the selected text, then click Cut on the Edit menu**

   The sentence is cut to the Office Clipboard.

3. **Select the sentence A detailed schedule is... (including the ¶ mark), right-click the selected text, then click Cut**

   The Office Clipboard displays the items you cut or copied, as shown in Figure B-5. The icon next to each item indicates the items are from a Word document. The last item collected displays at the top of the Clipboard task pane. As new items are collected, the first items collected move down the task pane.

QUICK TIP

An item remains on the Office Clipboard even after you paste it.

4. **Place the insertion point at the end of the second paragraph (after Quarter. but before the ¶ mark), then click the San Diego Union-Tribune... item on the Office Clipboard**

   Clicking an item on the Office Clipboard pastes the item in the document at the location of the insertion point. Items remain on the Office Clipboard until you delete them or close all open Office programs. Also, if you add a 25th item to the Office Clipboard, the first item is deleted.

5. **Place the insertion point at the end of the third paragraph (after Duong.), then click the A detailed schedule is... item on the Office Clipboard**

   The sentence is pasted in the document.

6. **Select the fourth paragraph, which begins with the sentence This is the first event... (including the ¶ mark), right-click the selected text, then click Cut**

   The paragraph is cut to the Office Clipboard.

QUICK TIP

Click the Paste All button on the Clipboard task pane to paste all the collected items at the location of the insertion point.

7. **Place the insertion point at the beginning of the third paragraph (before Our...), right-click, click Paste on the Edit menu, then press [Backspace]**

   The sentences from the "This is the first..." paragraph are pasted at the beginning of the "Our speaker list..." paragraph. You can paste the last item collected using either the Paste command or the Office Clipboard.

8. **Place the insertion point at the end of the third paragraph (after www.questspecialtytravel.com and before the ¶ mark), then press [Delete] twice**

   The ¶ symbols and the extra blank lines between the third and fourth paragraphs are deleted.

9. **Click the Show/Hide ¶ button in the Paragraph group**

   Compare your press release with Figure B-6. Note that many Word users prefer to work with formatting marks on at all times. Experiment to see which method you prefer.

QUICK TIP

To delete an individual item from the Office Clipboard, click the list arrow next to the item, then click Delete.

10. **Click the Clear All button on the Clipboard task pane to remove the items from the Office Clipboard, click the Close button on the Clipboard task pane, press [Ctrl][Home], then save the document**

    Pressing [Ctrl][Home] moves the insertion point to the top of the document.

FIGURE B-5: Office Clipboard in Clipboard task pane

Click to resize or move the Clipboard task pane

Clipboard task pane

Items stored on the Office Clipboard (yours may include additional items)

Click to change display options for the Office Clipboard

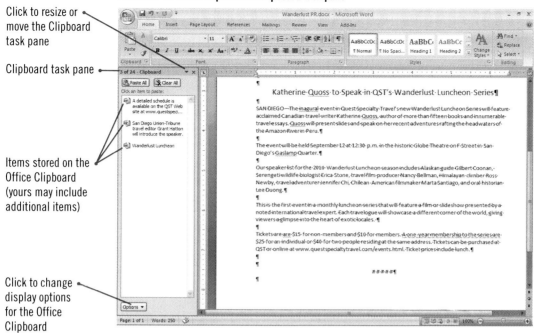

FIGURE B-6: Revised press release

Last item collected

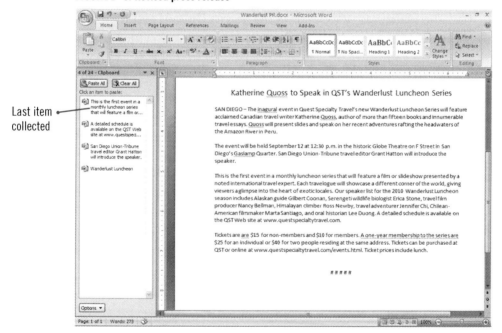

Copying and moving items between documents

The system and Office Clipboards also can be used to copy and move items between Word documents. To copy or cut items from one Word document and paste them into another, first open both documents and the Clipboard task pane in the program window. With multiple documents open, you can copy and move items between documents by copying or cutting the item(s) from one document and then switching to another document and pasting the item(s). To switch between open documents, click the button on the taskbar for the document you want to appear in the document window. You can also display both documents at the same time by clicking the Arrange All button or the View Side by Side button in the Window group on the View tab. The Office Clipboard stores all the items collected from all documents, regardless of which document is displayed in the document window. The system Clipboard stores the last item collected from any document.

Finding and Replacing Text

UNIT B — Word 2007

The Find and Replace feature in Word allows you to automatically search for and replace all instances of a word or phrase in a document. For example, you might need to substitute "tour" for "trip," and it would be very time-consuming to manually locate and replace each instance of "trip" in a long document. Using the Replace command you can automatically find and replace all occurrences of specific text at once, or you can choose to find and review each occurrence individually. You also can use the Find command to locate and select every occurrence of a specific word or phrase in a document. ▰▰▰ QST has decided to change the name of the lecture series from "Wanderlust Luncheon Series" to "Wanderlust Travelogue Series." You use the Replace command to search the document for all instances of "Luncheon" and replace them with "Travelogue."

STEPS

TROUBLE
If any of the Search Options check boxes are selected in your Find and Replace dialog box, deselect them. If Format appears under the Find what or Replace with text box, click in the text box, then click No Formatting.

1. **Click the Replace button in the Editing group, then click More in the Find and Replace dialog box**
   The Find and Replace dialog box opens, as shown in Figure B-7.

2. **Type Luncheon in the Find what text box**
   "Luncheon" is the text that will be replaced.

3. **Press [Tab], then type Travelogue in the Replace with text box**
   "Travelogue" is the text that will replace "Luncheon."

4. **Click the Match case check box in the Search Options section to select it**
   Selecting the Match case check box tells Word to find only exact matches for the uppercase and lowercase characters you entered in the Find what text box. You want to replace all instances of "Luncheon" in the proper name "Wanderlust Luncheon Series." You do not want to replace "luncheon" when it refers to a lunchtime event.

QUICK TIP
To find, review, and replace each occurrence individually, click Find Next.

5. **Click Replace All**
   Clicking Replace All changes all occurrences of "Luncheon" to "Travelogue" in the press release. A message box reports three replacements were made.

6. **Click OK to close the message box, then click Close in the Find and Replace dialog box**
   Word replaced "Luncheon" with "Travelogue" in three locations, but did not replace "luncheon."

7. **Click the Find button in the Editing group**
   The Find and Replace dialog box opens with the Find tab displayed. The Find command allows you to quickly locate all instances of text in a document. You can use it to verify that Word did not replace "luncheon."

QUICK TIP
To highlight all instances of specific text in a document, click Reading Highlight on the Find tab, then click Highlight All.

8. **Type luncheon in the Find what text box, make sure the Match case check box is still selected, click Find in, click Main Document on the menu that opens, then click Close**
   The Find and Replace dialog box closes and "luncheon" is selected in the document, as shown in Figure B-8.

9. **Deselect the text, press [Ctrl][Home], then save the document**

Navigating a document using the Go To command

Rather than scrolling to move to a different place in a longer document, you can use the Go To command to quickly move the insertion point to a specific location. To move to a specific page, section, line, table, graphic, or other item in a document, click the Page number button on the status bar to open the Find and Replace dialog box with the Go To tab displayed. On the Go To tab in the Find and Replace dialog box, select the type of item you want to find in the Go to what list box, enter the relevant information about that item, and then click Go To or Next to move the insertion point to the item.

FIGURE B-7: Find and Replace dialog box

Replace only exact matches of upper-case and lowercase characters

Find only complete words

Use wildcards (*) in a search string

Find words that sound like the Find what text

Find and replace all forms of a word

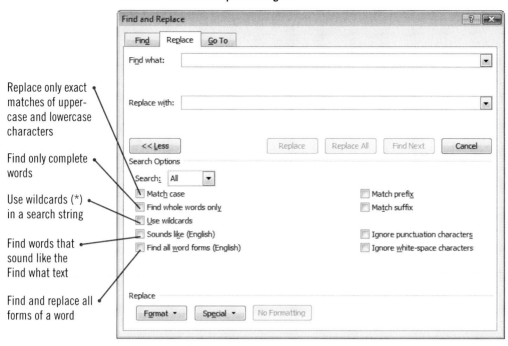

FIGURE B-8: Found text highlighted in document

Found text is highlighted

Checking Spelling and Grammar

When you finish typing and revising a document, you can use the Spelling and Grammar command to search the document for misspelled words and grammar errors. The Spelling and Grammar checker flags possible mistakes, suggests correct spellings, and offers remedies for grammar errors such as subject-verb agreement, repeated words, and punctuation. ▰▰▰ You use the Spelling and Grammar checker to search your press release for errors. Before beginning the search, you set the Spelling and Grammar checker to ignore words, such as Quoss, that you know are spelled correctly.

STEPS

1. **Right-click Quoss in the headline**

   A shortcut menu that includes suggestions for correcting the spelling of "Quoss" opens. You can correct individual spelling and grammar errors by right-clicking text that is underlined with a red or green wavy line and selecting a correction. Although "Quoss" is not in the Word dictionary, it is spelled correctly in the document.

2. **Click Ignore All**

   Clicking Ignore All tells Word not to flag "Quoss" as misspelled.

3. **Press [Ctrl][Home], click the Review tab, then click the Spelling and Grammar button in the Proofing group**

   The Spelling and Grammar: English (United States) dialog box opens, as shown in Figure B-9. The dialog box identifies "inagural" as misspelled and suggests possible corrections for the error. The word selected in the Suggestions box is the correct spelling.

4. **Click Change**

   Word replaces the misspelled word with the correctly spelled word. Next, the dialog box identifies "Gaslamp" as a misspelled word and suggests the correction "Gas lamp". The proper name "Gaslamp Quarter" is spelled correctly in the document.

5. **Click Ignore Once**

   Word ignores the spelling. Next, the dialog box indicates that "are" is repeated in a sentence.

6. **Click Delete**

   Word deletes the second occurrence of the repeated word. Next, the dialog box flags a subject-verb agreement error and suggests using "is" instead of "are," as shown in Figure B-10. The phrase selected in the Suggestions box is correct.

7. **Click Change**

   Word replaces "are" with "is" in the sentence and the Spelling and Grammar dialog box closes. Keep in mind that the Spelling and Grammar checker identifies many common errors, but you cannot rely on it to find and correct all spelling and grammar errors in your documents. Always proofread your documents carefully.

8. **Click OK to complete the spelling and grammar check, press [Ctrl][Home], then save the document**

FIGURE B-9: Spelling and Grammar: English (United States) dialog box

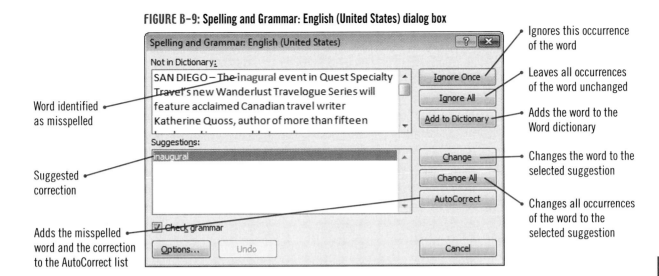

Word identified as misspelled

Suggested correction

Adds the misspelled word and the correction to the AutoCorrect list

Ignores this occurrence of the word

Leaves all occurrences of the word unchanged

Adds the word to the Word dictionary

Changes the word to the selected suggestion

Changes all occurrences of the word to the selected suggestion

FIGURE B-10: Grammar error identified in Spelling and Grammar dialog box

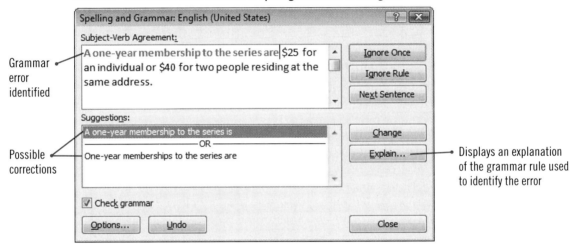

Grammar error identified

Possible corrections

Displays an explanation of the grammar rule used to identify the error

Inserting text with AutoCorrect

As you type, AutoCorrect automatically corrects many commonly misspelled words. By creating your own AutoCorrect entries, you can set Word to quickly insert text that you type often, such as your name or contact information, or to correct words you frequently misspell. For example, you could create an AutoCorrect entry so that the name "Ron Dawson" is automatically inserted whenever you type "rd" followed by a space. You create AutoCorrect entries and customize other AutoCorrect and AutoFormat options using the AutoCorrect dialog box. To open the AutoCorrect dialog box, click the Office button, click Word Options on the Office menu, click Proofing in the Word Options dialog box that opens, and then click

AutoCorrect Options. On the AutoCorrect tab in the AutoCorrect dialog box, type the text you want to be automatically corrected in the Replace text box (such as "rd"), type the text you want to be automatically inserted in its place in the With text box (such as "Ron Dawson"), and then click Add. The AutoCorrect entry is added to the list. Click OK to close the AutoCorrect dialog box, and then click OK to close the Word Options dialog box. Note that Word inserts an AutoCorrect entry in a document only when you press [Spacebar] after typing the text you want Word to correct. For example, Word will insert "Ron Dawson" when you type "rd" followed by a space, but not when you type "Mountain Rd."

Researching Information

The Word Research feature allows you to quickly search reference sources for information related to a word or phrase. Among the reference sources available in the Research task pane is a Thesaurus, which you can use to look up synonyms for awkward or repetitive words. When you are working with an active Internet connection, the Research task pane provides access to dictionary, encyclopedia, translation, and other reference sources, as well as third-party research services, such as medical and legal dictionaries. ▓▓▓ After proofreading your document for errors, you decide the press release would read better if several adjectives were more descriptive. You use the Thesaurus to find synonyms.

STEPS

QUICK TIP

You can also click the Research button in the Proofing group to open the Research task pane.

1. **Scroll down until the headline is displayed at the top of your screen**

2. **Select noted in the first sentence of the third paragraph, then click Thesaurus in the Proofing group**

   The Research task pane opens, as shown in Figure B-11. "Noted" appears in the Search for text box and possible synonyms for "noted" are listed under the Thesaurus: English (United States) heading in the task pane.

QUICK TIP

To look up synonyms for a different word, type the word in the Search for text box, then click the green Start searching button.

3. **Point to prominent in the list of synonyms**

   A box containing a list arrow appears around the word.

4. **Click the list arrow, click Insert on the menu that appears, then close the Research task pane**

   "Prominent" replaces "noted" in the press release.

5. **Right-click innumerable in the first sentence of the first paragraph, point to Synonyms on the Edit menu, then click numerous**

   "Numerous" replaces "innumerable" in the press release.

6. **Select the four paragraphs of body text (including the ¶ at the end of the last paragraph), then click the Word Count button ⚏ in the Proofing group**

   The Word Count dialog box opens, as shown in Figure B-12. The dialog box lists the number of pages, words, characters, paragraphs, and lines included in the selected text. Notice that the status bar also displays the number of words included in the selected text and the total number of words in the entire document. If you want to view the page, character, paragraph, and line count for the entire document, make sure nothing is selected in your document, and then click Word Count in the Proofing group.

QUICK TIP

To add or remove available reference sources, click Research options in the Research task pane.

7. **Click Close, press [Ctrl][Home], then save the document**

8. **Click the Office button 🔘, click Save As, type Wanderlust PR Public in the File name text box, then click Save**

   The Wanderlust PR file closes and the Wanderlust PR Public file is displayed in the document window. You will modify this file to prepare it for electronic release to the public.

FIGURE B-11: Research task pane

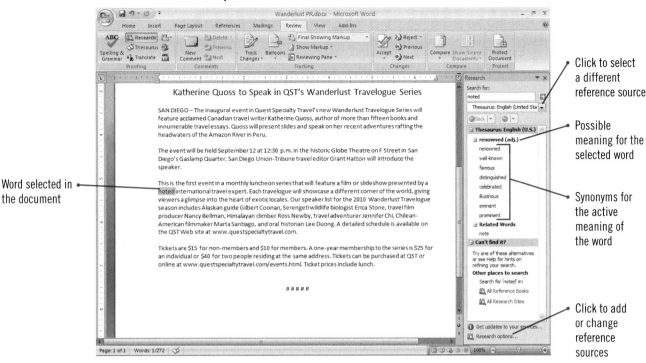

Word selected in the document

Click to select a different reference source

Possible meaning for the selected word

Synonyms for the active meaning of the word

Click to add or change reference sources

FIGURE B-12: Word Count dialog box

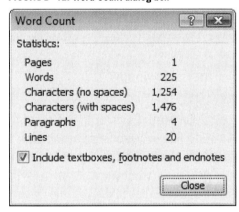

Publishing a blog directly from Word

A **blog**, which is short for weblog, is an informal journal that is created by an individual or a group and available to the public on the Internet. A blog usually conveys the ideas, comments, and opinions of the blogger and is written using a strong personal voice. The person who creates and maintains a blog, the **blogger**, typically updates the blog daily. If you have or want to start a blog, you can configure Word to link to your blog site, so that you can write, format, and publish blog entries directly from Word. To create a blog entry, click the Office button, click New, then double-click New blog post to open a predesigned blog post document that you can customize with your own text, formatting, and images. When you are ready to publish the entry to your blog, Word prompts you to log onto your personal blog account. To blog directly from Word, you must first obtain a blog account with a blog service provider. The Word Help system provides detailed information on obtaining and registering your personal blog account with Word.

Adding Hyperlinks

A **hyperlink** is text or a graphic that, when clicked, "jumps" the viewer to a different location or program. When a document is viewed on screen, hyperlinks allow readers to link (or "jump") to a Web page, an e-mail address, a file, or a specific location in a document. When you create a hyperlink in a document, you select the text or graphic you want to use as a hyperlink and then specify the location you want to jump to when the hyperlink is clicked. You create a hyperlink using the Hyperlink button in the Links group on the Insert tab. Text that is formatted as a hyperlink appears as colored, underlined text. ▓▓▓▓ Hundreds of people on your lists of press and client contacts will receive the press release by e-mail or Internet fax. To make it easier for these people to access additional information about the series, you add several hyperlinks to the press release.

STEPS

1. **Select your name, click the Insert tab, then click the Hyperlink button in the Links group**

   The Insert Hyperlink dialog box opens, as shown in Figure B-13. You use this dialog box to specify the location of the Web page, file, e-mail address, or position in the current document you want to jump to when the hyperlink—in this case, your name—is clicked.

2. **Click E-mail Address in the Link to section**

   The Insert Hyperlink dialog box changes so you can create a hyperlink to your e-mail address.

3. **Type your e-mail address in the E-mail address text box, type Wanderlust Travelogue Series in the Subject text box, then click OK**

   As you type, Word automatically adds mailto: in front of your e-mail address. After you close the dialog box, the hyperlink text—your name—is formatted in blue and underlined.

4. **Press and hold [Ctrl], then click the your name hyperlink**

   An e-mail message addressed to you with the subject "Wanderlust Travelogue Series" opens in the default e-mail program. People who receive the press release electronically can use the hyperlink to send you an e-mail message about the series.

5. **Close the e-mail message window**

   The hyperlink text changes to purple, indicating the hyperlink has been followed.

6. **Scroll down, select Gaslamp Quarter in the second paragraph, click the Hyperlink button, click Existing File or Web Page in the Link to section, type www.gaslamp.org in the Address text box, then click OK**

   As you type the Web address, Word automatically adds http:// in front of "www." The text "Gaslamp Quarter" is formatted as a hyperlink to the Gaslamp Quarter Association home page at www.gaslamp.org. When clicked, the hyperlink will open the Web page in the default browser window.

7. **Select detailed schedule in the last sentence of the third paragraph, click the Hyperlink button, type www.questspecialtytravel.com in the Address text box, then click OK**

   The text "detailed schedule" is formatted as a hyperlink to the QST Web site. If you point to a hyperlink in Word, the link to location appears in a ScreenTip. You can edit ScreenTip text to make it more descriptive.

8. **Right-click Quarter in the Gaslamp Quarter hyperlink, click Edit Hyperlink, click ScreenTip in the Edit Hyperlink dialog box, type Map, parking, and other information about the Gaslamp Quarter in the ScreenTip text text box, click OK, click OK, save your changes, then point to the Gaslamp Quarter hyperlink in the document**

   The ScreenTip you created appears above the Gaslamp Quarter hyperlink, as shown in Figure B-14.

9. **If you are working with an active Internet connection, press [Ctrl], click the Gaslamp Quarter hyperlink, close the browser window that opens, press [Ctrl], click the detailed schedule hyperlink, then close the browser window**

   Before distributing a document, it's important to test each hyperlink to verify it works as you intended.

FIGURE B-13: Insert Hyperlink dialog box

Create a hyperlink to a Web page or file

Create a hyperlink to a location in the current file

Create a hyperlink to a new blank document

Create a hyperlink to an e-mail address

Text selected to be formatted as a hyperlink

Files in the current drive or folder (yours might differ)

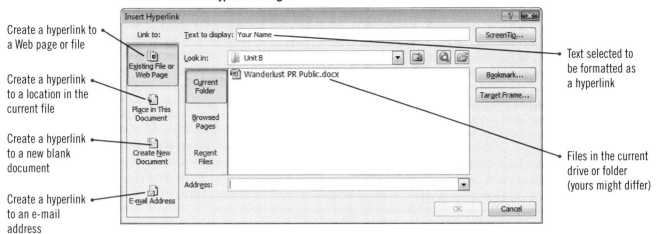

FIGURE B-14: Hyperlinks in the document

Purple indicates the hyperlink has been followed

Hyperlinks are colored and underlined

ScreenTip for the Gaslamp Quarter hyperlink

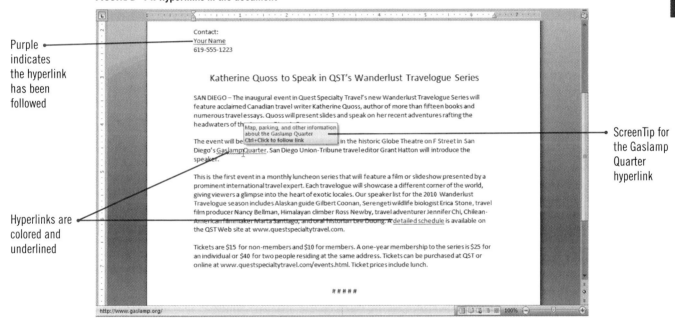

E-mailing and faxing documents directly from Word

Word includes several options for distributing and sharing documents over the Internet directly from within Word, including e-mailing and faxing documents. When you e-mail a document from within Word, the document is sent as an attachment to an e-mail message using your default e-mail program. To e-mail a file, open the file in Word, click the Office button, point to Send, and then click E-mail. A message window opens that includes the filename of the current file as the message subject and the file as an attachment. Type the e-mail address(es) of the recipient(s) in the To and Cc text boxes, any message you want in the message window,

and then click Send on the message window toolbar to send the message. The default e-mail program sends a copy of the document to each recipient. It's also possible to fax a document directly from within Word, although faxing a document requires registration with a third-party Internet fax service. To fax a document, open it in Word, click the Office button, point to Send, click Internet Fax, click OK to find and select a fax service if you don't already have one, and then follow the on-screen instructions. Fax services generally charge a monthly or per page fee for sending and receiving faxes.

Preparing a Document for Distribution

Before you distribute a document electronically to people outside your organization, it's wise to make sure the file does not include embedded private or confidential information. The Prepare command on the Office menu includes tools for stripping a document of sensitive information, for securing its authenticity, and for guarding it from unwanted changes once it is distributed to the public. See Table B-1. One of these tools, the Document Inspector, detects and removes unwanted private or confidential information from a document. Another tool, Mark as Final, allows you to make a document read-only so it cannot be modified by viewers. ▰▰▰▰▰ Before sending the press release to the public, you remove all identifying information from the file and mark it as final.

STEPS

QUICK TIP

To create or modify the standard document properties for a file, you type in the Document Information panel text boxes.

1. **Press [Ctrl][Home], click the Office button ⊙, point to Prepare, then click Properties**

   The Document Information panel opens above the document window, as shown in Figure B-15. It shows the standard document properties for the press release. **Document properties** are user-defined details about a file that describe its contents and origin, including the name of the author, the title of the document, and keywords that you can assign to help organize and search your files.

2. **Click ⊙, point to Prepare, click Inspect Document, then click Yes**

   The Document Inspector dialog box opens. You use this dialog box to indicate which private or identifying information you want to search for and remove from the document.

3. **Make sure all the check boxes are selected, then click Inspect**

   After a moment, the Document Inspector dialog box changes to indicate that the file contains document properties. You might not want this information to be available to the public.

4. **Click Remove All next to Document Properties, then click Close**

   The standard document property information is removed from the press release document.

5. **Click ⊙, point to Prepare, then click Mark as Final**

   A dialog box indicating that the document will be marked as final opens.

QUICK TIP

You can edit a document that is marked as final by turning off the Mark as Final status. Click the Office button, point to Prepare, and then click Mark as Final again.

6. **Click OK, then click OK if a second message box opens**

   The document is saved automatically, "Final" appears in the Status text box in the Document Information panel, and the commands on the Insert tab are disabled, indicating that the document is marked as final and cannot be changed. The Marked as Final icon also appears in the status bar.

7. **Click the Close button in the Document Information panel, click ⊙, point to Print, click Quick Print, close the file, then exit Word**

   The press release prints. The completed press release is shown in Figure B-16.

TABLE B-1: Prepare command options

feature	use to
Properties	View and modify the standard document properties and open the Properties dialog box
Inspect Document	Detect and remove unwanted private or proprietary information from a document, including document properties, comments, revisions, annotations, personal information, custom XML data, and hidden text
Encrypt Document	Add encryption to a document to make it more secure
Add a Digital Signature	Add an invisible digital signature to a document to verify its authenticity and integrity
Mark as Final	Indicate to readers that a document is read-only and cannot be edited
Run Compatibility Checker	Check the document for features that are not supported by previous versions of Microsoft Word

FIGURE B-15: Document Information panel

Document properties assigned when the original file was created

Your file location will differ

Document Information panel

Quest Specialty Travel Press Release

FIGURE B-16: Completed press release for electronic distribution

Quest Specialty Travel Press Release
340 West Market Street ● San Diego, CA 92101 ● Tel: 619-555-1223 ● Fax: 619-555-0937 ● www.questspecialtytravel.com

For Immediate Release
August 14, 2010

Contact:
Your Name
619-555-1223

Katherine Quoss to Speak in QST's Wanderlust Travelogue Series

SAN DIEGO – The inaugural event in Quest Specialty Travel's new Wanderlust Travelogue Series will feature acclaimed Canadian travel writer Katherine Quoss, author of more than fifteen books and numerous travel essays. Quoss will present slides and speak on her recent adventures rafting the headwaters of the Amazon River in Peru.

The event will be held September 12 at 12:30 p.m. in the historic Globe Theatre on F Street in San Diego's Gaslamp Quarter. San Diego Union-Tribune travel editor Grant Hatton will introduce the speaker.

This is the first event in a monthly luncheon series that will feature a film or slideshow presented by a prominent international travel expert. Each travelogue will showcase a different corner of the world, giving viewers a glimpse into the heart of exotic locales. Our speaker list for the 2010 Wanderlust Travelogue season includes Alaskan guide Gilbert Coonan, Serengeti wildlife biologist Erica Stone, travel film producer Nancy Bellman, Himalayan climber Ross Newby, travel adventurer Jennifer Chi, Chilean-American filmmaker Marta Santiago, and oral historian Lee Duong. A detailed schedule is available on the QST Web site at www.questspecialtytravel.com.

Tickets are $15 for non-members and $10 for members. A one-year membership to the series is $25 for an individual or $40 for two people residing at the same address. Tickets can be purchased at QST or online at www.questspecialtytravel.com/events.html. Ticket prices include lunch.

# # # # #

Viewing and modifying advanced document properties

The Document Information panel includes summary information about the document that you enter to suit your needs. To view more detailed document properties, including those entered automatically by Word when the document is created, click the Document Properties list arrow in the Document Information panel, and then click Advanced Properties to open the Properties dialog box. The General, Statistics, and Contents tabs of the Properties dialog box display information about the file that is automatically created and updated by Word. The General tab shows the file type, location, size, and date and time the file was created and last modified; the Statistics tab displays information about revisions to the document along with the number of pages, words, lines, paragraphs, and characters in the file; and the Contents tab shows the title of the document. You can define other document properties using the Summary and Custom tabs of the Properties dialog box. The Summary tab shows information similar to the information shown in the Document Information panel. The Custom tab allows you to create new document properties, such as client, project, or date completed. To create a custom property, select a property name in the Name list box on the Custom tab, use the Type list arrow to select the type of data you want for the property, type the identifying detail (such as a project name) in the Value text box, and then click Add. When you are finished viewing or modifying the document properties, click OK to close the Properties dialog box, then click the Close button in the Document Information panel.

Practice

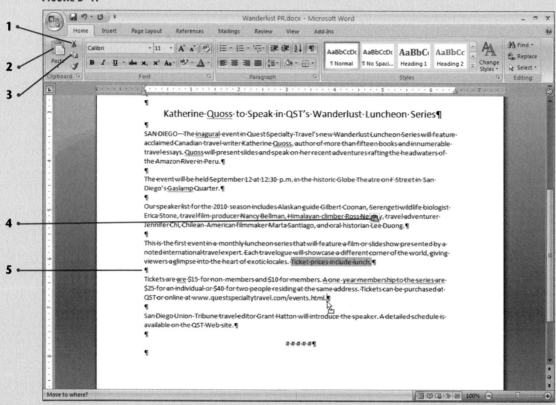

If you have a SAM user profile, you may have access to hands-on instruction, practice, and assessment of the skills covered in this unit. Log in to your SAM account (http://sam2007.course.com/) to launch any assigned training activities or exams that relate to the skills covered in this unit.

▼ CONCEPTS REVIEW

Label the elements of the Word program window shown in Figure B-17.

FIGURE B-17

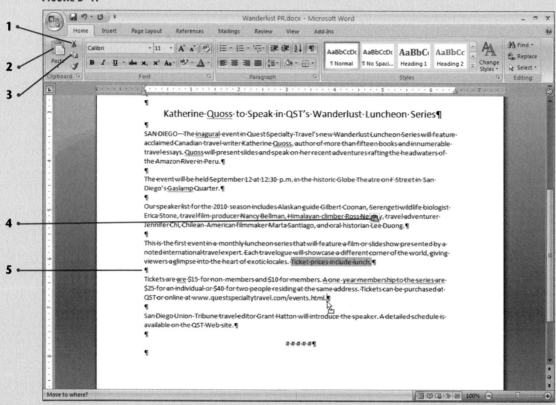

Match each term with the statement that best describes it.

6. **Hyperlink**

7. **Cut**

8. **Shortcut key**

9. **Document properties**

10. **Paste**

11. **Office Clipboard**

12. **System Clipboard**

13. **Blog**

14. **Thesaurus**

a. Command used to insert text stored on the Clipboard into a document

b. Temporary storage area for up to 24 items collected from Office files

c. Temporary storage area for only the last item cut or copied from a document

d. A function key or a combination of keys that perform a command when pressed

e. Text or a graphic that jumps the reader to a different location or program when clicked

f. An informal journal that is available to the public on the Internet

g. User-defined details about a file that describe its contents and origin

h. Feature used to suggest synonyms for words

i. Command used to remove text from a document and place it on the Clipboard

Select the best answer from the list of choices.

15. What is the keyboard shortcut for the Paste command?

   a. [Ctrl][C]
   c. [Ctrl][X]

   b. [Ctrl][V]
   d. [Ctrl][P]

16. Which of the following statements is *not* true?

   a. The Office Clipboard can hold more than one item.

   b. You can view the contents of the Office Clipboard.

   c. When you move text by dragging it, a copy of the text you move is stored on the system Clipboard.

   d. The last item cut or copied from a document is stored on the system Clipboard.

17. To locate and select all instances of a word in a document, which command do you use?

   a. Highlight
   c. Find

   b. Replace
   d. Search

18. Which command is used to display a document in two panes in the document window?

   a. New Window
   c. Two Pages

   b. Split
   d. Arrange All

19. Which of the following is an example of a document property?

   a. Keyword
   c. URL

   b. Language
   d. Permission

20. A hyperlink *cannot* be linked to which of the following?

   a. Web page
   c. ScreenTip

   b. E-mail address
   d. New blank document

▼ SKILLS REVIEW

1. Cut and paste text.

   a. Start Word, click the Office button, then open the file WD B-2.docx from the drive and folder where you store your Data Files.

   b. Save the document with the filename **PAOS 2010 PR**.

   c. Select **Your Name** and replace it with your name.

   d. Display paragraph and other formatting marks in your document if they are not already displayed.

   e. Use the Cut and Paste buttons to switch the order of the two sentences in the fourth paragraph (which begins New group shows...).

   f. Use the drag-and-drop method to switch the order of the second and third paragraphs.

   g. Adjust the spacing if necessary so that there is one blank line between paragraphs, then save your changes.

2. Copy and paste text.

   a. Use the Copy and Paste buttons to copy **PAOS 2008** from the headline and paste it before the word **map** in the third paragraph.

   b. Change the formatting of the pasted text to match the formatting of the third paragraph, then insert a space between **2008** and **map** if necessary.

   c. Use the drag-and-drop method to copy **PAOS** from the third paragraph and paste it before the word **group** in the second sentence of the fourth paragraph, then save your changes.

3. Use the Office Clipboard.

   a. Use the launcher in the Clipboard group to open the Clipboard task pane.

   b. Scroll so that the first body paragraph is displayed at the top of the document window.

   c. Select the fifth paragraph (which begins Studio location maps...) and cut it to the Office Clipboard.

   d. Select the third paragraph (which begins Portsmouth is easily accessible...) and cut it to the Office Clipboard.

   e. Use the Office Clipboard to paste the Studio location maps... item as the new fourth paragraph.

   f. Use the Office Clipboard to paste the Portsmouth is easily accessible... item as the new fifth paragraph.

   g. Adjust the spacing if necessary so that there is one blank line between each of the six body paragraphs.

   h. Turn off the display of formatting marks, clear and close the Office Clipboard, then save your changes.

4. Find and replace text.

a. Using the Replace command, replace all instances of 2008 with 2010.

b. Replace all instances of the abbreviation st with street, taking care to replace whole words only when you perform the replace. (*Hint*: Deselect Match case if it is selected.)

c. Use the Find command to find all instances of st in the document and to make sure no errors occurred when you replaced st with street. (*Hint*: Deselect the Find whole words only check box.)

d. Save your changes to the press release.

5. Check spelling and grammar and research information.

a. Switch to the Review tab.

b. Move the insertion point to the top of the document, then use the Spelling and Grammar command to search for and correct any spelling and grammar errors in the press release. (*Hint*: Jumpin' is not misspelled.)

c. Use the Thesaurus to replace thriving in the second paragraph with a different suitable word.

d. Check the word count of the press release.

e. Proofread your press release, correct any errors, then save your changes.

6. Add hyperlinks.

a. Save the document as PAOS 2010 PR Public, then switch to the Insert tab.

b. Select your name, then open the Insert Hyperlink dialog box.

c. Create a hyperlink to your e-mail address with the subject PAOS 2010.

d. Test the your name hyperlink, then close the message window that opens. (*Hint*: Press [Ctrl], then click the hyperlink.)

e. Select NEA in the last paragraph of the press release, then create a hyperlink to the URL www.nea.gov.

f. Right-click the NEA hyperlink, then edit the hyperlink ScreenTip to become Information on the National Endowment for the Arts.

g. Point to the NEA hyperlink to view the new ScreenTip, then save your changes.

h. If you are working with an active Internet connection, press [Ctrl], click the NEA hyperlink, view the NEA home page in the browser window, then close the browser window.

7. Prepare a document for distribution.

a. Click the Office button, point to Prepare, then view the document properties for the press release.

b. Use the Prepare command to run the Document Inspector.

c. Remove the document property data, then save your changes.

d. Use the Prepare command to mark the document as final. The finished press release is shown in Figure B-18.

e. Print the press release, close the file, then exit Word.

FIGURE B-18

PRESS RELEASE

FOR IMMEDIATE RELEASE
September 7, 2010

Contact:
Your Name
603-555-2938

PAOS 2010
Portsmouth Artists Open Their Studios to the Public

PORTSMOUTH, NH -- The fall 2010 Open Studios season kicks off with Portsmouth Artists Open Studios on Saturday and Sunday, October 13 and 14, from 11 a.m. to 6 p.m. More than 60 Portsmouth artists will open their studios and homes to the public for this annual event, now in its tenth year.

Portsmouth is an historic and diverse city, long home to a flourishing community of artists. Quiet residential streets lined with charming Victorians edge a vibrant commercial and industrial zone, all peppered with the studios of printmakers, sculptors, painters, glass and jewelry makers, illustrators, potters, photographers, watercolorists, and other artists working in a wide range of mediums.

Internationally celebrated sculptor Eva Russo will display her new work in the rotunda of City Hall. New PAOS group shows will open at the Atlantic Gallery and at Jumpin' Jay's Fish Café, both on Congress Street.

Studio location maps will be available prior to the opening at businesses and public libraries, and on the days of the event at Market Square. Market Square is located at the junction of Congress Street and Pleasant Street in downtown Portsmouth.

Portsmouth is easily accessible from all points in the Northeast by car or bus, and from Boston and Portland by train. On Saturday, non-Portsmouth residents may park in permit-only areas provided they display a copy of the PAOS 2010 map on the dashboard. There are no parking restrictions on Sundays in Portsmouth.

PAOS 2010 receives funds from participating artists and from the Portsmouth Arts Council, the New Hampshire Cultural Council, and the NEA, with valuable support from local universities and businesses.

#####

▼ INDEPENDENT CHALLENGE 1

Because of your success in revitalizing a historic theatre in Wellington, New Zealand, you were hired as the director of The Hobart Lyric Theatre in Hobart, Tasmania, to breathe life into its theatre revitalization efforts. After a year on the job, you are launching your first major fund-raising drive. You'll create a fund-raising letter for the Lyric Theatre by modifying a letter you wrote for the theatre in Wellington.

a. Start Word, open the file WD B-3.docx from the drive and folder where you store your Data Files, then save it as **Lyric Fundraising Letter**.

b. Replace the theatre name and address, the date, the inside address, and the salutation with the text shown in Figure B-19.

c. Use the Replace command to replace all instances of **Wellington** with **Hobart**.

d. Use the Replace command to replace all instances of **Town Hall** with **Lyric**.

e. Use the Replace command to replace all instances of **New Zealanders** with **Tasmanians**.

f. Use the Find command to locate the word **considerable**, then use the Thesaurus to replace the word with a synonym.

g. Move the fourth body paragraph so that it becomes the second body paragraph.

h. Create an AutoCorrect entry that inserts **Executive Director** whenever you type **exd**.

i. Replace Your Name with your name in the signature block, select Title, then type **exd** followed by a space.

j. Use the Spelling and Grammar command to check for and correct spelling and grammar errors.

The Hobart Lyric Theatre
60-62 Macquarie Street, Hobart, Tasmania 7001, Australia

November 10, 2010

Ms. Natasha Campbell
450 Elizabeth Street
North Hobart, TAS 7004

Dear Ms. Campbell:

Advanced Challenge Exercise

- Open the Document Information panel, change the title to **Hobart Lyric Theatre**, then add the keyword **fund-raising**.
- Open the Properties dialog box, add your name as author on the Summary tab, then review the paragraph, line, word, and character count on the Statistics tab.
- On the Custom tab, add a property named **Project** with the value **Capital Campaign**, then close the dialog box and the Document Information panel.

k. Proofread the letter, correct any errors, save your changes, print a copy, close the document, then exit Word.

An advertisement for job openings in Toronto caught your eye and you have decided to apply. The ad, shown in Figure B-20, was printed in last weekend's edition of your local newspaper. Instead of writing a cover letter from scratch, you revise a draft of a cover letter you wrote several years ago for a summer internship position.

a. Read the ad shown in Figure B-20 and decide which position to apply for. Choose the position that most closely matches your qualifications.

b. Start Word, open WD B-4.docx from the drive and folder where you store your Data Files, then save it as Cover Letter.

c. Replace the name, address, telephone number, and e-mail address in the letterhead with your own information.

d. Remove the hyperlink from the e-mail address.

e. Replace the date with today's date, then replace the inside address and the salutation with the information shown in Figure B-20.

f. Read the draft cover letter to get a feel for its contents.

g. Rework the text in the body of the letter to address your qualifications for the job you have chosen to apply for:

- Delete the third paragraph.
- Adjust the first sentence of the first paragraph as follows: specify the job you are applying for, including the position code, and indicate where you saw the position advertised.
- Move the first sentence in the last paragraph, which briefly states your qualifications and interest in the position, to the end of the first paragraph, then rework the sentence to describe your current qualifications.
- Adjust the second paragraph as follows: describe your work experience and skills. Be sure to relate your experience and qualifications to the position requirements listed in the advertisement. Add a third paragraph if your qualifications are extensive.
- Adjust the final paragraph as follows: politely request an interview for the position and provide your phone number and e-mail address.

h. Include your name in the signature block.

i. When you are finished revising the letter, check it for spelling and grammar errors and correct any mistakes. Make sure to remove any hyperlinks.

j. Save your changes to the letter, print a copy, close the document, then exit Word.

FIGURE B-20

*Global*Dynamics

Career Opportunities in Toronto

Global Dynamics, an established software development firm with offices in North America, Asia, and Europe, is seeking candidates for the following positions in its Toronto facility:

Instructor
Responsible for delivering software training to our expanding Canadian customer base. Duties include delivering hands-on training, keeping up-to-date with product development, and working with the Director of Training to ensure the high quality of course materials. Successful candidate will have excellent presentation skills and be proficient in Microsoft PowerPoint and Microsoft Word. **Position B12C6**

Administrative Assistant
Proficiency with Microsoft Word a must! Administrative office duties include making travel arrangements, scheduling meetings, taking notes and publishing meeting minutes, handling correspondence, and ordering office supplies. Must have superb multitasking abilities, excellent communication, organizational, and interpersonal skills, and be comfortable working with e-mail and the Internet. **Position B16F5**

Copywriter
The ideal candidate will have marketing or advertising writing experience in a high tech environment, including collateral, newsletters, and direct mail. Experience writing for the Web, broadcast, and multimedia is a plus. Fluency with Microsoft Word required. **Position C13D4**

Positions offer salary, excellent benefits, moving expenses, and career growth opportunities.

Send resume and cover letter referencing position code to:

Thomas Finlay
Director of Recruiting
Global Dynamics
330 University Avenue
Toronto, Ontario M5G 1R8
Canada

▼ INDEPENDENT CHALLENGE 3

As administrative director of continuing education, you drafted a memo to instructors asking them to help you finalize the course schedule for next semester. Today you'll examine the draft and make revisions before distributing it as an e-mail attachment.

a. Start Word, open the file WD B-5.docx from the drive and folder where you store your Data Files, then save it as **Business Courses Memo**.

b. Replace Your Name with your name in the From line, then scroll down until the first body paragraph is at the top of the screen.

Advanced Challenge Exercise

- Use the Split command on the View tab to split the window under the first body paragraph, then scroll until the last paragraph of the memo is displayed in the bottom pane.
- Use the Cut and Paste buttons to move the sentence **If you are planning to teach...** from the first body paragraph to become the first sentence in the last paragraph of the memo.
- Double-click the split bar to restore the window to a single pane.

c. Use the [Delete] key to merge the first two paragraphs into one paragraph.

d. Use the Office Clipboard to reorganize the list of twelve-week courses so that the courses are listed in alphabetical order.

e. Use the drag-and-drop method to reorganize the list of one-day seminars so that the seminars are listed in alphabetical order, then clear and close the Office Clipboard.

f. Select Web site in the first paragraph, then create a hyperlink to the URL **www.course.com** with the ScreenTip **Spring 2011 Business Course**.

g. Select e-mail me in the last paragraph, then create a hyperlink to your e-mail address with the subject **Final Business Course Schedule**.

h. Use the Spelling and Grammar command to check for and correct spelling and grammar errors.

i. Use the Document Inspector to strip the document of document property information, ignore any other content that is flagged by the Document Inspector, then close the Document Inspector.

j. Proofread the memo, correct any errors, save your changes, print a copy, close the document, then exit Word.

▼ REAL LIFE INDEPENDENT CHALLENGE

This Independent Challenge requires an Internet connection.

Reference sources—dictionaries, thesauri, style and grammar guides, and guides to business etiquette and procedure—are essential for day-to-day use in the workplace. Much of this reference information is available on the World Wide Web. In this independent challenge, you will locate reference sources on the Web and use some of them to look up definitions, synonyms, and antonyms for words. Your goal is to familiarize yourself with online reference sources so you can use them later in your work.

a. Start Word, open the file WD B-6.docx from the drive and folder where you store your Data Files, then save it as **Web Reference Sources**. This document contains the questions you will answer about the Web reference sources you find. You will type your answers to the questions in the document.

b. Replace the placeholder text at the top of the Web Reference Sources document with your name and the date.

c. Use your favorite search engine to search the Web for grammar and style guides, dictionaries, and thesauri. Use the keywords **grammar**, **usage**, **dictionary**, **glossary**, and **thesaurus** to conduct your search.

d. Complete the Web Reference Sources document, then proofread it and correct any mistakes.

e. Save the document, print a copy, close the document, then exit Word.

Open WD B-7.docx from the drive and folder where you store your Data Files, then save the document as Australian Visa Letter. Replace the placeholders for the date, letterhead, inside address, salutation, and closing with the information shown in Figure B-21, then use the Office Clipboard to reorganize the sentences to match Figure B-21. Correct spelling and grammar errors, remove the document property information from the file, mark the document as final, then print a copy.

FIGURE B-21

Your Name

4637 Baker Street, Chicago, IL 60627; Tel: 630-555-2840

1/3/2010

Embassy of Australia
1601 Massachusetts Avenue NW
Washington, DC 20036

Dear Sir or Madam:

I am applying for a long-stay tourist visa to Australia, valid for four years. I am scheduled to depart for Sydney on March 13, 2010, returning to Chicago on September 8, 2010.

During my stay in Australia, I will be interviewing musicians and recording footage for a film I am making on contemporary Australian music. I would like a multiple entry visa valid for four years so I can return to Australia after this trip to follow up on my initial research. I will be based in Sydney, but I will be traveling frequently to film performances and to meet with musicians and producers.

Included with this letter are my completed visa application form, my passport, a passport photo, a copy of my return air ticket, and the visa fee. Please contact me if you need further information.

Sincerely,

Your Name

Enc: 5

Formatting Text and Paragraphs

Files You Will Need:

WD C-1.docx
WD C-2.docx
WD C-3.docx
WD C-4.docx
WD C-5.docx
WD C-6.docx

Formatting can enhance the appearance of a document, create visual impact, and help illustrate a document's structure. The formatting of a document can also set the tone of the document, allowing readers to know at a glance if the document is business-like, serious, formal, informal, or fun. In this unit you learn how to format text using different fonts and font-formatting options. You also learn how to change the alignment, indentation, and spacing of paragraphs, how to spruce up documents with borders, shading, bullets, and other paragraph-formatting effects, and how to add footnotes and endnotes to a document. The Word live preview feature simplifies formatting by allowing you to quickly preview the different formatting options in your document before you apply them. You have finished drafting the text for a two-page flyer advertising last minute specials for October tours. Now, you need to format the flyer so it is attractive and highlights the significant information. The flyer will be distributed to clients with the quarterly newsletter.

OBJECTIVES

Format with fonts

Copy formats using the Format Painter

Change line and paragraph spacing

Align paragraphs

Work with tabs

Work with indents

Add bullets and numbering

Add borders and shading

Add footnotes and endnotes

Formatting with Fonts

Formatting text with different fonts is a quick and powerful way to enhance the appearance of a document. A **font** is a complete set of characters with the same typeface or design. Arial, Times New Roman, Comic Sans, Courier, Tahoma, and Calibri are some of the more common fonts, but there are hundreds of others, each with a specific design and feel. Another way to alter the impact of text is to increase or decrease its **font size**, which is measured in points. A **point** is ½ of an inch. You change the font and font size of the body text, title, and headings in the flyer, selecting fonts and font sizes that enhance the sales tone of the document and help to visually structure the report for readers.

STEPS

1. **Start Word, open the file** WD C-1.docx **from the drive and folder where you store your Data Files, then save it as** Last Minute Deals

   Notice that the name of the font used in the document, Calibri, is displayed in the Font list box in the Font group. The word "(Body)" in the Font list box indicates Calibri is the font used for body text in the current theme, the default theme. A **theme** is a related set of fonts, colors, styles, and effects that is applied to an entire document to give it a cohesive appearance. The font size, 11, appears next to it in the Font Size list box.

2. **Scroll the document to get a feel for its contents, press [Ctrl][Home], press [Ctrl][A] to select the entire document, then click the** Font list arrow **in the Font group**

   The Font list, which shows the fonts available on your computer, opens as shown in Figure C-1. The font names are formatted in the font and can appear in more than one location on the font list.

3. **Drag the pointer slowly down the font names in the Font list, use the scroll box to scroll down the Font list, then click** Garamond

   Dragging the pointer down the font list allows you to preview how the selected text will look if the highlighted font is applied. Clicking a font name applies the font. The font of the flyer changes to Garamond.

4. **Click the** Font Size list arrow **in the Font group, drag the pointer slowly up and down the Font Size list, then click** 12

   Dragging the pointer over the font sizes allows you to preview how the selected text will look if the highlighted font size is applied. The font size of the selected text increases to 12 points.

5. **Select the title** Quest Specialty Travel Last Minute Travel Deals, **click the** Font list arrow, **click** Trebuchet MS, **click the** Font Size list arrow, **click** 22, **then click the** Bold button **B** **in the Font group**

   The title is formatted in 22-point Trebuchet MS bold.

6. **Click the** Font Color list arrow **A·** **in the Font group**

   A gallery of colors opens. It includes the set of theme colors in a range of tints and shades as well as a set of standard colors. You can point to a color in the gallery to preview it applied to the selected text.

7. **Click the** Blue, Accent 1 **color as shown in Figure C-2, then deselect the text**

   The color of the title text changes to blue. The active color on the Font Color button also changes to blue.

8. **Select the heading** Rajasthan Desert Safari, **then, using the Mini toolbar, click the** Font list arrow, **click** Trebuchet MS, **click the** Font Size list arrow, **click** 14, **click** A·, **click the** Dark Blue, Text 2 **color, click** B, **then deselect the text**

   The heading is formatted in 14-point Trebuchet MS bold with a dark blue color. Notice that when you use the buttons on the Mini toolbar to format text, you cannot preview the formatting options in the document.

9. **Press [Ctrl][Home], then click the** Save button **📇** **on the Quick Access toolbar**

   Compare your document to Figure C-3.

Font list
arrow

FIGURE C-1: Font list

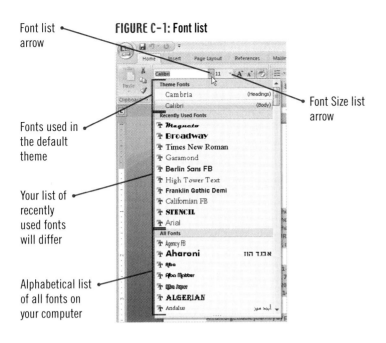

Font Size list
arrow

Fonts used in
the default
theme

Your list of
recently
used fonts
will differ

Alphabetical list
of all fonts on
your computer

FIGURE C-2: Font Color gallery

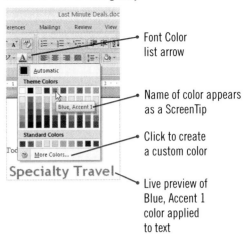

Font Color
list arrow

Name of color appears
as a ScreenTip

Click to create
a custom color

Live preview of
Blue, Accent 1
color applied
to text

FIGURE C-3: Document formatted with fonts

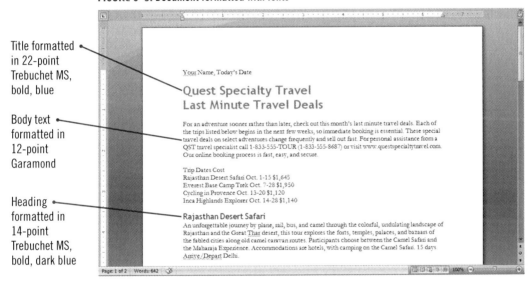

Title formatted
in 22-point
Trebuchet MS,
bold, blue

Body text
formatted in
12-point
Garamond

Heading
formatted in
14-point
Trebuchet MS,
bold, dark blue

Adding a drop cap

A fun way to illustrate a document with fonts is to add a drop cap to a paragraph. A **drop cap** is a large initial capital letter, often used to set off the first paragraph of an article. To create a drop cap, place the insertion point in the paragraph you want to format, click the Insert tab, and then click the Drop Cap button in the Text group to open a menu of Drop cap options. Preview and select one of the options on the menu, or click Drop Cap Options to open the Drop Cap dialog box, shown in Figure C-4. In the Drop Cap dialog box, select the position, font, number of lines to drop, and the distance you want the drop cap to be from the paragraph text, and then click OK. The drop cap is added to the paragraph as a graphic object.

Once a drop cap is inserted in a paragraph, you can modify it by selecting it and then changing the settings in the Drop Cap dialog box. For even more interesting effects, enhance a drop cap with font color, font styles, or font effects, fill the graphic object with shading, or add a border around it. To enhance a drop cap, first select it, and then experiment with the formatting options available in the Font dialog box and in the Borders and Shading dialog box.

FIGURE C-4: Drop Cap dialog box

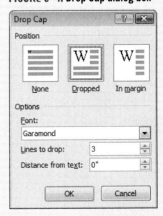

Copying Formats Using the Format Painter

You can dramatically change the appearance of text by applying different font styles, font effects, and character-spacing effects. For example, you can use the buttons in the Font group to make text darker by applying **bold** or to slant text by applying **italic**. You can also use the Font dialog box to apply font effects and character-spacing effects to text. When you are satisfied with the formatting of certain text, you can quickly apply the same formats to other text using the Format Painter. The **Format Painter** is a powerful Word feature that allows you to copy all the format settings applied to selected text to other text that you want to format the same way. You spice up the appearance of the text in the document by applying different font styles and effects. After formatting a heading and subheading, you use the Format Painter to apply the settings to other headings and subheadings.

STEPS

1. **Select** immediate booking is essential **in the first body paragraph, click the** Bold button **B** **on the Mini toolbar, select the entire** paragraph, **then click the** Italic button **I** **on the Mini toolbar**

   "Immediate booking is essential" is bold and the entire paragraph is formatted in italic.

2. **Select** Last Minute Travel Deals, **then click the** launcher **in the Font group**

   The Font dialog box opens, as shown in Figure C-5. You can use options on the Font tab to change the font, font style, size, and color of text, and to add an underline and apply font effects to text.

3. **Scroll down the Size list, click** 48, **click the** Font color list arrow, **click the** Red, Accent 2 **color in the Theme Colors, click the** Shadow check box, **click** OK, **then deselect the text**

   The text is larger, red, and has a shadow effect.

4. **Select** Last Minute Travel Deals, **right-click, click** Font **on the Edit menu, click the** Character Spacing tab, **click the** Scale list arrow, **click** 80%, **click** OK, **then deselect the text**

   You use the Character Spacing tab in the Font dialog box to change the scale, or width, of the selected characters, to alter the spacing between characters, or to raise or lower the characters. Decreasing the scale of the characters makes them narrower and gives the text a tall, thin appearance, as shown in Figure C-6.

5. **Scroll down, select the subheading** Camel Safari, **then, using the Mini toolbar, click the** Font list arrow, **click** Trebuchet MS, **click** **B**, **click** **I**, **click the** Font Color list arrow **A**, **click the** Red, Accent 2 **color in the Theme Colors, then deselect the text**

   The subheading is formatted in Trebuchet MS, bold, italic, and red.

6. **Select** Camel Safari, **then click the** Format Painter button **in the Clipboard group**

   The pointer changes to .

7. **Scroll down, select** Maharaja Experience **with the pointer, then deselect the text**

   The subheading is formatted in Trebuchet MS, bold, italic, and red, as shown in Figure C-7.

8. **Scroll up as needed, select** Rajasthan Desert Safari, **then double-click**

   Double-clicking the Format Painter button allows the Format Painter to remain active until you turn it off. By keeping the Format Painter turned on you can apply formatting to multiple items.

9. **Scroll down, select the headings** Everest Base Camp Trek, Cycling in Provence, **and** Inca Highlands Explorer **with the pointer, click** **to turn off the Format Painter, then save your changes**

   The headings are formatted in 14-point Trebuchet MS bold with a dark blue font color.

FIGURE C-5: Font tab in Font dialog box

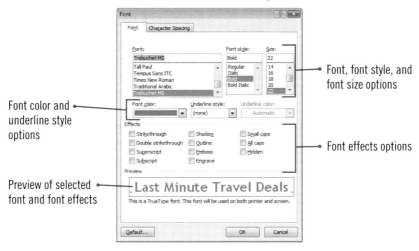

Font, font style, and font size options

Font color and underline style options

Font effects options

Preview of selected font and font effects

FIGURE C-6: Font and character spacing effects applied to text

Title formatted in 48-point, red, with a shadow effect and a character scale of 80%

Paragraph formatted in italic

FIGURE C-7: Formats copied and applied using the Format Painter

Format Painter button

Subhead formatted in Trebuchet MS, bold, italic, red

Same formats copied and applied to subhead using the Format Painter

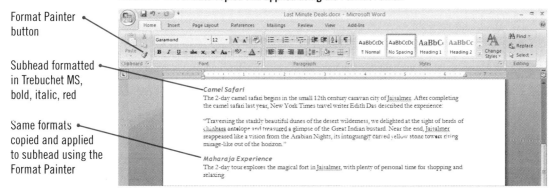

Underlining text

Another creative way to call attention to text and to jazz up the appearance of a document is to apply an underline style to words you want to highlight. The Underline list arrow in the Font group displays straight, dotted, wavy, dashed, and mixed style underlines, along with a gallery of colors to choose from. To apply an underline to text, simply select it, click the Underline list arrow, and then select an underline style from the list. For a wider variety of underline styles, click More Underlines in the list, and then select an underline style in the Font dialog box. You can change the color of an underline at any time by selecting the underlined text, clicking the Underline list arrow, pointing to Underline Color, and then choosing from the options in the color gallery. If you want to remove an underline from text, select the underlined text, and then click the Underline button.

Changing Line and Paragraph Spacing

Increasing the amount of space between lines adds more white space to a document and can make it easier to read. Adding space before and after paragraphs can also open up a document and improve its appearance. You use the Line Spacing list arrow in the Paragraph group on the Home tab to quickly change line spacing. To change paragraph spacing, you use the Spacing options in the Paragraph group on the Page Layout tab. Line and paragraph spacing are measured in points. ▰▰▰▰▰ You increase the line spacing of several paragraphs and add extra space under each heading to give the report a more open feel. You work with formatting marks turned on, so you can see the paragraph marks (¶).

STEPS

1. **Press [Ctrl][Home], click the** Show/Hide ¶ button ▣ **in the Paragraph group, place the insertion point in the italicized paragraph under the title, then click the** Line Spacing list arrow ▣ **in the Paragraph group on the Home tab**

   The Line Spacing list opens. This list includes options for increasing the space between lines. The check mark on the Line Spacing list indicates the current line spacing.

2. **Click** 1.15

   The space between the lines in the paragraph increases to 1.15 lines. Notice that you do not need to select an entire paragraph to change its paragraph formatting; simply place the insertion point in the paragraph you want to format.

> **QUICK TIP**
> Word recognizes any string of text that ends with a paragraph mark as a paragraph, including titles, headings, and single lines in a list.

3. **Select the** five-line list **that begins with Trip Dates Cost, click** ▣, **then click** 1.5

   The line spacing between the selected paragraphs changes to 1.5. To change the paragraph-formatting features of more than one paragraph, you must select the paragraphs.

4. **Scroll down, place the insertion point in the heading** Rajasthan Desert Safari, **then click the** Page Layout tab

   The paragraph spacing settings for the active paragraph are shown in the Before and After text boxes in the Paragraph group on the Page Layout tab.

5. **Click the** After up arrow **in the Spacing section of the Paragraph group so that 6 pt appears**

   Six points of space are added after the Rajasthan Desert Safari heading paragraph.

> **QUICK TIP**
> Using [F4] is not the same as using the Format Painter. Pressing [F4] repeats only the last action you took. You can use the Format Painter at any time to copy multiple format settings.

6. **Scroll down, place the insertion point in the heading** Everest Base Camp Trek, **then press** [F4]

   Pressing [F4] repeats the last action you took, in this case, adding six points of space after the paragraph. Six points of space are added below the Everest Base Camp Trek heading.

7. **Scroll down, select** Cycling in Provence, **press and hold [Ctrl], select** Inca Highlands Explorer, **release [Ctrl], then press** [F4]

   When you press [Ctrl] as you select items, you can select and format multiple items at once. Six points of space are added after each heading.

8. **Press [Ctrl][Home], place the insertion point in** Last Minute Travel Deals, **click the** Before up arrow **in the Spacing section of the Paragraph group twice so that 12 pt appears**

   The second line of the title has 12 points of space before it. Compare your document with Figure C-8.

> **QUICK TIP**
> Adjusting the space between paragraphs is a more precise way to add white space to a document than inserting blank lines.

9. **Click the** Home tab, **click** ▣, **then save your changes**

FIGURE C-8: Line and paragraph spacing applied to document

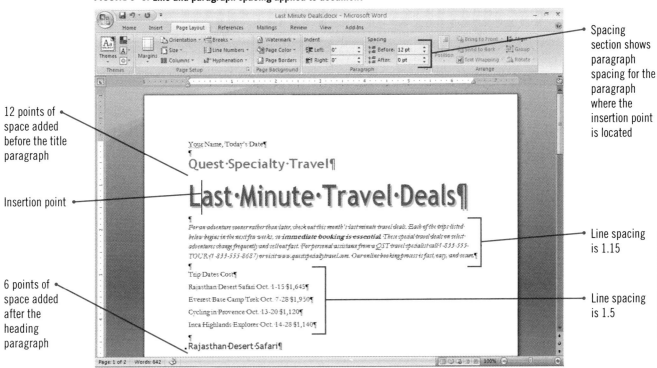

12 points of space added before the title paragraph

Insertion point

6 points of space added after the heading paragraph

Spacing section shows paragraph spacing for the paragraph where the insertion point is located

Line spacing is 1.15

Line spacing is 1.5

Formatting with Quick Styles

You can also apply multiple format settings to text in one step by applying a style. A **style** is a set of formats, such as font, font size, and paragraph alignment, that are named and stored together. Formatting a document with styles is a quick and easy way to give it a professional appearance. To make it even easier, Word includes sets of styles, called **Quick Styles**, that are designed to be used together in a document to make it attractive and readable. A Quick Style set includes styles for a title, several heading levels, body text, quotes, and lists. The styles in a Quick Style set use common fonts, colors, and formats, so that using the styles together in a document gives the document a cohesive look.

To view the active set of Quick Styles, click the More button ▼ in the Styles group on the Home tab to expand the Quick Styles gallery, shown in Figure C-9. As you move the pointer over each style in the gallery, a preview of the style is applied to the selected text. To apply a style to the selected text, you simply click the button for that style in the Quick Styles gallery. To remove a style from selected text, you click the Clear Formatting button ⌫ in the Font group or in the Quick Styles gallery.

If you want to change the active set of Quick Styles to a Quick Style set with a different design, click the Change Styles button in the Styles group, point to Style Set, and then select the Quick Style set that best suits your document's content, tone, and audience. Distinctive, Traditional, Modern, Fancy, and Formal are some examples of the Quick Style sets you can choose to apply. When you

change the Quick Style set, a complete set of new fonts and colors is applied to the entire document. You can also change the color scheme or font used in the active Quick Style set by clicking the Change Styles button, pointing to Colors or to Fonts, and then selecting from the available color schemes or font options.

FIGURE C-9: Quick Styles gallery

AaBbCcDc	AaBbCcDc	AaBbC	AaBbCc
¶ Normal	No Spacing	Heading 1	Heading 2
AaBbCcI	AaB	*AaBbCc.*	AaBbCcD
Heading 3	Title	Subtitle	Subtle Em...
AaBbCcL	AABBCCDL	**AaBbCcD**	*AaBbCcD*
Emphasis	Intense E...	Strong	Quote
AaBbCcD	AABBCCDL	AABBCCDL	AABBCCDL
Intense Q...	Subtle Ref...	Intense R...	Book Title
AaBbCcDc			
¶ List Para...			

Save Selection as a New Quick Style...
⌫ Clear Formatting
⌦ Apply Styles...

Aligning Paragraphs

Changing paragraph alignment is another way to enhance a document's appearance. Paragraphs are aligned relative to the left and right margins in a document. By default, text is **left-aligned**, which means it is flush with the left margin and has a ragged right edge. Using the alignment buttons in the Paragraph group, you can **right-align** a paragraph—make it flush with the right margin—or **center** a paragraph so that it is positioned evenly between the left and right margins. You can also **justify** a paragraph so that both the left and right edges of the paragraph are flush with the left and right margins. You change the alignment of several paragraphs at the beginning of the report to make it more visually interesting.

STEPS

1. **Replace** Your Name, Today's Date **with your name, a comma, and the date**

2. **Select your name, the comma, and the date, then click the** Align Text Right button ▤ **in the Paragraph group**
   The text is aligned with the right margin. In Page Layout view, the junction of the white and shaded sections of the horizontal ruler indicates the location of the left and right margins.

3. **Place the insertion point between your name and the comma, press** [Delete] **to delete the comma, then press** [Enter]
   The new paragraph containing the date is also right-aligned. Pressing [Enter] in the middle of a paragraph creates a new paragraph with the same text and paragraph formatting as the original paragraph.

4. **Select the two-line** title, **then click the** Center button ▤ **in the Paragraph group**
   The two paragraphs that make up the title are centered between the left and right margins.

5. **Scroll down as needed, place the insertion point in the** Rajasthan Desert Safari **heading, then click** ▤
   The Rajasthan Desert Safari heading is centered.

6. **Place the insertion point in the italicized paragraph under the title, then click the** Justify button ▤ **in the Paragraph group**
   The paragraph is aligned with both the left and right margins, as shown in Figure C-10. When you justify a paragraph, Word adjusts the spacing between words so that each line in the paragraph is flush with the left and the right margins.

7. **Place the insertion point in** Rajasthan Desert Safari, **then click the** launcher ▣ **in the Paragraph group**
   The Paragraph dialog box opens, as shown in Figure C-11. The Indents and Spacing tab shows the paragraph format settings for the paragraph where the insertion point is located. You can check or change paragraph format settings using this dialog box.

8. **Click the** Alignment list arrow, **click** Left, **click** OK, **then save your changes**
   The Rajasthan Desert Safari heading is left-aligned.

FIGURE C-10: Modified paragraph alignment

Right margin on the ruler

View Ruler button

Right-aligned

Center-aligned

Justified

Left-aligned

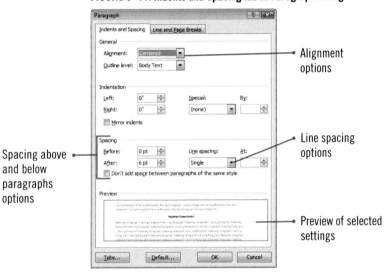

FIGURE C-11: Indents and Spacing tab in Paragraph dialog box

Alignment options

Spacing above and below paragraphs options

Line spacing options

Preview of selected settings

Formatting a document using themes

Changing the theme applied to a document is another powerful and efficient way to tailor a document's look and feel, particularly when a document is formatted with a Quick Style set. By default, all documents created in Word are formatted with the default Office theme—which uses Calibri as the font for the body text—but you can change the theme at any time to fit the content, tone, and purpose of a document. When you change the theme for a document, a complete set of new theme colors, fonts, and effects is applied to the whole document.

To preview how various themes look when applied to the current document, click the Themes button in the Themes group on the Page Layout tab, and then move the pointer over each theme in the gallery and notice how the document changes. When you click the theme you like, all document content that uses theme colors, all text that is formatted with a style, including default body text, and all table styles and graphic effects change to the colors, fonts, and effects used by the theme. In addition, the gallery of colors changes to display the set of theme colors, and the active Quick Style set changes to employ the theme colors and fonts. Note that changing the theme does not affect the formatting of text to which font formatting has already been applied, nor does it change any standard or custom colors used in the document.

If you want to tweak the document design further, you can modify it by applying a different set of theme colors, heading and body text fonts, or graphic effects. To do this, simply click the Theme Colors, Theme Fonts, or Theme Effects button in the Themes group, move the pointer over each option in the gallery to preview it in the document, and then click the option you like best.

Working with Tabs

Tabs allow you to align text at a specific location in a document. A **tab stop** is a point on the horizontal ruler that indicates the location at which to align text. By default, tab stops are located every ½" from the left margin, but you can also set custom tab stops. Using tabs, you can align text to the left, right, or center of a tab stop, or you can align text at a decimal point or insert a bar character. Table C-1 describes the different types of tab stops. You set tabs using the horizontal ruler or the Tabs dialog box. You use tabs to format the summary information on last minute tour deals so it is easy to read.

STEPS

1. **Scroll as needed, then select the** five-line list **beginning with Trip Dates Cost**

   Before you set tab stops for existing text, you must select the paragraphs for which you want to set tabs.

2. **Point to the** tab indicator ☐ **at the left end of the horizontal ruler**

   The icon that appears in the tab indicator indicates the active type of tab; pointing to the tab indicator displays a ScreenTip with the name of the active tab type. By default, left tab is the active tab type. Clicking the tab indicator scrolls through the types of tabs and indents.

> **QUICK TIP**
> To remove a tab stop, drag it up or down off the ruler.

3. **Click the** tab indicator **to see each of the available tab and indent types, make** Left Tab ☐ **the active tab type, click the** 1" **mark on the horizontal ruler, then click the** 3½" **mark on the horizontal ruler**

   A left tab stop is inserted at the 1" mark and the 3½" on the horizontal ruler. Clicking the horizontal ruler inserts a tab stop of the active type for the selected paragraph or paragraphs.

4. **Click the tab indicator twice so the** Right Tab icon ☐ **is active, then click the** 5" **mark on the horizontal ruler**

   A right tab stop is inserted at the 5" mark on the horizontal ruler, as shown in Figure C-12.

5. **Place the insertion point before** Trip **in the first line in the list, press** [Tab], **place the insertion point before** Dates, **press** [Tab], **place the insertion point before** Cost, **then press** [Tab]

   Inserting a tab before Trip left-aligns the text at the 1" mark, inserting a tab before Dates left-aligns the text at the 3½" mark, and inserting a tab before Cost right-aligns Cost at the 5" mark.

6. **Insert a tab at the beginning of each remaining line in the list**

   The paragraphs left-align at the 1" mark.

> **QUICK TIP**
> Place the insertion point in a paragraph to see the tab stops for that paragraph on the horizontal ruler.

7. **Insert a tab before each** Oct. **in the list, then insert a tab before each** $ **in the list**

   The dates left-align at the 3½" mark. The prices right-align at the 5" mark.

8. **Select the five lines of tabbed text, drag the right tab stop to the** 5½" **mark on the horizontal ruler, then deselect the text**

   Dragging the tab stop moves it to a new location. The prices right-align at the 5½" mark.

> **QUICK TIP**
> Double-click a tab stop on the ruler to open the Tabs dialog box.

9. **Select the last** four lines **of tabbed text, click the** launcher ☐ **in the Paragraph group, then click** Tabs **in the Paragraph dialog box**

   The Tabs dialog box opens, as shown in Figure C-13. You can use the Tabs dialog box to set tab stops, change the position or alignment of existing tab stops, clear tab stops, and apply tab leaders to tabs. **Tab leaders** are lines that appear in front of tabbed text.

10. **Click** 3.5" **in the Tab stop position list box, click the** 2 option button **in the Leader section, click** Set, **click** 5.5" **in the Tab stop position list box, click the** 2 option button **in the Leader section, click** Set, **click** OK, **deselect the text, then save your changes**

    A dotted tab leader is added before each 3.5" and 5.5" tab stop in the last four lines of tabbed text, as shown in Figure C-14.

Formatting Text and Paragraphs

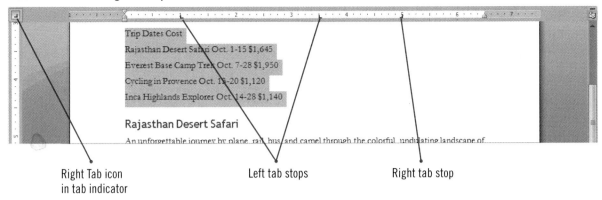

FIGURE C-12: Left and right tab stops on the horizontal ruler

Right Tab icon
in tab indicator

Left tab stops

Right tab stop

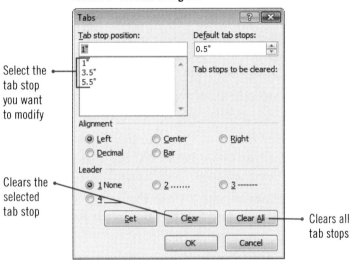

FIGURE C-13: Tabs dialog box

Select the
tab stop
you want
to modify

Clears the
selected
tab stop

Clears all
tab stops

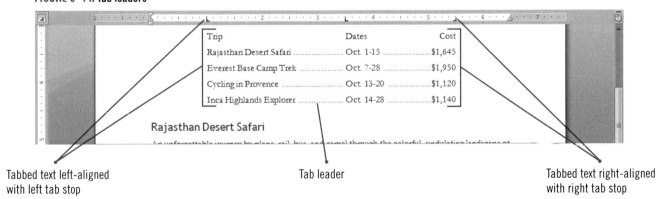

FIGURE C-14: Tab leaders

Tabbed text left-aligned
with left tab stop

Tab leader

Tabbed text right-aligned
with right tab stop

TABLE C-1: Types of tabs

tab	use to
⌊ Left tab	Set the start position of text so that text runs to the right of the tab stop as you type
⊥ Center tab	Set the center align position of text so that text stays centered on the tab stop as you type
⌋ Right tab	Set the right or end position of text so that text moves to the left of the tab stop as you type
⊥ Decimal tab	Set the position of the decimal point so that numbers align around the decimal point as you type
⎮ Bar tab	Insert a vertical bar at the tab position

Working with Indents

When you **indent** a paragraph, you move its edge in from the left or right margin. You can indent the entire left or right edge of a paragraph, just the first line, or all lines except the first line. The **indent markers** on the horizontal ruler indicate the indent settings for the paragraph in which the insertion point is located. Dragging an indent marker to a new location on the ruler is one way to change the indentation of a paragraph; changing the indent settings in the Paragraph group on the Page Layout tab is another; and using the indent buttons in the Paragraph group on the Home tab is a third. Table C-2 describes different types of indents and some of the methods for creating each.　　 You indent several paragraphs in the report.

STEPS

QUICK TIP
Press [Tab] at the beginning of a paragraph to indent the first line ½".

1. **Press [Ctrl][Home], place the insertion point in the italicized paragraph under the title, then click the** Increase Indent button 📑 **in the Paragraph group on the Home tab**

   The entire paragraph is indented ½" from the left margin, as shown in Figure C-15. The indent marker 🔻 also moves to the ½" mark on the horizontal ruler. Each time you click the Increase Indent button, the left edge of a paragraph moves another ½" to the right.

2. **Click the** Decrease Indent button 📑 **in the Paragraph group**

   The left edge of the paragraph moves ½" to the left, and the indent marker moves back to the left margin.

TROUBLE
Take care to drag only the First Line Indent marker. If you make a mistake, click the Undo button, then try again.

3. **Drag the** First Line Indent marker 🔻 **to the ¾" mark on the horizontal ruler**

   Figure C-16 shows the First Line Indent marker being dragged. The first line of the paragraph is indented ¾". Dragging the First Line Indent marker indents only the first line of a paragraph.

4. **Scroll to the bottom of page 1, place the insertion point in the quotation, click the** Page Layout tab, **click the** Indent Left text box **in the Paragraph group, type .5, click the** Indent Right text box, **type .5, then press [Enter]**

   The left and right edges of the paragraph are indented ½" from the margins, as shown in Figure C-17.

5. **Press [Ctrl][Home], place the insertion point in the italicized paragraph, then click the** launcher 🔲 **in the Paragraph group**

   The Paragraph dialog box opens. You can use the Indents and Spacing tab to check or change the alignment, indentation, and paragraph and line spacing settings applied to a paragraph.

6. **Click the** Special list arrow, **click (none), click OK, then save your changes**

   The first line indent is removed from the paragraph.

TABLE C-2: Types of indents

indent type: description	to create
Left indent: The left edge of a paragraph is moved in from the left margin	Enter the position you want the left edge of the paragraph to align in the Indent Left text box in the Paragraph group on the Page Layout tab; or drag the Left Indent marker 🔲 on the ruler right to the position where you want the left edge of the paragraph to align
Right indent: The right edge of a paragraph is moved in from the right margin	Enter the position you want the right edge of the paragraph to align in the Indent Right text box in the Paragraph group on the Page Layout tab; or drag the Right Indent marker 🔺 on the ruler left to the position where you want the right edge of the paragraph to end
First line indent: The first line of a paragraph is indented more than the subsequent lines	Drag 🔻 on the ruler right to the position where you want the first line of the paragraph to begin; or activate the First Line Indent marker 🔻 in the tab indicator, and then click the ruler at the position where you want the first line of the paragraph to begin
Hanging indent: The subsequent lines of a paragraph are indented more than the first line	Drag the Hanging Indent marker 🔺 on the ruler right to the position where you want the hanging indent to begin; or activate the Hanging Indent marker 🔺 in the tab indicator, and then click the ruler at the position where you want the second and remaining lines of the paragraph to begin
Negative indent (or Outdent): The left edge of a paragraph is moved to the left of the left margin	Enter the negative position you want the left edge of the paragraph to align in the Indent Left text box in the Paragraph group on the Page Layout tab; or drag the Left Indent marker 🔲 on the ruler left to the position where you want the negative indent to begin

FIGURE C-15: Indented paragraph

First Line Indent marker

Hanging Indent marker

Left Indent marker

Indented paragraph

Right Indent marker

Increase Indent button

Decrease Indent button

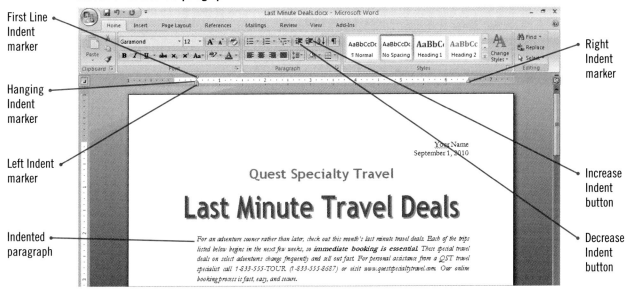

FIGURE C-16: Dragging the First Line Indent marker

First Line Indent marker being dragged

Dotted line shows the position of indent in the document

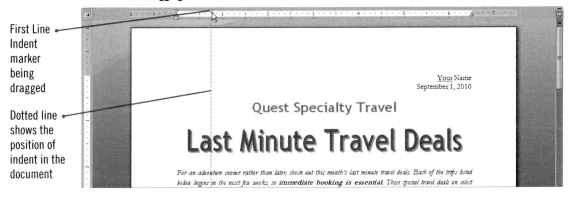

FIGURE C-17: Paragraph indented from the left and right

Paragraph indented ½" from left margin

Paragraph indented ½" from right margin

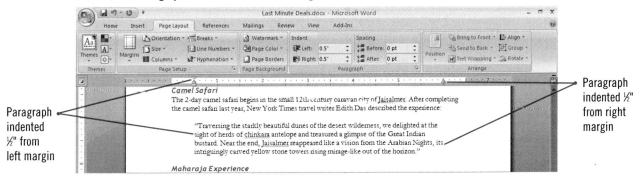

Clearing formatting

If you are unhappy with the way text is formatted, you can use the Clear Formatting command to return the text to the default format settings. The default format includes font and paragraph formatting: text is formatted in 11-point Calibri, and paragraphs are left-aligned with 1.15 point line spacing, 10 points of space below, and no indents. To clear formatting from text and return it to the default format, select the text you want to clear, and then click the Clear Formatting button in the Font group on the Home tab. If you prefer to return the text to the default font and remove all paragraph formatting, making the text 11-point Calibri, left-aligned, single spaced, with no paragraph spacing or indents, select the text and then simply click the No Spacing button in the Styles group on the Home tab.

Adding Bullets and Numbering

Formatting a list with bullets or numbering can help to organize the ideas in a document. A **bullet** is a character, often a small circle, that appears before the items in a list to add emphasis. Formatting a list as a numbered list helps illustrate sequences and priorities. You can quickly format a list with bullets or numbering by using the Bullets and Numbering buttons in the Paragraph group on the Home tab. You format the lists in your report with numbers and bullets.

STEPS

1. **Scroll until the Everest Base Camp Trek heading is at the top of your screen**

2. **Select the three-line list of 3-day add-ons, click the Home tab, then click the Numbering list arrow ▤▾ in the Paragraph group**

    The Numbering Library opens, as shown in Figure C-18. You use this list to choose or change the numbering style applied to a list.

3. **Drag the pointer over different numbering styles, then click the numbering style shown in Figure C-18**

    Dragging the pointer over the numbering styles allows you to preview how the selected text will look if the highlighted numbering style is applied. After clicking, the paragraphs are formatted as a numbered list.

4. **Place the insertion point after Pokhara — Valley of Lakes, press [Enter], then type Temples of Janakpur**

    Pressing [Enter] in the middle of the numbered list creates a new numbered paragraph and automatically renumbers the remainder of the list. Similarly, if you delete a paragraph from a numbered list, Word automatically renumbers the remaining paragraphs.

5. **Click 1 in the list**

    Clicking a number in a list selects all the numbers, as shown in Figure C-19.

6. **Click the Bold button ⓑ in the Font group**

    The numbers are all formatted in bold. Notice that the formatting of the items in the list does not change when you change the formatting of the numbers. You can also use this technique to change the formatting of bullets in a bulleted list.

7. **Select the list of items under Last minute participants in the Everest Base Camp trek..., then click the Bullets button ▤ in the Paragraph group**

    The four paragraphs are formatted as a bulleted list using the most recently used bullet style.

8. **Click a bullet in the list to select all the bullets, click the Bullets list arrow ▤▾ in the Paragraph group, click the check mark bullet style, then save your changes**

    The bullet character changes to a check mark, as shown in Figure C-20.

Creating multilevel lists

You can create lists with hierarchical structures by applying a multilevel list style to a list. To create a **multilevel list**, also called an outline, begin by applying a multilevel list style using the Multilevel List list arrow ▤▾ in the Paragraph group on the Home tab, then type your outline, pressing [Enter] after each item. To demote items to a lower level of importance in the outline, place the insertion point in the item, then click the Increase Indent button ▤ in the Paragraph group on the Home tab. Each time you indent a paragraph, the item is demoted to a lower level in the outline. Similarly, you can use the Decrease Indent button ▤ to promote an item to a higher level in the outline. You can also create a hierarchical structure in any bulleted or numbered list by using ▤ and ▤ to demote and promote items in the list. To change the multilevel list style applied to a list, select the list, click ▤▾, then select a new style.

FIGURE C-18: Numbering Library

Numbering list arrow

Number format will be applied to selected text

Choose this numbering style

Click to change the style, format, and alignment of the numbers in a list

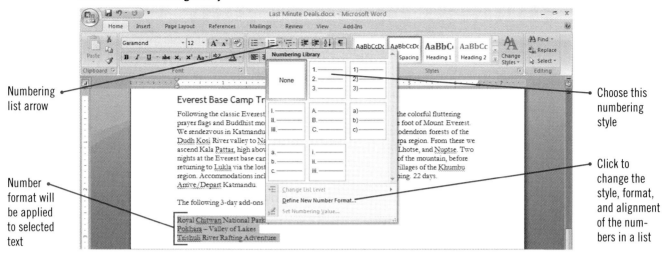

FIGURE C-19: Numbered list

Bullets button

Numbers selected in numbered list

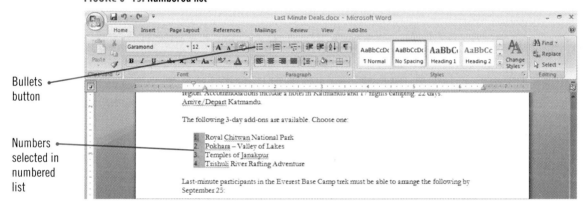

FIGURE C-20: Check mark bullets applied to list

Numbers are bold

Check mark bullets

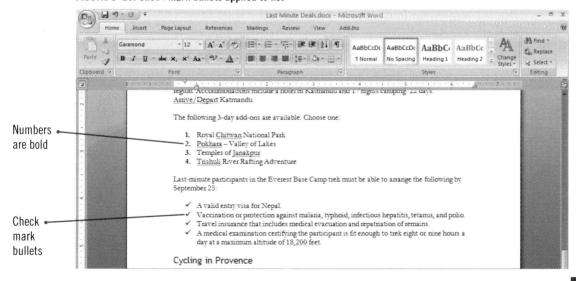

Adding Borders and Shading

Borders and shading can add color and splash to a document. **Borders** are lines you add above, below, to the side, or around words or paragraphs. You can format borders using different line styles, colors, and widths. **Shading** is a color or pattern you apply behind words or paragraphs to make them stand out on a page. You apply borders and shading using the Borders button and the Shading button in the Paragraph group on the Home tab. ▓▓▓▓ You enhance the tabbed text of the last minute tours schedule by adding shading to it. You also apply a border around the tabbed text to set it off from the rest of the document.

STEPS

1. **Press [Ctrl][Home], then scroll down until the tabbed text is at the top of your screen**

2. **Select the five paragraphs of tabbed text, click the Shading list arrow ▣ ▾ in the Paragraph group on the Home tab, click the Blue, Accent 1, Lighter 60% color, then deselect the text**

   Light blue shading is applied to the five paragraphs. Notice that the shading is applied to the entire width of the paragraphs, despite the tab settings.

3. **Select the five paragraphs, drag the Left Indent marker ▢ to the ¾" mark on the horizontal ruler, drag the Right Indent marker ▢ to the 5¾" mark, then deselect the text**

   The shading for the paragraphs is indented from the left and right, which makes it look more attractive, as shown in Figure C-21.

4. **Select the five paragraphs, click the Bottom Border list arrow ▣ ▾ in the Paragraph group, click Outside Borders, then deselect the text**

   A black outside border is added around the selected text. You can use the Borders list arrow to add a border above, below, to the side of, or around the selected text, among other options. The style of the border added is the most recently used border style, in this case the default, a thin black line.

5. **Select the five paragraphs, click the Outside Borders list arrow ▣ ▾, click No Border, click the No Border list arrow ▣ ▾, then click Borders and Shading**

   The Borders and Shading dialog box opens, as shown in Figure C-22. You use the Borders tab to change the border style, color, and width, and to add boxes and lines to words or paragraphs.

6. **Click the Box box in the Setting section, scroll down the Style list, click the double line style, click the Color list arrow, click the Dark Blue, Text 2 color, click the Width list arrow, click 1½ pt, click OK, then deselect the text**

   A 1½-point dark blue double line border is added around the tabbed text.

7. **Select the five paragraphs, click the Bold button 🅱 in the Font group, click the Font Color list arrow 🅰 ▾ in the Font group, click the Dark Blue, Text 2 color, then deselect the text**

   The text changes to bold dark blue.

8. **Select the first line in the tabbed text, click the launcher ▣ in the Font group, click the Font tab if it is not the active tab, click 14 in the Size list, click the Font Color list arrow, click the Red, Accent 2 color, click the Small caps check box in the Effects section, click OK, deselect the text, then save your changes**

   The text in the first line of the tabbed text is enlarged and changed to red small caps, as shown in Figure C-23. When you change text to small caps, the lowercase letters are changed to uppercase letters in a smaller font size.

FIGURE C-21: Shading applied to the tabbed text

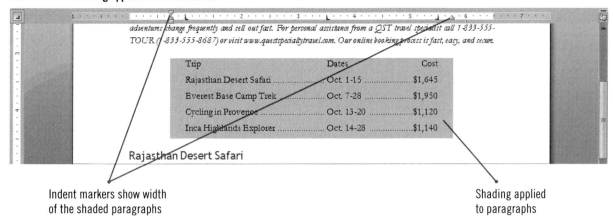

Indent markers show width
of the shaded paragraphs

Shading applied
to paragraphs

FIGURE C-22: Borders tab in Borders and Shading dialog box

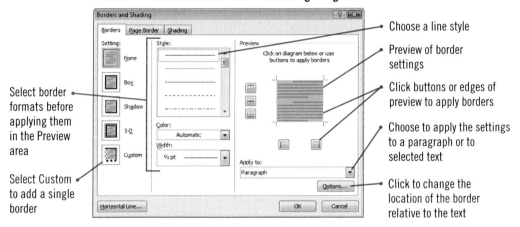

Select border
formats before
applying them
in the Preview
area

Select Custom
to add a single
border

Choose a line style

Preview of border
settings

Click buttons or edges of
preview to apply borders

Choose to apply the settings
to a paragraph or to
selected text

Click to change the
location of the border
relative to the text

FIGURE C-23: Border and font formatting applied to tabbed text

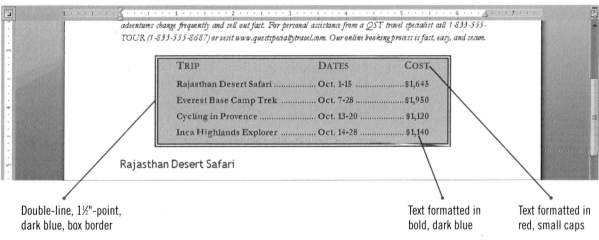

Double-line, 1½"-point,
dark blue, box border

Text formatted in
bold, dark blue

Text formatted in
red, small caps

Highlighting text in a document

The Highlight tool allows you to mark and find important text in a document. **Highlighting** is transparent color that is applied to text using the Highlight pointer ✎. To highlight text, click the Text Highlight Color list arrow in the Font group on the Home tab, select a color, then use the I-beam part of the ✎ pointer to select the text. Click to turn off the Highlight pointer. To remove highlighting, select the highlighted text, click , then click No Color. Highlighting prints, but it is used most effectively when a document is viewed on screen.

Word 2007

Adding Footnotes and Endnotes

Footnotes and endnotes are used in printed documents to provide further information, comment on, or supply references for text in a document. A **footnote** or **endnote** is an explanatory note that consists of two linked parts: the note reference mark that appears next to text to indicate that additional information is offered in a footnote or endnote, and the corresponding footnote or endnote text. Word places footnotes at the end of each page and endnotes at the end of the document. You insert and manage footnotes and endnotes in a document using the tools in the Footnotes group on the References tab. ▰▰▰▰ Before finalizing the document, you add several footnotes to expand upon the document information.

STEPS

TROUBLE
Scroll up as needed to see the note reference mark; then scroll down to see the footnote.

1. **Place the insertion point after Cost in the top row of the tabbed text, click the References tab, then click the Insert Footnote button in the Footnotes group**

   A note reference mark, in this case a superscript 1, appears after Cost, and the insertion point moves below a separator line at the bottom of the page. A note reference mark can be a number, a symbol, a character, or a combination of characters.

2. **Type International flights, travel insurance, visas, and taxes are not included in the tour price.**

   The footnote text appears below the separator line at the bottom of page 1.

3. **Place the insertion point at the end of the quotation at the bottom of page 1, click the Insert Footnote button, then type April 12, 2009**

   The footnote text for the second footnote appears under the first footnote at the bottom of page 1, as shown in Figure C-24.

QUICK TIP
To change the number format of the note reference mark or to use a symbol instead of a character, click the launcher in the Footnotes group, select from the options in the Footnote and Endnote dialog box, then click Apply.

4. **Scroll to the middle of page 2, place the insertion point at the end of the second line in the bulleted list, click the Insert Footnote button, then type Vaccination requirements are subject to change and should be confirmed before departure.**

   The footnote text for the third footnote appears at the bottom of page 2.

5. **Scroll up, place the insertion point after the Everest Base Camp Trek heading, click the Insert Footnote button, then type Due to altitude, terrain, and distance walked, this trek is for strong mountain walkers only.**

   Notice that when you inserted a new footnote between existing footnotes, Word automatically renumbered the footnotes. The new footnote appears above the final footnote at the bottom of page 2.

6. **Press [Ctrl][Home], click the Next Footnote button in the Footnotes group**

   The insertion point moves to the first reference mark in the document.

QUICK TIP
To convert all footnotes to endnotes, click the launcher in the Footnotes group, click Convert, click OK, then click Close.

7. **Click the Next Footnote button, press [Delete] to select the number 2 reference mark, then press [Delete] again**

   The reference mark and associated footnote are deleted from the document and the footnotes are automatically renumbered. You must select a reference mark to delete a footnote; you can not simply delete the footnote text itself.

8. **Scroll to the bottom of page 2, notice the remaining footnotes have been renumbered, press [Ctrl][Home], then save your changes**

   The completed document is shown in Figure C-25.

9. **Click the Office button 📄, point to Print, click Quick Print, close the document, then exit Word**

   A copy of the flyer prints. Depending on your printer, colors might appear differently when you print. If you are using a black-and-white printer, colors will print in shades of gray.

FIGURE C-24: Footnotes in the document

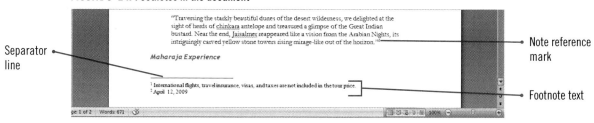

Separator line

"Traversing the starkly beautiful dunes of the desert wilderness, we delighted at the sight of herds of chinkara antelope and treasured a glimpse of the Great Indian bustard. Near the end, Jaisalmer reappeared like a vision from the Arabian Nights, its intriguingly carved yellow stone towers rising mirage-like out of the horizon."²

Maharaja Experience

¹ International flights, travel insurance, visas, and taxes are not included in the tour price.
² April 12, 2009

Note reference mark

Footnote text

ge: 1 of 2 | Words: 671 | 100%

FIGURE C-25: Completed document

Your Name
September 1, 2010

Quest Specialty Travel

Last Minute Travel Deals

*For an adventure sooner rather than later, check out this month's last minute travel deals. Each of the trips listed below begins in the next few weeks, so **immediate booking is essential** These special travel deals on select adventures change frequently and sell out fast. For personal assistance from a QST travel specialist call 1-833-555-TOUR (1-833-555-8687) or visit www.questspecialtytravel.com. Our online booking process is fast, easy, and secure.*

TRIP	DATES	COST¹
Rajasthan Desert Safari	Oct. 1-15	$1,645
Everest Base Camp Trek	Oct. 7-28	$1,950
Cycling in Provence	Oct. 13-20	$1,120
Inca Highlands Explorer	Oct. 14-28	$1,140

Rajasthan Desert Safari

An unforgettable journey by plane, rail, bus, and camel through the colorful, undulating landscape of Rajasthan and the Great Thar desert, this tour explores the forts, temples, palaces, and bazaars of the fabled cities along old camel caravan routes. Participants choose between the Camel Safari and the Maharaja Experience. Accommodations are hotels, with camping on the Camel Safari. 15 days. Arrive/Depart Delhi.

Camel Safari
The 2-day camel safari begins in the small 12th century caravan city of Jaisalmer. After completing the camel safari last year, New York Times travel writer Edith Das described the experience:

"Traversing the starkly beautiful dunes of the desert wilderness, we delighted at the sight of herds of chinkara antelope and treasured a glimpse of the Great Indian bustard. Near the end, Jaisalmer reappeared like a vision from the Arabian Nights, its intriguingly carved yellow stone towers rising mirage-like out of the horizon."

Maharaja Experience
The 2-day tour explores the magical fort in Jaisalmer, with plenty of personal time for shopping and relaxing.

¹ International flights, travel insurance, visas, and taxes are no included in the tour price.

Everest Base Camp Trek²

Following the classic Everest expedition route, this trek leads hikers past the colorful fluttering prayer flags and Buddhist monasteries of traditional Sherpa villages, to the foot of Mount Everest. We rendezvous in Katmandu, fly to Lukla, and traverse the pine and rhododendron forests of the Dudh Kosi River valley to Namche Bazaar, the bustling center of the Sherpa region. From there we ascend Kala Pattar, high above the tree line, for suburb views of Everest, Lhotse, and Nuptse. Two nights at the Everest base camp allows us ample time to explore the base of the mountain, before returning to Lukla via the lost valleys, high mountain passes, and remote villages of the Khumbu region. Accommodations include a hotel in Katmandu and 17 nights camping. 22 days. Arrive/Depart Katmandu.

The following 3-day add-ons are available. Choose one:

1. Royal Chitwan National Park
2. Pokhara – Valley of Lakes
3. Temples of Janakpur
4. Trishuli River Rafting Adventure

Last-minute participants in the Everest Base Camp trek must be able to arrange the following by September 25:

✓ A valid entry visa for Nepal.
✓ Vaccination or protection against malaria, typhoid, infectious hepatitis, tetanus, and polio.³
✓ Travel insurance that includes medical evacuation and repatriation of remains.
✓ A medical examination certifying the participant is fit enough to trek eight or nine hours a day at a maximum altitude of 18,200 feet.

Cycling in Provence

The fertile, rambling terrain of Provence provides the backdrop for this easy-going trip. Days are spent cycling between pleasant medieval towns and delightful villages, with ample time to linger at the sights along the way. At night, we relax in the comfort and warmth of small, local hotels. The average daily ride is 30 miles, but there are options for longer routes if you want to cycle more. 8 days. Arrive/Depart Nice.

Inca Highlands Explorer

This epic overland adventure combines the highlights of Inca civilization with an astonishing five-day Andean trek through cloud forests and snow-capped peaks to the ancient Inca site of Machu Picchu. We then travel by road to gorgeous Lake Titicaca, birthplace of the Inca legend, and on to La Paz, Bolivia, the world's highest capital city. Accommodations include camping and hotels. 15 days. Arrive Lima/Depart La Paz.

² Due to altitude, terrain, and distance walked, this trek is for strong mountain walkers only.
³ Vaccination requirements are subject to change and should be confirmed before departure.

Creating a bibliography

Many documents require a **bibliography**, a list of sources that you consulted or cited in creating the document. The Word bibliography feature allows you to quickly create sources, add citations to a document, and automatically generate a bibliography based on the source information you provide for the document. Each time you create a new source, the source information is saved on your computer so that it is available for use in any document.

To add a citation and source to a document, begin by selecting the style you want to use for the citation and source using the Style list arrow in the Citations & Bibliography group on the References tab. APA, Chicago, and MLA are commonly used styles. Next, place the insertion point at the end of the sentence where you want to add the citation, click the Insert Citation button in the Citations & Bibliography group, click Add New Source, and then enter the relevant information about the reference source in the Create Source dialog box. When you have finished adding citations to a document and are ready to create a bibliography, place the insertion point where you want the bibliography, usually at the end of the document, click the Bibliography button in the Citations & Bibliography group, and then click a built-in bibliography style from the gallery, or click Insert Bibliography. The bibliography is inserted in the document as a field, and can be formatted any way you choose.

Practice

If you have a SAM user profile, you may have access to hands-on instruction, practice, and assessment of the skills covered in this unit. Log in to your SAM account (http://sam2007.course.com/) to launch any assigned training activities or exams that relate to the skills covered in this unit.

▼ CONCEPTS REVIEW

Label each element of the Word program window shown in Figure C-26.

FIGURE C-26

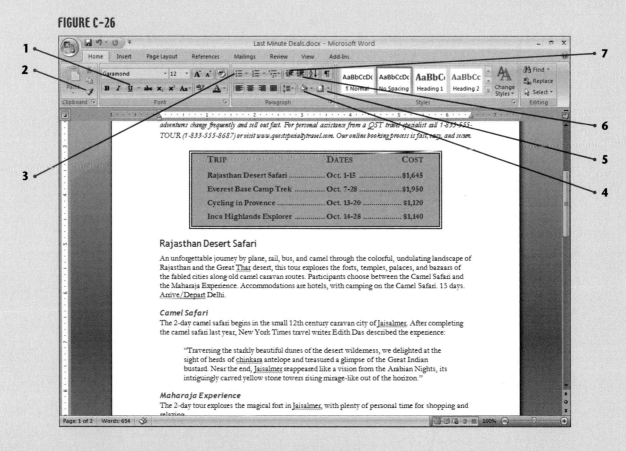

Match each term with the statement that best describes it.

8. **Footnote**

9. **Shading**

10. **Point**

11. **Style**

12. **Bibliography**

13. **Highlight**

14. **Bullet**

15. **Border**

a. Color or pattern that is applied behind text to make it look attractive

b. A note placed at the bottom of a page that comments on part of the document text

c. A list of sources consulted or cited in creating a document

d. A line that can be applied above, below, or to the sides of a paragraph

e. Transparent color that is applied to text to mark it in a document

f. A unit of measurement equal to ½ of an inch

g. A character that appears at the beginning of a paragraph to add emphasis

h. A set of format settings

Select the best answer from the list of choices.

16. What is Garamond?
  a. A character format
  b. A style
  c. A font
  d. A text effect

17. What is the most precise way to increase the amount of white space between two paragraphs?
  a. Change the before paragraph spacing for the second paragraph
  b. Indent the paragraphs
  c. Change the line spacing of the paragraphs
  d. Insert an extra blank line between the paragraphs

18. In which type of indent are the subsequent lines of a paragraph indented more than the first line?
  a. Hanging indent
  b. Negative indent
  c. First Line indent
  d. Right indent

19. Which dialog box is used to change the scale of characters?
  a. Paragraph
  b. Borders and Shading
  c. Tabs
  d. Font

20. Which button is used to align a paragraph with both the left and right margins?
  a.
  b.
  c.
  d.

▼ SKILLS REVIEW

1. Format with fonts.
  a. Start Word, open the file WD C-2.docx from the drive and folder where you store your Data Files, save it as **Franklin EDA Report**, then scroll through the document to get a feel for its contents.
  b. Press [Ctrl][A], then format the text in 12-point Californian FB. Choose a different serif font if Californian FB is not available to you.
  c. Press [Ctrl][Home], format the report title **Town of Franklin Economic Development Authority Report Executive Summary** in 26-point Berlin Sans FB. Choose a different sans serif font if Berlin Sans FB is not available to you.
  d. Change the font color of the report title to Purple, Accent 4, Darker 25%, then press [Enter] after Franklin in the title.
  e. Place the insertion point in the first body paragraph under the title, then add a two-line drop cap to the paragraph using the Dropped position.
  f. Format the heading **Mission Statement** in 14-point Berlin Sans FB with the Purple, Accent 4, Darker 25% font color.
  g. Press [Ctrl][Home], then save your changes to the report.

2. Copy formats using the Format Painter.
  a. Use the Format Painter to copy the format of the Mission Statement heading to the following headings: **Guiding Principles, Issues, Proposed Actions**.
  b. Show formatting marks, then format the paragraph under the Mission Statement heading in italic.
  c. Format **Years Population Growth**, the first line in the four-line list under the Issues heading, in bold, small caps, with Purple, Accent 4, Darker 50% font color.
  d. Change the font color of the next two lines under Years Population Growth to Purple, Accent 4, Darker 50%.
  e. Format the line **Source: Office of State Planning** in italic.

    f. Scroll to the top of the report, then change the character scale of Town of Franklin Economic Development Authority Report to 90%.

    g. Change the character scale of Executive Summary to 150%, then save your changes.

3. Change line and paragraph spacing.

    a. Change the line spacing of the three-line list under the first body paragraph to 1.5 lines.

    b. Add 24 points of space before and 6 points of space after the Executive Summary line in the title.

    c. Add 12 points of space after the Mission Statement heading, then use the F4 key to add 12 points of space after each additional heading in the report (Guiding Principles, Issues, Proposed Actions).

    d. Add 6 points of space after each paragraph in the list under the Guiding Principles heading.

    e. Change the line spacing of the 4-line list under the Issues heading that begins with Years Population Growth to 1.15.

    f. Add 6 points of space after each paragraph under the Proposed Actions heading.

    g. Press [Ctrl][Home], then save your changes to the report.

4. Align paragraphs.

    a. Press [Ctrl][A] to select the entire document, then justify all the paragraphs.

    b. Center the three-line report title.

    c. Press [Ctrl][End], type your name, press [Enter], type the current date, then right-align your name and the date.

    d. Save your changes to the report.

5. Work with tabs.

    a. Scroll up and select the four-line list of population information under the Issues heading.

    b. Set left tab stops at the 2" mark and the 3¾" mark.

    c. Insert a tab at the beginning of each line in the list.

    d. In the first line, insert a tab before Population. In the second line, insert a tab before 4.5%. In the third line, insert a tab before 53%.

    e. Select the first three lines, then drag the second tab stop to the 3" mark on the horizontal ruler.

    f. Press [Ctrl][Home], then save your changes to the report.

6. Work with indents.

    a. Indent the paragraph under the Mission Statement heading ½" from the left and ½" from the right.

    b. Indent the first line of the paragraph under the Guiding Principles heading ½".

    c. Indent the first line of the three body paragraphs under the Issues heading ½".

    d. Press [Ctrl][Home], then save your changes to the report.

7. Add bullets and numbering.

    a. Apply bullets to the three-line list under the first body paragraph. Change the bullet style to small black circles if necessary.

    b. Change the font color of the bullets to Purple, Accent 4, Darker 25%.

    c. Scroll down until the Guiding Principles heading is at the top of your screen.

    d. Format the six-paragraph list under Guiding Principles as a numbered list.

    e. Format the numbers in 14-point Berlin Sans FB, then change the font color to Purple, Accent 4, Darker 25%.

    f. Scroll down until the Proposed Actions heading is at the top of your screen, then format the paragraphs under the heading as a bulleted list using check marks as the bullet style.

    g. Change the font color of the bullets to Purple, Accent 4, Darker 25%, press [Ctrl][Home], then save your changes to the report.

▼ SKILLS REVIEW (CONTINUED)

8. Add borders and shading.

a. Change the font color of **Town of Franklin Economic Development Authority Report** to White, Background 1, then apply Orange, Accent 6 shading.

b. Add a 1-point Orange, Accent 6 border below the Mission Statement heading.

c. Use the F4 key to add the same border to the other headings in the report (Guiding Principles, Issues, Proposed Actions).

d. Under the Issues heading, select the first three lines of tabbed text, which are formatted in purple, then apply Purple, Accent 4, Lighter 60% shading to the paragraphs.

e. Select the first three lines of tabbed text again if necessary, then add a 1½ -point Orange, Accent 6 single line box border around the paragraphs.

f. Indent the shading and border around the paragraphs 1¾" from the left and 1¾" from the right, then save your changes.

9. Add footnotes and endnotes.

a. Place the insertion point at the end of item 5 under the Guiding Principles heading, insert an endnote, then type **A capital reserve fund was established in 2009**.

b. Place the insertion point at the end of item 3, insert an endnote, then type **See the Downtown District EDA Report**.

c. Place the insertion point at the end of the third item in the list under the Proposed Actions heading, insert an endnote, then type **Scheduled for February 2010**.

d. Locate and delete the first endnote from the document. Scroll to the end of the document and verify the endnotes are correct.

e. Press [Ctrl][Home], save your changes to the report, view the report in Print Preview, then print a copy. The formatted report is shown in Figure C-27.

f. Turn off formatting marks, close the file and exit Word.

Word 2007

FIGURE C-27

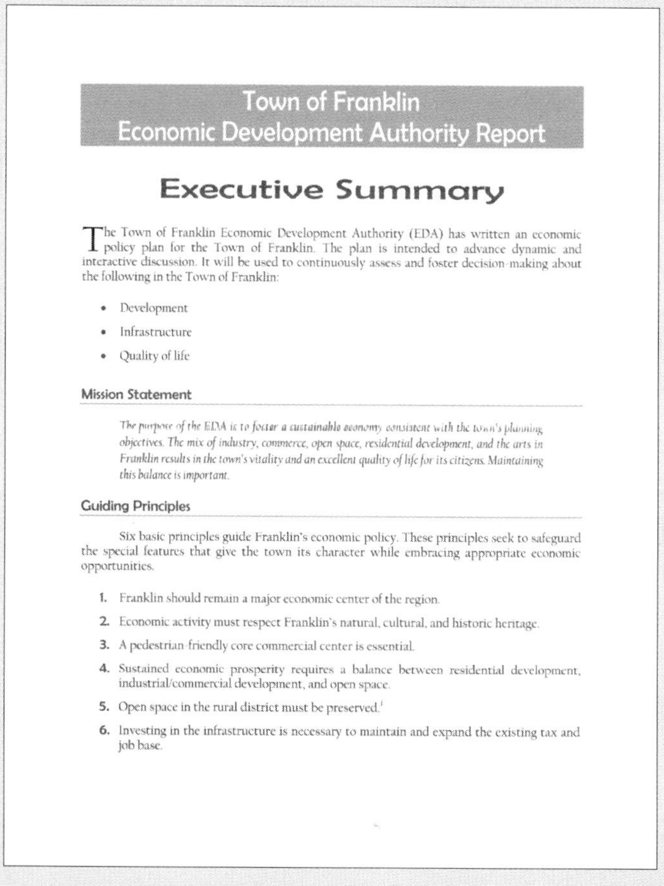
Town of Franklin
Economic Development Authority Report

Executive Summary

The Town of Franklin Economic Development Authority (EDA) has written an economic policy plan for the Town of Franklin. The plan is intended to advance dynamic and interactive discussion. It will be used to continuously assess and foster decision-making about the following in the Town of Franklin:

- Development
- Infrastructure
- Quality of life

Mission Statement

The purpose of the EDA is to foster a sustainable economy consistent with the town's planning objectives. The mix of industry, commerce, open space, residential development, and the arts in Franklin results in the town's vitality and an excellent quality of life for its citizens. Maintaining this balance is important.

Guiding Principles

Six basic principles guide Franklin's economic policy. These principles seek to safeguard the special features that give the town its character while embracing appropriate economic opportunities.

1. Franklin should remain a major economic center of the region.
2. Economic activity must respect Franklin's natural, cultural, and historic heritage.
3. A pedestrian-friendly core commercial center is essential.
4. Sustained economic prosperity requires a balance between residential development, industrial/commercial development, and open space.
5. Open space in the rural district must be preserved.[i]
6. Investing in the infrastructure is necessary to maintain and expand the existing tax and job base.

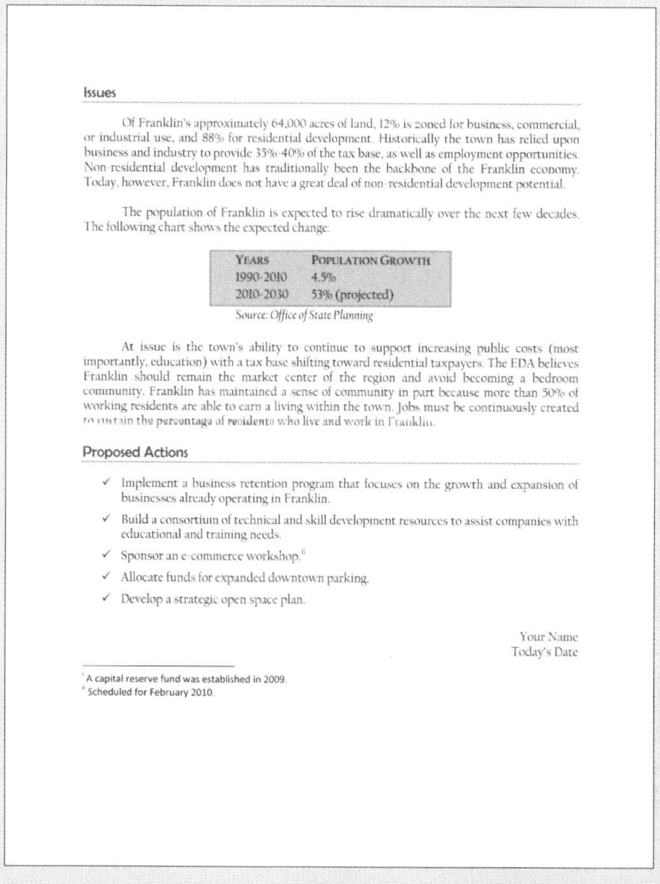
Issues

Of Franklin's approximately 64,000 acres of land, 12% is zoned for business, commercial, or industrial use, and 88% for residential development. Historically the town has relied upon business and industry to provide 35%-40% of the tax base, as well as employment opportunities. Non-residential development has traditionally been the backbone of the Franklin economy. Today, however, Franklin does not have a great deal of non-residential development potential.

The population of Franklin is expected to rise dramatically over the next few decades. The following chart shows the expected change:

YEARS	POPULATION GROWTH
1990-2010	4.5%
2010-2030	53% (projected)

Source: Office of State Planning

At issue is the town's ability to continue to support increasing public costs (most importantly, education) with a tax base shifting toward residential taxpayers. The EDA believes Franklin should remain the market center of the region and avoid becoming a bedroom community. Franklin has maintained a sense of community in part because more than 50% of working residents are able to earn a living within the town. Jobs must be continuously created to sustain the percentage of residents who live and work in Franklin.

Proposed Actions

- ✓ Implement a business retention program that focuses on the growth and expansion of businesses already operating in Franklin.
- ✓ Build a consortium of technical and skill development resources to assist companies with educational and training needs.
- ✓ Sponsor an e-commerce workshop.[ii]
- ✓ Allocate funds for expanded downtown parking.
- ✓ Develop a strategic open space plan.

Your Name
Today's Date

[i] A capital reserve fund was established in 2009.
[ii] Scheduled for February 2010.

▼ INDEPENDENT CHALLENGE 1

You are an estimator for Jermanok Construction in the Australian city of Wollongong. You have drafted an estimate for a home renovation job, and need to format it. It's important that your estimate have a clean, striking design, and reflect your company's professionalism.

a. Start Word, open the file WD C-3.docx from the drive and folder where you store your Data Files, save it as Jermanok Construction, then read the document to get a feel for its contents. Figure C-28 shows how you will format the letterhead.

JERMANOK *Construction*

26-38 Corrimal Street, Wollongong, NSW 2500; Tel: 02-4225-3202; www.jermanok.com.au

b. Select the entire document, change the style to No Spacing, then change the font to 12-point Times New Roman.

c. In the first paragraph, format Jermanok in 24-point Arial Black and change the case to All caps. Format Construction in 24-point Arial, apply italic, then delete the space between the two words. (*Hint*: Select a similar font if Arial Black is not available to you.)

d. Format the next line in 10-point Arial, then right-align the two-line letterhead.

e. Add a 2¼ -point dotted black border below the address line paragraph.

f. With the insertion point in the address line, open the Borders and Shading dialog box, click Options to open the Border and Shading Options dialog box, change the Bottom setting to 5 points, then click OK twice to adjust the location of the border relative to the line of text.

g. Format the title Proposal of Renovation in 14-point Arial Black, then center the title.

h. Format the following headings (including the colons) in 11-point Arial Black: Date, Work to be performed for and at, Scope of work, Payment schedule, and Agreement.

i. Select the 14-line list under Scope of work that begins with Demo of all..., then change the paragraph spacing to add 4 points of space after each paragraph in the list. (*Hint*: Select 0 pt in the After text box, type 4, then press Enter.)

j. With the list selected, set a right tab stop at the 6¼" mark, insert tabs before every price in the list, then apply dotted line tab leaders.

k. Format the list as a numbered list, then apply bold to the numbers.

l. Apply bold to the two lines, Total estimated job cost... and Approximate job time... below the list.

m. Replace Your Name with your name in the signature block, select the signature block (Respectfully submitted through your name), set a left tab stop at the 3¼" mark, then indent the signature block using tabs.

n. Examine the document carefully for formatting errors and make any necessary adjustments.

o. Save and print the document, then close the file and exit Word.

Your employer, The Lange Center for Contemporary Arts in Halifax, Nova Scotia, is launching a membership drive. Your boss has written the text for a flyer advertising Lange membership, and asks you to format it so that it is eye catching and attractive.

a. Open the file WD C-4.docx from the drive and folder where you store your Data Files, save it as Membership Drive 2010, then read the document. Figure C-29 shows how you will format the first several paragraphs of the flyer.

FIGURE C-29

b. Select the entire document, change the style to No Spacing, then change the font to 11-point Arial Narrow.
c. Center the first line, Membership Drive, and apply shading to the paragraph. Choose a dark custom shading color of your choice for the shading color. (*Hint*: Click More Colors, then select a color from the Standard or Custom tab.) Format the text in 26-point Arial Narrow, bold, with a white font color. Expand the character spacing by 10 points.
d. Format the second line, 2010, in 36-point Arial Black. Expand the character spacing by 25 points and change the character scale to 250%. Center the line.
e. Format each What we do for... heading in 12-point Arial, bold. Change the font color to the same custom color used for shading the title. (*Note*: The color now appears in the Recent Colors section of the Font Color gallery.) Add a single line ½-point black border under each heading.
f. Format each subheading (Gallery, Lectures, Library, All members..., and Membership Levels) in 10-point Arial, bold. Add 3 points of spacing before each paragraph. (*Hint*: Select 0 in the Before text box, type 3, then press Enter.)
g. Indent each body paragraph ¼", except for the lines under the What we do for YOU heading.
h. Format the four lines under the All members... subheading as a bulleted list. Use a bullet symbol of your choice and format the bullets in the custom font color.
i. Indent the five lines under the Membership Levels heading ¼". For these five lines, set left tab stops at the 1¼" mark and the 2" mark on the horizontal ruler. Insert tabs before the price and before the word All in each of the five lines.
j. Format the name of each membership level (Artistic, Conceptual, etc.) in 10-point Arial, bold, italic, with the custom font color.
k. Format the For more information heading in 14-point Arial, bold, with the custom font color, then center the heading.
l. Format the last two lines in 11-point Arial Narrow, and center the lines. In the contact information, replace Your Name with your name, then apply bold to your name.

Advanced Challenge Exercise

■ Change the font color of 2010 to a dark gray and add a shadow effect.
■ Add a shadow effect to each What we do for... heading.
■ Add a 3-point dotted black border above the For more information heading.

m. Examine the document carefully for formatting errors and make any necessary adjustments.
n. Save and print the flyer, then close the file and exit Word.

▼ INDEPENDENT CHALLENGE 3

One of your responsibilities as program coordinator at Solstice Mountain Sports is to develop a program of winter outdoor learning and adventure workshops. You have drafted a memo to your boss to update her on your progress. You need to format the memo so it is professional looking and easy to read.

a. Start Word, open the file WD C-5.docx from the drive and folder where you store your Data Files, then save it as **Solstice Winter Memo**.

b. Select the heading **Solstice Mountain Sports Memorandum**, apply the Quick Style Title to it, then center the heading. (*Hint*: Open the Quick Style gallery, then click the Title button.)

c. In the memo header, replace Today's Date and Your Name with the current date and your name.

d. Select the four-line memo header, set a left tab stop at the ¾" mark, then insert tabs before the date, the recipient's name, your name, and the subject of the memo.

e. Apply the Quick Style Strong to **Date:**, **To:**, **From:**, and **Re:**.

f. Apply the Quick Style Heading 2 to the headings **Overview**, **Workshops**, **Accommodations**, **Fees**, and **Proposed winter programming**.

g. Under the Fees heading, apply the Quick Style Emphasis to the words **Workshop fees** and **Accommodations fees**.

h. On the second page of the document, format the list under the **Proposed winter programming** heading as a multilevel list. Figure C-30 shows the hierarchical structure of the outline. (*Hint*: Apply a multilevel list style, then use the Increase Indent and Decrease Indent buttons to change the level of importance of each item.)

i. Change the outline numbering style to the bullet numbering style shown in Figure C-30, if necessary.

Advanced Challenge Exercise

- Zoom out on the memo so that two pages display in the document window, then, using the Change Styles button, change the style set to Modern.
- Using the Change Case button, change the title Solstice Mountain Sports Memorandum so that only the initial letter of each word is capitalized.
- Using the Themes button, change the theme applied to the document.
- Using the Theme Fonts button, change the fonts to a font set of your choice. Choose fonts that allow the document to fit on two pages.
- Using the Theme Colors button, change the colors to a color palette of your choice.
- Apply different styles and adjust other formatting elements as necessary to make the memo attractive, eye-catching, and readable.

j. Save and print the document, then close the file and exit Word.

FIGURE C-30

Proposed winter programming
- ❖ Skiing, Snowboarding, and Snowshoeing
  - ➢ Skiing and Snowboarding
    - ▪ Cross-country skiing
      - • Cross-country skiing for beginners
      - • Intermediate cross-country skiing
      - • Inn-to-inn ski touring
      - • Moonlight cross-country skiing
    - ▪ Telemarking
      - • Basic telemark skiing
      - • Introduction to backcountry skiing
      - • Exploring on skis
    - ▪ Snowboarding
      - • Backcountry snowboarding
  - ➢ Snowshoeing
    - ▪ Beginner
      - • Snowshoeing for beginners
      - • Snowshoeing and winter ecology
    - ▪ Intermediate and Advanced
      - • Intermediate snowshoeing
      - • Guided snowshoe trek
      - • Above tree line snowshoeing
- ❖ Winter Hiking, Camping, and Survival
  - ➢ Hiking
    - ▪ Beginner
      - • Long-distance hiking
      - • Winter summits
      - • Hiking for women
  - ➢ Winter camping and survival
    - ▪ Beginner
      - • Introduction to winter camping
      - • Basic winter mountain skills
      - • Building snow shelters
    - ▪ Intermediate
      - • Basic winter mountain skills II
      - • Ice climbing
      - • Avalanche awareness and rescue

▼ REAL LIFE INDEPENDENT CHALLENGE

The fonts you choose for a document can have a major effect on the document's tone. Not all fonts are appropriate for use in a business document, and some fonts, especially those with a definite theme, are appropriate only for specific purposes. In this Independent Challenge, you will use font formatting and other formatting features to design a letterhead and a fax coversheet for yourself or your business. The letterhead and coversheet should not only look professional and attract interest; the design should say something about the character of your business or your personality. Figure C-31 shows an example of a business letterhead.

FIGURE C-31

jenniferweizenbaumcommunications

167 East 12ᵗʰ Street, 4ᵗʰ floor, New York, NY 10003   Tel: 212-555-9767   Fax: 212-555-2992   www.jweizenbaum.com

a. Start Word, and save a new blank document as **Personal Letterhead** to the drive and folder where you store your Data Files.

b. Type your name or the name of your business, your address, your phone number, your fax number, and your Web site or e-mail address.

c. Format your name or the name of your business in a font that expresses your personality or says something about the nature of your business. Use fonts, font colors, font effects, borders, shading, paragraph formatting, and other formatting features to design a letterhead that is appealing and professional.

d. Save your changes, print a copy, then close the file.

e. Open a new blank document and save it as **Personal Fax Coversheet**. Type FAX, your name or the name of your business, your address, your phone number, your fax number, and your Web site or e-mail address at the top of the document.

f. Type a fax header that includes the following: Date; To; From; Re; Number of pages, including cover sheet; and Comments.

g. Format the information in the fax coversheet using fonts, font effects, borders, shading, paragraph formatting, and other formatting features. Since a fax coversheet is designed to be faxed, all fonts and other formatting elements should be black. Format the fax header using tabs.

h. Save your changes, print a copy, close the file, then exit Word.

▼ VISUAL WORKSHOP

Open the file WD C-6.docx from the drive and folder where you store your Data Files. Create the menu shown in Figure C-32. (*Hints:* Use Harlow Solid Italic and Eras Light ITC or similar fonts. Change the font size of the heading to 48 points, the font size of Daily Specials to 20 points, the font size of the days and the specials to 16 points, and the font size of the descriptions to 12 points. Format the prices using tabs. Use paragraph spacing to adjust the spacing between paragraphs so that all the text fits on one page.) Save the menu as **Nina's Trackside**, then print a copy.

FIGURE C-32

Nina's Trackside Café

Daily Specials

Monday
Chicken Cajun Bleu: Cajun chicken, chunky blue cheese, cucumbers, leaf lettuce, and tomato on our roasted garlic roll. $6.50

Tuesday
Clam Chowder: Classic New England thick, rich, clam chowder in our peasant French bread bowl. Served with a garden salad. $5.95

Wednesday
Veggie Chili: Hearty veggie chili with melted cheddar in our peasant French bread bowl. Topped with sour cream & scallions. $5.95

Thursday
French Dip: Lean roast beef topped with melted cheddar on our roasted garlic roll. Served with a side of au jus and red bliss mashed potatoes. $6.95

Friday
Turkey-Bacon Club: Double-decker roasted turkey, crisp bacon, leaf lettuce, tomato, and sun-dried tomato mayo on toasted triple seed. $6.50

Saturday
Greek Salad: Our large garden salad with Kalamata olives, feta cheese, and garlic vinaigrette. Served with an assortment of rolls. $5.95

Sunday
Hot Chicken and Gravy: Delicious chicken and savory gravy served on a thick slice of toasted honest white. Served with a garden salad. $6.95

Chef: Your Name

Formatting Documents

Files You Will Need:

WD D-1.docx
WD D-2.docx
WD D-3.docx
WD D-4.docx
WD D-5.docx
WD D-6.docx
WD D-7.docx

The page-formatting features of Word allow you to lay out and design the pages of your documents creatively. In this unit, you learn how to change the document margins, determine page orientation, add page numbers, and insert headers and footers. You also learn how to format text in columns and how to illustrate your documents with tables and clip art.  You have written and formatted the text for the quarterly newsletter for QST clients. You are now ready to lay out and design the newsletter pages. You plan to organize the articles in columns and to enhance the visual appeal of the newsletter by adding a table and clip art.

OBJECTIVES

Set document margins

Divide a document into sections

Insert page breaks

Format columns

Insert page numbers

Add headers and footers

Edit headers and footers

Insert a table

Insert clip art

Setting Document Margins

Changing a document's margins is one way to change the appearance of a document and control the amount of text that fits on a page. The **margins** of a document are the blank areas between the edge of the text and the edge of the page. When you create a document in Word, the default margins are 1" at the top, bottom, left, and right sides of the page. You can adjust the size of a document's margins using the Margins command on the Page Layout tab, or using the rulers. The newsletter should be a four-page document when finished. You begin formatting the pages by reducing the size of the document margins so that more text fits on each page.

STEPS

1. **Start Word, open the file WD D-1.docx from the drive and folder where you store your Data Files, then save it as Footprints**

   The newsletter opens in Print Layout view.

2. **Scroll through the newsletter to get a feel for its contents, then press [Ctrl][Home]**

   The newsletter is currently five pages long. Notice that the status bar indicates the page where the insertion point is located and the total number of pages in the document.

3. **Click the Page Layout tab, then click the Margins button in the Page Setup group**

   The Margins menu opens. You can select predefined margin settings from this menu, or click Custom Margins to create different margin settings.

4. **Click Custom Margins**

   The Page Setup dialog box opens with the Margins tab displayed, as shown in Figure D-1. You can use the Margins tab to change the top, bottom, left, or right document margin, to change the orientation of the pages from portrait to landscape, and to alter other page layout settings. **Portrait orientation** means a page is taller than it is wide; **landscape orientation** means a page is wider than it is tall. This newsletter uses portrait orientation. You can also use the Orientation button in the Page Setup group on the Page Layout tab to change the orientation of a document.

5. **Click the Top down arrow three times until 0.7" appears, then click the Bottom down arrow until 0.7" appears**

   The top and bottom margins of the newsletter will be .7". Notice that the margins in the Preview section of the dialog box change as you adjust the margin settings.

6. **Press [Tab], type .7 in the Left text box, press [Tab], then type .7 in the Right text box**

   The left and right margins of the newsletter will also be .7". You can change the margin settings by using the arrows or by typing a value in the appropriate text box.

7. **Click OK**

   The document margins change to .7", as shown in Figure D-2. The location of each margin (right, left, top, and bottom) is shown on the horizontal and vertical rulers at the intersection of the white and shaded areas. You can also change a margin setting by using the ⟺ pointer to drag the intersection to a new location on the ruler.

8. **Click the View tab, then click the Two Pages button in the Zoom group**

   The first two pages of the document appear in the document window.

9. **Scroll down to view all five pages of the newsletter, press [Ctrl][Home], click the Page Width button in the Zoom group, then save your changes**

FIGURE D-1: Margins tab in Page Setup dialog box

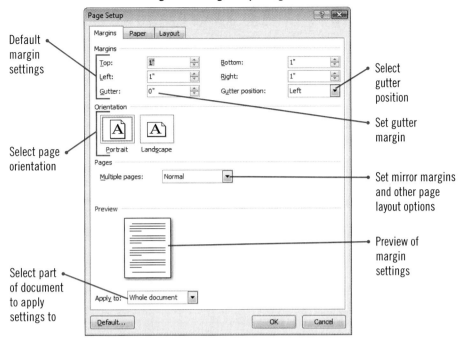

Default margin settings

Select page orientation

Select part of document to apply settings to

Select gutter position

Set gutter margin

Set mirror margins and other page layout options

Preview of margin settings

FIGURE D-2: Newsletter with smaller margins

Left margin on ruler

Top margin on ruler

Document margins are narrower

Page 1 is the active page

Right margin on ruler

Document is five pages long

Changing orientation, margin settings, and paper size

By default, the documents you create in Word use an 8½" × 11" paper size in portrait orientation with the default margin settings. You can change the orientation, margin settings, and paper size to common settings using the Orientation, Margins, and Size buttons in the Page Setup group on the Page Layout tab. You can also adjust these settings and others in the Page Setup dialog box. For example, to change the layout of multiple pages, use the Multiple pages list arrow on the Margins tab to create pages that use mirror margins, that include two pages per sheet of paper, or that are formatted like a folded booklet. **Mirror margins** are used in a document with facing pages, such as a magazine, where the margins on the left page

of the document are a mirror image of the margins on the right page. Documents with mirror margins have inside and outside margins, rather than right and left margins. Another type of margin is a gutter margin, which is used in documents that are bound, such as books. A **gutter** adds extra space to the left, top, or inside margin to allow for the binding. Add a gutter to a document by adjusting the setting in the Gutter position text box on the Margins tab. To change the size of the paper used, use the Paper size list arrow on the Paper tab to select a standard paper size, or enter custom measurements in the Width and Height text boxes.

Dividing a Document into Sections

Dividing a document into sections allows you to format each section of the document with different page layout settings. A **section** is a portion of a document that is separated from the rest of the document by section breaks. **Section breaks** are formatting marks that you insert in a document to show the end of a section. Once you have divided a document into sections, you can format each section with different column, margin, page orientation, header and footer, and other page layout settings. By default, a document is formatted as a single section, but you can divide a document into as many sections as you like. ▰▰▰ You insert a section break to divide the document into two sections, and then format the text in the second section in two columns. First, you customize the status bar to display section information.

STEPS

1. **Right-click the status bar, click Section on the Customize Status Bar menu that opens (if it is not already checked), then click the document to close the menu**
   The status bar indicates the insertion point is located in section 1 of the document.

2. **Click the Home tab, then click the Show/Hide ¶ button ¶ in the Paragraph group**
   Turning on formatting marks allows you to see the section breaks you insert in a document.

3. **Place the insertion point before the headline QST Launches New Tours to South Africa, click the Page Layout tab, then click the Breaks button in the Page Setup group**
   The Breaks menu opens. You use this menu to insert different types of section breaks. See Table D-1.

4. **Click Continuous**
   Word inserts a continuous section break, shown as a dotted double line, above the headline. The document now has two sections. Notice that the status bar indicates the insertion point is in section 2.

5. **Click the Columns button in the Page Setup group**
   The columns menu opens. You use this menu to format text in one, two, or three columns of equal width, or to create two columns of different widths, one narrow and one wider. To create columns with custom widths and spacing, you click More Columns on the Columns menu.

6. **Click Two**
   Section 2 is formatted in two columns of equal width, as shown in Figure D-3. The text in section 1 remains formatted in a single column. Notice that the status bar now indicates the document is four pages long. Formatting text in columns is another way to increase the amount of text that fits on a page.

7. **Click the View tab, click the Two Pages button in the Zoom group, scroll down to examine all four pages of the document, press [Ctrl][Home], then save the document**
   The text in section 2—all the text below the continuous section break—is formatted in two columns. Text in columns flows automatically from the bottom of one column to the top of the next column.

TABLE D-1: Types of section breaks

section	function
Next page	Begins a new section and moves the text following the break to the top of the next page
Continuous	Begins a new section on the same page
Even page	Begins a new section and moves the text following the break to the top of the next even-numbered page
Odd page	Begins a new section and moves the text following the break to the top of the next odd-numbered page

Formatting Documents

FIGURE D-3: Continuous section break and columns

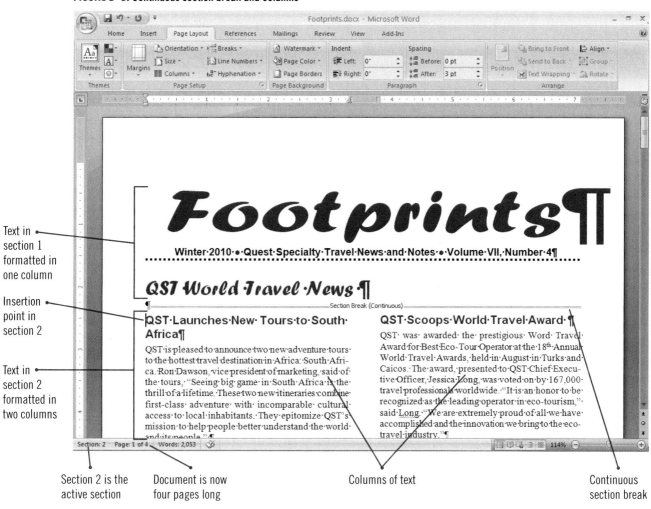

Text in section 1 formatted in one column

Insertion point in section 2

Text in section 2 formatted in two columns

Section 2 is the active section

Document is now four pages long

Columns of text

Continuous section break

Changing page layout settings for a section

Dividing a document into sections allows you to vary the layout of a document. In addition to applying different column settings to sections, you can apply different margins, page orientation, paper size, vertical alignment, header and footer, page numbering, footnotes, endnotes, and other page layout settings. For example, if you are formatting a report that includes a table with many columns, you might want to change the table's page orientation to landscape so that it is easier to read. To do this, you would insert a section break before and after the table to create a section that contains only the table, and then you would change the page orientation of the section that contains the table to landscape. Or, you might be creating a title page for a report, and want to center the text on the title page between the top and bottom margins. To do this you would insert a next page section break after the title page and then use the

Vertical alignment list arrow on the Layout tab of the Page Setup dialog box to change the **vertical alignment** of the section to Center. You can vertically align text on a page only when the text does not fill the page—for example, if you are creating a flyer or a title page.

To check or change the page layout settings for an individual section, place the insertion point in the section, then open the Page Setup dialog box. Select any options you want to change, click the Apply to list arrow, click This section, then click OK. When you select This section in the Apply to list box, the settings are applied to the current section only. If you select Whole document in the Apply to list box, the settings are applied to all the sections in the document. Use the Apply to list arrow in the Columns dialog box or the Footnote and Endnote dialog box to change those settings for a section.

Inserting Page Breaks

As you type text in a document, Word inserts an **automatic page break** (also called a soft page break) when you reach the bottom of a page, allowing you to continue typing on the next page. You can also force text onto the next page of a document by using the Breaks command to insert a **manual page break** (also called a hard page break). You insert manual page breaks where you know you want to begin each new page of the newsletter.

STEPS

1. **Place the insertion point before the headline Spotlight on Japan on page 2, click the Page Layout tab, then click the Breaks button in the Page Setup group**

   The Breaks menu opens. You also use this menu to insert page, column, and text-wrapping breaks. Table D-2 describes these types of breaks.

   QUICK TIP

   Manual and automatic page breaks are always visible in Draft view.

2. **Click Page**

   Word inserts a manual page break before "Spotlight on Japan" and moves all the text following the page break to the beginning of the next page. The page break appears as a dotted line in Print Layout view when formatting marks are displayed. Page break marks are visible on the screen but do not print.

3. **Scroll down to pages 3 and 4, place the insertion point before the headline Language and Culture Immersion: Antigua, Guatemala, press and hold [Ctrl], then press [Enter]**

   Pressing [Ctrl][Enter] is a fast way to insert a manual page break. The headline is forced to the top of the fourth page, as shown in Figure D-4.

   QUICK TIP

   You can also double-click a page break to select it, and then press [Delete] to delete it.

4. **Place the insertion point before the headline Traveler's Corner on page 4, then press [Ctrl][Enter]**

   The headline is forced to the top of the fifth page.

5. **Press [Ctrl][Home], click to the left of the page break at the top of page 2 to select it, then press [Delete]**

   The manual page break is deleted and the text from pages 2 and 3 flows together. You can also click to the left of a section or a column break to select it.

   QUICK TIP

   To add line numbers in the margin to the left of each line on a page, in a section, or in a document, click the Line Numbers button in the Page Setup group, and then select an option.

6. **Click the Breaks button, then click Next Page**

   A next page section break is inserted at the top of page 2 and the text following the break is forced to the top of page 3, as shown in Figure D-5. The document now contains three sections.

7. **Place the insertion point in section 2 on page 1 (the body text), then save the document**

   The status bar indicates the insertion point is in section 2. In the next lesson you will format the columns in section 2 so that the entire section fits on the first page of the newsletter.

Controlling automatic pagination

Another way to control the flow of text between pages (or between columns) is to apply pagination settings to specify where Word positions automatic page breaks. For example, you might want to make sure an article appears on the same page as its heading, or you might want to prevent a page from breaking in the middle of the last paragraph of a report. To manipulate automatic pagination, simply select the paragraphs(s) or line(s) you want to control, click the launcher in the Paragraph group on the Home or Page Layout tab, click the Line and Page Breaks tab in the Paragraph dialog box, select one or more of the following settings from the Pagination section, and then click OK. Apply the Keep with next setting to any paragraph you want to appear together with the next paragraph on a single page, in order to prevent the page from breaking between the paragraphs. To prevent a page from breaking in the middle of a paragraph or between certain lines, select the paragraph or lines and apply the Keep lines together setting. Finally, to specify that a certain paragraph follows an automatic page break, apply the Page break before setting to the paragraph. Note that the Widow/Orphan control setting is turned on by default in the Pagination section of the dialog box. This setting ensures that at least two lines of a paragraph appear at the top and bottom of every page. In other words, it prevents a page from beginning with just the last line of a paragraph (a **widow**), and prevents a page from ending with only the first line of a new paragraph (an **orphan**).

FIGURE D-4: Manual page break in document

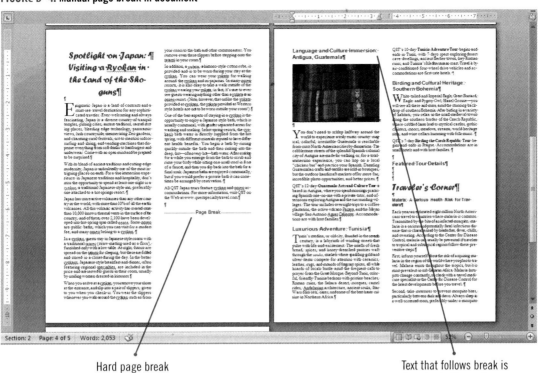

Hard page break

Text that follows break is forced onto the next page

FIGURE D-5: Next page section break in document

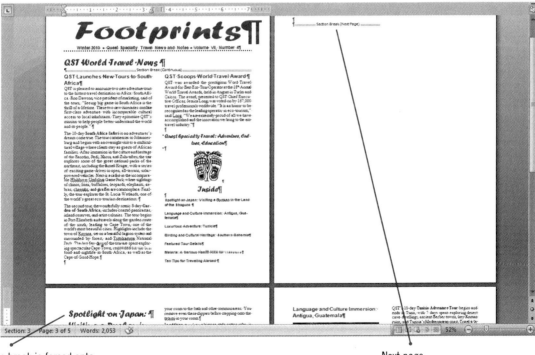

Text that follows break is forced onto the next page and is in a new section

Next page section break

TABLE D-2: Types of breaks

break	function
Page	Forces the text following the break to begin at the top of the next page
Column	Forces the text following the break to begin at the top of the next column
Text Wrapping	Forces the text following the break to begin at the beginning of the next line

Formatting Columns

Formatting text in columns often makes the text easier to read. You can apply column formatting to a whole document, to a section, or to selected text. The Columns command on the Page Layout tab allows you to quickly create columns of equal width and spacing, and to customize the width and spacing of columns. To control the way text flows between columns, you can insert a **column break**, which forces the text following the break to move to the top of the next column. You can also balance columns of unequal length on a page by inserting a continuous section break at the end of the last column on the page. You continue to format the newsletter using columns.

STEPS

1. **Make sure the insertion point is in section 2, click the** Columns button **in the Page Setup group, then click** Right.

   The text in section 2 is reformatted into two columns of unequal width. The formatting of the text in section 3 does not change. All the text now fits on four pages.

QUICK TIP

To change the width and spacing of existing columns, you can use the Columns dialog box or drag the column markers on the horizontal ruler.

2. **Select the headline** Spotlight on Japan: Visiting a Ryokan in the Land of the Shoguns **and the** paragraph mark **below it, click the** Columns button, **then click** One

   A continuous section break is added below the headline. The headline is formatted as a single column in its own new section, section 3, where the insertion point is located. The newsletter now contains 4 sections, each with different column formatting.

3. **Scroll down, place the insertion point before Malaria: A Serious... on page 4, click the** Zoom Level button 52% **on the status bar, click the** Page width option button, **click** OK, **click the** Breaks button **in the Page Setup group, then click** Continuous

   A continuous section break is inserted before the Malaria headline, and the insertion point is in the new section, section 5.

QUICK TIP

To fit more text on the screen, you can hide the white space on the top and bottom of each page by moving the pointer between the pages until it changes to ⊥⊤, and then double-clicking. To show the white space again, double-click with the ⊤⊥ pointer.

4. **Click the** Columns button, **then click** More Columns

   The Columns dialog box opens, as shown in Figure D-6.

5. **Select** Three **in the Presets section, click the** Spacing down arrow **twice until 0.3" appears, select the** Line between check box, **then click** OK

   All the text in section 5 is formatted in three columns of equal width with a line between the columns, as shown in Figure D-7.

6. **Click the** Zoom Level button 114% **on the status bar, click the** Whole page option button, **then click** OK

   Page 4 would look better if the three columns were balanced—each the same length.

7. **Place the insertion point at the end of the third column (before the final paragraph mark), click the** Breaks button, **then click** Continuous

   The columns in section 5 adjust to become roughly the same length.

QUICK TIP

If a section contains a column break, you cannot balance the columns by inserting a continuous section break.

8. **Scroll up to page 3, place the insertion point before the heading Luxurious Adventure: Tunisia, click the** Breaks button, **then click** Column

   The text following the column break is forced to the top of the next column. The page looks cleaner when the Tunisia article does not break across the columns.

9. **Click the** View tab, **click the** Two Pages button **in the Zoom group, then save the document**

   The columns on pages 3 and 4 are formatted as shown in Figure D-8.

FIGURE D-6: Columns dialog box

Select a preset format for columns

Change the number of columns

Set custom widths and spacing for columns

Select to add a line between columns

Preview of current settings

Select to create columns of equal width

Select part of document to apply format to

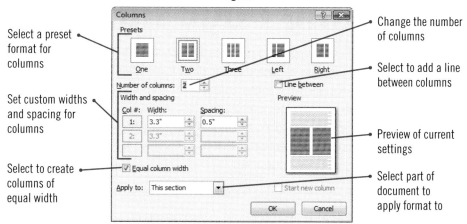

FIGURE D-7: Text formatted in three columns

Section break at end of section 4

Section 5 formatted in three columns

Column markers show width and spacing of columns

Line added between columns

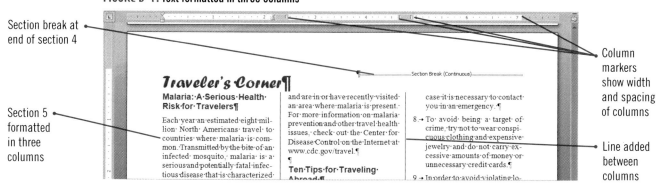

FIGURE D-8: Columns on pages 3 and 4 of the newsletter

Text following column break forced to top of next column

Column break

Continuous section break

Columns in section 5 are balanced

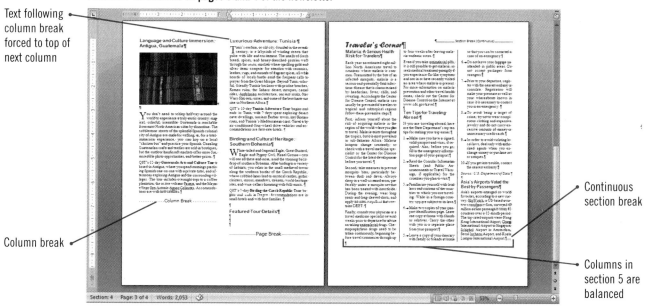

Hyphenating text in a document

Hyphenating a document is another way to control the flow of text in columns. Hyphens are small dashes that break words that fall at the end of a line. Hyphenation diminishes the gaps between words in justified text and reduces ragged right edges in left-aligned text. If a document includes narrow columns, hyphenating the text can help give the pages a cleaner look. To hyphenate a document automatically, click the Hyphenation button in the Page Setup group on the Page Layout tab, and then click Automatic. To set the hyphenation zone—the distance between the margin and the end of the last word in the line—click the Hyphenation button and then click Hyphenation Options to open the Hyphenation dialog box. A smaller hyphenation zone results in a greater number of hyphenated words.

Inserting Page Numbers

If you want to number the pages of a multiple-page document, you can insert a page number field in the top, bottom, or side margin of each page. A **field** is a code that serves as a placeholder for data that changes in a document, such as a page number or the current date. When you use the Page Number button on the Insert tab to add page numbers to a document, you insert the page number field at the top, bottom, or side of any page and Word automatically numbers all the pages in the document for you. You insert a page number field so that page numbers will appear centered between the margins at the bottom of each page in the document.

STEPS

QUICK TIP

Point to Current Position to insert a page number field at the location of the insertion point.

1. **Click the Page Width button in the Zoom group on the View tab, press [Ctrl][Home], click the Insert tab, then click the Page Number button in the Header & Footer group**

   The Page Number menu opens. You use this menu to select the position for the page numbers. If you choose to add a page number field to the top, bottom, or side of a document, a page number will appear on every page in the document. If you choose to insert it in the document at the location of the insertion point, the field will appear on that page only.

2. **Point to Bottom of Page**

   A gallery of formatting and alignment options for page numbers located at the bottom of a page opens, as shown in Figure D-9.

QUICK TIP

To change the location or formatting of page numbers, click the Page Number button, point to a page number location, then select a format from the gallery.

3. **Drag the scroll box down the gallery to view the options, scroll to the top of the gallery, then click Plain Number 2 in the Simple section**

   The page number 1 appears centered in the Footer area at the bottom of the first page, as shown in Figure D-10. The document text is gray, or dimmed, because the Footer area is open. Text that is inserted in a Footer area appears at the bottom of every page in a document.

4. **Double-click the document text, then scroll to the bottom of page 1**

   Double-clicking the document text closes the Footer area. The page number is now dimmed because it is located in the Footer area, which is no longer the active area. When the document is printed, the page numbers appear as normal text. You will learn more about working with the Footer area in the next lesson.

QUICK TIP

To remove page numbers from a document, click the Page Number button, then click Remove Page Numbers.

5. **Scroll down the document to see the page number at the bottom of each page**

   Word automatically numbered each page of the newsletter, and each page number is centered at the bottom of the page. If you want to change the numbering format or to start page numbering with a different number, you can simply click the Page Number button, click Format Page Numbers, and then choose from the options in the Page Number Format dialog box.

6. **Press [Ctrl][Home], then save the document**

Moving around in a long document

Rather than scrolling to move to a different place in a long document, you can use the Browse by Object feature to quickly move the insertion point to a specific location. Browse by Object allows you to browse to the next or previous page, section, line, table, graphic, or other item of the same type in a document. To do this, first click the Select Browse Object button ⊙ below the vertical scroll bar to open a palette of object types. On this palette, click the button for the type of item by which you want to browse, and then click the Next ⬇ or Previous ⬆ buttons to scroll through the items of that type in the document.

FIGURE D-9: Gallery of options for page numbers located at the bottom of the page

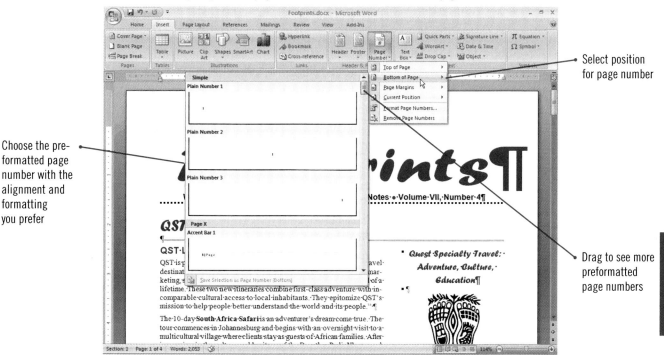

Choose the pre-formatted page number with the alignment and formatting you prefer

Select position for page number

Drag to see more preformatted page numbers

FIGURE D-10: Page number in document

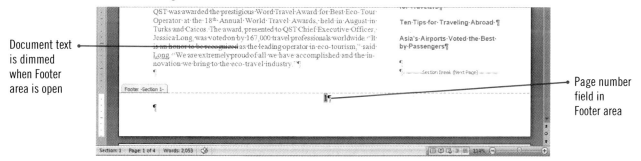

Document text is dimmed when Footer area is open

Page number field in Footer area

Inserting Quick Parts

The Word Quick Parts feature makes it easy to insert reusable pieces of content into a document quickly. The **Quick Parts** items you can insert include fields, such as for the current date or the total number of pages in a document; document property information, such as the author and title of a document; and building blocks, which are customized content that you create, format, and save for future use.

To insert a Quick Part into a document at the location of the insertion point, click the Quick Parts button in the Text group on the Insert tab (or, if headers and footers are open, click the Quick Parts button in the Insert group on the Header and Footer Tools Design tab), and then select the type of Quick Part you want to insert. To insert a field into a document, click Field on the Quick Parts menu that opens, click the name of the field you want to insert in the Field dialog box, and then click OK. Field information is updated automatically each time the document is opened or saved.

To insert a document property, point to Document Property on the Quick Parts menu and then click the property you want to insert. The property is added to the document as a content control and contains the document property information you entered in the Document Information panel. If you did not assign a document property, the content control contains a placeholder, which you can replace with your own text. Once you replace the placeholder text—or edit the document property information that appears in the content control—this text replaces the document property information in the Document Information panel.

To insert a building block, click Building Blocks Organizer on the Quick Parts menu, select the building block you want, and then click Insert. You will learn more about working with building blocks in later lessons.

Adding Headers and Footers

A **header** is text or graphics that appears at the top of every page of a document. A **footer** is text or graphics that appears at the bottom of every page. In longer documents, headers and footers often contain information such as the title of the publication, the title of the chapter, the name of the author, the date, or a page number. You can add headers and footers to a document by double-clicking the top or bottom margin of a document to open the Header and Footer areas, and then inserting text and graphics into them. You can also use the Header or Footer command on the Insert tab to insert predesigned headers and footers that you can modify to include your own information. ▰▰▰ You create a header that includes the name of the newsletter and the current date, and add the word "Page" to the footer.

STEPS

1. **Click the Insert tab, then click the Header button in the Header & Footer group**

   A gallery of built-in header designs opens.

2. **Scroll down the gallery to view the header designs, scroll to the top of the gallery, then click Blank**

   The Header and Footer areas open and the document text is dimmed. When the document text is dimmed, it cannot be edited. The Header & Footer Tools Design tab also opens and is the active tab, as shown in Figure D-11. This tab is available whenever the Header and Footer areas are open. The Header and Footer areas of a document are independent of the document itself and must be formatted separately. For example, if you select all the text in a document and then change the font, the header and footer font does not change.

3. **Type Footprints in the content control in the Header area, press [Spacebar] twice, then click the Date & Time button in the Insert group**

   The Date and Time dialog box opens. You use this dialog box to select the format for the date or time and to indicate whether you want the date or time inserted in the document as a field that is updated automatically, or as static text. Word uses the clock on your computer to compute the date and time.

4. **Make sure the Update Automatically check box is selected, then click OK**

   A date field is inserted into the header using the default month/date/year (M/d/yyyy) format. The word "Footprints" and the current date will appear at the top of every page in the document.

5. **Select Footprints and the date, click the Font list arrow on the Mini toolbar, click Forte, click the Center button ▤ on the Mini toolbar, then click in the Header area to deselect the text**

   The text is formatted in Forte and centered in the Header area. In addition to the alignment buttons, you can use the Insert Alignment Tab button in the Position group on the Header & Footer Tools Design tab to left-, center-, and right-align text in the Header and Footer areas with the document margins.

6. **Click the Go to Footer button in the Navigation group**

   The insertion point moves to the Footer area, where a page number field is centered in the Footer area. You can use the buttons in the Navigation group to move quickly between the Header and Footer areas on the current page or to a header or a footer in the previous or next section of the document.

7. **Verify that the insertion point is before the page number field, type Page, press [Spacebar], select the text and the field in the footer, click the Font list arrow on the Mini toolbar, click Forte, then click in the Footer area to deselect the text and field**

   The footer text is formatted in Forte.

8. **Click the Close Header and Footer button in the Close group, save the document, then scroll down until the bottom of page 1 and the top of page 2 appear in the document window**

   The Header and Footer areas close and the header and footer text is dimmed, as shown in Figure D-12.

FIGURE D-11: Header area open

Header & Footer Tools Design tab

Header area is open

Content control

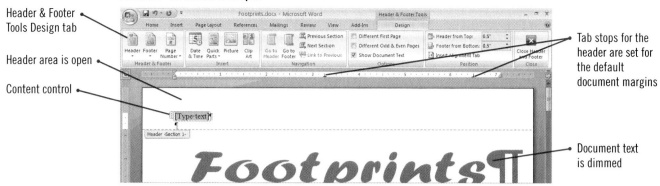

Tab stops for the header are set for the default document margins

Document text is dimmed

FIGURE D-12: Header and footer in document

Page number appears in footer on every page

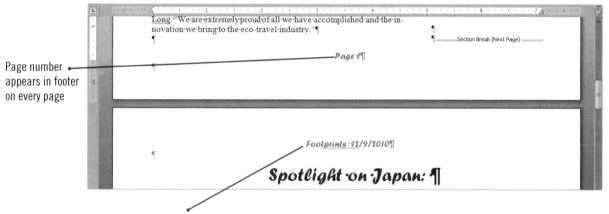

Header text appears centered in the header on every page (your date will differ)

Adding a custom header or footer to the gallery

When you design a header that you want to use again in other documents, you can add it to the Header gallery by saving it as a building block. **Building blocks** are reusable pieces of formatted content or document parts, including headers and footers, page numbers, and text boxes, that are stored in galleries. Building blocks include predesigned content that comes with Word, as well as content that you create and save for future use. For example, you might create a custom header that contains your company name and logo and is formatted using the fonts, border, and colors you use in all company documents.

To add a custom header to the Header gallery, select all the text in the header, including the last paragraph mark, click the Header button, and then click Save Selection to Header Gallery. In the

Create New Building Block dialog box that opens, type a unique name for the header in the Name text box, click the Gallery list arrow and select the appropriate gallery, verify that the Category is General, and then type a brief description of the new header design in the Description text box. This description appears in a ScreenTip when you point to the custom header in the gallery. When you are finished, click OK. The new header appears in the Header gallery under the General category.

To remove a custom header from the Header gallery, right-click it, click Organize and Delete, make sure the appropriate building block is selected in the Building Blocks Organizer that opens, click Delete, click Yes, and then click Close. You can follow the same process to add or remove a custom footer to the Footer gallery.

Editing Headers and Footers

To change header and footer text or to alter the formatting of headers and footers, you must first open the Header and Footer areas. You open headers and footers by using the Edit Header or Edit Footer command in the Header and Footer galleries, or by double-clicking a header or footer in Print Layout view. You modify the header by adding a small circle symbol between "Footprints" and the date. You also add a border under the header text to set it off from the rest of the page. Finally, you remove the header and footer text from the first page of the document.

STEPS

1. **Scroll down, place the insertion point at the top of page 2, position the pointer over the header text at the top of page 2, then double-click**

   The Header and Footer areas open. The insertion point is located in the Header area at the top of page 2.

2. **Place the insertion point between the two spaces after Footprints, click the Insert tab, click the Symbol button in the Symbols group, then click More Symbols in the gallery of recently used symbols**

   The Symbol dialog box opens and is similar to Figure D-13. **Symbols** are special characters, such as graphics, shapes, and foreign language characters, that you can insert into a document. The symbols shown in Figure D-13 are the symbols included with the (normal text) font. You can use the Font list arrow on the Symbols tab to view the symbols included with each font on your computer.

3. **Scroll the list of symbols if necessary to locate the bullet symbol shown in Figure D-13, select the bullet symbol, click Insert, then click Close**

   A bullet symbol is added at the location of the insertion point.

4. **With the insertion point in the header text, click the Home tab, click the Bottom Border list arrow [⊞ ▾] in the Paragraph group, then click Borders and Shading**

   The Borders and Shading dialog box opens.

5. **Click the Borders tab if it is not already selected, click Custom in the Setting section, click the dotted line in the Style list box (the second line style), click the Width list arrow, click 2¼ pt, click the Bottom border button in the Preview section, make sure Paragraph is selected in the Apply to list box, click OK, double-click the document text to close the Header and Footer areas, then click the Show/Hide button [¶] in the Paragraph group**

   A dotted line border is added below the header text, as shown in Figure D-14.

6. **Press [Ctrl][Home] to move the insertion point to the beginning of the document**

   The newsletter already includes the name of the document at the top of the first page, making the header information redundant. You can modify headers and footers so that the header and footer text does not appear on the first page of a document or a section.

7. **Position the pointer over the header text at the top of page 1, then double-click**

   The Header and Footer areas open. The Options group on the Header & Footer Tools Design tab includes options for creating a different header and footer for the first page of a document or a section, and for creating different headers and footers for odd- and even-numbered pages. For example, in a document with facing pages, such as a magazine, you might want the publication title to appear in the left-page header and the publication date to appear in the right-page header.

8. **Click the Different First Page check box to select it, then click the Close Header and Footer button**

   The header and footer text is removed from the Header and Footer areas on the first page.

9. **Scroll to see the header and footer on pages 2, 3, and 4, then save the document**

FIGURE D-13: Symbol dialog box

Special Characters tab

Bullet symbol

Name of selected symbol

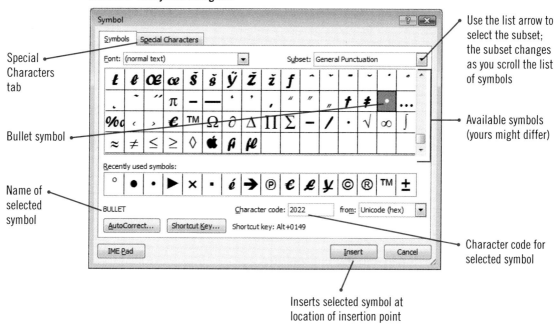

Use the list arrow to select the subset; the subset changes as you scroll the list of symbols

Available symbols (yours might differ)

Character code for selected symbol

Inserts selected symbol at location of insertion point

FIGURE D-14: Symbol and border added to header

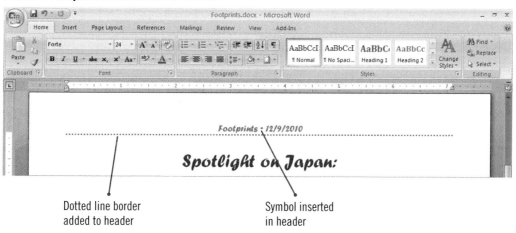

Dotted line border added to header

Symbol inserted in header

Creating an AutoText building block

AutoText is a type of building block that allows you to store text and graphics that you use frequently so that you can easily insert them in a document. AutoText entries are stored in the Building Blocks Organizer, and each AutoText entry has a unique name, so that you can find it when you need it. For example, you might want to store your company letterhead or a list of staff names and titles, so that you can easily insert them in a document without having to retype or reformat the information.

To create a custom AutoText entry, enter the text or graphic you want to store—such as a company letterhead or staff list—in a document, select it, click the Quick Parts button in the Text group on the

Insert tab, and then click Save Selection to Quick Part Gallery. In the Create New Building Block dialog box that opens, enter a unique name for the new building block, select AutoText for the Gallery, enter any other relevant information, such as a description, and then click OK to save the text or graphic as an AutoText entry in the Building Blocks Organizer.

To insert an AutoText entry or any other building block into a document at the location of the insertion point, click the Quick Parts button, click Building Blocks Organizer, scroll the list of building blocks to find the building block you want, select it, and then click Insert.

Inserting a Table

Adding a table to a document is a useful way to illustrate information that is intended for quick reference and analysis. A **table** is a grid of columns and rows of cells that you can fill with text and graphics. A **cell** is the box formed by the intersection of a column and a row. The lines that divide the columns and rows of a table and help you see the grid-like structure of the table are called **borders**. A simple way to insert a table into a document is to use the Insert Table command on the Insert tab. This command allows you to determine the dimensions and format of a table before it is inserted. ▰▰▰▰ You add a table showing the details for the QST tours mentioned by name in the newsletter.

STEPS

1. **Click the** Show/Hide button ¶ **in the Paragraph group, then scroll until the heading Featured Tour Details on page 3 is at the top of your document window**

2. **Place the insertion point before the heading Featured Tour Details, click the** Page Layout tab**, click the** Breaks button **in the Page Setup group, then click** Continuous
   A continuous section break is inserted before the heading. The document now includes six sections, with the heading Featured Tour Details in the fifth section.

3. **Click the** Columns button **in the Page Setup group, then click** One
   Section 5 is formatted as a single column.

4. **Place the insertion point before the second paragraph mark below the heading, click the** Insert tab**, click the** Table button **in the Tables group, then click** Insert Table
   The Insert Table dialog box opens. You use this dialog box to create a blank table with a set number of columns and rows, and to choose an option for sizing the width of the columns in the table.

5. **Type** 4 **in the Number of columns text box, press [Tab], type** 6 **in the Number of rows text box, make sure the** Fixed column width option button **is selected, then click** OK
   A blank table with four columns and six rows is inserted in the document at the location of the insertion point. The insertion point is in the upper-left cell of the table, the first cell in the header row. When the insertion point is in a table, the Table Tools Design tab becomes the active tab.

6. **Type** Tour **in the first cell in the first row, press [Tab], type** Season**, press [Tab], type** Length**, press [Tab], type** Cost**, then press [Tab]**
   Pressing [Tab] moves the insertion point to the next cell in the row. At the end of a row, pressing [Tab] moves the insertion point to the first cell in the next row. You can also click in a cell to move the insertion point to it.

7. **Type the text shown in Figure D-15 in the table cells, pressing [Tab] to move from cell to cell**
   Don't be concerned if the text wraps to the next line in a cell as you type: you will adjust the width of the columns after you finish typing.

8. **Click the** Table Tools Layout tab**, click the** AutoFit button **in the Cell Size group, click** AutoFit Contents**, click the** AutoFit button **again, then click** AutoFit Window
   The width of the table columns is adjusted to fit the text and then the window. You modify the structure of a table using the commands on the Table Tools Layout tab. To edit the text in a table, simply place the insertion point in a cell and then type.

9. **Click the** Table Tools Design tab**, click the** More button ▾ **in the Table Styles group to expand the Table Styles gallery, click the** Light List – Accent 2 style**, then clear the** First Column check box **in the Table Style Options group**
   The Light List - Accent 2 style table style is applied to the table, as shown in Figure D-16. A **table style** includes format settings for the text, borders, and shading in a table.

10. **Click the** View tab**, click the** Two Pages button**, then save the document**
    Completed pages 3 and 4 are shown in Figure D-17.

FIGURE D-15: Text in table

Header row

Row

Cell

Column

Section 5 is one column

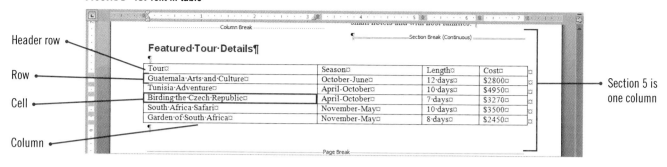

FIGURE D-16: Completed table

First Column check box

Light List – Accent 2 table style

Header row

Nonprinting, vertical gridlines might not appear on your screen

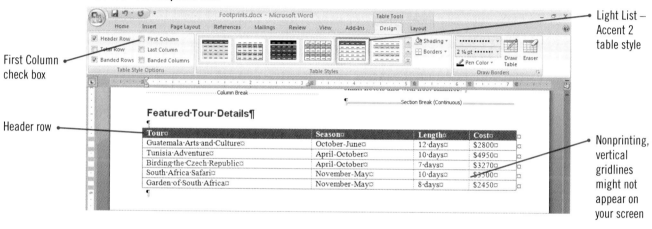

FIGURE D-17: Completed pages 3 and 4

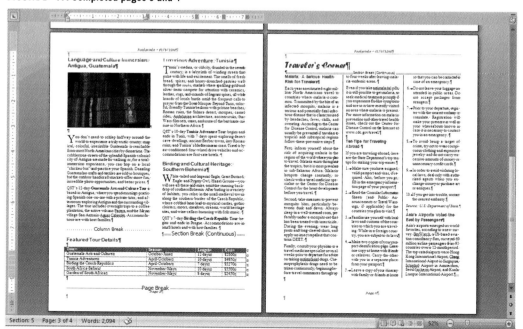

Inserting Clip Art

Clip art is a collection of graphic images that you can insert into a document. Clip art images are stored in the **Clip Organizer**, a library of the **clips**—media files such as graphics, photographs, sounds, movies, and animations—that come with Word. You can add a clip to a document using the Clip Art command on the Insert tab. Once you insert a clip art image, you can wrap text around it, resize it, enhance it, and move it to a different location. ⬛⬛⬛⬛ You illustrate the second page of the newsletter with a clip art image.

STEPS

1. **Click the Page Width button in the Zoom group, scroll to the top of page 2, place the insertion point before the second body paragraph, which begins With its blend..., click the Insert tab, then click the Clip Art button in the Illustrations group**
   The Clip Art task pane opens. You can use this task pane to search for clips related to a keyword.

2. **Select the text in the Search for text box if necessary, type pagoda, click the Search in list arrow, make sure Everywhere has a check mark, click the Results should be list arrow, make sure All media types has a check mark, then click Go**
   Clips that include the keyword "pagoda" appear in the Clip Art task pane, as shown in Figure D-18.

3. **Point to the clip called out in Figure D-18, click the list arrow that appears next to the clip, click Insert on the menu, then close the Clip Art task pane**
   The clip is inserted at the location of the insertion point. When a graphic is selected, the active tab changes to the Picture Tools Format tab. This tab contains commands used to adjust, enhance, arrange, and size graphics. Until you apply text wrapping to a graphic, it is part of the line of text in which it was inserted (an **inline graphic**). To move a graphic independently of text, you must wrap the text around it to make it a **floating graphic**, which can be moved anywhere on a page.

4. **Click the Position button in the Arrange group, then click Position in Middle Right with Square Text Wrapping**
   The photo is moved to the middle right side of the page and the text wraps around it. The white circles that appear on the square edges of the graphic are the **sizing handles**. Applying text wrapping to the photo made it a floating graphic.

5. **Click the Shape Width up arrow in the Size group until 3.8" appears**
   The photo is enlarged. Notice that when you increased the width of the photo, the height increased proportionally. You can also resize a graphic proportionally by dragging a corner sizing handle.

6. **Scroll to the top of page 2, position the pointer over the graphic, when the pointer changes to ⁺⇱ drag the graphic up and to the left so it is centered on the page and its top is just under the second line of text as shown in Figure D-19, then release the mouse button**
   The graphic is moved up and is roughly centered between the margins.

7. **Click the Position button, click More Layout Options, click the Picture Position tab if necessary, click the Alignment option button in the Horizontal section, click the Alignment list arrow, click Centered, then click OK**
   The Advanced Layout dialog box allows you to position a graphic using precise measurements.

8. **Click the More button ⬇ in the Picture Styles group, select the Soft Edge Oval picture style, click the Text Wrapping button in the Arrange group, click Tight, then deselect the graphic**
   A picture style is applied to the photo and the text wraps tight to the oval shape.

9. **Click the View tab, then click the Two Pages button**
   The completed pages 1 and 2 are displayed, as shown in Figure D-20.

10. **Click the Page Width button, press [Ctrl][End], press [Enter], type your name, save your changes, print the document, then close the document and exit Word**

Formatting Documents

FIGURE D-18: Clip Art task pane

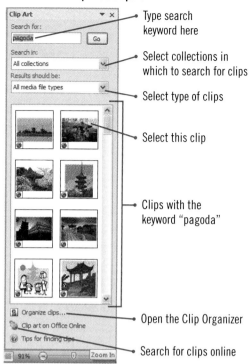

Type search keyword here

Select collections in which to search for clips

Select type of clips

Select this clip

Clips with the keyword "pagoda"

Open the Clip Organizer

Search for clips online

FIGURE D-19: Graphic being moved to a new location

Faded image shows graphic as it is being dragged; position the graphic as shown

Sizing handles

FIGURE D-20: Completed pages 1 and 2 of newsletter

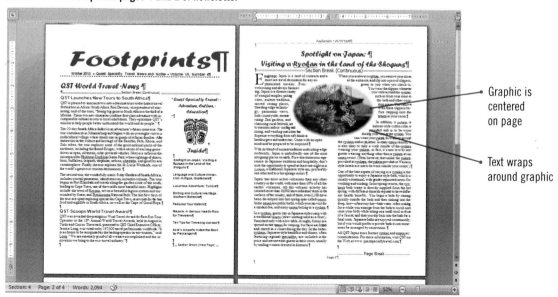

Graphic is centered on page

Text wraps around graphic

Practice

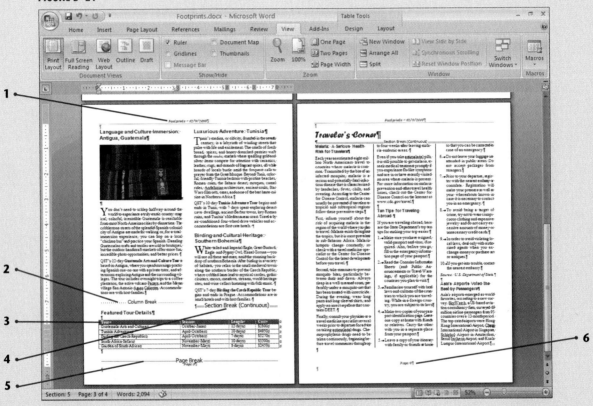

SAM

If you have a SAM user profile, you may have access to hands-on instruction, practice, and assessment of the skills covered in this unit. Log in to your SAM account (http://sam2007.course.com/) to launch any assigned training activities or exams that relate to the skills covered in this unit.

▼ CONCEPTS REVIEW

Label each element shown in Figure D-21.

FIGURE D-21

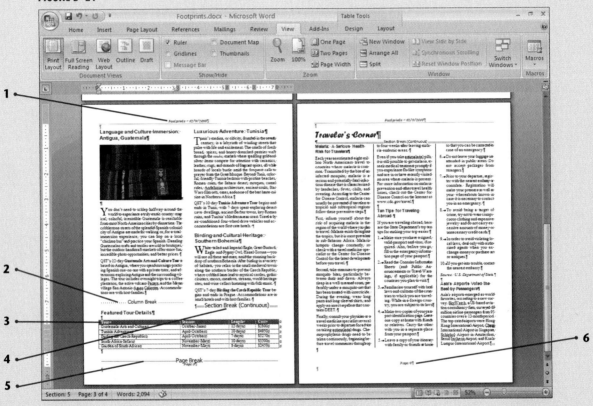

Match each term with the statement that best describes it.

7. **Footer**	**a.** An image that is inserted as part of a line of text
8. **Header**	**b.** The blank area between the edge of the text and the edge of the page
9. **Manual page break**	**c.** A formatting mark that divides a document into parts that can be formatted differently
10. **Section break**	
11. **Field**	**d.** Text or graphics that appear at the bottom of every page in a document
12. **Inline graphic**	**e.** A placeholder for information that changes
13. **Floating graphic**	**f.** A formatting mark that forces the text following the mark to begin at the top of the next page
14. **Margin**	
	g. Text or graphics that appear at the top of every page in a document
	h. An image to which text wrapping has been applied

Select the best answer from the list of choices.

15. Which type of break can you insert if you want to force text to begin on the next page?

    a. Automatic page break   **c.** Text wrapping break

    b. Continuous section break   **d.** Next page section break

16. Which type of break do you insert if you want to balance the columns in a section?

    a. Column break   **c.** Manual page break

    b. Continuous section break   **d.** Text wrapping break

17. Which of the following cannot be inserted using the Quick Parts command?

    a. AutoText building block   **c.** Page number field

    b. Document property   **d.** Page break

18. Which of the following do documents with mirror margins always have?

    a. Gutters   **c.** Inside and outside margins

    b. Landscape orientation   **d.** Different first page headers and footers

19. What name describes formatted pieces of content that are stored in galleries?

    a. Header   **c.** Building Block

    b. Field   **d.** Property

20. What must you do to change an inline graphic to a floating graphic?

    a. Apply text wrapping to the graphic   **c.** Anchor the graphic

    b. Resize the graphic   **d.** Move the graphic

▼ SKILLS REVIEW

1. Set document margins.

    a. Start Word, open the file WD D-2.docx from the drive and folder where you store your Data Files, then save it as Greenwood Fitness.

    b. Change the top and bottom margins settings to Moderate: 1" top and bottom, and .75" left and right.

    c. Save your changes to the document.

2. Divide a document into sections.

    a. Hide the white space in the document by moving the pointer to the top of a page, then double-clicking with the Hide White Space pointer that appears.

    b. Turn on the display of formatting marks, then customize the status bar to display sections if necessary.

    c. Scroll down, then insert a continuous section break before the Facilities heading.

    d. Format the text in section 2 in two columns, then save your changes to the document.

3. Insert page breaks.

    a. Insert a manual page break before the heading Welcome to the Greenwood Fitness Center!.

    b. Scroll down and insert a manual page break before the heading Services.

    c. Scroll down and insert a manual page break before the heading Membership.

    d. Show the white space in the document by moving the pointer over the thick black line that separates the pages, and then double-clicking with the Show White Space pointer that appears.

    e. Press [Ctrl][Home], then save your changes to the document.

4. Format columns.

    a. On page 2, select Facilities and the paragraph mark below it, use the Columns button to format the selected text as one column, then center Facilities on the page.

    b. Balance the columns on page 2 by inserting a continuous section break at the bottom of the second column.

    c. On page 3, select Services and the paragraph mark below it, format the selected text as one column, then center the text.

    d. Balance the columns on page 3.

    e. On page 4, select Membership and the paragraph mark below it, format the selected text as one column, then center the text.

    f. Insert a column break before the Membership Cards heading, press [Ctrl][Home], then save your changes to the document.

▼ SKILLS REVIEW (CONTINUED)

5. Insert page numbers.

   a. Insert page numbers in the document at the bottom of the page. Select the Plain Number 2 page number style from the gallery.

   b. Scroll through the document to view the page numbers on each page, then save your changes to the document.

6. Add headers and footers.

   a. Double-click the margin at the top of a page to open the Header and Footer areas.

   b. With the insertion point in the Header area, click the Quick Parts button in the Insert Group on the Header & Footer Tools Design tab, point to Document Property, then click Author.

   c. Replace the text in the Author content control with your name, press [End] to move the insertion point out of the content control, then press [Spacebar]. (*Note*: If your name does not appear in the header, right-click the Author content control, click Remove Content Control, then type your name in the header.)

   d. Click the Insert Alignment Tab button in the Position group, select the Right option button and keep the alignment relative to the margin, then click OK in the dialog box to move the insertion point to the right margin.

   e. Use the Insert Date and Time command in the Insert group to insert the current date as static text.

   f. Move the insertion point to the Footer area.

   g. Double-click the page number to select it, then format the page number in bold italic.

   h. Close headers and footers, view the header and footer on each page, then save your changes to the document.

7. Edit headers and footers.

   a. Open headers and footers, then apply italic to the text in the header.

   b. Move the insertion point to the Footer area, then change the footer style to Plain Number 3. (*Hint*: Click the Page Number button, point to Bottom of Page, then click the new style.)

   c. Use the Symbol command on the Insert tab to open the Symbol dialog box, insert a black right-pointing triangle symbol (character code: 25BA), then close the Symbol dialog box. (*Note*: Select a different symbol if 25BA is not available to you.)

   d. Use the Header & Footer Tools Design tab to create a different header and footer for the first page of the document.

   e. Scroll to the beginning of the document, type your name in the First Page Header area, then apply italic to your name.

   f. Close headers and footers, preview the header and footer on each page in Print Preview, close Print Preview, then save your changes to the document.

8. Insert a table.

   a. On page 4, select the word Table at the end of the Membership Rates section, press [Delete], open the Insert Table dialog box, then create a table with two columns and five rows.

   b. Apply the green Light List - Accent 3 table style to the table.

   c. Press [Tab] to leave the first cell in the header row blank, then type Rate.

   d. Press [Tab], then type the following text in the table, pressing [Tab] to move from cell to cell.

Enrollment/Individual	$100
Enrollment/Couple	$150
Monthly membership/Individual	$35
Monthly membership/Couple	$60

   e. With the insertion point in the table, right-click the table, use the AutoFit command to AutoFit to Contents, and then AutoFit to Window.

   f. Save your changes to the document.

9. Insert clip art.

    a. On page 1, place the insertion point in the second blank paragraph below A Rehabilitation and Exercise Facility. (*Hint*: Place the insertion point to the left of the paragraph mark.)

    b. Open the Clip Art task pane. Search for clips related to the keyword fitness.

    c. Insert the clip shown in Figure D-22. (*Note*: An active Internet connection is needed to select the clip shown in the figure. Select a different clip if this one is not available to you. If you are working offline, you might need to search using a keyword such as sports.)

    d. Select the graphic, then drag the lower-right sizing handle down and to the right so that the graphic is about 3.75" wide and 3.1" tall. Size the graphic so that all the text and the manual page break fit on page 1. You can use the Shape Height and Shape Width text boxes in the Size group on the Format tab to size the graphic precisely if necessary.

    e. Apply a Drop Shadow Rectangle picture style to the graphic.

    f. Move the insertion point to page 3, search for clips related to the keyword massage, then insert an appropriate clip. Select a clip that works with the design of the document.

    g. Use the Position command to position the clip at the bottom center of the document with square text wrapping.

    h. Save your changes to the document. Preview the document, print a copy, then close the document and exit Word.

FIGURE D-22

The Greenwood Fitness Center

A Rehabilitation and Exercise Facility

Member Services

Hours of Operation

Monday – Friday:
6:00 a.m. to 10:00 p.m.

Saturday:
7:00 a.m. to 10:00 p.m.

Sunday:
1:00 p.m. to 5:00 p.m.

▼ INDEPENDENT CHALLENGE 1

You are the owner of a small business in White Horse, Yukon Territory, called Blue Chair Catering. You have begun work on the text for a brochure advertising your business and are now ready to lay out the pages and prepare the final copy. The brochure will be printed on both sides of an 8½" × 11" sheet of paper, and folded in thirds.

a. Start Word, open the file WD D-3.docx from the drive and folder where you store your Data Files, then save it as **Blue Chair**. Read the document to get a feel for its contents.

b. Change the page orientation to landscape, and change all four margins to .6".

c. Format the document in three columns of equal width.

d. Insert a next page section break before the heading **Catering Services**.

e. On page 1, insert column breaks before the headings **Sample Tuscan Banquet Menu** and **Sample Indian Banquet Menu**.

f. Change the column spacing on the first page to .4", add lines between the columns on the first page, then center the text in the columns.

g. Double-click the bottom margin to open the footer area, create a different header and footer for the first page, then type **Call for custom menus designed to your taste and budget** in the First Page Footer area.

h. Center the text in the footer area, format it in 20-point Papyrus, with a Blue, Accent 1 font color, then close headers and footers.

i. On page 2, insert a column break before Your Name. Press [Enter] as many times as necessary to move the contact information to the bottom of the second column. Be sure all five lines of the contact information are in column 2 and do not flow to the next column.

j. Replace Your Name with your name, then center the contact information in the column.

k. Insert a column break at the bottom of the second column. Then, type the text shown in Figure D-23 in the third column and apply the No Spacing style. Refer to the figure as you follow the instructions for formatting the text in the third column.

l. Format Blue Chair Catering in 30-point Papyrus, bold.

m. Format the remaining text in 12-point Papyrus. Center the text in the third column.

n. Insert the clip art graphic shown in Figure D-23 or another appropriate clip art graphic. Do not wrap text around the graphic.

o. Resize the graphic and add or remove blank paragraphs in the third column of your brochure so that the spacing between elements roughly matches the spacing shown in Figure D-23.

Advanced Challenge Exercise

- Insert a different appropriate clip art graphic at the bottom of the first column on page 2.
- Apply text wrapping to the graphic, then resize the graphic and position it so it enhances the design of the brochure.
- Apply a suitable picture style to the graphic.

p. Save your changes, preview the brochure in Print Preview, then print a copy. If possible, print the two pages of the brochure back to back so that the brochure can be folded in thirds.

q. Close the document and exit Word.

FIGURE D-23

Blue Chair Catering

Complete catering services available for all types of events. Menus and estimates provided upon request.

▼ INDEPENDENT CHALLENGE 2

You work in the Campus Safety Department at Pacific State College. You have written the text for an informational flyer about parking regulations on campus, and now you need to format the flyer so it is attractive and readable.

a. Start Word, open the file WD D-4.docx from the drive and folder where you store your Data Files, then save it as **Pacific Parking FAQ**. Read the document to get a feel for its contents.
b. Change all four margins to .7".
c. Insert a continuous section break before **1. May I bring a car to school?** (*Hint*: Place the insertion point before May.)
d. Scroll down and insert a next page section break before **Sample Parking Permit**.
e. Format the text in section 2 in three columns of equal width with .3" of space between the columns.
f. Hyphenate the document using the automatic hyphenation feature. (*Hint*: If the Hyphenation feature is not installed on your computer, skip this step.)
g. Add a 3-point dotted-line bottom border to the blank paragraph under Pacific State College. (*Hint*: Place the insertion point before the paragraph mark under Pacific State College.)
h. Open the Header area and insert your name in the header. Right-align your name and format it in 10-point Arial.
i. Add the following text to the footer, inserting symbols between words as indicated:
Parking and Shuttle Service Office • 54 Buckley Street • Pacific State College • 942-555-2227.
j. Format the footer text in 9-point Arial Black and center it in the footer. Use a different font if Arial Black is not available to you. If necessary, adjust the font and font size so that the entire address fits on one line.
k. Apply a 3-point dotted-line border above the footer text. Make sure to apply the border to the paragraph.
l. Balance the columns in section 2.
m. Add the clip art graphic shown in Figure D-24 (or another appropriate clip art graphic) to the upper-right corner of the document, above the border. Make sure the graphic does not obscure the border. (*Hint*: Apply text wrapping to the graphic before positioning it.)
n. Place the insertion point on page 2 (which is section 4). Change the left and right margins in section 4 to 1". Also change the page orientation of section 4 to landscape.
o. Change the vertical alignment of section 4 to center. (*Hint*: Use the Layout tab in the Page Setup dialog box.)
p. Apply a table style to the table similar to the style shown in Figure D-25.
q. Save your changes, preview the flyer in Print Preview, then print a copy. If possible, print the two pages of the flyer back to back.
r. Close the document and exit Word.

FIGURE D-24

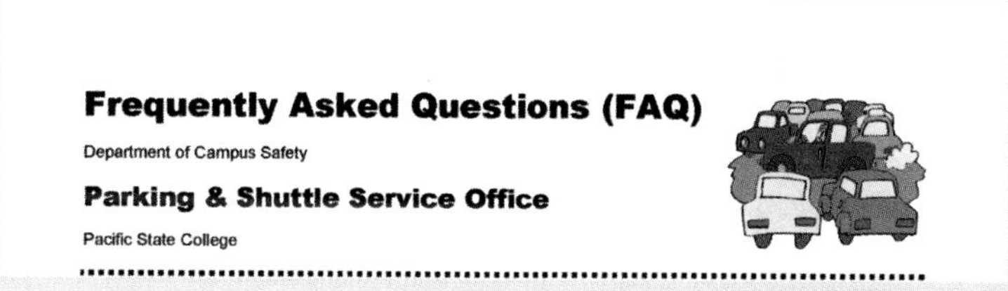

FIGURE D-25

Sample Parking Permit

Pacific State College
Office of Parking and Shuttle Service

2010-11 Student Parking Permit

License number:	VA 498 359
Make:	Subaru
Model:	Forester
Year:	2004
Color:	Red
Permit Issue Date:	September 8, 2010
Permit Expiration Date:	June 4, 2011

Restrictions:
Parking is permitted in the Pacific State College Greene Street lot 24 hours a day, 7 days a week. Shuttle service is available from the Greene Street lot to campus from 7 a.m. to 7 p.m. Monday through Friday. Parking is also permitted in any on-campus lot from 4:30 p.m. Friday to midnight Sunday.

▼ INDEPENDENT CHALLENGE 3

A book publisher would like to publish an article you wrote on stormwater pollution in Australia as a chapter in a forthcoming book called *Environmental Issues for the New Millennium*. The publisher has requested that you format your article like a book chapter before submitting it for publication, and has provided you with a style sheet.

a. Start Word, open the file WD D-5.docx from the drive and folder where you store your Data Files, then save it as Chapter 9.

b. Change the font of the entire document to 11-point High Tower Text. If this font is not available to you, select a different font suitable for the pages of a book. Change the alignment to justified.

c. Change the paper size to 6" × 9".

d. Create mirror margins. (*Hint*: Use the Multiple Pages list arrow.) Change the top and bottom margins to .8", change the inside margin to .4", change the outside margin to .6", and create a .3" gutter to allow room for the book's binding.

e. Change the Zoom level to Page Width, open the Header and Footer areas, then apply the setting to create different headers and footers for odd- and even-numbered pages.

f. In the odd-page header, type Chapter 9, insert a symbol of your choice, then type Stormwater Pollution in the Fairy Creek Catchment.

g. Format the header text in 9-point High Tower Text italic, then right-align the text.

h. In the even-page header, type your name, insert a symbol of your choice, then insert a date field that updates automatically. (*Hint*: Scroll down or use the Next Section button to move the insertion point to the even-page header.)

i. Change the format of the date to include just the month and the year. (*Hint*: Right-click the date field, click Edit Field, then type MMMM yyyy in the Date Formats text box.)

j. Format the header text in 9-point High Tower Text italic. The even-page header should be left-aligned.

k. Insert a left-aligned page number field in the even-page footer area, format it in 10-point High Tower Text, insert a right-aligned page number field in the odd-page footer area, then format it in 10-point High Tower Text.

l. Format the page numbers so that the first page of your chapter, which is Chapter 9 in the book, begins on page 135. (*Hint*: Select a page number field, click the Page Number button, then click Format Page Numbers.)

m. Go to the beginning of the document, press [Enter] 10 times, type Chapter 9: Stormwater Pollution in the Fairy Creek Catchment, press [Enter] twice, type your name, then press [Enter] twice.

n. Format the chapter title in 16-point Calibri bold, format your name in 14-point Calibri, then left-align the title text and your name, as shown in Figure D-26.

FIGURE D-26

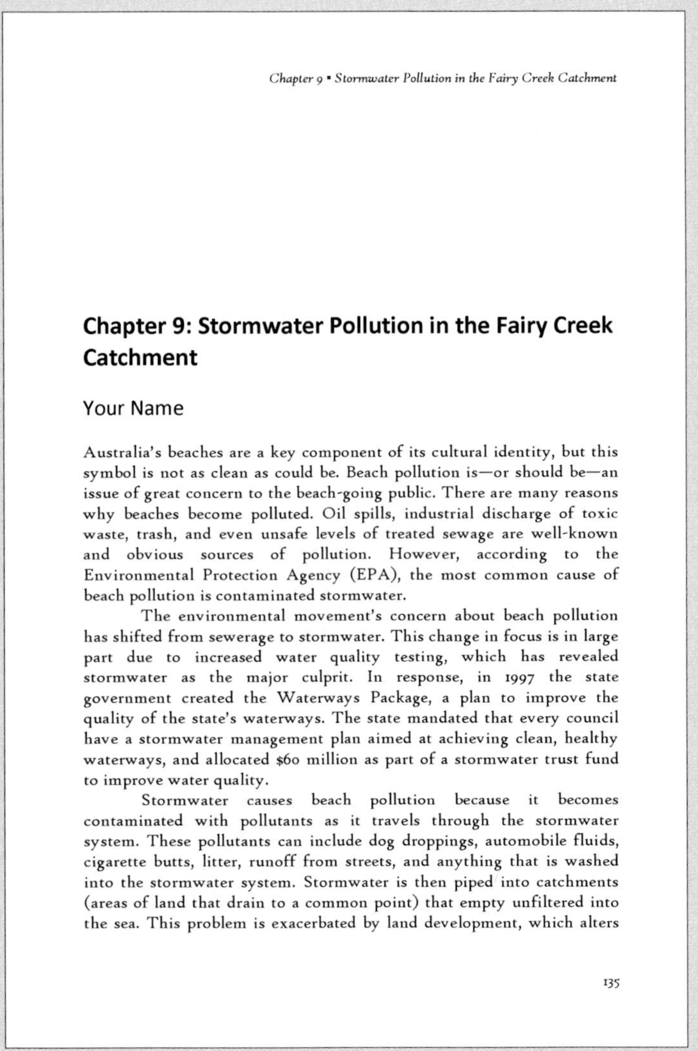

Chapter 9 • Stormwater Pollution in the Fairy Creek Catchment

Chapter 9: Stormwater Pollution in the Fairy Creek Catchment

Your Name

Australia's beaches are a key component of its cultural identity, but this symbol is not as clean as could be. Beach pollution is—or should be—an issue of great concern to the beach-going public. There are many reasons why beaches become polluted. Oil spills, industrial discharge of toxic waste, trash, and even unsafe levels of treated sewage are well-known and obvious sources of pollution. However, according to the Environmental Protection Agency (EPA), the most common cause of beach pollution is contaminated stormwater.

The environmental movement's concern about beach pollution has shifted from sewerage to stormwater. This change in focus is in large part due to increased water quality testing, which has revealed stormwater as the major culprit. In response, in 1997 the state government created the Waterways Package, a plan to improve the quality of the state's waterways. The state mandated that every council have a stormwater management plan aimed at achieving clean, healthy waterways, and allocated $60 million as part of a stormwater trust fund to improve water quality.

Stormwater causes beach pollution because it becomes contaminated with pollutants as it travels through the stormwater system. These pollutants can include dog droppings, automobile fluids, cigarette butts, litter, runoff from streets, and anything that is washed into the stormwater system. Stormwater is then piped into catchments (areas of land that drain to a common point) that empty unfiltered into the sea. This problem is exacerbated by land development, which alters

135

▼ INDEPENDENT CHALLENGE 3 (CONTINUED)

Advanced Challenge Exercise

- Scroll to page 4 in the document, place the insertion point at the end of the paragraph above the Potential health effects... heading, press [Enter] twice, type **Table 1: Total annual pollutant loads per year in the Fairy Creek Catchment**, format the text as bold, then press [Enter] twice.
- Insert a table with four columns and four rows.
- Type the text shown in Figure D-27 in the table. Do not be concerned when the text wraps to the next line in a cell.

FIGURE D-27

Area	Nitrogen	Phosphorus	Suspended solids
Fairy Creek	9.3 tonnes	1.2 tonnes	756.4 tonnes
Durras Arm	6.2 tonnes	.9 tonnes	348.2 tonnes
Cabbage Tree Creek	9.8 tonnes	2.3 tonnes	485.7 tonnes

- Apply the Light List Table style. Make sure the text in the header row is bold, then remove any bold formatting from the text in the remaining rows.
- AutoFit the table to fit the contents, then AutoFit the table to fit the window.

o. Save your changes, preview the chapter in Print Preview, print the first four pages of the chapter, then close the document and exit Word.

▼ REAL LIFE INDEPENDENT CHALLENGE

One of the most common opportunities to use the page layout features of Word is when formatting a research paper. The format recommended by the *MLA Handbook for Writers of Research Papers*, a style guide that includes information on preparing, writing, and formatting research papers, is the standard format used by many schools, colleges, and universities. In this independent challenge, you will research the MLA (Modern Language Association) guidelines for formatting a research paper and use the guidelines you find to prepare a sample research report.

a. Use your favorite search engine to search the Web for information on the MLA guidelines for formatting a research report. Use the keywords **MLA Style** and **research paper format** to conduct your search.

b. Look for information on the proper formatting for the following aspects of a research paper: paper size, margins, title page or first page of the report, line spacing, paragraph indentation, and page numbers. Print the information you find.

c. Start Word, open the file WD D-6.docx from the drive and folder where you store your Data Files, then save it as **Research Paper**. Using the information you learned, format this document as a research report.

d. Adjust the margins, set the line spacing, and add page numbers to the document in the format recommended by the MLA. Use **The Maori History of New Zealand** as the title for your sample report, use your name as the author name, and make up information about the course and instructor, if necessary. Make sure to format the title page exactly as the MLA style dictates.

e. Format the remaining text as the body of the research report. Indent the first line of each paragraph rather than use quadruple spacing between paragraphs.

f. Save the document, print a copy, close the document, then exit Word.

▼ VISUAL WORKSHOP

Open the file WD D-7.docx from the drive and folder where you store your Data Files, then modify it to create the article shown in Figure D-28. (*Hint*: Change all four margins to .6". To locate the flower clip art image, search using the keyword **dahlias**, and be sure only the Photographs check box in the Results should be in list box in the Clip Art task pane has a check mark. Select a different clip if the clip shown in the figure is not available to you.) Save the document with the filename **Gardener's Corner**, then print a copy.

FIGURE D-28

GARDENER'S CORNER

Putting a Perennial Garden to Bed

By Your Name

A certain sense of peace descends when a perennial garden is put to bed for the season. The plants are safely tucked in against the elements, and the garden is ready to welcome the first signs of life. When the work is done, you can sit back and anticipate the bright blooms of spring. Many gardeners are uncertain of how to close a perennial garden. This week's column demystifies the process.

Clean up

Garden clean up can be a gradual process—plants will deteriorate at different rates, allowing you to do a little bit each week.

- Edge beds and borders and remove stakes and other plant supports.
- Dig and divide irises, daylilies, and other early bloomers.
- Cut back plants when foliage starts to deteriorate, then rake all debris out of the garden and pull any weeds that remain.

Plant perennials

Fall is the perfect time to plant perennials! The warm, sunny days and cool nights provide optimal conditions for new root growth.

- Dig deeply and enhance soil with organic matter.
- Use a good starter fertilizer to speed up new root growth.
- Untangle the roots of new plants before planting.
- Water deeply after planting as the weather dictates, and keep plants moist for several days after planting.

Add compost

Organic matter is the key ingredient to healthy garden soil. Composting adds nutrients to the soil, helps the soil retain water and nutrients, and keeps the soil well aerated. If you take care of the soil, your plants will become strong and disease resistant. Before adding compost, use an iron rake to loosen the top few inches of soil. Spread a one to two inch layer of compost over the entire garden— the best compost is made up of yard waste and kitchen scraps—and then refrain from stepping on the area and compacting the soil.

To mulch or not to mulch?

Winter protection for perennial beds can only help plants survive the winter. Winter mulch prevents the freezing and thawing cycles, which cause plants to heave and eventually die. Here's what works and what doesn't:

- Always apply mulch after the ground is frozen.
- Never apply generic hay because is contains billions of weed seeds. Also, whole leaves and bark mulch hold too much moisture.
- Use a loose material to allow air filtration. Straw and salt marsh hay are excellent choices for mulch. If using leaves, use only stiff leaves such as Oak or Beech. Soft leaves, such as Maple, make it difficult for air and water to filtrate.
- Remove the winter mulch in the spring as soon as new growth begins.

For copies of earlier Gardener's Corner columns, call 1-800-555-3827.

Creating and Formatting Tables

Files You Will Need:

WD E-1.docx
WD E-2.docx

Tables are commonly used to display information for quick reference and analysis. In this unit, you learn how to create and modify a table in Word, how to sort table data and perform calculations, and how to format a table with borders and shading. You also learn how to use a table to structure the layout of a page. You are preparing a summary budget for an advertising campaign aimed at the Chicago market. The goal of the ad campaign is to promote winter tours to tropical destinations. You decide to format the budget information as a table so that it is easy to read and analyze.

OBJECTIVES

Insert a table

Insert and delete rows and columns

Modify rows and columns

Sort table data

Split and merge cells

Perform calculations in tables

Apply a table style

Create a custom format for a table

Inserting a Table

A **table** is a grid made up of rows and columns of cells that you can fill with text and graphics. A **cell** is the box formed by the intersection of a column and a row. The lines that divide the columns and rows and help you see the grid-like structure of a table are called **borders**. You can create a table in a document by using the Table command in the Tables group on the Insert tab. Once you have created a table, you can add text and graphics to it. ████████ You begin by inserting a blank table and adding text to it.

STEPS

QUICK TIP
Click the View Ruler button at the top of the vertical scroll bar to display the rulers if they are not already displayed.

1. **Start Word, click the View tab, then click the Page Width button in the Zoom group**

2. **Click the Insert tab, then click the Table button in the Tables group**
   The Table menu opens. It includes a grid for selecting the number of columns and rows you want the table to contain, as well as several commands for inserting a table. Table E-1 describes the function of these commands. As you move the pointer across the grid, a preview of the table with the specified number of columns and rows appears in the document at the location of the insertion point.

3. **Point to the second box in the fourth row to select 2x4 Table, then click**
   A table with two columns and four rows is inserted in the document, as shown in Figure E-1. Black borders surround the table cells. The insertion point is in the first cell in the first row.

TROUBLE
Don't be concerned if the paragraph spacing under the text in your table is different from that shown in the figures.

4. **Type Location, then press [Tab]**
   Pressing [Tab] moves the insertion point to the next cell in the row.

5. **Type Cost, press [Tab], then type Chicago Tribune**
   Pressing [Tab] at the end of a row moves the insertion point to the first cell in the next row.

6. **Press [Tab], type 27,600, press [Tab], then type the following text in the table, pressing [Tab] to move from cell to cell**

Chicagotribune.com	**25,000**
Taxi tops	**18,000**

7. **Press [Tab]**
   Pressing [Tab] at the end of the last cell of a table creates a new row at the bottom of the table, as shown in Figure E-2. The insertion point is located in the first cell in the new row.

TROUBLE
If you pressed [Tab] after the last row, click the Undo button ↺ on the Quick Access toolbar to remove the new blank row.

8. **Type the following, pressing [Tab] to move from cell to cell and to create new rows**

Chicago Defender	**18,760**
Hellochicago.com	**3,250**
Bus stops	**12,000**
Chicago Magazine	**12,400**

9. **Click the Save button 💾 on the Quick Access toolbar, then save the document as Chicago Ad Budget to the drive and folder where you store your Data Files**
   The table is shown in Figure E-3.

TABLE E-1: Table menu commands

command	use to
Insert Table	Create a table with any number of columns and rows and select an AutoFit behavior
Draw Table	Create a complex table by drawing the table columns and rows
Convert Text to Table	Convert selected text that is separated by tabs, commas, or another separator character into a table
Excel Spreadsheet	Insert a blank Excel worksheet into the document as an embedded object
Quick Tables	Insert a table template chosen from a gallery of preformatted tables and replace the placeholder data with your own data

FIGURE E-1: Blank table

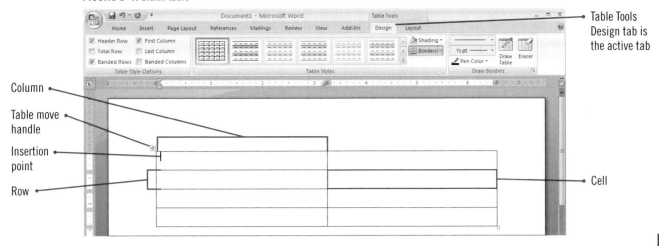

Column

Table move handle

Insertion point

Row

Cell

Table Tools Design tab is the active tab

FIGURE E-2: New row in table

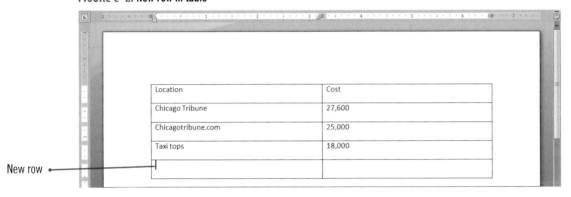

New row

FIGURE E-3: Text in the table

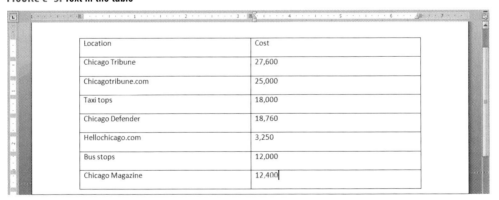

Converting text to a table and a table to text

Another way to create a table is to convert text that is separated by a tab, a comma, or another separator character into a table. For example, to create a two-column table of last and first names, you could type the names as a list with a comma separating the last and first name in each line, and then convert the text to a table. The separator character—a comma in this example—indicates where you want to divide the table into columns, and a paragraph mark indicates where you want to begin a new row. To convert text to a table, select the text, click the Table button in the Tables group on the Insert tab, and then click Convert Text to Table. In the Convert Text to Table dialog box, select from the options for structuring and formatting the table, and then click OK to create the table.

Conversely, you can convert a table to text that is separated by tabs, commas, or some other character by selecting the table, clicking the Table Tools Layout tab, and then clicking the Convert to Text button in the Data group.

Inserting and Deleting Rows and Columns

You can easily modify the structure of a table by adding and removing rows and columns. First, you must click or select an existing row or column in the table to indicate where you want to insert or delete a row or a column. You can select any element of a table using the Select command in the Table group on the Table Tools Layout tab, but it is often easier to select rows and columns using the mouse. To insert or delete rows and columns, you use the commands in the Rows & Columns group on the Table Tools Layout tab. ▨▨▨ You add new rows and columns to the table and delete unnecessary rows.

STEPS

1. **Click the Home tab, then click the Show/Hide ¶ button ¶ in the Paragraph group to display formatting marks**

   An end of cell mark appears at the end of each cell and an end of row mark appears at the end of each row.

2. **Click the Table Tools Layout tab, click the first cell of the Hellochicago.com row, then click the Insert Above button in the Rows & Columns group**

   A new row is inserted directly above the Hellochicago.com row, as shown in Figure E-4. To insert a single row, you simply place the insertion point in the row above or below where you want the new row to be inserted, and then insert the row.

3. **Click the first cell of the new row, type Chicago Sun Times, press [Tab], then type 15,300**

QUICK TIP
If the end of row mark is not selected, you have selected only the text in the row, not the row itself.

4. **Place the pointer in the margin to the left of the Chicagotribune.com row until the pointer changes to ⬦, click to select the row, press and hold the mouse button, drag down to select the Taxi tops row, then release the mouse button**

   The two rows are selected, including the end of row marks.

5. **Click the Insert Below button in the Rows & Columns group**

   Two new rows are added below the selected rows. To insert multiple rows, you select the number of rows you want to insert before inserting the rows.

QUICK TIP
You can also delete a row or column by pressing [Shift][Delete].

6. **Click the Chicago Defender row, click the Delete button in the Rows & Columns group, click Delete Rows, select the two blank rows, right-click the selected rows, then click Delete Rows on the shortcut menu**

   The Chicago Defender row and the two blank rows are deleted. If you select a row and press [Delete], you delete only the contents of the row, not the row itself.

7. **Place the pointer over the top border of the Location column until the pointer changes to ↓, then click**

   The entire column is selected.

QUICK TIP
To select a cell, place the ◢ pointer over the left border of the cell, then click.

8. **Click the Insert Left button in the Rows & Columns group, then type Type**

   A new column is inserted to the left of the Location column, as shown in Figure E-5.

9. **Click in the Location column, click the Insert Right button in the Rows & Columns group, then type Details in the first cell of the new column**

   A new column is added to the right of the Location column.

10. **Press [↓] to move the insertion point to the next cell in the Details column, click the Home tab, click ¶ to turn off the display of formatting marks, enter the text shown in Figure E-6 in each cell in the Details and Type columns, then save your changes**

    You can use the arrow keys to move the insertion point from cell to cell. Notice that text wraps to the next line in the cell as you type. Compare your table to Figure E-6.

FIGURE E-4: Inserted row

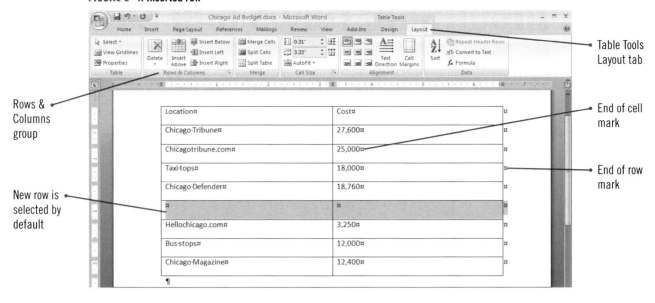

Table Tools Layout tab

Rows & Columns group

End of cell mark

End of row mark

New row is selected by default

FIGURE E-5: Inserted column

New column

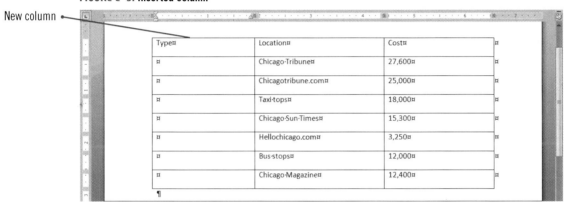

FIGURE E-6: Text in Type and Details column

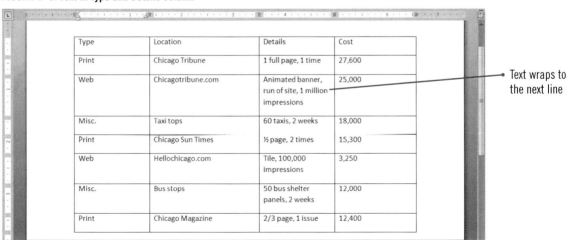

Text wraps to the next line

Copying and moving rows and columns

You can copy and move rows and columns within a table in the same manner you copy and move text. Select the row or column you want to move, then use the Copy or Cut button to place the selection on the Clipboard. Place the insertion point in the location where you want to insert the row or column, then click the Paste button to paste the selection. Rows are inserted above the row containing the insertion point; columns are inserted to the left of the column containing the insertion point. You can also copy or move columns and rows by selecting them and using the pointer to drag them to a new location in the table.

Modifying Rows and Columns

Once you create a table, you can easily adjust the size of columns and rows to make the table easier to read. You can change the width of columns and the height of rows by dragging a border, by using the AutoFit command in the Cell Size group on the Table Tools Layout tab, or by setting exact measurements using the Table Row Height and Table Column Width text boxes in the Cell Size group or the Table Properties dialog box. ▰▰▰▰ You adjust the size of the columns and rows to make the table more attractive and easier to read. You also center the text vertically in each table cell.

STEPS

1. **Position the pointer over the border between the first and second columns until the pointer changes to ◄║►, then drag the border to approximately the ½" mark on the horizontal ruler**

   The dotted line that appears as you drag represents the border. Dragging the column border changes the width of the first and second columns: the first column is narrower and the second column is wider. When dragging a border to change the width of an entire column, make sure no cells are selected in the column. You can also drag a row border to change the height of the row above it.

2. **Position the pointer over the right border of the Location column until the pointer changes to ◄║►, then double-click**

   Double-clicking a column border automatically resizes the column to fit the text.

3. **Double-click the right border of the Details column with the ◄║► pointer, then double-click the right border of the Cost column with the ◄║► pointer**

   The widths of the Details and Cost columns are adjusted.

4. **Move the pointer over the table, then click the table move handle ⊞ that appears outside the upper-left corner of the table**

   Clicking the table move handle selects the entire table. You can also use the Select button in the Table group on the Table Tools Layout tab to select an entire table.

5. **Click the Home tab, then click the No Spacing button in the Styles group**

   Changing the style to No Spacing removes the paragraph spacing below the text in each table cell.

6. **With the table still selected, click the Table Tools Layout tab, click the Distribute Rows button ▤ in the Cell Size group, then click in the table to deselect it**

   All the rows in the table become the same height, as shown in Figure E-7. You can also use the Distribute Columns button to make all the columns the same width, or use the AutoFit button to make the width of the columns fit the text, to adjust the width of the columns so the table is justified between the margins, or to set fixed column widths.

7. **Click in the Details column, click the Table Column Width text box in the Cell Size group, type 3.5, then press [Enter]**

   The width of the Details column changes to 3.5".

8. **Click the Select button in the Table group, click Select Table, click the Align Center Left button ▤ in the Alignment group, deselect the table, then save your changes**

   The text is centered vertically in each table cell, as shown in Figure E-8. You can use the alignment buttons in the Alignment group to change the vertical and horizontal alignment of the text in selected cells or in the entire table.

Creating and Formatting Tables

FIGURE E-7: Resized columns and rows

Table move handle: click to select the table; drag to move the table

Rows are all the same height

Table resize handle; drag to change the size of all the rows and columns

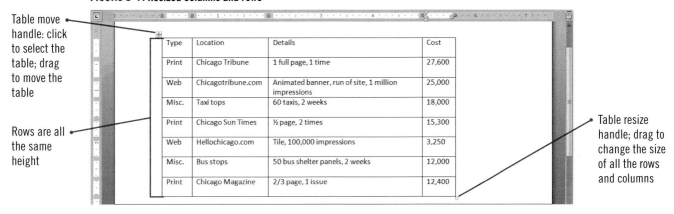

Type	Location	Details	Cost
Print	Chicago Tribune	1 full page, 1 time	27,600
Web	Chicagotribune.com	Animated banner, run of site, 1 million impressions	25,000
Misc.	Taxi tops	60 taxis, 2 weeks	18,000
Print	Chicago Sun Times	½ page, 2 times	15,300
Web	Hellochicago.com	Tile, 100,000 impressions	3,250
Misc.	Bus stops	50 bus shelter panels, 2 weeks	12,000
Print	Chicago Magazine	2/3 page, 1 issue	12,400

FIGURE E-8: Text centered vertically in cells

Column is widened

Text is centered vertically in the cell

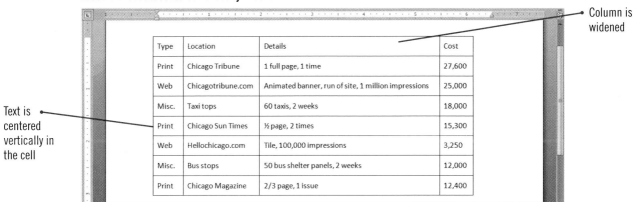

Type	Location	Details	Cost
Print	Chicago Tribune	1 full page, 1 time	27,600
Web	Chicagotribune.com	Animated banner, run of site, 1 million impressions	25,000
Misc.	Taxi tops	60 taxis, 2 weeks	18,000
Print	Chicago Sun Times	½ page, 2 times	15,300
Web	Hellochicago.com	Tile, 100,000 impressions	3,250
Misc.	Bus stops	50 bus shelter panels, 2 weeks	12,000
Print	Chicago Magazine	2/3 page, 1 issue	12,400

Setting advanced table properties

When you want to wrap text around a table, indent a table, or set other advanced table properties, you click the Properties command in the Table group on the Table Tools Layout tab to open the Table Properties dialog box, shown in Figure E-9. Using the Table tab in this dialog box, you can set a precise width for the table, change the horizontal alignment of the table between the margins, indent the table, and set text wrapping options for the table. You can also click Options on the Table tab to open the Table Options dialog box, which you use to customize the table's default cell margins and the spacing between table cells. Alternatively, click Borders and Shading on the Table tab to open the Borders and Shading dialog box, which you can use to create a custom format for the table. The other tabs in the Table Properties dialog box, the Column, Row, and Cell tabs, allow you to set an exact width for columns, to specify an exact height for rows, and to indicate an exact size for individual cells.

FIGURE E-9: Table Properties dialog box

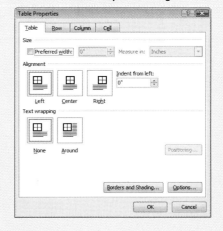

Sorting Table Data

Tables are often easier to interpret and analyze when the data is **sorted**, which means the rows are organized in alphabetical or sequential order based on the data in one or more columns. When you sort a table, Word arranges all the table data according to the criteria you set. You set sort criteria by specifying the column (or columns) by which you want to sort, and indicating the sort order—ascending or descending—you want to use. **Ascending order** lists data alphabetically or sequentially (from A to Z, 0 to 9, or earliest to latest). **Descending order** lists data in reverse alphabetical or sequential order (from Z to A, 9 to 0, or latest to earliest). You can sort using the data in one column or multiple columns. When you sort by multiple columns you must select primary, secondary, and tertiary sort criteria. You use the Sort command in the Data group on the Table Tools Layout tab to sort a table. You sort the table so that all ads of the same type are listed together. You also add secondary sort criteria so that the ads within each type are listed in descending order by cost.

STEPS

1. **Place the insertion point anywhere in the table**

   To sort an entire table, you simply need to place the insertion point anywhere in the table. If you want to sort specific rows only, then you must select the rows you want to sort.

2. **Click the Sort button in the Data group on the Table Tools Layout tab**

   The Sort dialog box opens, as shown in Figure E-10. You use this dialog box to specify the column or columns by which you want to sort, the type of information you are sorting (text, numbers, or dates), and the sort order (ascending or descending). Column 1 is selected by default in the Sort by list box. Since you want to sort your table first by the information in the first column—the type of ad (Print, Web, or Misc.)—you don't change the Sort by criteria.

3. **Click the Descending option button in the Sort by section**

   The ad type information will be sorted in descending—or reverse alphabetical—order, so that the "Web" ads will be listed first, followed by the "Print" ads, and then the "Misc." ads.

4. **In the first Then by section click the Then by list arrow, click Column 4, click the Type list arrow, click Number if it is not already selected, then click the Descending option button**

   Within the Web, Print, and Misc. groups, the rows will be sorted by the cost of the ad—the information contained in the fourth column, which is numbers, not dates or text. The rows will appear in descending order within each group, with the most expensive ad listed first.

QUICK TIP
To repeat the header row on every page of a table that spans multiple pages, click the Repeat Header Rows button in the Data group on the Table Tools Layout tab.

5. **Click the Header row option button in the My list has section to select it**

   The table includes a header row that you do not want included in the sort. A **header row** is the first row of a table that contains the column headings.

6. **Click OK, then deselect the table**

   The rows in the table are sorted first by the information in the Type column and second by the information in the Cost column, as shown in Figure E-11. The first row of the table, which is the header row, is not included in the sort.

7. **Save your changes to the document**

Creating and Formatting Tables

Select the primary sort column

Select the type of data in the sort column

Choose the sort order

Include or exclude the header row in the sort

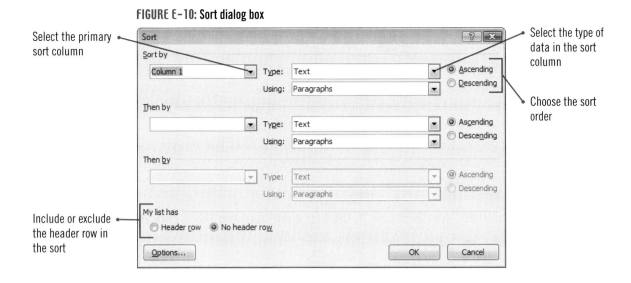

Header row is not included in the sort

First, rows are sorted by type in descending order

Second, within each type, rows are sorted by cost in descending order

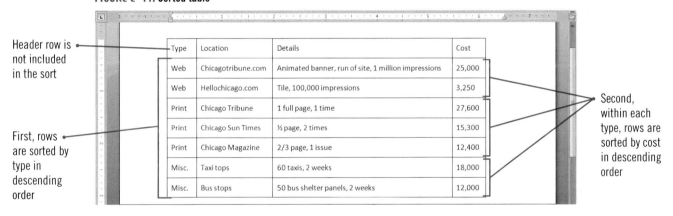

Type	Location	Details	Cost
Web	Chicagotribune.com	Animated banner, run of site, 1 million impressions	25,000
Web	Hellochicago.com	Tile, 100,000 impressions	3,250
Print	Chicago Tribune	1 full page, 1 time	27,600
Print	Chicago Sun Times	½ page, 2 times	15,300
Print	Chicago Magazine	2/3 page, 1 issue	12,400
Misc.	Taxi tops	60 taxis, 2 weeks	18,000
Misc.	Bus stops	50 bus shelter panels, 2 weeks	12,000

Sorting lists and paragraphs

In addition to sorting table data, you can use the Sort command to alphabetize text or sort numerical data. When you want to sort data that is not formatted as a table, such as lists and paragraphs, you use the Sort command in the Paragraph group on the Home tab. To sort lists and paragraphs, select the items you want included in the sort, then click the Sort button. In the Sort Text dialog box, use the Sort by list arrow to select the sort by criteria (paragraphs or fields), use the Type list arrow to select the type of data (text, numbers, or dates), and then click the Ascending or Descending option button to choose a sort order.

When sorting text information in a document, the term "fields" refers to text or numbers that are separated by a character, such as a tab or a comma. For example, you might want to sort a list of names alphabetically. If the names you want to sort are listed in "Last name, First name" order, then last name and first name are each considered a field. You can choose to sort the list in alphabetical order by last name or by first name. Use the Options button in the Sort Text dialog box to specify the character that separates the fields in your lists or paragraphs, along with other sort options.

Word 2007

Splitting and Merging Cells

A convenient way to change the format and structure of a table is to merge and split the table cells. When you **merge** cells, you combine adjacent cells into a single larger cell. When you **split** a cell, you divide an existing cell into multiple cells. You can merge and split cells using the Merge Cells and Split Cells commands in the Merge group on the Table Tools Layout tab. You merge cells in the first column to create a single cell for each ad type—Web, Print, and Misc. You also add a new row to the bottom of the table, and split the cells in the row to create three new rows with a different structure.

STEPS

1. **Select the two Web cells in the first column of the table, click the Merge Cells button in the Merge group on the Table Tools Layout tab, then deselect the text**
   The two Web cells merge to become a single cell. When you merge cells, Word converts the text in each cell into a separate paragraph in the merged cell.

2. **Select the first Web in the cell, then press [Delete]**

3. **Select the three Print cells in the first column, click the Merge Cells button, type Print, select the two Misc. cells, click the Merge Cells button, then type Misc.**
   The three Print cells merge to become one cell and the two Misc. cells merge to become one cell.

4. **Click the Bus stops cell, then click the Insert Below button in the Rows & Columns group**
   A row is added to the bottom of the table.

5. **Select the first three cells in the new last row of the table, click the Merge Cells button, then deselect the cell**
   The three cells in the row merge to become a single cell.

6. **Click the first cell in the last row, then click the Split Cells button in the Merge group**
   The Split Cells dialog box opens, as shown in Figure E-12. You use this dialog box to split the selected cell or cells into a specific number of columns and rows.

7. **Type 1 in the Number of columns text box, press [Tab], type 3 in the Number of rows text box, click OK, then deselect the cells**
   The single cell is divided into three rows of equal height. When you split a cell into multiple rows, the width of the original column does not change. When you split a cell into multiple columns, the height of the original row does not change. If the cell you split contains text, all the text appears in the upper-left cell.

8. **Click the last cell in the Cost column, click the Split Cells button, repeat Step 7, then save your changes**
   The cell is split into three rows, as shown in Figure E-13. The last three rows of the table now have only two columns.

Creating and Formatting Tables

FIGURE E-12: Split Cells dialog box

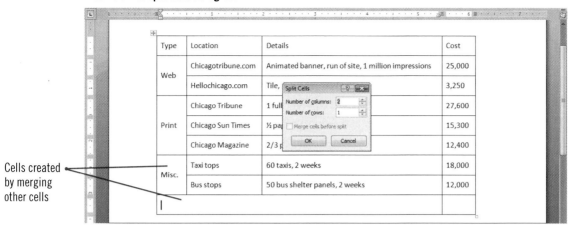

Cells created
by merging
other cells

FIGURE E-13: Cells split into three rows

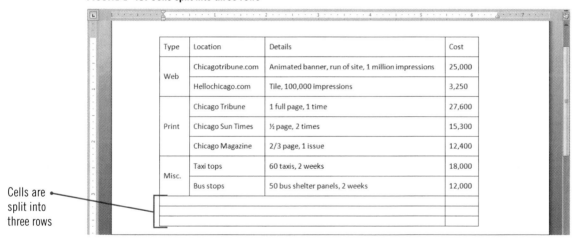

Cells are
split into
three rows

Changing cell margins

By default, table cells have .08" left and right cell margins with no spacing between the cells, but you can adjust these settings for a table using the Cell Margins button in the Alignment group on the Table Tools Layout tab. First, place the insertion point in the table, and then click the Cell Margins button to open the Table Options dialog box. Enter new settings for the top, bottom, left, and right cell margins in the text boxes in the Default cell margins section of the dialog box, or select the Allow spacing between cells check box and then enter a setting in the Cell spacing section to increase the spacing between table cells. You can also deselect the Automatically resize to fit contents check box in the Options section of the dialog box to turn off the setting that causes table cells to widen to fit the text as you type. Any settings you change in the Table Options dialog box are applied to the entire table.

Performing Calculations in Tables

If your table includes numerical information, you can perform simple calculations in the table. The Formula command allows you to quickly total the numbers in a column or row, and to perform other standard calculations, such as averages. When you calculate data in a table using formulas, you use cell references to refer to the cells in the table. Each cell has a unique **cell reference** composed of a letter and a number; the letter represents its column and the number represents its row. For example, the cell in the third row of the fourth column is cell D3. Figure E-14 shows the cell references in a simple table. ◣▚▟▞ You use the Formula command to calculate the total cost of the Chicago ad campaign. You also add information about the budgeted cost and create a formula to calculate the difference between the actual and budgeted costs.

STEPS

QUICK TIP
If a column or row contains blank cells, you must type a zero in any blank cell before using the SUM function.

1. **Click the first blank cell in column 1, type Total Cost, press [Tab], then click the Formula button in the Data group on the Table Tools Layout tab**

   The Formula dialog box opens, as shown in Figure E-15. The SUM function appears in the Formula text box followed by the reference for the cells to include in the calculation, (ABOVE). The formula =SUM(ABOVE) indicates that Word will sum the numbers in the cells above the active cell.

2. **Click OK**

   Word totals the numbers in the cells above the active cell and inserts the sum as a field. You can use the SUM function to quickly total the numbers in a column or a row. If the cell you select is at the bottom of a column of numbers, Word totals the column. If the cell is at the right end of a row of numbers, Word totals the row.

3. **Select 12,000 in the cell above the total, then type 13,500**

   If you change a number that is part of a calculation, you must recalculate the field result.

QUICK TIP
To change a field result to regular text, click the field to select it, then press [Ctrl][Shift][F9].

4. **Press [↓], then press [F9]**

   When the insertion point is in a cell that contains a formula, pressing [F9] updates the field result.

5. **Press [Tab], type Budgeted, press [Tab], type 113,780, press [Tab], type Difference, then press [Tab]**

   The insertion point is in the last cell of the table.

6. **Click the Formula button**

   The Formula dialog box opens. Word proposes to sum the numbers above the active cell, but you want to insert a formula that calculates the difference between the actual and budgeted costs. You can type simple custom formulas using a plus sign (+) for addition, a minus sign (–) for subtraction, an asterisk (*) for multiplication, and a slash (/) for division.

QUICK TIP
Cell references are determined by the number of columns in each row, not by the number of columns in the table. Therefore, rows 9 and 10 have only two columns.

7. **Select =SUM(ABOVE) in the Formula text box, then type =B9-B10**

   You must type an equal sign (=) to indicate that the text following it is a formula. You want to subtract the budgeted cost in the second column of row 10 from the actual cost in the second column of row 9; therefore, you type a formula to subtract the value in cell B10 from the value in cell B9.

8. **Click OK, then save your changes**

   The difference appears in the cell, as shown in Figure E-16.

FIGURE E-14: Cell references in a table

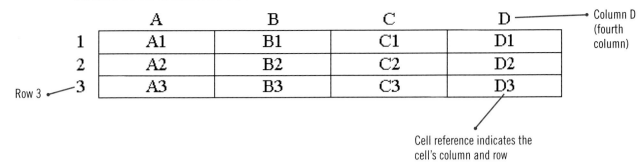

FIGURE E-15: Formula dialog box

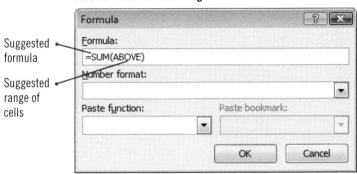

FIGURE E-16: Difference calculated in table

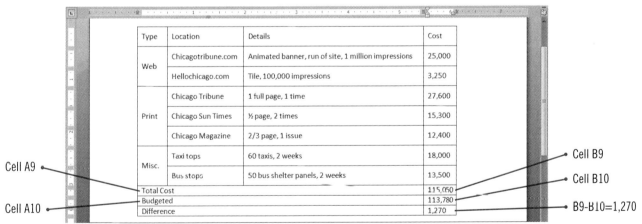

Working with formulas

In addition to the SUM function, Word includes formulas for averaging, counting, and rounding data, to name a few. To use a Word formula, click the Paste function list arrow in the Formula dialog box, select a function, and then insert the cell references of the cells you want included in the calculation in parentheses after the name of the function. When entering formulas, you must separate cell references by a comma. For example, if you want to average the values in cells A1, B3, and C4, enter the formula =AVERAGE(A1,B3,C4). You must separate cell ranges by a colon. For example, to total the values in cells A1 through A9, enter the formula =SUM(A1:A9). To display the result of a calculation in a particular number format, such as a decimal percentage (0.00%), click the Number format list arrow in the Formula dialog box and select a number format. Word inserts the result of a calculation as a field in the selected cell.

Applying a Table Style

Adding shading and other design elements to a table can help give it a polished appearance and make the data easier to read. Word includes built-in table styles that you can apply to a table to format it quickly. Table styles include borders, shading, fonts, alignment, colors, and other formatting effects. You can apply a table style to a table using the buttons in the Table Styles group on the Table Tools Design tab. ▰▰▰ You want to enhance the appearance of the table with shading, borders, and other formats, so you apply a table style to the table. After applying a style, you change the theme colors to a more pleasing palette.

STEPS

1. **Click the Table Tools Design tab**

   The Table Tools Design tab includes buttons for applying table styles and for adding, removing, and customizing borders and shading in a table.

2. **Click the More button ▼ in the Table Styles group**

   The gallery of table styles opens, as shown in Figure E-17. You point to a table style in the gallery to preview the style applied to the table.

3. **Move the pointer over several styles in the gallery, then click the Light Grid – Accent 2 style**

   The Light Grid – Accent 2 style is applied to the table, as shown in Figure E-18. Because of the structure of the table, this style neither enhances the table nor helps make the data more readable.

4. **Click the More button ▼ in the Table Style group, then click the Light List – Accent 2 style**

   This style works better with the structure of the table, and makes the table data easier to read.

5. **In the Table Style Options group, click the First Column check box to clear it, then click the Banded Columns check box to select it**

   The bold formatting is removed from the first column and column borders are added to the table. When the banded columns or banded rows setting is active, the odd columns or rows are formatted differently from the even columns or rows to make the table data easier to read.

6. **Click the Page Layout tab, click the Theme Colors list arrow ▦▾ in the Themes group, then click Origin in the gallery that opens**

   The color palette for the document changes to the colors used in the Origin theme, and the table color changes to Ice Blue.

7. **Click the Table Tools Design tab, click the More button ▼ in the Table Styles group, then click the Light List – Accent 1 style**

   The table color changes to Blue-Gray. Notice that the alignment of the text in the table changed back to top left when you applied a table style.

8. **Click the Table Tools Layout tab, click the table move handle ⊕ to select the table, click the Align Center Left button ▤ in the Alignment group, select the Type column, click the Align Center button ▤ in the Alignment group, select the Cost column, then click the Align Center Right button ▤ in the Alignment group**

   First, the data in the table is left-aligned and centered vertically, then the data in the Type column is centered, and finally the data in the Cost column is right-aligned.

9. **Select the last three rows of the table, click the Bold button B on the Mini toolbar, then click ▤**

   The text in the last three rows is right-aligned and bold is applied.

10. **Select the first row of the table, click the Center button ▤ on the Mini toolbar, click the Font Size list arrow on the Mini toolbar, click 14, deselect the row, then save your changes**

    The text in the header row is centered and enlarged, as shown in Figure E-19. You can also use the alignment buttons in the Paragraph group on the Home tab to change the alignment of text in a table.

Creating and Formatting Tables

FIGURE E-17: Gallery of table styles

Options for customizing table style settings

Modify an existing table style

Remove a table style from a table

Create a new table style

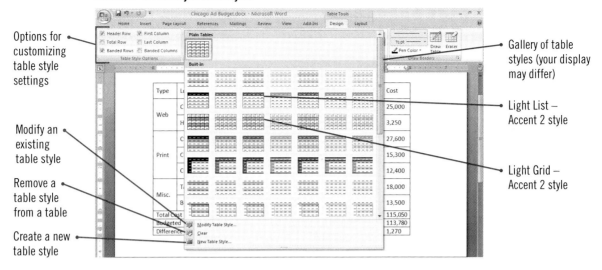

Gallery of table styles (your display may differ)

Light List – Accent 2 style

Light Grid – Accent 2 style

FIGURE E-18: Light Grid – Accent 2 style applied to table

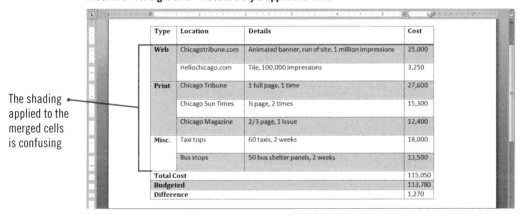

The shading applied to the merged cells is confusing

FIGURE E-19: Light List – Accent 1 style (Origin theme) applied to table

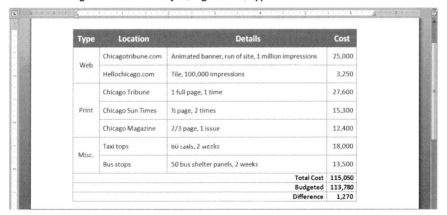

Using tables to lay out a page

Tables are often used to display information for quick reference and analysis, but you can also use tables to structure the layout of a page. You can insert any kind of information in the cell of a table—including graphics, bulleted lists, charts, and other tables (called **nested tables**). For example, you might use a table to lay out a résumé, a newsletter, or a Web page. When you use a table to lay out a page, you generally remove the table borders to hide the table structure from the reader. After you remove borders, it can be help-ful to display the table gridlines onscreen while you work. **Gridlines** are blue dotted lines that show the boundaries of cells, but do not print. If your document will be viewed online—for example, if you are planning to e-mail your résumé to potential employers—you should turn off the display of gridlines before you distribute the doc-ument so that it looks the same online as it looks when printed. To turn gridlines off or on, click the View Gridlines button in the Table group on the Table Tools Layout tab.

Creating a Custom Format for a Table

You can also use the formatting tools available in Word to create your own table designs. For example, you can add or remove borders and shading, vary the line style, thickness, and color of borders, and change the orientation of text from horizontal to vertical. ▓▓▓▓ You adjust the text direction, shading, and borders in the table to make it easier to understand at a glance.

STEPS

1. **Select the Type and Location cells in the first row, click the Merge Cells button in the Merge group on the Table Tools Layout tab, then type Ad Location**
   The two cells are combined into a single cell containing the text "Ad Location."

2. **Select the Web, Print, and Misc. cells in the first column, click the Bold button B on the Mini toolbar, click the Text Direction button in the Alignment group twice, then deselect the cells**
   The text is rotated 270 degrees.

3. **Position the pointer over the right border of the Web cell until the pointer changes to ◄╫►, then drag the border to approximately the ¼" mark on the horizontal ruler**
   The width of the column containing the vertical text narrows.

4. **Place the insertion point in the Web cell, click the Table Tools Design tab, then click the Shading list arrow in the Table Styles group**
   The gallery of shading colors for the Origin theme opens.

5. **Click Light Yellow, Accent 4 in the gallery as shown in Figure E-20, click the Print cell, click the Shading list arrow, click Lime, Accent 3, click the Misc. cell, click the Shading list arrow, then click Ice Blue, Accent 2**
   Shading is applied to each cell.

6. **Drag to select the six white cells in the Web rows (rows 2 and 3), click the Shading list arrow, then click Light Yellow, Accent 4, Lighter 40%**

7. **Repeat Step 6 to apply Lime, Accent 3, Lighter 40% shading to the Print rows and Ice Blue, Accent 2, Lighter 40% shading to the Misc. rows**
   Shading is applied to all the cells in rows 1-8.

8. **Select the last three rows of the table, click the Borders list arrow in the Table Styles group, click No Border on the menu that appears, then click in the table to deselect the rows**
   The top, bottom, left, and right borders are removed from each cell in the selected rows.

9. **Click the Pen Color list arrow in the Draw Borders group, click Blue-Gray, Accent 1, select the Total Cost row, click the Borders list arrow, click Top Border, click the 113,780 cell, click the Borders list arrow, then click the Bottom Border**
   The active pen color for borders changes to Blue-Gray, Accent 1. You use the buttons in the Draw Borders group to change the active pen color, line weight, and line style settings before adding a border to a table. A top border is added to each cell in the Total Cost row, and a bottom border is added below 113,780. The completed table is shown in Figure E-21.

10. **Press [Ctrl][Home], press [Enter], type your name, save your changes, print a copy of the document, close the document, then exit Word**
    Press [Enter] at the beginning of a table to move the table down one line in a document.

FIGURE E-20: Gallery of shading colors from the Origin theme

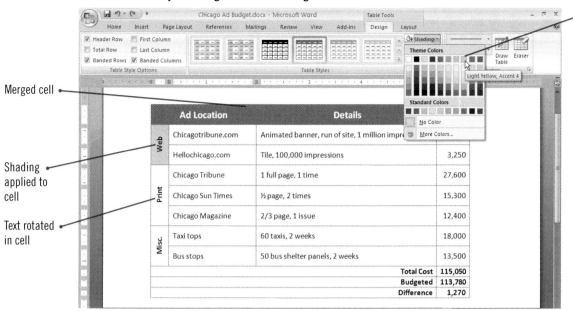

Merged cell

Shading applied to cell

Text rotated in cell

Light Yellow, Accent 4: use ScreenTips as needed to identify colors

FIGURE E-21: Completed table

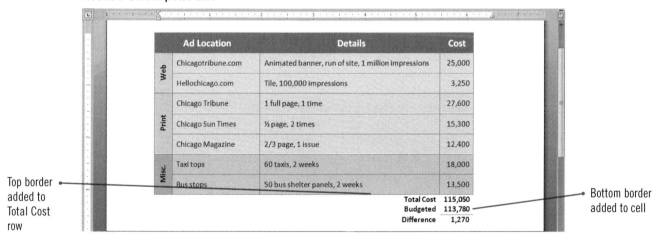

Top border added to Total Cost row

Bottom border added to cell

Drawing a table

The Word Draw Table feature allows you to draw table cells exactly where you want them. To draw a table, click the Table button on the Insert tab, and then click Draw Table. If a table is already started, you can click the Draw Table button in the Draw Borders group on the Table Tools Design tab to turn on the Draw pointer, and then click and drag to draw a cell. Using the same method, you can draw borders within the cell to create columns and rows, or draw additional cells attached to the first cell. Click the Draw Table button to turn off the draw feature. The borders you draw are added using the active line style, line weight, and pen color settings.

If you want to remove a border from a table, click the Eraser button in the Draw Borders group to activate the Eraser pointer, and then click the border you want to remove. Click the Eraser button to turn off the erase feature. You can use the Draw pointer and the Eraser pointer to change the structure of any table, not just the tables you draw from scratch.

Practice

▼ CONCEPTS REVIEW

Label each element shown in Figure E-22.

FIGURE E-22

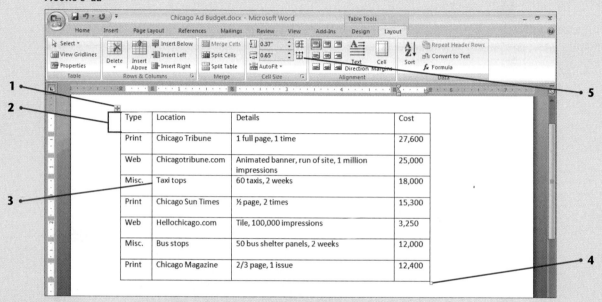

Match each term with the statement that best describes it.

6. Header row
7. Gridlines
8. Split
9. Ascending order
10. Borders
11. Cell
12. Nested table
13. Descending order
14. Merge
15. Cell reference

a. To combine two or more adjacent cells into one larger cell
b. The first row of a table that contains the column headings
c. Lines that separate columns and rows in a table and that print
d. An object inserted in a table cell
e. To divide an existing cell into multiple cells
f. The box formed by the intersection of a column and a row
g. Lines that show columns and rows in a table, but do not print
h. Sort order that organizes text from A to Z
i. Sort order that organizes text from Z to A
j. A cell address composed of a column letter and a row number

Select the best answer from the list of choices.

16. Which of the following is the cell reference for the third cell in the second column?
   a. C2
   b. 2C
   c. 3B
   d. B3

17. Which button do you use to change the alignment of text in a cell?
   a. ![icon]
   b. ![icon]
   c. ![icon]
   d. ![icon]

Creating and Formatting Tables

18. Which of the following is *not* a correct formula for adding the values in cells A1, A2, and A3?

a. =SUM(A1~A3)   **c.** =SUM(A1:A3)

b. =A1+A2+A3   **d.** =SUM(A1,A2,A3)

19. Which of the following is *not* a valid way to add a new row to the bottom of a table?

a. Right-click the bottom row, point to Insert, then click Insert Rows Below.

b. Click in the bottom row, then click the Insert Below button in the Rows & Columns group on the Table Tools Layout tab.

c. Click in the bottom row, open the Properties dialog box, then insert a row using the options on the Row tab.

d. Place the insertion point in the last cell of the last row, then press [Tab].

20. What happens when you double-click a column border?

a. The columns in the table are distributed evenly.   **c.** A new column is added to the right.

b. The column width is adjusted to fit the text.   **d.** A new column is added to the left.

▼ **SKILLS REVIEW**

1. Insert a table.

a. Start Word, then save the new blank document as **Mutual Funds** to the drive and folder where you store your Data Files.

b. Type your name, press [Enter] twice, type **Mutual Funds Performance**, then press [Enter].

c. Insert a table that contains four columns and four rows.

d. Type the text shown in Figure E-23, pressing [Tab] to add rows as necessary. (*Note*: Do not format text or the table at this time.)

e. Save your changes.

FIGURE E-23

Fund Name	1 Year	5 Year	10 Year
Computers	16.47	25.56	27.09
Europe	-6.15	13.89	10.61
Natural Resources	19.47	12.30	15.38
Health Care	32.45	24.26	23.25
Financial Services	22.18	21.07	24.44
500 Index	9.13	15.34	13.69

2. Insert and delete rows and columns.

a. Insert a row above the Health Care row, then type the following text in the new row:

Canada   8.24   8.12   8.56

b. Delete the Europe row.

c. Insert a column to the right of the 10 Year column, type **Date Purchased** in the header row, then enter a date in each cell in the column using the format MM/DD/YY (for example, 11/27/02).

d. Move the Date Purchased column to the right of the Fund Name column, then save your changes.

3. Modify rows and columns.

a. Double-click the border between the first and second columns to resize the columns.

b. Drag the border between the second and third columns to the 2¼" mark on the horizontal ruler.

c. Double-click the right border of the 1 Year, 5 Year, and 10 Year columns.

d. Select the 1 Year, 5 Year, and 10 Year columns, then distribute the columns evenly.

e. Select the table, apply the No Spacing style, select rows 2-7, set the row height to exactly .3", then save your changes.

4. Sort table data.

a. Sort the table data, excluding the header row, in descending order by the information in the 1 Year column.

b. Sort the table data, excluding the header row, in ascending order by date purchased.

c. Sort the table data, excluding the header row, by fund name in alphabetical order, then save your changes.

5. Split and merge cells.

a. Insert a row above the header row, then merge the first cell in the new row with the Fund Name cell.

b. Merge the second cell in the new row with the Date Purchased cell.

c. Merge the three remaining blank cells in the first row into a single cell, then type **Average Annual Returns** in the merged cell.

d. Add a new row to the bottom of the table.

e. Merge the first two cells in the new row, then type **Average Return** in the merged cell.

f. Select the first seven cells in the first column (from Fund Name to Natural Resources), open the Split Cells dialog box, clear the Merge cells before split check box, then split the cells into two columns.

g. Type Trading Symbol as the heading for the new column, then enter the following text in the remaining cells in the column: FINX, CAND, COMP, FINS, HCRX, NARS.

h. Double-click the right border of the first column to resize the column, then save your changes.

6. **Perform calculations in tables.**

a. Place the insertion point in the last cell in the 1 Year column.

b. Open the Formula dialog box, delete the text in the Formula text box, type =average(above), click the Number Format list arrow, scroll down, click 0.00%, then click OK.

c. Repeat Step b to insert the average return in the last cell in the 5 Year and 10 Year columns.

d. Change the value of the 1-year return for the Natural Resources fund to 10.35.

e. Use [F9] to recalculate the average return for 1 year, then save your changes.

7. **Apply a table style.**

a. Click the Table Tools Design tab, preview table styles applied to the table, and then apply an appropriate style. Was the style you chose effective?

b. Apply the Light Shading style to the table, then remove the style from First Column and Banded Rows.

c. Apply bold to the 1 Year, 5 Year, and 10 Year column headings, and to the bottom row of the table.

d. Center the table between the margins, center the table title Mutual Funds Performance, increase the font size of the title to 14-points, apply bold, then save your changes.

8. **Create a custom format for a table.**

a. Select the entire table, then use the Align Center button in the Alignment group on the Table Tools Layout tab to center the text in every cell vertically and horizontally.

b. Center right-align the dates in column 3 and the numbers in columns 4-6.

c. Center left-align the fund names and trading symbols in columns 1 and 2, but not the column headings.

d. Center right-align the text in the bottom row. Make sure the text in the header row is still centered.

e. Change the theme colors to Apex.

f. Select all the cells in the header row, including the 1 Year, 5 Year, and 10 Year column headings, change the shading color to Lavender, Accent 5, then change the font color to white.

g. Apply Lavender, Accent 5, Lighter 60% shading to the cells containing the fund names and trading symbols, and Lavender Accent 5, Lighter 80% shading to the cells containing the purchase dates.

h. To the cells containing the 1 Year, 5 Year, and 10 Year data, respectively, apply Tan, Accent 1, Lighter 60% shading, Lavender, Accent 6, Lighter 60% shading, and Olive Green, Accent 2, Lighter 60% shading.

i. Apply Lavender Accent 5, Lighter 80% shading to the last row of the table.

j. Add a ½-point white bottom border to the Average Annual Returns cell.

k. Add a 1½-point black border around the outside of the table.

l. Add a ½-point black top border to the 500 Index row and to the last row of the table. (*Hint*: Do not remove any borders.)

m. Compare your table to Figure E-24, make any necessary adjustments, save your changes, print a copy, close the file, then exit Word.

FIGURE E-24

Mutual Funds Performance

Fund Name	Trading Symbol	Date Purchased	Average Annual Returns		
			1 Year	5 Year	10 Year
500 Index	FINX	5/9/96	9.13	15.34	13.69
Canada	CAND	11/13/03	8.24	8.12	8.56
Computers	COMP	9/23/01	16.47	25.56	27.09
Financial Services	FINS	2/12/01	22.18	21.07	24.44
Health Care	HCRX	3/24/96	32.45	24.26	23.25
Natural Resources	NARS	6/2/98	10.35	12.30	15.38
		Average Return	16.47%	17.78%	18.74%

▼ INDEPENDENT CHALLENGE 1

You are the director of sales for a publishing company with branch offices in six cities around the globe. In preparation for the upcoming sales meeting, you create a table showing your sales projections for the fiscal year 2010.

a. Start Word, then save the new blank document as **2010 Sales** to the drive and folder where you store your Data Files.

b. Type the table heading **Projected Sales in Millions, Fiscal Year 2010** at the top of the document, then press [Enter] twice.

c. Insert a table with five columns and four rows, then enter the data shown in Figure E-25 into the table, adding rows as necessary. (*Note*: Do not format text or the table at this time.)

d. Resize the columns to fit the text.

e. Sort the table rows in alphabetical order by Office.

f. Add a new row to the bottom of the table, type **Total** in the first cell, then enter a formula in each remaining cell in the new row to calculate the sum of the cells above it.

FIGURE E-25

Office	Q1	Q2	Q3	Q4
Paris	9500	5800	3900	9800
Tokyo	6700	8900	4500	4900
Berlin	8800	8500	6800	7400
Shanghai	5800	7200	4700	8200
New York	8500	7800	9800	9400
Melbourne	7900	6800	3800	6200

g. Add a new column at the right end of the table, type **Total** in the first cell, then enter a formula in each remaining cell in the new column to calculate the sum of the cells to the left of it. (*Hint*: Make sure the formula you insert in each cell sums the cells to the left, not the cells above. In the last cell in the last column, you can sum the cells to the left or the cells above; either way the total should be the same.)

h. Apply a table style to the table. Select a style that enhances the information contained in the table, and adjust the Table Style Options to suit the content.

i. Center the text in the header row, left-align the remaining text in the first column, then right-align the numerical data in the table.

j. Enhance the table with fonts, font colors, shading, and borders to make the table attractive and easy to read at a glance.

k. Increase the font size of the table heading to 18 points, then center the table heading and the table on the page.

l. Press [Ctrl][End], press [Enter], type your name, save your changes, print the table, close the file, then exit Word.

▼ INDEPENDENT CHALLENGE 2

You have been invited to speak to your local board of realtors about the economic benefits of living in your city. To illustrate some of your points, you want to distribute a handout comparing the cost of living and other economic indicators in the U.S. cities that offer features similar to your city. You decide to format the data as a table.

a. Start Word, open the file WD E-1.docx, then save it as **City Data** to the drive and folder where you store your Data Files.

b. Center the table heading, then increase the font size to 18 points.

c. Turn on formatting marks, select the tabbed text in the document, then convert the text to a table.

d. Add a row above the first row in the table, then enter the following column headings in the new header row: **City**, **Cost of Living**, **Median Income**, **Average House Cost**, **Bachelor Degree Rate**.

e. Apply an appropriate Table style to the table. Add or remove the style from various elements of the table using the options in the Table Style Options group, as necessary.

f. Adjust the column widths so that the table is attractive and readable. (*Hint*: Allow the column headings to wrap to two lines.)

g. Make the height of each row at least .25".

h. Center Left align the text in each cell in the first column, including the column head.

i. Center Right align the text in each cell in the remaining columns, including the column heads.

j. Center the entire table on the page.

k. Sort the table by cost of living in descending order.

▼ INDEPENDENT CHALLENGE 2 (CONTINUED)

Advanced Challenge Exercise

- Add a new row to the bottom of the table, then type **Average** in the first cell in the new row.
- In each subsequent cell in the Average row, insert a formula that calculates the averages of the cells above it. (*Hint*: For each cell, replace SUM with AVERAGE in the Formula text box, but do not make other changes.)
- Format the Average row with borders, shading, fonts, and other formats, as necessary to enhance the data.

l. On the blank line below the table, type **Note: The average cost of living in the United States is 100.**, italicize the text, then use a tab stop and indents to align the text with the left side of the table if it is not aligned.

m. Enhance the table with borders, shading, fonts, and other formats, if necessary, to make it attractive and readable.

n. Type your name at the bottom of the document, save your changes, print a copy of the table, close the document, then exit Word.

▼ INDEPENDENT CHALLENGE 3

You work in the advertising department at a magazine. Your boss has asked you to create a fact sheet on the ad dimensions for the magazine. The fact sheet should include the dimensions for each type of ad. As a bonus, you could also add a visual representation of the different ad shapes and sizes, shown in Figure E-26. You'll use tables to lay out the fact sheet, present the dimension information, and, if you are performing the ACE steps, illustrate the ad shapes and sizes.

FIGURE E-26

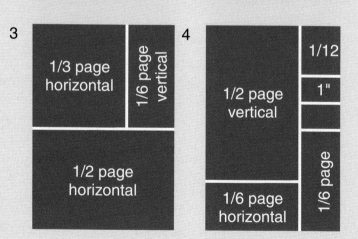

a. Start Word, open the file WD E-2.doc from the drive and folder where you store your Data Files, then save it as **Ad Fact Sheet**. Turn on the display of gridlines, then read the document to get a feel for its contents.

b. Drag the border between the first and second column to approximately the 2¾" mark on the horizontal ruler, resize the second and third columns to fit the text, then make each row in the table .5".

c. Change the alignment of the text in the first column to center left, then change the alignment of the text in the second and third columns to center right.

d. Remove all the borders from the table, then apply a 2¼-point, dark blue, dotted line, inside horizontal border to the entire table. This creates a dark blue dotted line between each row. (*Hint*: Use the Dark Blue, Text 2 color.)

e. In the second blank paragraph under the table heading, insert a new table with three columns and four rows, then merge the cells in the third column of the new blank table.

f. Drag the border between the first and second columns of the new blank table to the 1¼" mark on the horizontal ruler. Drag the border between the second and third columns to the 1½" mark.

g. Select the table that contains text, cut it to the Clipboard, then paste it in the merged cell in the blank table. The table with text is now a nested table in the main table.

h. Split the nested table above the Unit Size (Bleed) row. (*Hint*: Place the insertion point in the Unit Size (Bleed) row, then use the Split Table button.)

▼ INDEPENDENT CHALLENGE 3 (CONTINUED)

i. Scroll up, merge the four cells in the first column of the main table, then merge the four cells in the second column.

j. Split the first column into one column and seven rows.

k. Using the Table Row Height text box in the Cell Size group, change the row height of each cell in the first column so that the rows alternate between exactly 1.8" and .25" in height. Make the height of the first, third, fifth, and seventh rows 1.8". (*Hint*: You can also use the Table Properties dialog box.)

l. Add Dark Blue, Text 2 shading to the first, third, fifth, and seventh cells in the first column, remove all the borders from the main table, then turn off the display of gridlines. The dark blue dotted line borders in the nested table remain.

Advanced Challenge Exercise

- In the first dark blue cell, type **Full Page**, change the font color to white, then center the text vertically in the cell.
- In the Draw Borders group on the Table Tools Design tab, change the Line Style to a single line, change the Line Weight to 2¼ pt, then change the Pen Color to white.
- Be sure the Draw Table pointer is active, then, referring to Figure E-26, draw a vertical border that divides the second dark blue cell into ⅔ and ⅓.
- Label the cells and align the text as shown in the figure. (*Hint*: Change the text direction and alignment before typing text. Take care not to change the size of the cells when you type. If necessary, press [Enter] to start a new line of text in a cell, or reduce the font size of the text.)
- Referring to Figure E-26, divide the third and fourth dark blue cells, then label the cells as shown in the figure.

m. Examine the document for errors, then make any necessary adjustments.

n. Press [Ctrl][End], type your name, save your changes to the document, preview it, print a copy, close the file, then exit Word.

▼ REAL LIFE INDEPENDENT CHALLENGE

This Independent Challenge requires an Internet connection.

A well-written and well-formatted résumé gives you an advantage when it comes to getting a job interview. In a winning résumé, the content and format support your career objective and effectively present your background and qualifications. One simple way to create a résumé is to lay out the page using a table. In this exercise you research guidelines for writing and formatting résumés. You then create your own résumé using a table for its layout.

a. Use your favorite search engine to search the Web for information on writing and formatting résumés. Use the keywords **resume advice**.

b. Print helpful advice on writing and formatting résumés from at least two Web sites.

c. Think about the information you want to include in your résumé. The header should include your name, address, telephone number, and e-mail address. The body should include your career objective and information on your education, work experience, and skills. You may want to add additional information.

d. Sketch a layout for your résumé using a table as the underlying grid. Include the table rows and columns in your sketch.

e. Start Word, open a new blank document, then save it as **My Resume** to the drive and folder where you store your Data Files.

f. Set appropriate margins, then insert a table to serve as the underlying grid for your résumé. Split and merge cells and adjust the size of the table columns as necessary.

g. Type your résumé in the table cells. Take care to use a professional tone and keep your language to the point.

h. Format your résumé with fonts, bullets, and other formatting features. Adjust the spacing between sections by resizing the table columns and rows.

i. When you are satisfied with the content and format of your résumé, remove the borders from the table, then hide the gridlines if they are visible.

j. Check your résumé for spelling and grammar errors.

k. Save your changes, preview your résumé, print a copy, close the file, then exit Word.

Word 2007

▼ VISUAL WORKSHOP

Create the calendar shown in Figure E-27 using a table to lay out the entire page. (*Hints*: The top and bottom margins are .9", the left and right margins are 1", and the font is Century Gothic. The clip art image is inserted in the table. The clip art image is found using the keyword coast. Use a different clip art image or font if the ones shown in the figure are not available.) Type your name in the last table cell, save the calendar with the filename June 2010 to the drive and folder where you store your Data Files, then print a copy.

FIGURE E-27

June 2010

Sunday	Monday	Tuesday	Wednesday	Thursday	Friday	Saturday
		1	2	3	4	5
6	7	8	9	10	11	12
13	14	15	16	17	18	19
20	21	22	23	24	25	26
27	28	29	30			

Illustrating Documents with Graphics

Files You Will Need:

WD F-1.docx
WD F-2.docx
WD F-3.docx
Fishing Boats.jpg
Stone Barn.jpg

Graphics can help illustrate the ideas in your documents, provide visual interest on a page, and give your documents punch and flair. In addition to clip art, you can add photos or graphics created in other programs to a document, or you can use the graphic features of Word to create your own images. In this unit, you learn how to insert, modify, and position graphics and text boxes, how to draw your own images, and how to illustrate a document with WordArt and charts. You are preparing a flyer advertising QST tours to Mexico. You use the graphic features of Word to illustrate the flyer so that it promotes Mexico as a colorful, warm, lively, and inviting travel destination.

OBJECTIVES

Insert a graphic

Size and scale a graphic

Position a graphic

Create a text box

Create WordArt

Draw shapes

Create a chart

Finalize page layout

Inserting a Graphic

Graphic images you can insert in a document include the clip art images that come with Word, photos taken with a digital camera, scanned art, and graphics created in other graphics programs. To insert a graphic file into a document, you use the Picture command in the Illustrations group on the Insert tab. Once you insert a graphic, you can apply a Picture style to it to enhance its appearance. You have written the text for the Mexico flyer, and now want to illustrate it with digital photographs. You insert a photo file in the document, apply a shadow to the photo, and then wrap text around it to make it a floating graphic.

STEPS

1. **Start Word, open the file** WD F-1.docx **from the drive and folder where you store your Data Files, save it as** Mexico Flyer, **click the** Show/Hide ¶ button ¶ **in the Paragraph group to display formatting marks if necessary, read the flyer to get a feel for its format and contents, then press** [Ctrl][Home]

   The flyer is divided into five sections and includes a hard page break and several inline graphics. The second and fourth sections are formatted in three columns.

2. **Click the** Insert tab, **then click the** Picture button **in the Illustrations group**

   The Insert Picture dialog box opens. You use this dialog box to locate and insert graphic files. Most graphic files are **bitmap graphics**, which are often saved with a .bmp, .png, .jpg, .tif, or .gif file extension. To view all the graphic files in a particular location, use the File type list arrow to select All Pictures.

   TROUBLE
   If you do not see All Pictures, click the File type list arrow, then click All Pictures.

3. **Verify that** All Pictures **appears in the File type text box, navigate to the location where you store your Data Files, click the file** Fishing Boats.jpg, **then click** Insert

   The photo is inserted as an inline graphic at the location of the insertion point, as shown in Figure F-1. When a graphic is selected, white circles and squares, called **sizing handles**, appear on the sides and corners of the graphic, a green **rotate handle** appears, and the Picture Tools Format tab appears on the Ribbon. You use this tab to size, crop, position, wrap text around, format, and adjust a graphic.

4. **Click the** Picture Effects button **in the Picture Styles group, point to** Shadow, **move the pointer over the shadow styles in the gallery to preview them in the document, then click** Offset Diagonal Bottom Right **in the Outer section**

   A drop shadow is applied to the photo. You can use the Picture Effects button to apply other visual effects to a graphic, such as a glow, soft edge, reflection, or 3-D rotation.

5. **Click the** Picture Effects button, **point to** Shadow, **then click** Shadow Options

   The Format Picture dialog box opens. You use this dialog box to adjust the format settings applied to graphic objects.

   QUICK TIP
   Change a floating graphic to an inline graphic by changing the text wrapping style to In Line with Text.

6. **Click the** Distance up arrow **in the Shadow section four times until 7 pt appears, then click** Close

   The distance of the shadow from the picture is increased to 7 points. Notice that as you adjust the settings in the dialog box, the change is immediately applied to the photo.

7. **Click the** Text Wrapping button **in the Arrange group, then click** Tight

   The text wraps around the sides of the graphic, as shown in Figure F-2, making the graphic a floating object. A floating object is part of the drawing layer in a document and can be moved anywhere on a page, including in front of or behind text and other objects. Notice the anchor that appears in the upper-right corner of the photo next to the Adventure Mexico paragraph. The anchor indicates the floating graphic is **anchored** to the nearest paragraph so that the graphic moves with the paragraph if the paragraph is moved. The anchor symbol appears only when formatting marks are displayed.

   QUICK TIP
   To position a graphic anywhere on a page, you must apply text-wrapping to it even if there is no text on the page.

8. **Deselect the graphic, then click the** Save button 🖫 **on the Quick Access toolbar**

FIGURE F-1: Inline graphic

Rotate handle

Sizing handles

Picture Tools Format tab

Graphic is part of the same line of text as "Adventure"

FIGURE F-2: Floating graphic

Anchor symbol indicates photo is anchored to the paragraph next to it

Text wraps around the shape of the graphic

Adjusting the brightness, contrast, or colors of a picture

The Word picture editing features give you the power to enhance the color of photographs and clip art and create interesting visual effects. Using the commands in the Adjust group on the Picture Tools Format tab, you can adjust a picture's relative lightness (**brightness**), alter the difference between its darkest and lightest areas (**contrast**), and recolor a picture to give it a stylized effect, such as sepia tone, grayscale, or duotone.

When you want to alter the brightness or contrast of a picture, you select it, click the Brightness or Contrast button in the Adjust group to open a gallery of percentages that you can preview applied to the picture, and then click the percentage you want to apply. You can also fine tune the brightness or contrast applied to a picture by clicking Picture Corrections Options in the gallery, and then using the sliders in the Picture pane of the Format Picture dialog box to adjust the percentage. See Figure F-3.

If you want to change the colors of a picture, simply select it, click the Recolor button in the Adjust group, and then select one of the color modes or variations in the gallery that opens. After you edit a picture, you can undo any changes that you made to the

brightness, contrast, or color by clicking the Reset Picture button in the Adjust group. This command also resets any changes you made to a picture's size, cropping, border, and effects.

FIGURE F-3: Format Picture dialog box

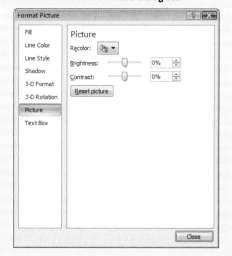

Sizing and Scaling a Graphic

Once you insert a graphic into a document, you can change its shape or size by using the mouse to drag a sizing handle, by using the Shape Width and Shape Height text boxes in the Size group on the Picture Tools Format tab to specify an exact height and width for the graphic, or by changing the scale of the graphic using the Size dialog box. Resizing a graphic with the mouse allows you to see how the image looks as you modify it. Using the text boxes in the Size group or the Size dialog box allows you to set precise measurements. ░░░░░ You enlarge the photograph.

STEPS

1. **Double-click the photo to select it, place the pointer over the middle-right sizing handle, when the pointer changes to ⟷, drag to the right until the graphic is about 5" wide**

   As you drag, the transparent image indicates the size and shape of the graphic. You can refer to the ruler to gauge the measurements as you drag. When you release the mouse button, the image is stretched to be wider. Dragging a side, top, or bottom sizing handle changes only the width or height of a graphic.

2. **Click the Undo button 🔄 on the Quick Access toolbar, place the pointer over the lower-right sizing handle, when the pointer changes to ⬂ drag down and to the right until the graphic is about 2 ¾ " tall and 4" wide, then release the mouse button**

   The image is enlarged. Dragging a corner sizing handle resizes the photo proportionally so that its width and height are reduced or enlarged by the same percentage. Table F-1 describes other ways to resize objects using the mouse.

3. **Click the launcher 🔳 in the Size group**

   The Size dialog box opens, as shown in Figure F-4. It allows you to enter precise height and width measurements for a graphic or to scale a graphic by entering the percentage by which you want to reduce or enlarge it. When a graphic is sized to scale (or **scaled**), its height to width ratio remains the same.

4. **Select the measurement in the Height text box in the Scale section, type 130, then click the Width text box in the Scale section**

   The scale of the width changes to 130% and the Height and Width measurements in the Size and rotate section increase proportionally. When the Lock aspect ratio check box is selected, you need to enter only a height or width measurement. Word calculates the other measurement so that the resized graphic is proportional.

5. **Click Close**

   The photo is enlarged to 130% its original size.

6. **Type 4.6 in the Shape Width text box in the Size group, press [Enter], then save your changes**

   The photo is enlarged to be precisely 4.6" wide and approximately 3.07" tall, as shown in Figure F-5. Because the Lock aspect ratio check box is selected in the Size dialog box for this graphic, the photo is sized proportionally when you adjust a setting in either the Shape Height or the Shape Width text box.

Cropping graphics

If you want to use only part of a picture in a document, you can **crop** the graphic to trim the parts you don't want to use. To crop a graphic, select it, then click the Crop button in the Size group on the Picture Tools Format tab. The pointer changes to the cropping pointer ⌐, and cropping handles (solid black lines) appear on all four corners and sides of the graphic. To crop one side of a graphic, drag a side cropping handle inward to where you want to trim the graphic. To crop two adjacent sides at once, drag a corner cropping handle inward to the point where you want the corner of the cropped image to be. When you finish adjusting the parameters of the graphic, click the Crop button again to turn off the crop feature. You can also crop a graphic by entering precise crop measurements on the Size tab in the Size dialog box.

FIGURE F-4: Size tab in the Size dialog box

Set specific height and
width measurements
(yours might differ)

Change the scale
of an object

Select to keep height and
width proportional

Select to make scaled
measurements relative
to the original size

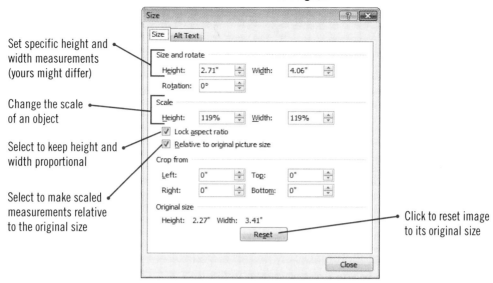

Click to reset image
to its original size

FIGURE F-5: Enlarged photo

Shape Height and
Shape Width text
boxes show the
size of the
selected object

TABLE F-1: Methods for resizing an object using the mouse

do this	to
Drag a corner sizing handle	Resize a clip art or bitmap graphic and maintain its proportions
Press [Shift] and drag a corner sizing handle	Resize any graphic object and maintain its proportions
Press [Ctrl] and drag a side, top, or bottom sizing handle	Resize any graphic object vertically or horizontally while keeping the center position fixed
Press [Ctrl] and drag a corner sizing handle	Resize any graphic object diagonally while keeping the center position fixed
Press [Shift][Ctrl] and drag a corner sizing handle	Resize any graphic object while keeping the center position fixed and maintaining its proportions

Positioning a Graphic

Once you insert a graphic into a document and make it a floating graphic, you can move it by dragging it with the mouse, nudging it with the arrow keys, or setting an exact location for the graphic using the Position command. ▄▄▟▛▜ You experiment with different positions for the photo, and then you move an inline graphic from page 2 to page 1 using Cut and Paste.

STEPS

QUICK TIP
Press an arrow key to nudge an object in small increments.

1. **Select the photo if it is not already selected, click the Position button in the Arrange group, then click Position in Middle Center with Square Text Wrapping**
   The photo is centered vertically and horizontally on the page and the text wraps around the graphic. Moving an inline graphic using the Position button is a fast way to make it a floating graphic and position it so it is centered or aligned with the margins.

QUICK TIP
To move an object only horizontally or vertically, press [Shift] as you drag.

2. **Be sure the section break is at the top of your screen, then use the ⬚ pointer to drag the photo up and to the right as shown in Figure F-6**
   As you drag, the transparent image indicates the position of the photo. When you release the mouse button, the photo is moved. Notice that the anchor symbol moved when you moved the graphic.

3. **Click the Position button, click More Layout Options, then click the Picture Position tab in the Advanced Layout dialog box if it is not already selected**
   The Picture Position tab allows you to specify an exact position for a graphic relative to some aspect of the document, such as a margin, column, or paragraph.

QUICK TIP
You can place a floating graphic anywhere on a page, including outside the margins.

4. **Type 2.44 in the Absolute position text box in the Horizontal section, then type 2.25 in the Absolute position text box in the Vertical section**
   The left side of the photo will be positioned exactly 2.44" from the right margin and the top of the photo will be positioned precisely 2.25" below the top margin.

5. **Click the Text Wrapping tab**
   You use the Text Wrapping tab to change the text wrapping style, to wrap text around only one side of a graphic, and to change the distance between the edge of the graphic and the edge of the wrapped text.

QUICK TIP
Use the Change Picture button in the Adjust group to replace the current picture with another picture while preserving the formatting and size of the current picture.

6. **Type .1 in the Bottom text box, then click OK**
   The position of the photo is adjusted and the amount of white space under the photo is increased to .1".

7. **Change the Zoom level to 75%, scroll until the section break is at the top of your screen, be sure the photo is still selected, then drag the anchor symbol to the left margin near the top of the first body paragraph if it is not already located there**
   Dragging the anchor symbol to a different paragraph anchors the selected graphic to that paragraph.

8. **Press [Ctrl][End], select the pyramid photo, press [Ctrl][X] to cut the photo, scroll up until the section break at the top of page 1 is at the top of your screen, click the blank paragraph in the first column, then press [Ctrl][V]**
   The inline graphic is pasted above the Quest Specialty Travel Mexico Destinations heading.

9. **Double-click the pyramid photo, click the Position button, click Position in Bottom Left with Square Text Wrapping, then drag the anchor symbol to the margin left of the first body paragraph**
   The pyramid photo becomes a floating graphic aligned in the lower-left corner of the page and anchored to the first body paragraph. Both photos are now anchored to the same paragraph.

10. **Click the Fishing boats photo, click the Home tab, click the Format Painter button ✪ in the Clipboard group, click the pyramid photo with the ▟▙ pointer, then click ▣**
    The shadow format settings are copied from the fishing boats photo to the pyramid photo. Compare your document to Figure F-7.

FIGURE F-6: Dragging a graphic to move it

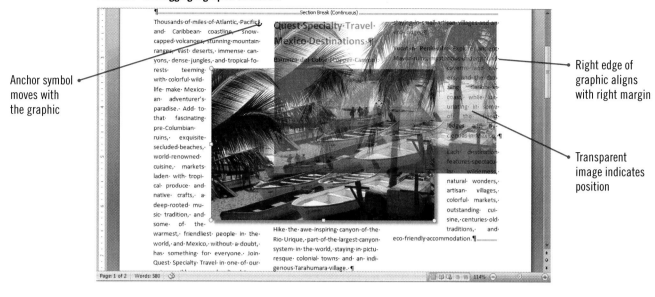

Anchor symbol moves with the graphic

Right edge of graphic aligns with right margin

Transparent image indicates position

FIGURE F-7: Repositioned photos

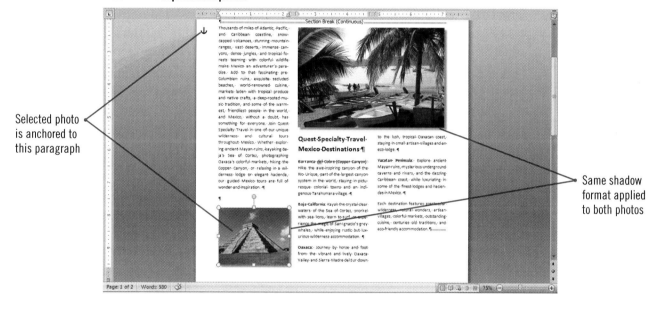

Selected photo is anchored to this paragraph

Same shadow format applied to both photos

Changing the shape of a picture and enhancing it with visual effects

A fun way to alter the appearance of a picture in a document is to change its shape, either to something sophisticated, such as an oval or a rectangle, or to something playful, such as a star, sun, triangle, or arrow. Another fun way to give a document personality and flair, and help to communicate its message, is to apply a visual effect to a picture, such as a glow, a shadow, a reflection, soft edges, a bevel, or some other effect. When you change the shape of a picture or apply a visual effect, any other formatting you have applied to the picture is preserved. To change the shape of a picture, simply select it, click the Picture Shape button in the Picture Styles group on the Picture Tools Format tab, and then select one of the shapes from the Shape menu that opens. To apply a visual effect, select the picture, click the Picture Effects button in the Picture Styles group, point to a type of

effect, and then select from the gallery choices. Figure F-8 shows a photo that is shaped like a cloud and has a bevel effect applied.

FIGURE F-8: Photograph with picture shape and effects applied

Creating a Text Box

When you want to illustrate your documents with text, you can create a text box. A **text box** is a container that you can fill with text and graphics. Like other drawing objects, a text box can be resized, formatted with colors, lines, and text-wrapping, and positioned anywhere on a page. You can choose to insert a pre-formatted text box that you customize with your own text, draw an empty text box and then fill it with text, or select existing text and then draw a text box around it. You use the Text Box button in the Text group or the Shapes button in the Illustrations group on the Insert tab to create a text box. You draw a text box around the QST Mexico Destinations information, resize and position the text box on the page, and then format it using a text box style.

STEPS

1. **Select all the text in columns 2 and 3, including the heading and the last paragraph mark before the section break**

   The text in columns 2 and 3 is selected.

2. **Click the Insert tab, then click the Text Box button in the Text group**

   A gallery of preformatted text boxes and sidebars opens.

3. **Click Draw Text Box**

   The selected text is formatted as a text box, as shown in Figure F-9. When you draw a text box around existing text or graphics, the text box becomes part of the drawing layer (a floating object).

4. **Click the Text Box Tools Format tab, type 4.1 in the Shape Height text box in the Size group, type 4.65 in the Shape Width text box in the Size group, then press [Enter]**

   The text box is resized to be exactly 4.1" tall and 4.65" wide.

5. **Click the Position button in the Arrange group, then click Position in Bottom Right with Square Text Wrapping**

   The text box is moved to the lower-right corner of the page.

6. **Delete the paragraph mark above the pyramid photo, click the Show/Hide ¶ button ¶ in the Paragraph group on the Home tab, then double-click the text box frame with the ⬚ pointer**

   Double-clicking the text box frame selects the text box and activates the Text Box Tools Format tab. Clicking inside a text box with the I pointer moves the insertion point inside the text box so the text can be edited.

7. **Click the More button ▾ in the Text Box Styles group, move the pointer over the styles in the gallery to preview them applied to the text box, then click Diagonal Gradient – Accent 1**

   A style that includes green gradient shading, a thin green border, and a slight shadow is applied to the text box. You can also create your own designs using the Shape Fill and Shape Outline buttons in the Text Box Styles group.

8. **Click the Shadow On/Off button ▨ in the Shadow Effects group**

   The shadow is removed from the text box.

9. **Place the insertion point in the paragraph above the pyramid photo, click the Insert tab, click the Drop Cap button in the Text group, click Drop Cap Options, click Dropped in the Position section, click the Font list arrow, scroll down, click Segoe Script, click the Lines to drop up arrow once, click the Distance from text up arrow once, click OK, deselect the drop cap, then save your changes**

   A drop cap is added to the paragraph. Compare your document to Figure F-10.

Illustrating Documents with Graphics

FIGURE F-9: Text box

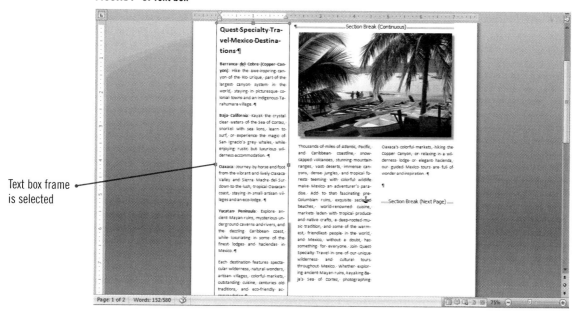

Text box frame is selected

FIGURE F-10: Formatted text box and drop cap

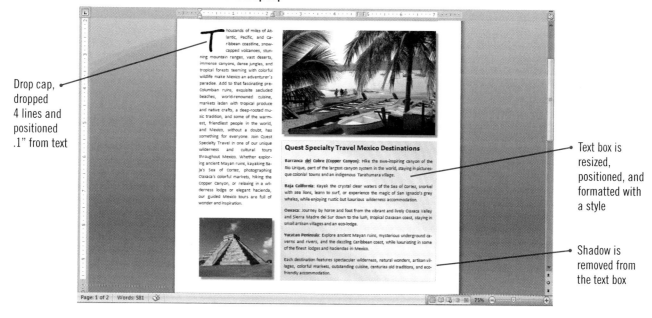

Drop cap, dropped 4 lines and positioned .1" from text

Text box is resized, positioned, and formatted with a style

Shadow is removed from the text box

Linking text boxes

If you are working on a longer document, you might want text to begin in a text box on one page and then continue in a text box on another page. By creating a **link** between two or more text boxes, you can force text to flow automatically from one text box to another, allowing you to size and format the text boxes any way you wish. To link two or more text boxes, you must first create the original text box, fill it with text, and then create a second, empty text box. Then, to create the link, select the first text box, click the

Create Link button in the Text group on the Text Box Tools Format tab to activate the pointer, and then click the second text box with the pointer. Any overflow text from the first text box flows seamlessly into the second text box. As you resize the first text box, the flow of text adjusts automatically between the two linked text boxes. If you want to break a link between two linked text boxes so that all the text is contained in the original text box, select the original text box, and then click the Break Link button in the Text group.

Creating WordArt

Another way to give your documents punch and flair is to use WordArt. **WordArt** is a drawing object that contains text formatted with special shapes, patterns, and orientations. You create WordArt using the WordArt button in the Text group on the Insert tab. Once you have created a WordArt object, you can use the buttons on the WordArt Tools Format tab to change its shape, font, colors, borders, shadows, and other effects to create the impact you desire. You use WordArt to create an impressive heading for the flyer.

STEPS

1. **Press [Ctrl][Home], click the View tab, click the Page Width button in the Zoom group, triple-click Adventure Mexico to select it, click the Insert tab, then click the WordArt button in the Text group**

   The WordArt Gallery opens. It includes the styles you can choose for your WordArt.

2. **Click WordArt style 14 (the second style in the third row)**

   The Edit WordArt Text dialog box opens. You enter or edit the text you want to format as WordArt in this dialog box and, if you wish, change the font and font size of the WordArt text.

3. **Click OK**

   The WordArt object appears at the location of the insertion point and the WordArt Tools Format tab becomes the active tab. Like other graphic objects, the WordArt object is an inline graphic until you wrap text around it. Since the object is located where you want it, aligned with the top margin, you decide to leave it as an inline graphic.

4. **Type 7 in the Shape Width text box in the Size group, press [Enter], then click the Shape Height down arrow once**

   The WordArt is enlarged to span the page between the left and right margins.

5. **Click the Spacing button in the Text group, click Tight, click the Even Height button [Aa] in the Text group, click the Change WordArt Shape button in the WordArt Styles group, then click Double Wave 2**

   The spacing between the characters is decreased, the characters become a uniform height, and the shape of the WordArt text changes, as shown in Figure F-11.

6. **Click the More button ⊽ in the WordArt Styles group, point to several styles in the gallery to see a preview in the document, then click WordArt style 13 (the first style in the third row)**

   The style of the WordArt object changes.

7. **Click the Shape Fill list arrow in the WordArt Styles group, point to Gradient, then click More Gradients**

   The Fill Effects dialog box opens, as shown in Figure F-12. You use this dialog box to change the fill colors and effects of the WordArt object. Using the Gradient tab, you can select a preset gradient effect or choose colors and shading styles to create your own gradient effect. You can also apply a preset texture using the Texture tab, design a two-color pattern using the Pattern tab, or fill the object with a graphic using the Picture tab.

8. **Make sure the Two colors option button is selected in the Colors section on the Gradient tab, click the Color 1 list arrow, click Light Blue, Accent 5, click the Color 2 list arrow, click Lime, Accent 1, click the Diagonal up option button in the Shading styles section, click the lower-right box in the Variants section, click OK, deselect the object, then save your changes**

   The new fill effects are applied to the WordArt, as shown in Figure F-13.

WordArt object is enlarged

Double Wave 2 shape applied

Upper- and lower-case characters are the same height

FIGURE F-12: Fill Effects dialog box

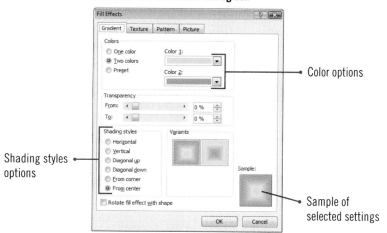

Color options

Shading styles options

Sample of selected settings

FIGURE F-13: Completed WordArt object

Customized WordArt style

Explore Wild Mexico with Quest Specialty Travel

Thousands of miles of Atlantic, Pacific, and Caribbean coastline, snow-capped volcanoes, stunning mountain ranges, vast deserts, immense canyons, dense jungles, and tropical forests teeming with colorful wildlife make Mexico an adventurer's paradise. Add to that fascinating pre-Columbian ruins, exquisite secluded beaches, world-renowned cuisine,

Enhancing an object with shadows and 3-D effects

A fun way to enliven the look of a WordArt or other graphic object is to enhance it with a shadow or three-dimensional effect. The commands in the Shadow Effects group on the active Format tab for that type of object give you the power to apply a variety of shadow styles to an object, change the color of a shadow, and nudge a shadow up, down, right, or left to fine-tune the shadow's placement and depth. The 3-D Effects command on the Format tab is a powerful feature that allows you not only to select from a variety of 3-D styles for an object, but to adjust the tilt, color, direction, and depth of the 3-D effect. In addition, you can alter the direction and intensity of the lighting cast on the object, and change the surface of the 3-D effect to have a matte look, or to resemble plastic, metal, or wire. The best way to learn about shadow and three-dimensional effects is to experiment by applying the effects to an object and seeing what works.

Drawing Shapes

One way you can create your own graphics in Word is to draw shapes. **Shapes** are the rectangles, ovals, lines, callouts, block arrows, stars, banners, hearts, suns, and other drawing objects you can create using the Shapes command in the Illustrations group on the Insert tab. Once you draw a shape, you can add colors, borders, fill effects, shadows, and three-dimensional effects to it to make it come alive in a document. ██████ You use the Shapes feature to draw a Mayan pyramid in the document.

STEPS

1. **Scroll to the bottom of the document, click the Insert tab, click the Shapes button in the Illustrations group, then click Bevel in the Basic Shapes section of the Shapes menu**
   The Shapes menu contains categories of shapes and lines that you can draw. When you click a shape in the Shapes menu, the pointer changes to ╋. You draw a shape by clicking and dragging with this pointer.

2. **Position the ╋ pointer in the blank area at the bottom of the page, press [Shift], then drag down and to the right to create a square bevel that is approximately 2" tall and wide**
   Pressing [Shift] as you drag creates a bevel that is perfectly square. When you release the mouse button, sizing handles appear around the bevel to indicate it is selected, as shown in Figure F-14.

3. **Click the Bevel shape in the Insert Shapes group, place the ╋ pointer exactly over the inside upper-left corner of the last bevel you drew, press [Shift], drag down and to the right to create a square bevel that fills the inside of the previous bevel, then repeat this step to create two more bevel shapes inside the stack of bevels**
   When you are finished, the stack of bevels looks like an aerial view of a pyramid.

4. **With the inside bevel still selected, press and hold [Ctrl], click the other three bevel shapes to select them, click the Group button ⊞▾ in the Arrange group, then click Group**
   Grouping converts multiple shapes into a single object that can be sized, positioned, and formatted together.

5. **Click the More button ▾ in the Insert Shapes group, click Sun in the Basic Shapes section, place the ╋ pointer in the upper-left inside corner of the inside bevel, then drag down and to the right to create a sun that fills the top of the pyramid**
   The sun shape includes a yellow diamond-shaped **adjustment handle**.

6. **Position the pointer over the adjustment handle until it changes to ▷, drag the handle to the right about ⅛", click the Shape Fill list arrow ◆▾ in the Shape Styles group, then click Gold, Accent 3**
   The sun shape becomes narrower and filled with color.

7. **Click ▾ in the Insert Shapes group, click Rectangle in the Basic Shapes section, place the ╋ pointer over the topmost horizontal line in the pyramid, draw a rectangle similar to that shown in Figure F-15, click ◆▾, click Pattern, click the fourth pattern in the second row, click the Foreground Color list arrow, click Blue, Accent 4, then click OK**
   The rectangle is filled with thin blue lines that resemble stairs, as shown in Figure F-15.

8. **With the rectangle selected, press and hold [Ctrl], click the grouped bevel shape and the sun shape to select them, click ⊞▾, click Group, click the Shape Outline list arrow ✎▾ in the Shape Styles group, then click Blue, Accent 4**
   The pyramid shape, sun shape, and rectangle are grouped into a single object, and the lines change to blue.

9. **Click the Rotate button ⟳▾ in the Arrange group, click Rotate Right 90°, then press [F4]**
   The pyramid drawing is rotated 180°. You can also rotate a graphic by dragging the green rotate handle.

10. **Drag the pyramid drawing up to position it temporarily over the third column of text, as shown in Figure F-16, then save your changes**
    The drawing object is automatically formatted as a floating graphic with the In Front of Text wrapping style applied, making it part of the drawing layer. You will finalize the object's position in a later lesson.

QUICK TIP
To draw a circle, click the Oval, then press [Shift] while you drag with the pointer.

TROUBLE
If the shape is not as expected, click the Undo button on the Quick Access toolbar and try again.

QUICK TIP
Drag an adjustment handle to modify the shape, but not the size, of a shape.

QUICK TIP
To convert a shape to a text box, right-click it, then click Add Text.

QUICK TIP
Use the Bring to Front and Send to Back list arrows to shift the order of the layers in a stack of graphic objects.

Illustrating Documents with Graphics

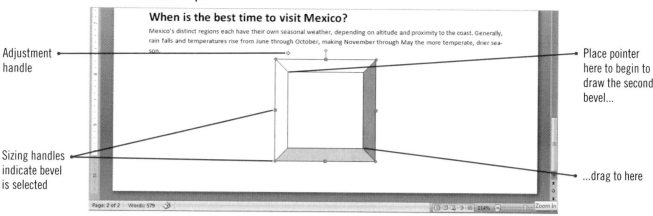
FIGURE F-14: Bevel shape

Adjustment handle

Sizing handles indicate bevel is selected

Place pointer here to begin to draw the second bevel...

...drag to here

FIGURE F-15: Rectangle added to pyramid

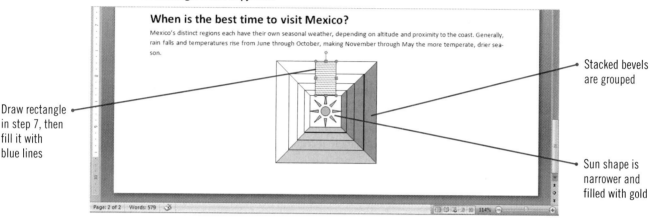

Draw rectangle in step 7, then fill it with blue lines

Stacked bevels are grouped

Sun shape is narrower and filled with gold

FIGURE F-16: Rotated drawing

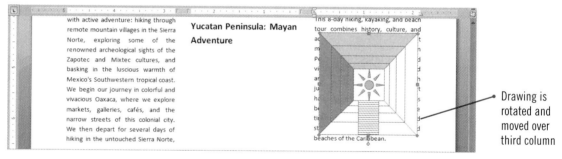

Drawing is rotated and moved over third column

Creating an illustration in a drawing canvas

A **drawing canvas** is a workspace for creating your own graphics. It provides a frame-like boundary between an illustration and the rest of the document so that the illustration can be sized, formatted, and positioned like a single graphic object. If you are creating an illustration that includes multiple shapes, such as a flow chart, it is helpful to create the illustration in a drawing canvas. To draw shapes or lines in a drawing canvas, click the Shapes button in the Illustrations group, click New Drawing Canvas to open a drawing canvas in the document, and then create and format your illustration in the drawing canvas. When you are finished, right-click the drawing canvas

and then click Fit to automatically resize the drawing canvas to fit the illustration. Right-click the drawing canvas again and click Scale Drawing to change the cropping handles on the drawing canvas to sizing handles that you can use to resize the illustration. Once you have resized a drawing canvas, you can wrap text around it and position it by using the Ribbon or dragging the drawing canvas frame. By default, a drawing canvas has no border or background so that it is transparent in a document, but you can add fill and borders to it if you wish.

Creating a Chart

Adding a chart can be an attractive way to illustrate a document that includes numerical information. A **chart** is a visual representation of numerical data and usually is used to illustrate trends, patterns, or relationships. The Word chart feature allows you to create many types of charts, including bar, column, pie, area, and line charts. To create a chart, you use the Chart button in the Illustrations group on the Insert tab. ██████ You create a chart that shows the average temperature for each season in the four geographic areas where QST Mexico tours are located.

STEPS

1. **Press [Ctrl][End], click the Insert tab, then click the Chart button in the Illustrations group**
   The Insert Chart dialog box opens. You use this dialog box to select the type and style of chart you intend to create. The chart types are listed in the left pane of the dialog box, and the styles for each chart type are listed in the right pane. You want to create a simple column chart.

QUICK TIP
Click the Change Chart Type button in the Type group on the Chart Tools Design tab to change the type of chart.

2. **Click OK**
   A worksheet opens in a Microsoft Excel window and a column chart appears in the Word document. The worksheet and the chart contain placeholder data that you replace with your own data. The chart is based on the data in the worksheet. Any change you make to the data is made automatically to the chart.

3. **Drag the scroll box down to the bottom of the Word document, then click an empty cell in the Excel worksheet**
   The pointer changes to ✛. You use this pointer to select the cells in the worksheet. The blue lines in the worksheet indicate the range of data to include in the chart.

4. **Move the pointer over the lower-right corner of the blue box, when the pointer changes to ◥ drag the range one column to the right, then release the mouse button**
   The range is enlarged to include five columns and five rows.

TROUBLE
Click the Edit Data button in the Data group on the Chart Tools Design tab to open the worksheet and edit the chart data.

5. **Click the Category 1 cell, type Baja California, click the Category 2 cell, type Oaxaca, press [Enter], type Copper Canyon, replace the remaining placeholder text with the data shown in Figure F-17, click an empty cell, then click the Close button in the Excel window**
   When you click a cell and type, the data in the cell is replaced with the text you type. As you edit the worksheet, the changes you make are reflected in the chart.

6. **Click the chart border to select the object if necessary, click the More button ▼ in the Chart Styles group on the Chart Tools Design tab, then click Style 26**
   A chart style is applied to the chart.

QUICK TIP
Point to any part of a chart to see a ScreenTip that identifies the part.

7. **Click the Layout tab, click the Chart Title button in the Labels group, click Above Chart, type Average Temperature, click the Axis Titles button in the Labels group, point to Primary Vertical Axis Title, click Rotated Title, then type Degrees Celsius**
   A chart title and vertical axis title are added to the chart.

8. **Click the Legend button in the Labels group, then click Show Legend at Top**
   The legend moves above the chart.

QUICK TIP
To change the formatting of any chart element, select it, then click the Format Selection button in the Current Selection group to open the Format Chart Element dialog box.

9. **Right-click Yucatan to select the Horizontal axis, click the Shrink Font button ᴀˇ on the Mini toolbar, right-click the chart title, then click ᴀˇ twice**
   The font sizes of the destination names in the horizontal axis and the chart title are reduced. You can also click a chart element in the chart to select it.

10. **Click the border of the chart object to select the chart area, click the Format tab, click the More button ▼ in the Shape Styles group, click Colored Outline, Dark 1, type 2.5 in the Shape Height text box in the Size group, type 4.1 in the Shape Width text box in the Size group, press [Enter], deselect the chart, then save your changes**
    The completed chart is shown in Figure F-18.

FIGURE F-17: Chart object in Word and worksheet in Excel

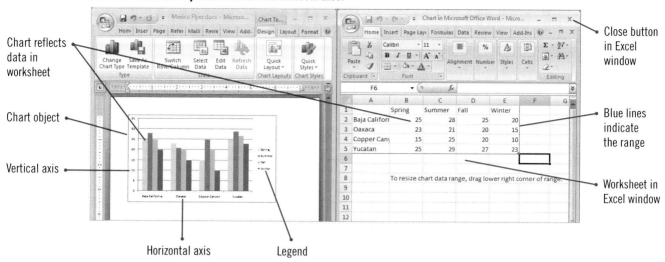

Chart reflects data in worksheet

Chart object

Vertical axis

Horizontal axis

Legend

Close button in Excel window

Blue lines indicate the range

Worksheet in Excel window

FIGURE F-18: Completed chart

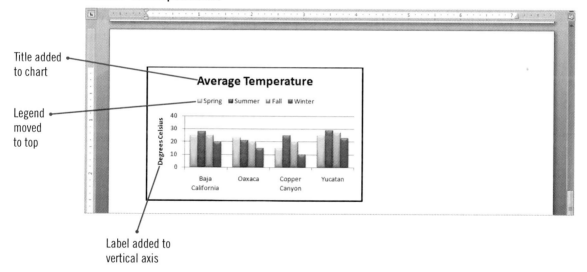

Title added to chart

Legend moved to top

Label added to vertical axis

Creating SmartArt graphics

Diagrams are another way to illustrate concepts in your documents. The powerful Word **SmartArt** feature makes it easy for you to quickly create and format many types of diagrams, including pyramid, target, cycle, and radial diagrams, as well as lists and organization charts. To insert a SmartArt graphic in a document, click the SmartArt button in the Illustrations group on the Insert tab to open the Choose a SmartArt Graphic dialog box. In this dialog box, select a category of diagrams in the left pane, select a specific diagram layout and design in the middle pane, preview the selected diagram layout in the right pane, and then click OK. The SmartArt object appears in the document with placeholder text, and the SmartArt Tools Design and Format tabs are enabled. These tabs contain commands and styles for customizing and formatting the SmartArt graphic and for sizing and positioning the graphic in the document.

Finalizing Page Layout

When you finish creating the illustrations for a document, it is time to fine-tune the position and formatting of the text and graphics on each page. One way to vary the layout of a page that includes many graphics is to format some of the graphic elements in a text box. ▓▓▓▓▓ You format the Mexico weather information in a text box and adjust the size and position of the other graphic objects so that the text flows smoothly between the columns. Finally, you add a small text box that includes the QST address.

STEPS

1. **Move the pointer to the top of page 3, double-click with the ⊞ pointer, scroll up, move the pointer to the left margin, then drag the ⟋ pointer to select the heading** When is the best time..., **the** paragraph **under it, and the** chart object

2. **Click the** Insert tab, **click the** Text Box button, **click** Draw Text Box, **click the** View tab, **click the** One Page button **in the Zoom group, double-click the** top of the page **with the ⊞ pointer, then scroll as needed so the text box is visible on your screen**
   The heading, body text, and chart object are moved into a text box.

TROUBLE
Don't be concerned if your text box jumps to another location.

3. **Right-click the** chart object, **click the** Center button ▤ **on the Mini toolbar, double-click the** text box frame, **type** 4.1 **in the Shape Height text box in the Size group, type** 4.65 **in the Shape Width text box, then press [Enter]**
   The chart object is centered in the text box and the text box is resized.

4. **Scroll to display all of page 2, then with the text box selected, click the** Position button **in the Arrange group, click** Position in Bottom Left..., **click the** More button ▾ **in the Text Box Styles group, then click** Horizontal Gradient – Accent 5
   The text box is moved to the lower-left corner of page 2, the text wraps around it, and a style is applied.

5. **Click the** View tab, **click the** Gridlines check box **in the Show/Hide group, click the** Page Width button **in the Zoom group, then scroll down to view the bottom of the page**
   Non-printing **drawing gridlines** appear within the document margins in Print Layout view. You use drawing gridlines to help you size, align, and position objects.

QUICK TIP
You can confirm or modify the size of the selected object by checking the height and width measurements in the Size group on the Drawing Tools Format tab.

6. **Double-click the** pyramid drawing **to select it, drag the object down using the ⬚ pointer onto a blank area of the drawing grid, press [Shift], then with the ⟋ pointer, drag the lower-left sizing handle up and to the right until the object is about** 1" square
   Use the ruler and the gridlines to help judge the size of the object as you drag.

7. **Drag the object to position it as shown in Figure F-19**
   You can nudge the drawing with the arrow keys if necessary to position it more precisely on the grid.

QUICK TIP
To align two or more objects to each other, select the objects, click the Align button in the Arrange group, then select an option.

8. **Click the** Text Box button **in the Insert Shapes group, click under the pyramid with the ＋ pointer, resize the new text box similar to Figure F-19, click the** More button ▾ **in the Text Box Styles group, then click** Horizontal Gradient – Accent 2
   Clicking with the ＋ pointer inserts a 1" square text box. After resizing the text box, it should be approximately .9" tall and 2.1" wide and aligned with the column and the bottom margin.

TROUBLE
Reduce the font size of the text in the text box if all the text doesn't fit.

9. **Click** inside the text box, **right-click, then using the Mini toolbar, click the** Style list arrow ▾, **click** No Spacing, **click the** Center button ▤, **click the** Bold button **B**, **and then type the text shown in Figure F-19 in the text box**
   Figure F-19 shows the pyramid drawing reduced and repositioned and the new text box.

10. **Click the** View tab, **click the** Gridlines check box, **click the** Two Pages button, **save your changes, print the file, then close the file and exit Word**
   The completed document is shown in Figure F-20.

FIGURE F-19: Repositioned object and new text box

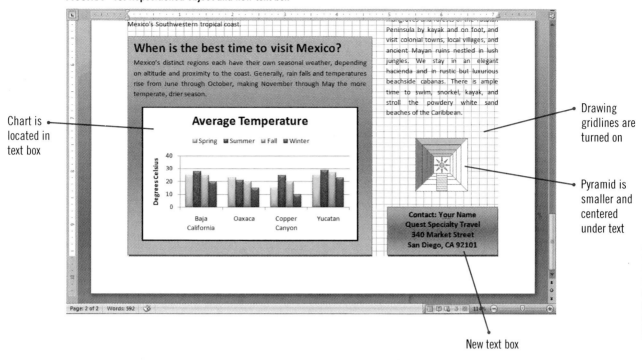

Chart is located in text box

Drawing gridlines are turned on

Pyramid is smaller and centered under text

New text box

FIGURE F-20: Completed flyer

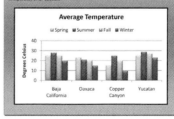

Practice

If you have a SAM user profile, you may have access to hands-on instruction, practice, and assessment of the skills covered in this unit. Log in to your SAM account (http://sam2007.course.com/) to launch any assigned training activities or exams that relate to the skills covered in this unit.

▼ CONCEPTS REVIEW

Label the elements shown in Figure F-21.

FIGURE F-21

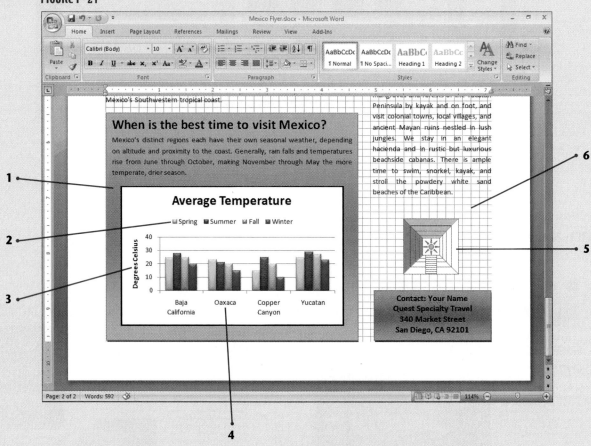

Match each term with the statement that best describes it.

7. Brightness
8. WordArt
9. Drawing gridlines
10. Drawing canvas
11. Floating graphic
12. Text box
13. Chart
14. Contrast

a. Nonprinting lines that are used to align, size, and position objects
b. A graphic to which a text wrapping style has been applied
c. The relative lightness of a picture
d. A graphic object that is a container for text and graphics
e. A workspace for creating graphics
f. A visual representation of numerical data
g. A graphic object composed of specially formatted text
h. The difference between the darkest and lightest areas in a picture

Select the best answer from the list of choices.

15. **Which button is used to change an inline graphic to a floating graphic?**
    a. Position
    b. Bring to Front
    c. Send to Back
    d. Change Picture

16. **Which button is used to change a photograph to sepia tone?**
    a. Brightness
    b. Contrast
    c. Recolor
    d. Picture Effects

17. **What do you drag to change a drawing object's shape, but not its size or dimensions?**
    a. Rotate handle
    b. Cropping handle
    c. Sizing handle
    d. Adjustment handle

18. **Which method do you use to nudge a picture?**
    a. Select the picture, then press an arrow key.
    b. Select the picture, then drag a corner sizing handle.
    c. Select the picture, then drag it to a new location.
    d. Select the picture, then drag a top, bottom, or side sizing handle.

19. **Which is not an example of a Fill Effect?**
    a. Texture
    b. Pattern
    c. Gradient
    d. Glow

20. **What style of text wrapping is applied to a shape by default?**
    a. Square
    b. In line with text
    c. In front of text
    d. Tight

▼ SKILLS REVIEW

1. **Insert a graphic.**
    a. Start Word, open the file WD F-2.docx from the drive and folder where you store your Data Files, then save it as **Stone Barn CSA Flyer**.
    b. Display formatting marks, scroll down, read the document to get a feel for its contents and formatting, then press [Ctrl][Home].
    c. Select the vegetables photo on page 1, apply square text wrapping, then apply the picture style Simple Frame, Black to the photo.
    d. Use the Format Painter to copy the format settings from the vegetables photo to the photo of the boy, then apply square text wrapping to the photo of the boy.
    e. Scroll down, place the insertion point at the top of page 2, insert the file Stone Barn.jpg from the drive and folder where you store your Data Files, then save your changes.

2. **Size and scale a graphic.**
    a. With the Stone Barn photo still selected, click the Crop button in the Size group.
    b. Drag the bottom-middle cropping handle up approximately 1", drag the top-middle cropping handle down approximately .5", verify that the photo is approximately 2.8" tall, adjust if necessary using the cropping handles, then click the Crop button again.
    c. Deselect the photo, then scroll to page 1.
    d. Resize the vegetable photo proportionally so that it is about 2.7" high and 1.8" wide.
    e. Resize the photo of the boy proportionally so that it is about 1.7" high and 1.1" wide.
    f. Scroll to page 2, then resize the photo of the scale proportionally to be precisely 2.7" high.
    g. Press [Ctrl][Home], then save your changes.

3. **Position a graphic.**
    a. Drag the vegetable photo up so its top is aligned with the first line of body text and its right side is aligned with the right margin.
    b. Change the zoom level to Whole Page, then use the Position command to align the photo of the boy with the middle of the left margin.

   c. Scroll to page 2, use the Position command to align the scale photo with the bottom and right margins, then save your changes.

4. Create a text box.

   a. Change the zoom level to Page Width, then scroll to the top of page 1.

   b. Add a drop cap using the default settings for the Dropped option to the first body paragraph, then change the font color of the drop cap to Dark Green, Accent 4.

   c. Select the heading What does Stone Barn Community Farm do?, the paragraph under it, and the two paragraph marks above the page break, then insert a text box.

   d. Delete the paragraph mark after 7 p.m. in the last line of body text on page 1.

   e. Apply the text box style Horizontal Gradient – Accent 4 to the text box, use the Position command to align it with the bottom and right margins, then drag the anchor symbol to the How does it work? paragraph. (*Hint*: The anchor symbol is over the photo of the boy.)

   f. Scroll to page 2, then draw a text box over the bottom of the Stone Barn photo that spans the width of the photo and is approximately .4" high.

   g. Type **Welcome to Stone Barn Community Farm – A USDA Certified Organic Farm** in the text box, center the text, change the font to 12-point Arial Rounded MT Bold, then change the font color to Orange, Accent 1, Lighter 80%.

   h. Remove the fill from the text box, adjust the placement of the text box as necessary so the text is attractively placed over the bottom of the photo, then remove the border from the text box.

   i. Scroll down, select all the green and brown text, then insert a text box.

   j. Resize the text box to be approximately 2.7" tall and 5.4" wide, align it with the lower-left corner of the page, then remove the border from the text box.

   k. Turn off paragraph marks, then save your changes.

5. Create WordArt.

   a. Press [Ctrl][Home], triple-click to select Stone Barn Community Farm, insert a WordArt object, select any horizontal WordArt style, then click OK.

   b. Resize the WordArt object to be 7.1" wide and 1.1" tall, then center it between the margins.

   c. Open the WordArt Gallery, then change the style to WordArt style 11.

   d. Change the fill of the object to the texture Green marble.

   e. Change the border color to Dark Green, Accent 4, Lighter 40%.

   f. Change the shadow color to Orange, Accent 1, Darker 25%, then save your changes.

6. Draw shapes.

   a. Scroll down to the middle of page 2, select the three-line address, then draw a text box around it.

   b. Move the text box approximately ¾" to the right.

   c. Click the Shapes button, then click the Sun shape.

   d. In a blank area, draw a sun that is approximately .5" tall and wide.

   e. Fill the sun with Orange, Accent 1, apply the gradient style From Center in the Light Variations section, then change the border color to Dark Green, Accent 4.

   f. Move the sun left of the address text box if necessary, then remove the border from the address text box.

   g. Click the Shapes button in the Illustrations group on the Insert tab, then click Rounded rectangle.

   h. Draw a rounded rectangle around the sun and the address, then click the Send to Back button.

   i. Adjust the size of the rectangle to resemble an address label, then save your changes.

7. Create a chart.

   a. Scroll up, place the insertion point in the text box on page 1, press [▼] many times as necessary to move the insertion point to the last line in the text box.

   b. Insert a chart, select Bar chart, select Clustered Bar for the style, then click OK.

c. Type the information shown in Figure F-22, adjust the range to include just the columns and rows that include data, then close Excel.

d. Apply the chart style Style 22 to the chart.

e. Select the chart title text, type Harvest Sales, change the font of the title to 12-point Arial Rounded MT Bold, remove the bold formatting, then change the font color to Orange, Accent 1, Darker 25%.

f. Click the Legend button, then remove the legend from the chart.

g. Click the Axes button, point to Primary Horizontal Axis, then click More Primary Horizontal Axis Options to open the Format Axis dialog box.

h. Click Number in the Left pane, select Percentage in the Category list, change the number of decimal places to 0, then click Close.

i. Resize the chart object to be approximately 2" tall and 3.3" wide, center the chart object in the text box, then save your changes.

FIGURE F-22

	A	B	C
1		Series 1	
2	CSA	0.42	
3	U-Pick	0.09	
4	Farm Stand	0.2	
5	Farmers' Market	0.22	
6	Other	0.07	
7			

8. Finalize page layout.

a. Resize the text box that includes the chart to be approximately 3.2" tall and 4.4" wide.

b. Scroll up to page 1, turn on the drawing gridlines in the Show/Hide group on the View tab, then change the zoom level to One Page.

c. Select the vegetable photo, then use the arrow keys to nudge the photo so it extends approximately ¼" outside the right margin.

d. Select the photo of the boy, then use the arrow keys to nudge the photo so it extends approximately ¼" outside the left margin.

e. Select the text box, then use arrow keys to nudge the text box so it extends approximately ¼" outside the right and bottom margins.

f. Using the mouse, carefully enlarge the vegetable photo by dragging the lower-left sizing handle out approximately ¼".

g. Using the mouse, carefully enlarge the photo of the boy by dragging the lower-right sizing handle out approximately ¼".

h. Continue to resize and shift the position of the photographs until all the text fits on page 1 and the layout of page 1 of the flyer looks similar to the completed flyer shown in Figure F-23. Your flyer does not need to match exactly.

i. Type your name in the document footer, save your changes, print the document, close the file, then exit Word.

FIGURE F-23

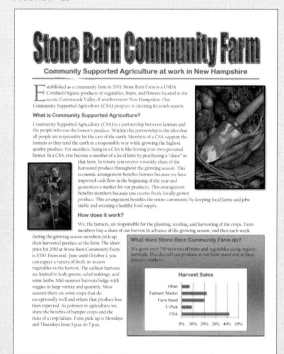

▼ INDEPENDENT CHALLENGE 1

Your company just completed a major survey of its customer base, and your boss has asked you to prepare a summary of the results for your colleagues. You create a chart for the summary that shows the distribution of customers by age and gender.

a. Start Word, then save a blank document as *Age and Gender Chart* to the location where you store your Data Files.

b. Type *Prepared by* followed by your name at the top of the document, press [Enter] twice, then insert a clustered column chart object into the document.

c. Enter the data shown in Figure F-24 into the worksheet. To begin, delete the data in rows 4 and 5 of the worksheet, and then adjust the range to include 5 columns and 3 rows. When you are finished, minimize the Excel window and maximize the Word window.

FIGURE F-24

	18-34	35-44	45-54	55+
Male	.11	.19	.09	.06
Female	.14	.22	.1	.09

d. Use the Switch Row/Column button in the Data group on the Design tab to switch the data so the age groups appear on the horizontal axis.

e. Apply a chart style to the chart, then add the title *Customers by Age and Gender* above the chart.

f. Move the legend to the left side of the chart, then add the horizontal axis title *Age Range*.

g. Click the Axes button, point to Primary Vertical Axis, then click More Primary Vertical Axis Options to open the Format Axis dialog box. Click Number in the Left pane, select Percentage in the Category list, change the number of decimal places to **0**, then click Close.

h. Use the Change Chart Type button in the Type group on the Design tab to change to a different type of column chart, taking care to choose an appropriate type for the data, then format the chart with styles, fills, outlines, and other effects so it is attractive and readable.

i. Save your changes, print the chart, close the file, then exit Word.

▼ INDEPENDENT CHALLENGE 2

You design ads for bestskivacations.com, a company that specializes in custom ski vacation packages. Your next assignment is to design a full-page ad for a travel magazine. Your ad needs to contain three photographs of ski vacation scenes, such as the photos shown in Figure F-25, the text "Your ski vacation begins here and now," and the Web address "www.bestskivacations.com." If you are performing the ACE steps, your ad will also include a company logo.

a. Start Word, then save a blank document as *Ski Ad* to the drive and folder where your Data Files are located.

b. Change all four page margins to .7".

c. Using keywords such as ski, snowboard, snow, and mountain, find and insert at least three appropriate clip art photographs into the document.

d. Using pencil and paper, sketch the layout for your ad.

e. Change the photos to floating graphics, then format them. You can crop, resize, move, and combine them with other design elements, or enhance them with styles, shapes, borders, and effects.

f. Using text boxes or WordArt, add the text *Your ski vacation begins here and now* and the Web address *www.bestskivacations.com* to the ad.

FIGURE F-25

Advanced Challenge Exercise

■ Using shapes and a text box, create a logo that includes a graphic and the company name bestskivacations.com.

■ Using the Fill Effects dialog box, fill the shapes with color, gradients, patterns, or textures.

■ Group the objects and resize the grouped object to suit your needs, then position the logo in the ad.

g. Adjust the layout, design, and colors in the ad as necessary. When you are satisfied with your ad, type your name in the document header, save your changes, print a copy, close the document, then exit Word.

▼ INDEPENDENT CHALLENGE 3

You are a graphic designer. The public library has hired you to design a bookmark for Literacy Week. Their only request is that the bookmark includes the words Literacy Week. You'll create three different bookmarks for the library.

a. Start Word, then save a blank document as **Literacy Bookmarks** to the location where you store your Data Files.

b. Change all four page margins to .7", change the page orientation to landscape, and change the zoom level to Whole Page.

c. Draw three rectangles. Resize the rectangles to be 6.5" tall x 2.5" wide and move them so they do not overlap. Each rectangle will become a bookmark.

d. In the first rectangle, design a bookmark using shapes.

e. In the second rectangle, design a bookmark using WordArt.

f. In the third rectangle, design a bookmark using clip art.

g. Format the bookmarks with fills, colors, lines, shapes, shadows, and other effects. Be sure to add the words **Literacy Week** to each bookmark.

Advanced Challenge Exercise

- ■ Fill one bookmark with a gradient, one with a texture, and one with a pattern. You might need to revise some aspects of the bookmarks you created in the previous steps.
- ■ To one bookmark, add a photograph and change the shape of the photograph.
- ■ To one bookmark, add curved, scribble, or freeform lines.

h. Type your name in the document header, save your changes, print, close the document, then exit Word.

▼ REAL LIFE INDEPENDENT CHALLENGE

One way to find graphic images to use in your documents is to download them from the Web. Many Web sites feature images that are in the public domain, which means they have no copyright restrictions and permission is not required to use the images. You are free to download these images and use them in your documents, although you must acknowledge the artist or identify the source. Other Web sites include images that are copyrighted and require written permission, and often payment, to use. Before downloading and using graphics from the Web, it's important to research and establish their copyright status and permission requirements. In this exercise you download photographs from the Web and research their copyright restrictions.

a. Start Word, then save a blank document as **Copyright Photos** to the drive and folder where you store your Data Files.

b. Type your name at the top of the page, press [Enter], then create a table with four rows and three columns. Type the following column headings in the header row: **Photo**, **URL**, **Copyright Restrictions**. You will fill this table with the photos you find on the Web and the copyright restrictions for those photos.

c. Use your favorite search engine to search the Web for photographs that you might use for your work or a personal project. Use the keywords **free photo archives** or **free public domain photos**. You can also add a keyword that describes the subject of the photos you want to find.

d. Find at least three Web sites that contain photos you could use in a document. Save a photo from each Web site to your computer, and note the URL and copyright restrictions. To save an image from a Web page, right-click the image, then click the appropriate command on the shortcut menu.

e. Insert the photos you saved from the Web in the Photo column of the table. Resize the photos proportionally so that they are no more than 1.5" tall or 1.5" wide. Wrap text around the photos and center them in the table cells.

f. Enter the URL and the copyright restrictions for the photos in the table. In the Copyright Restrictions column, indicate if the photo is copyrighted or in the public domain, and note the requirements for using that photo in a document.

g. Adjust the formatting of the table so it is easy to read, save your changes, print a copy, close the file, then exit Word.

VISUAL WORKSHOP

Using the file WD F-3.docx (located where you store your Data Files), create the flyer shown in Figure F-26. The photograph is a clip art image found using the keyword "surfer". (*Hints*: To wrap text around the photo, draw a rectangle, layer it behind the photo, remove the border, and then apply Square text wrapping to the rectangle. The photograph uses In Front of Text text wrapping and is formatted with a reflection (Full Reflection, 4 pt offset) and a bevel (Circle).) Type your name in the footer, save the flyer as **Surf Safe**, then print a copy.

FIGURE F-26

Follow the rules
All surfers need to follow basic safety rules before heading into the waves. The key to safe surfing is caution and awareness.

Study the surf
Always study the surf before going in. Select a safe beach with waves under 1 meter, and pick waves that are suitable for your ability.

Use a safe surfboard
A safe surfboard is a surfboard that suits your ability. Beginners need a big, thick surfboard for stability.

Dress appropriately and wear sunscreen
Wear a wet suit that is appropriate for the water temperature or a rash vest to help protect against UV rays. Wear at least SPF 30 broad spectrum sunscreen. Zinc cream also prevents sunburn and guards against UV rays.

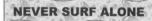

NEVER SURF ALONE

Recognize a rip current
A rip current is a volume of water moving out to sea: the bigger the surf, the stronger the rip. Indicators of rips include:
- Brown water from stirred up sand
- Foam on the surface of the water that trails past the break
- Waves breaking on both sides of a rip current
- A rippled appearance between calm water
- Debris floating out to sea

Learn how to escape rips
If you are dragged out by a rip, don't panic! Stay calm and examine the rip conditions before trying to escape the current. Poor swimmers should ride the rip out from the beach and then swim parallel to the shore for 30 or 40 meters. Once you have escaped the rip, swim toward the shore where the waves are breaking or probe with your feet to feel if a sand bar has formed near the edge of the rip. Strong swimmers should swim at a 45 degree angle across the rip.

Working with Themes and Building Blocks

The theme and building block features of Word 2007 streamline the process of designing a professional looking document. Document themes provide coordinated fonts, colors, and effects that you can apply to a document in one easy step, and building blocks offer dozens of preformatted document parts to insert and customize in a document. In this unit you learn how to work with themes, how to add and format sidebars and cover pages, and how to tailor preformatted content quickly and efficiently. You also learn how to create and save your own reusable building blocks for use in other documents. You are preparing a tour summary report for a new QST tour to Kenya. You create a customized theme for the report and simplify the process of designing the layout by using predesigned building blocks. Once the tour report is finished, you save the theme and several reusable pieces of customized content to use in other tour reports.

OBJECTIVES

Apply quick styles to text
Apply a theme
Customize a theme
Insert a sidebar
Insert quick parts
Add a cover page
Create building blocks
Insert building blocks

Applying Quick Styles to Text

Applying a style to text allows you to apply multiple format settings to text in one easy step. A **style** is a set of format settings, such as font, font size, font color, paragraph spacing, and alignment, that are named and stored together. Word includes many **Quick Style sets** — groups of related styles that share common fonts, colors, and formats, and are designed to be used together in a document — that you can use to give your documents a polished and cohesive look. Each Quick Style set includes styles for a title, subtitle, headings, body text, lists, quotes, and other text elements. ⬛⬛⬛⬛ You apply styles to the tour summary report to help organize the text attractively and make the report easy to read at a glance.

STEPS

1. **Start** Word, **open the file** WD G-1.docx **from the drive and folder where you store your Data Files, save it as** Mount Kenya Tour, **scroll the document to get a feel for its contents, then press** [Ctrl][Home]

   The four-page document includes text, photographs, and a chart.

QUICK TIP

To change the active Quick Style set, click the Change Styles button in the Styles group, point to Style Set, then click a new set.

2. **Select** Mount Kenya, Safari, and Beach, **click the** More button ⬇ **in the Styles group, then move the pointer over the styles in the Quick Styles gallery**

   As you move the pointer over a style in the gallery, a preview of that style is applied to the selected text.

3. **Click** Title

   The Title style is applied to selected text.

4. **Select** 15 days/14 nights, Nairobi to Mombasa, **click** Subtitle **in the Styles group, click the** Font Color list arrow ⬛ **in the Font group, then click** Olive Green, Accent 3, Darker 25%

   The Subtitle style is applied to the paragraph under the title, and then the font color is changed to olive green. You can modify the format of text to which a style has been applied without changing the style itself.

QUICK TIP

To change the color scheme or fonts used in the active Quick Style set, click the Change Styles button, point to Colors or Fonts, and then select from the options.

5. **Select** Tour Highlights, **click the** More button ⬇ **in the Styles group, click** Heading 1, **then deselect the text**

   The Heading 1 style is applied to the Tour Highlights heading, as shown in Figure G-1.

6. **Scroll down, then apply the** Heading 1 style **to each red heading in the document**

   The Heading 1 style is applied to the Tour Highlights, Tour Summary, Planning Your Trip, and What to Bring headings in the report.

7. **Scroll to page 2, select** Climate, **then click** Heading 2 **in the Styles group**

   The Heading 2 style is applied to the Climate subheading. The style seems too similar to the Heading 1 style for your purposes.

8. **Select** Climate **if necessary, click the** More button ⬇ **in the Styles group, click** Heading 3, **click the** Font Color list arrow ⬛, **click** Red, Accent 2, **then deselect the text**

   The Heading 3 style is applied to the Climate subheading, and the font color is changed to Red, Accent 2, as shown in Figure G-2.

9. **Scroll down, apply the** Heading 3 style **and the** Red, Accent 2 font color **to each purple subheading in the document, then save your changes**

   The Heading 3 style and the Red, Accent 2 font color are applied to the Climate, Visa and Vaccination Requirements, Luggage, Clothing and Footwear, and Equipment subheadings in the report.

FIGURE G-1: Styles applied to the report

Title style applied

Subtitle style applied and font color changed to green

Heading 1 style applied

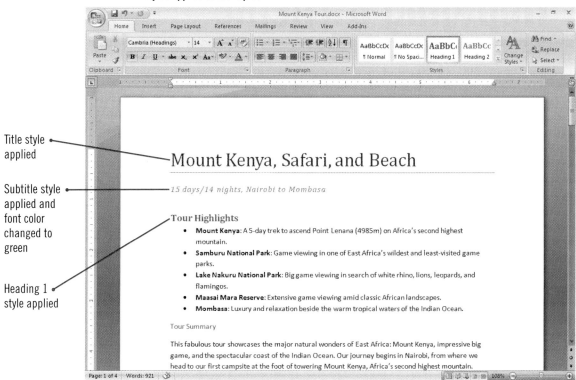

FIGURE G-2: Heading 3 style

Heading 3 style applied and font color changed to red

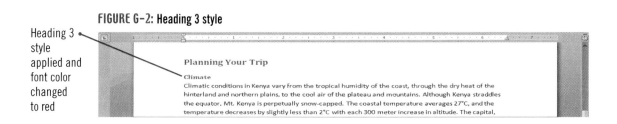

Saving a document as a Web page

Creating a Web page and posting it on the Internet or an intranet is a powerful way to share information with other people. You can design a Web page from scratch in Word, or you can use the Save As command to save an existing document in HTML format so it can be viewed with a browser. When you save an existing document as a Web page, Word converts the content and formatting of the Word file to HTML and displays the Web page in Web Layout view, which shows the Web page as it will appear in a browser. Any formatting that is not supported by Web browsers is either converted to similar supported formatting or removed from the Web page. For example, if you save a document that contains a floating graphic in HTML format, the graphic will be left- or right-aligned on the Web page. To be able to position text and graphics precisely on a document you plan to save as a Web page, it's best to create a table in the document, and then insert text and graphics in the table cells.

To save a document as a Web page, open the Save As dialog box, and then select a Web page format in the Save as type list box. You have the option of saving the document in Single File Web Page (.mht or .mhtml) format or in Web Page (.htm or .html) format. In a single file Web page, all the elements of the Web page, including the text and graphics, are saved together in a single MIME encapsulated aggregate HTML (MHTML) file, making it simple to publish your Web page or send it via e-mail. By contrast, if you choose to save a Web page as an .htm file, Word automatically creates a supporting folder in the same location as the .htm file. This folder has the same name as the .htm file plus the suffix _files, and it houses the supporting files associated with the Web page, such as graphics.

Applying a Theme

Changing the theme applied to a document is another quick way to set the tone of a document and give it a polished and cohesive appearance, particularly if the text and any tables, charts, shapes, SmartArt objects, or text boxes in the document are formatted with styles. A **theme** is a set of unified design elements, including theme colors, theme fonts for body text and headings, and theme effects for graphics. By default, all documents that you create in Word are formatted with the Office theme, but you can easily apply a different built-in theme to a document. To apply a theme to a document, you use the Themes command in the Themes group on the Page Layout tab. You experiment with different built-in themes and then apply a theme that more closely suits the message you want to convey with the tour summary report.

STEPS

1. **Press [Ctrl][Home], click the Page Layout tab, click the Themes button in the Themes group, then point to Aspect**

   A gallery of built-in Themes opens. When you point to the Aspect theme in the gallery, a preview of the theme is applied to the document, as shown in Figure G-3.

2. **Move the pointer over each theme in the gallery**

   When you point to a theme in the gallery, a preview of the theme is applied to the document. Notice that the font colors and the fonts for the body text and headings to which a style has been applied change when you preview each theme.

3. **Click Opulent, then scroll down to view the theme applied to each page in the document**

   A complete set of new theme colors, fonts, styles, and effects is applied to the document. Notice that while the font of the body text changed, the bold formatting applied to the text under the Tour Highlights heading at the top of page 1 remains. Changing the document theme does not affect the formatting of text to which font formatting has been applied. Only document content that uses theme colors, text that is formatted with a style (including default body text), and table styles and graphic effects change when a new theme is applied.

QUICK TIP
To restore the document to the default theme for the template on which the document is based, click the Themes button, and then click Reset to Theme from Template.

4. **Click the View tab, click the Two Pages button in the Zoom group, then scroll down to see pages 3 and 4**

   The fill effect in the chart at the bottom of the last page is changed to a fill effect from the Opulent theme, as shown in Figure G-4.

5. **Click the Page Layout tab, click the Themes button, then point to each built-in theme in the gallery**

   Notice how each theme affects the formatting of the chart, and, in some cases, the pagination of the document. It's important to choose a theme that not only mirrors the tone, content, and purpose of your document, but also meets your goal for document length.

6. **Click Median**

   The Median theme is applied to the document.

7. **Click the View tab, click the Page Width button in the Zoom group, press [Ctrl][Home], then save your changes**

FIGURE G-3: Aspect theme previewed in document

Aspect theme •

Themes • gallery

Preview of • Aspect theme applied to document

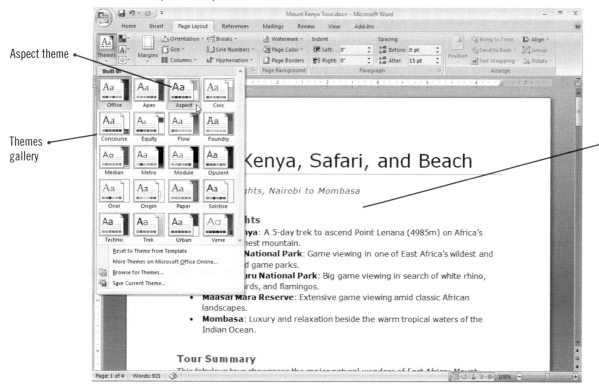

FIGURE G-4: Opulent theme applied to document

Fonts and • colors used in Opulent theme

Chart shows • fill effects from Opulent theme

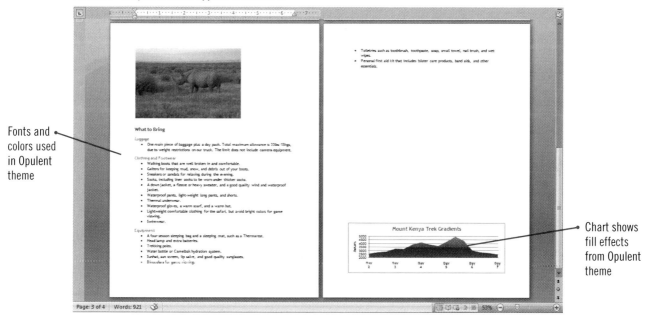

Changing the default theme

By default, all new documents created in Word are formatted with the Office theme, but you can change your settings to use a different theme as the default. To change the default theme to a different built-in or custom theme, press [Ctrl][N] to open a new blank document, click the Themes button in the Themes group on the Page Layout tab, and then click the theme you want to use as the default. If you want to customize the theme before saving it as the new default, use the Theme Colors, Theme Fonts, and Theme Effects buttons in the Themes group to customize the settings for theme colors, fonts, and effects. Alternatively, click the Change Styles button in the Styles group on the Home tab, and then use the Style Set, Colors, and Fonts options to select a new style set, new colors, or new fonts to use in the new default theme. When you are satisfied with the settings for the new default theme, click the Change Styles button again, and then click Set as Default. The Themes gallery will be updated to reflect your changes.

Customizing a Theme

When one of the built-in Word themes is not just right for your document, you can customize the theme by changing the theme colors, selecting new theme fonts for headings and body text, and changing the theme effects. You can then save the customized theme as a new theme that you can apply to other documents. ▓▓▓▓ You tweak the theme colors, fonts, and effects in the active theme to create a new theme that uses the colors and textures of Kenya and employs fonts that are attractive and easy to read. You then save the settings as a new theme so you can apply the theme to all documents related to Kenya tours.

STEPS

1. **Click the Page Layout tab, then click the Theme Colors button** 🔳 **in the Themes group**
   The gallery of theme colors opens. You can select from a palette of built-in theme colors or choose to customize the colors in the active palette. You want a palette that picks up the colors of the Kenyan landscape used in the photographs in the tour report.

2. **Click Oriel, click the Theme Colors button** 🔳**, then click Create New Theme Colors**
   The Oriel colors are applied to the document and the Create New Theme Colors dialog box opens, as shown in Figure G-5. You use this dialog box to change the colors in the active palette and to save the set of colors you create with a new name.

3. **Click the Accent 3 list arrow, click More Colors, click the Custom tab in the Colors dialog box, type 155 in the Red text box, type 187 in the Green text box, type 89 in the Blue text box, then click OK**
   The Accent 3 color changes from dark red to olive green.

QUICK TIP
To remove a custom theme from the gallery, right-click the theme, then click Delete.

4. **Type Kenya in the Name text box in the dialog box, click Save, then click** 🔳
   The new color scheme is saved with the name Kenya, the red subtitle in the document changes to green, and the Kenya color scheme appears in the Custom section in the Theme Colors gallery. The Kenya colors can now be applied to any document.

5. **Click the document to close the Theme Colors gallery if necessary, click the Theme Fonts button** 🅰 **in the Themes group, scroll down the gallery of theme fonts, point to several options to preview the fonts applied to the document, then click Equity**
   The heading and body text fonts from the Equity theme are applied to the document.

6. **Click the Theme Fonts button** 🅰**, then click Create New Theme Fonts**
   The Create New Theme Fonts dialog box opens, as shown in Figure G-6. You use this dialog box to select different fonts for headings and body text, and to save the font combination as a new theme font set.

7. **Click the Heading font list arrow, scroll down, click Trebuchet MS, type Tour Reports in the Name text box in the dialog box, then click Save**
   The font of the headings in the report changes to Trebuchet MS, and the Tour Reports theme font set is added to the Custom section of the Theme Fonts gallery.

TROUBLE
Scroll down if necessary to see the chart.

8. **Press [Ctrl][End], click the Theme Effects button** 🔳 **in the Themes group, point to each effect in the gallery to see it previewed in the chart, then click Paper**
   The effects from the Paper theme are applied to the document.

9. **Click the Themes button, click Save Current Theme, type Kenya Tour Report in the File name text box in the Save Current Theme dialog box, then click Save**
   The Kenya theme colors, Tour Reports theme fonts, and theme effects from the Paper theme are saved together as a new theme called Kenya Tour Report in the default location for document themes.

10. **Save your changes, then click the Themes button**
    The new theme appears in the Custom section of the Themes gallery, as shown in Figure G-7.

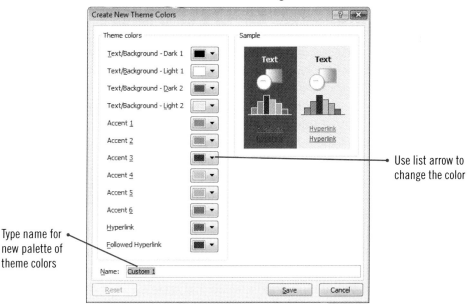

Type name for new palette of theme colors

Use list arrow to change the color

FIGURE G-6: Create New Theme Fonts dialog box

Select font for headings

Select font for body text

Type name for new set of theme fonts

Preview fonts

FIGURE G-7: Custom theme in the Themes gallery

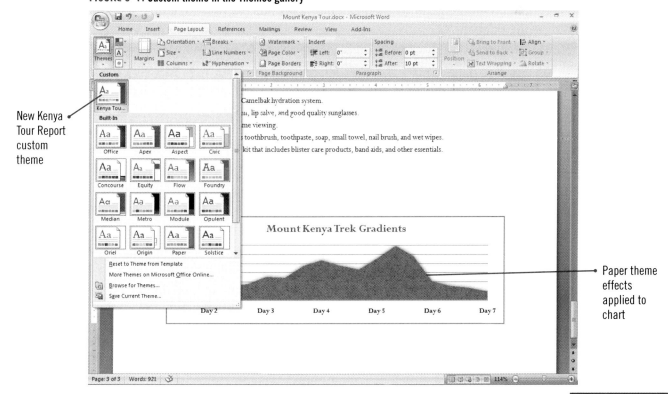

New Kenya Tour Report custom theme

Paper theme effects applied to chart

Inserting a Sidebar

Another way to design a document quickly and professionally is to use preformatted building blocks. **Building blocks** are the reusable pieces of formatted content or document parts that are stored in galleries, including headers and footers, cover pages, and text boxes. Sidebars and pull quotes are two types of text box building blocks that are frequently used to jazz up the appearance of a text-heavy page and to highlight information. A **sidebar** is a text box that is positioned adjacent to the body of a document and contains auxiliary information. A **pull quote** is a text box that contains a quote or excerpt from an article, formatted in a larger font size and placed on the same page. You use the Text Box command on the Insert tab to insert sidebars and pull quotes. 🖦️🔧 You create a sidebar to display the Tour Highlights information on page 1 and a second sidebar to display information for travelers to Kenya on page 2.

STEPS

1. **Click the document to close the Themes gallery if necessary, press [Ctrl][Home], click the Insert tab, then click the Text Box button in the Text group**
   The Text Box gallery opens. It includes built-in styles for sidebars and pull quotes.

QUICK TIP
The sidebar is anchored to the paragraph where the insertion point is located.

2. **Scroll down the gallery, then click the Tiles Sidebar**
   The Tiles sidebar is inserted at the top of the page. It is composed of a green text box with placeholder text, and a grey shadow. You can type directly in the text box to replace the placeholder text or you can paste text from the document into the text box.

3. **Select Tour Highlights and the bulleted list beneath it, press [Ctrl][X] to cut the text, click the text box, press [Ctrl][V] to paste the text, then press [Backspace]**
   The text is cut from the body of the document and pasted in the sidebar.

QUICK TIP
You can change the format of a sidebar by applying a text box style, adding a shadow, or using the other commands on the Text Box Tools Format tab.

4. **Select Tour Highlights, click the Font Color list arrow A▾ on the Mini toolbar, click Blue, Accent 2, Darker 25%, select the bulleted list, click the Font Color list arrow A▾, then click White, Background 1**
   The font colors of the text in the sidebar change to blue and white.

5. **Click the Text Box Tools Format tab, click the Shadow Effects button in the Shadow Effects group, point to Shadow Color, click Blue, Accent 2, Lighter 40%, then deselect the sidebar**
   The shadow color changes to light blue. The completed sidebar is shown in Figure G-8.

QUICK TIP
Sidebars are inserted on the left side of an even-numbered page and on the right side of an odd-numbered page.

6. **Scroll to page 2, place the insertion point in Planning Your Trip, click the View tab, click the One Page button in the Zoom group, click the Insert tab, click the Text Box button, then click Annual Sidebar**
   The Annual Sidebar, an orange text box, is inserted on the left side of the page and anchored to the Planning Your Trip heading paragraph. Rather than type text in the sidebar, you will insert text from a file.

7. **Click the Insert tab, click the Object list arrow in the Text group, then click Text from File**
   The Insert File dialog box opens. You use this dialog box to select the file you want to insert in the sidebar.

8. **Navigate to the drive and folder where you store your Data Files, click the file WD G-2.docx, click Insert, deselect the sidebar, then save your changes**
   The contents of the file WD G-2.docx is inserted in the sidebar, as shown in Figure G-9. When you insert a text file into a text box, it's important to verify that all the text from the file fits in the text box. If not, adjust the size of the text box accordingly.

FIGURE G-8: Tiles sidebar

Blue shadow color

Tiles sidebar

Text pasted in text box and formatted

FIGURE G-9: Annual sidebar

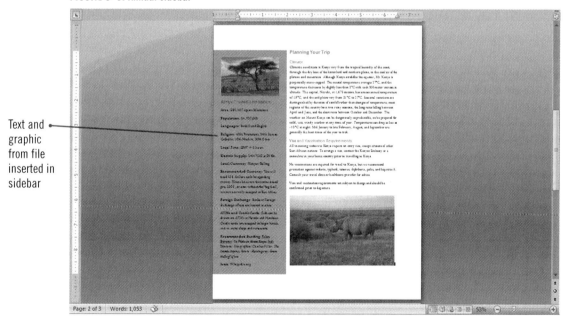

Text and graphic from file inserted in sidebar

Inserting Quick Parts

The Word Quick Parts feature makes it easy to insert reusable pieces of content into a document. Quick Parts items include fields, such as for the date or a page number, document properties, such as the document title or author, and building blocks. You insert a Quick Part into a document using the Quick Parts command on the Insert tab or on the Header & Footer Tools Design tab. You finalize the design of the three pages by adding a header and a footer building block to the document. You then customize the footer by adding document properties to it using the Quick Parts command.

STEPS

1. **Click the** View tab, **click the** Page Width button **in the Zoom group, click the** Insert tab, **then click the** Header button **in the Header & Footer group**

   The Header gallery opens and displays the list of predesigned headers.

2. **Scroll down the Header gallery, then click** Exposure

   The Exposure header is added to the document and the Header area opens. The Exposure header includes a property control for the Title document property as well as a content control for the date. A **property control** contains the document property information you entered in the Document Information Panel, or if you did not assign a document property, placeholder text. You can assign or update a document property by typing directly in a property control or by typing in the Document Information Panel.

3. **Click** Type the document title **to select the Title property control, type** Mount Kenya, Safari, and Beach, **click** Pick the date, **click the** Date list arrow, **then click** Today

   The title and the current date are added to the header. When you assign or update a document property by typing in a property control, all controls of the same type in the document are updated with the change, as well as the property field in the Document Information Panel.

4. **Click the** Header button **in the Header & Footer group, then click** Annual

   The header design changes to the Annual design, as shown in Figure G-10.

5. **Click the** Footer button **in the Header & Footer group, scroll down the Footer gallery, then click** Sideline

   The Sideline footer includes a page number field. Notice that this footer is formatted as a table.

6. **Press** [Tab] **to move the insertion point to the next table cell, click the** Quick Parts button **in the Insert group, point to** Document Property, **click** Company, **then type** Quest Specialty Travel

   The Company property control is added to the footer and updated to become "Quest Specialty Travel".

7. **Press** [→], **press** [Spacebar], **click the** Insert tab, **click the** Symbol list arrow **in the Symbols group, click** More Symbols, **be sure the Font is set to (normal text), type** 2022 **in the Character code text box, click** Insert **twice, then click** Close

   Two bullet symbols are added to the footer, as shown in Figure G-11.

8. **Place the insertion point between the two bullet symbols, press** [Spacebar], **click the** Quick Parts button **in the Text group, point to** Document Property, **click** Company Phone, **type** 1-800-555-TOUR, **press** [→], **press** [Spacebar], **then press** [End]

   The Company Phone property control is added to the footer and updated.

9. **Press** [Spacebar], **click the** Quick Parts button, **point to** Document Property, **click** Company Address, **type** www.questspecialtytravel.com, **then press** [→]

   The Company Address property control is added to the footer and updated.

10. **Move the pointer over the footer, click the** Table move handle **to select the table, click the** Bold button **B** **on the Mini toolbar, close the Footer area, then save your changes**

    Bold is applied to the text in the footer. The customized footer is shown in Figure G-12.

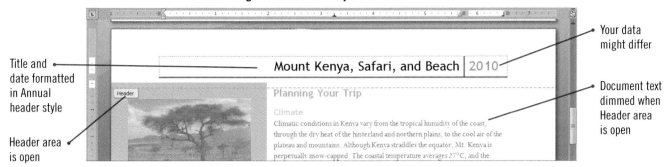

Title and date formatted in Annual header style

Header area is open

Your data might differ

Document text dimmed when Header area is open

FIGURE G-11: Bullet symbols in Sideline footer

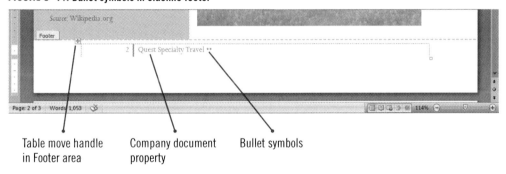

Table move handle in Footer area

Company document property

Bullet symbols

FIGURE G-12: Customized footer

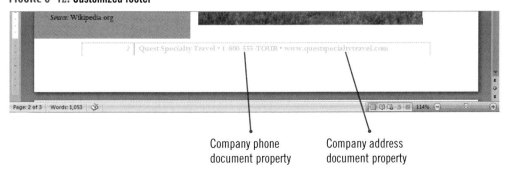

Company phone document property

Company address document property

Adding a Cover Page

To quickly finalize a report with simplicity or flair, you can insert one of the many predesigned cover pages that come with Word. Cover page designs range from conservative and business-like to colorful and attention-grabbing. Each cover page design includes placeholder text and property controls that you can replace with your own information. ▪▪▪▪ You finalize the tour report by inserting an eye-catching cover page that mirrors the design of the report.

STEPS

QUICK TIP

Click the Blank Page button in the Pages group to insert a blank page at the location of the insertion point.

1. **Click the View tab, click the One Page button in the Zoom group, click the Insert tab, then click the Cover Page list arrow in the Pages group**

   The gallery of cover pages opens. Each page design includes placeholder text and property controls.

2. **Scroll down the gallery, then click Motion**

   The Motion cover page is added at the beginning of the document. Notice that the tour name was added automatically to the Title property control and the current year was added automatically to the Date content control.

QUICK TIP

To change the user name and initials, click the Office button, click Word Options, then type a new user name and initials in the User name and Initials text boxes in the Word Options dialog box.

3. **Drag the Zoom slider right to zoom in on the cover page, then scroll down to view the author, company name, and current date controls at the bottom of the page**

   The company name is entered in the Company property control, and today's date is entered in the date control.

4. **Click the Author property control (the first line of text)**

   The text in the Author property control is the default author name for all new documents created on your computer. This information is based on the user name entered in the Word Options dialog box.

5. **Select the text in the Author property control, type your name, click the View tab, then click the One Page button**

   Your name replaces the user name as the Author property for the document.

QUICK TIP

To change to a different cover page design, simply insert a different cover page.

6. **Select the photograph, press [Delete], click the Insert tab, click the Clip Art button in the Illustrations group, type safari in the Search for text box in the Clip Art task pane, click Go, click the lion photograph, then close the Clip Art task pane**

   A photograph of a lion is inserted in the cover page. You can choose a different photograph if the lion photo is not available to you.

7. **Click the Text Wrapping list arrow in the Arrange group on the Picture Tools Format tab, click In Front of Text, then drag the photograph down and to the right to position it under the title and flush with the right edge of the page, as shown in Figure G-13**

QUICK TIP

To remove a cover page from a document, click the Cover Page list arrow in the Pages group, then click Remove Current Cover Page.

8. **Press [Ctrl][Home], click the Insert tab, click the Picture button in the Illustrations group, navigate to the drive and folder where you store your Data Files, click the file QST Logo.jpg, then click Insert**

   The QST logo is added to the cover page.

9. **Click the Position button in the Arrange group, click Position in Bottom Left with Square Text Wrapping, deselect the logo, then save your changes**

   The logo is moved to the bottom left corner of the page.

10. **Print the document**

    The completed tour report is shown in Figure G-14.

FIGURE G-13: Cover page

Date, title, and company are automatically entered

Lion photo is flush with edge of page

Author property control

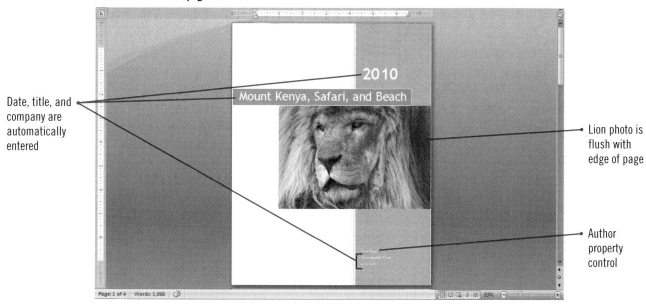

FIGURE G-14: Completed tour report

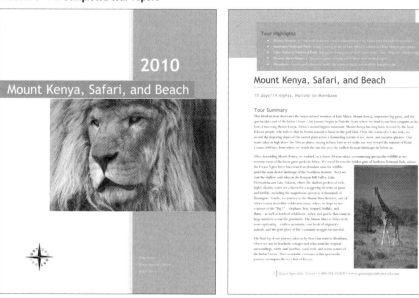

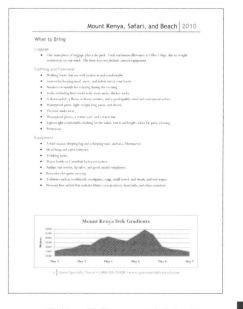

Creating Building Blocks

When you design a piece of content that you want to use again in other documents, you can save it as a building block in one of the Word galleries. For example, you might want to save your company mission statement or a list of staff names so that you don't have to type and format the information each time you use it in a document. You save an item as a building block using the Quick Parts command. ▰▰▰ You save the QST logo, the Kenya Travel Information sidebar, the Climate heading and paragraph, and the footer as building blocks so that you can easily include them in other tour reports.

STEPS

1. **Click the** logo **at the bottom of page 1 to select it, click the** Insert tab**, click the** Quick Parts button **in the Text group, then click** Save Selection to Quick Part Gallery

   The Create New Building Block dialog box opens, as shown in Figure G-15. You use this dialog box to enter a unique name and a description for the item and to specify the gallery where you want it to appear. You want the logo to appear in the Quick Parts gallery.

2. **Type** QST Logo **in the Name text box, click the Description text box, type** QST Logo in bottom left corner of tour report cover page**, then click** OK

   The logo is added to the Quick Parts gallery.

3. **Scroll to page 3, select the** orange sidebar**, click the** Quick Parts button**, click** Save Selection to Quick Part Gallery**, type** Kenya Travel Info Sidebar **in the Name text box, click the** Gallery list arrow**, click** Text Boxes**, click the** Category list arrow**, click** Create New Category**, type** Kenya**, click** OK**, click the** Description text box**, type** Generic info for travelers to Kenya**, click** OK**, then deselect the text box**

   You add the sidebar to the Text Box gallery and create a new category called Kenya. It's a good idea to assign a descriptive category name to a building block item so that you can sort, organize, and find your building blocks easily.

4. **Click the** Text Box button **in the Text group, then scroll to the bottom of the Text Box gallery**

   The Kenya Travel Info Sidebar building block is displayed in the Text Box gallery in the Kenya category, as shown in Figure G-16.

5. **Click the document to close the gallery, select the** Climate heading and paragraph **on page 3, click the** Quick Parts button**, click** Save Selection to Quick Part Gallery**, type** Kenya Climate Info **in the Name text box, click the** Category list arrow**, click** Create New Category**, type** Kenya**, click** OK**, then click** OK

   The Climate heading and paragraph are saved in the Quick Parts gallery in the Kenya category.

6. **Click the** Quick Parts button **to verify that the item was added to the gallery, then point to the** QST Logo item **in the gallery**

   The gallery includes the QST Logo item in the General category and the Kenya Climate Info item in the Kenya category. When you point to the QST Logo item in the gallery, the name and description appear in a ScreenTip, as shown in Figure G-17.

7. **Click the document, scroll down, double-click the** footer**, click the** Table move handle **to select the table in the footer, click the** Footer button **in the Header & Footer group on the Header & Footer Tools Design tab, then click** Save Selection to Footer Gallery

   The Create New Building Block dialog box opens with Footers automatically selected as the gallery.

8. **Type** Tour Report Footer **in the Name text box, click** OK**, then save and close the document**

   The footer is added to the Footers gallery under the General category. In the next lesson you will insert the building blocks you created into a different tour report document.

FIGURE G-15: Create New Building Block dialog box

Type name for item

Specify gallery for item

Select category for item

FIGURE G-16: Kenya Tour Info Sidebar in Text Box gallery

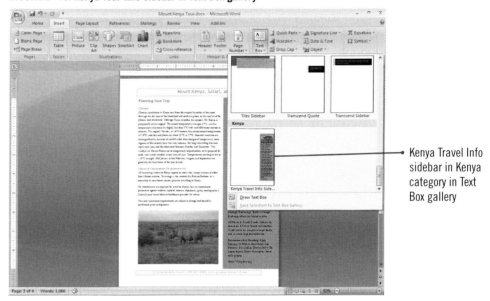

Kenya Travel Info sidebar in Kenya category in Text Box gallery

FIGURE G-17: Items in Quick Parts gallery

Quick Parts gallery (yours might include other items)

Selected text is added to Quick Parts gallery

ScreenTip shows name and description for QST Logo item

Climate heading and paragraph item in gallery

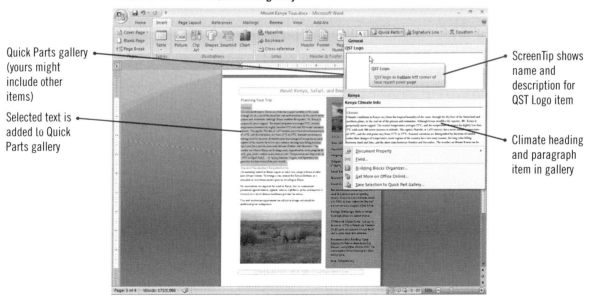

Renaming a building block and editing other properties

You can edit the properties of a building block at any time, including changing its name, gallery location, category, and description. To modify building block properties, simply right-click the item in a gallery, and then click Edit Properties. In the Modify Building Block dialog box that opens, edit the item's name or description, or assign it to a new gallery or category. When you are finished, click OK, and then click Yes in the warning box that opens. You can also modify the properties of a building block by selecting the item in the Building Blocks Organizer, and then clicking Edit Properties.

Inserting Building Blocks

Once you have created customized building blocks, it is easy to insert them in your documents. You can insert a building block directly from a gallery, or you can use the Building Blocks Organizer to search for, organize, and insert building blocks. You need to create a tour report for a different QST tour to Kenya. You open the tour report file, apply the Kenya theme, and then insert the building blocks you created so that all the Kenya tour reports have common content and a consistent look and feel.

STEPS

1. **Open the file** WD G-3.docx **from the drive and folder where you store your Data Files, save it as** Kenya Family Safari, **scroll down, replace** Ron Dawson **with your name at the bottom of page 1, click the** View tab, **then click the** Two Pages button **in the Zoom group**

   The Kenya Family Safari tour report includes a cover page, two pages of text formatted with styles, a sidebar, photographs, and a chart.

2. **Click the** Page Layout tab, **click the** Themes button **in the Themes group, then click the** Kenya Tour Report theme **in the Custom section of the gallery**

   The Kenya Tour Report theme you created is applied to the document.

   > **QUICK TIP**
   > Right-click an item in the Quick Parts gallery to open a menu of locations in which to insert the item.

3. **Press** [Ctrl][Home], **click the** Insert tab, **click the** Quick Parts button **in the Text group, then click the** QST Logo **item in the Quick Parts gallery**

   The logo is added to the lower-left corner of the cover page.

   > **TROUBLE**
   > If the insertion point is located on the cover page, the footer will appear on the cover page only.

4. **Click anywhere on page 2, click the** Footer button **in the Header & Footer group, scroll down the Footer gallery, click** Tour Report Footer **in the General section, zoom as needed to examine the footer in the document, then close headers and footers**

   The custom footer you created is added to the Footer area on pages 2 and 3. The property information is automatically entered in the property controls in the footer because the property information was saved previously with the document.

   > **QUICK TIP**
   > To edit the content of a building block, insert the item in a document, edit the item, then save the selection to the same Quick Part gallery using the same name.

5. **Scroll to page 3, click the** Practical Information heading, **click the** Insert tab, **click the** Quick Parts button **in the Text group, then click** Building Blocks Organizer

   The Building Blocks Organizer opens as shown in Figure G-18. The Building Blocks Organizer includes a complete list of the built-in and customized building blocks from every gallery. You use the Building Blocks Organizer to sort, preview, insert, delete, and edit the properties of building blocks.

6. **Click the** Category column heading **in the list of building blocks**

   The building blocks are sorted and grouped by category.

   > **QUICK TIP**
   > To delete a building block, select it in the Building Blocks Organizer, then click Delete.

7. **Scroll down the list to locate the two items in the Kenya category, click the** Kenya Travel Info Sidebar **item to select it, click** Insert, **click the** Text Box Tools Format tab **if necessary, click the** Shape Fill list arrow **in the Text Box Styles group, then click** Blue, Accent 2

   The Kenya Travel Information sidebar is inserted on page 3 and the color changes to blue. The sidebar is anchored to the Practical Information heading, where the insertion point is located.

   > **TROUBLE**
   > If you are working on your personal computer, and you want to save the building blocks you created, click Yes to save the Building Blocks.docx file.

8. **Click the** blank paragraph **above the chart, click the** Quick Parts button, **click the** Kenya Climate Info **item, then save your changes**

   The Climate heading and associated paragraph are inserted above the chart. The completed Kenya Family Safari tour report is shown in Figure G-19.

9. **Print the document, close the file, exit** Word, **then click** No **in the warning box to not save the changes to the BuildingBlocks.docx file**

   You can choose to save the customized building blocks you created in this session for use in other documents, or you can remove them from the Building Blocks Organizer.

FIGURE G-18: Building Blocks Organizer

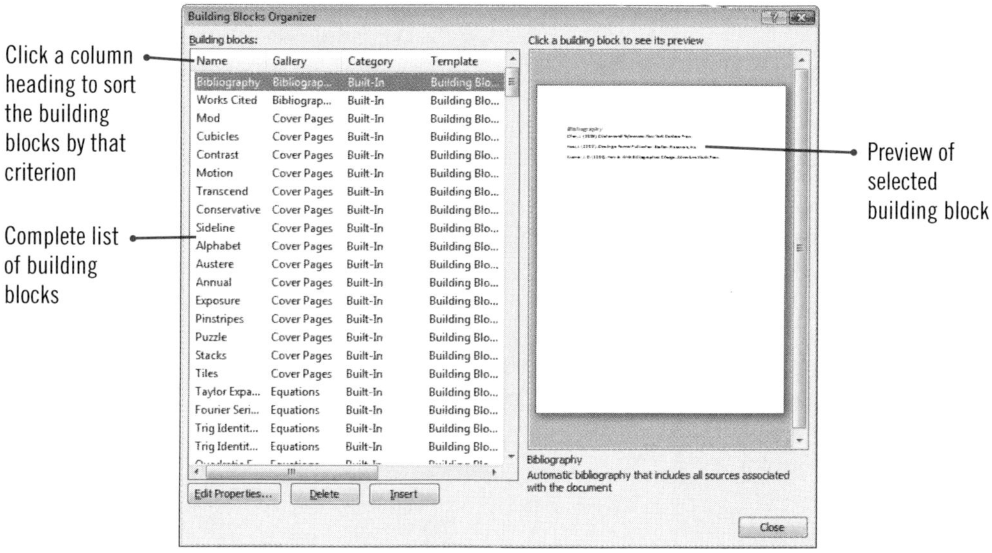

Click a column heading to sort the building blocks by that criterion

Complete list of building blocks

Preview of selected building block

FIGURE G-19: Completed Kenya Family Safari tour report

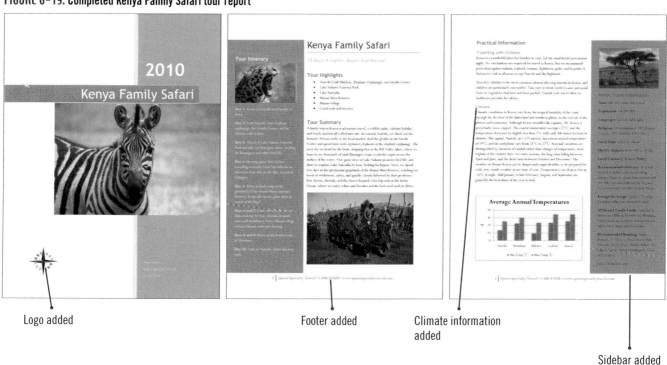

Logo added

Footer added

Climate information added

Sidebar added

Practice

▼ CONCEPTS REVIEW

Label each element shown in Figure G-20.

FIGURE G-20

Match each term with the statement that best describes it.

6. **Gallery**

7. **Building block**

8. **Theme**

9. **Quick Style set**

10. **Quick Part**

11. **Pull quote**

12. **Style**

13. **Sidebar**

a. A set of unified design elements, including colors, fonts, and effects that are named and stored together

b. A set of format settings, such as font, font color, and paragraph alignment, that are named and stored together

c. A group of related styles that share common fonts, colors, and formats

d. A reusable piece of formatted content or a document part that is stored in a gallery

e. A text box that is positioned adjacent to the body of a document and contains auxiliary information

f. A text box that contains a quote or excerpt from an article, formatted in a larger font size and placed on the same page

g. A field, document property, or other piece of content that can be inserted in a document

h. A location where styles or building blocks are stored

Select the best answer from the list of choices.

14. **Which of the following is *not* a design element included in a theme?**

   a. Fonts

   b. Picture styles

   c. Colors

   d. Effects

15. **Changing which of the following does not change the font used for body text in a document?**

   a. Style Set

   b. Theme fonts

   c. Theme

   d. Theme effects

16. **Which of the following elements uses theme effects?**

   a. SmartArt

   b. ClipArt

   c. Tables

   d. Headers and footers

17. **Which of the following is not an example of a building block?**

   a. Pull quote

   b. Document property

   c. Footer

   d. Cover page

18. Which of the following statements is false?

   a. Changing a document property in a property control updates the property in the Document Information Panel.

   b. When you change a document theme, the format of text to which font formatting has been applied does not change.

   c. You use the Object command to create a new building block.

   d. When you add a building block to a gallery, it is also added to the Building Block Organizer.

▼ SKILLS REVIEW

1. Apply quick styles to text.

   a. Start Word, open the file WD G-4.docx from the drive and folder where you store your Data Files, save it as Green Home, read the document, then press [Ctrl][Home].

   b. Apply the Title style to the Greening Your Home heading.

   c. Apply the Subtitle style to the Reducing your personal greenhouse gas emissions heading.

   d. Apply the Heading 1 style to the red headings: Small Steps to Take in Your Home and Yard and Use Green Power.

   e. Apply the Heading 3 style to the purple subheadings, then save your changes. (*Hint*: To make the Heading 3 style available, first apply the Heading 2 style to a subheading, then apply the Heading 3 style to the same subheading.)

2. Apply a theme.

   a. Change the view to Two Pages, then open the Themes gallery and preview each theme applied to the document.

   b. Apply the Urban theme, then scroll down to view page 3.

   c. Apply the Concourse theme, apply the Solstice theme, then save your changes.

3. Customize a theme.

   a. Change the theme colors to Flow.

   b. Create new theme colors by changing the Accent 1 color to dark green: click the Accent 1 list arrow, click More Colors, click the Custom tab if necessary, type 51 in the Red text box, type 102 in the Green text box, type 0 in the Blue text box, then click OK.

   c. Save the palette of new theme colors with the name Earth.

   d. Change the theme fonts to Median, scroll to the bottom of the document, then change the theme effects to Urban.

   e. Save the current theme with the name Earth.

   f. Press [Ctrl][Home], change the font color of the title to Dark Green, Accent 1, Darker 25%, then save your changes.

4. Insert a sidebar.

   a. Place the insertion point in the title, then insert the Contrast Sidebar.

   b. Select the second paragraph of body text, cut it, paste it in the sidebar, click the Paste Options button, click Match Destination Formatting, then press [Backspace].

   c. Select the sidebar text, use the Shading list arrow to change the Shading Color to Lime, Accent 6, click the Bottom Border list arrow, click Borders and Shading, then change the border color to Lime, Accent 6.

   d. Change the view to One Page, click the subheading Be green in your yard on page 2, then insert the Annual Sidebar.

   e. Insert the text file WD G-5.docx, found in the drive and folder where you store your Data Files, in the sidebar, select all the text in the sidebar, then change the font color to White, Background 1.

   f. Scroll to page 3, click the heading Use Green Power, then insert the Annual Sidebar.

   g. Insert the text file WD G-6.docx, found in the drive and folder where you store your Data Files, in the sidebar, select all the text in the sidebar, change the font color to White, Background 1, then save your changes.

5. Insert quick parts.

   a. Change the view to Page Width, insert the Sideline header from the Header gallery, click the Title property control, type Greening Your Home, then press [End] to move the insertion point out of the control.

   b. Press [Spacebar], insert a small bullet symbol of your choice, press [Spacebar], insert an Author property control, then add your name to the control as the author.

   c. Insert the Sideline footer from the Footer gallery, close headers and footers, then save your changes.

6. Add a cover page.

a. Change the view to Two Pages, then press [Ctrl][Home], insert the Pinstripes cover page, zoom in, click the Subtitle control, then type **Reducing your personal greenhouse gas emissions**.

b. Verify that your name appears in the Author control, then use the Date control to select the current date.

c. Change the cover page design to the Sideline cover page, right-click the Company control, click Remove Content Control, then verify that the remaining information is accurate.

d. Save your changes, then print the document. The completed document is shown in Figure G-21.

7. Create building blocks.

a. Change the view to Two Pages, click the upper right corner of the sidebar on page 2 to select it (*Note*: Sizing handles appear around the dark green box when the sidebar is selected.), then use the Quick Parts button to save the selection as a quick part.

b. Name the building block **Intro Sidebar**, assign it to the Text Boxes gallery, create a category called **Green Reports**, and then click OK.

c. Scroll down, select the sidebar on page 4, save it as a quick part, name the building block **Measure Your Impact Sidebar**, assign it to the Text Boxes gallery, assign it to the Green Reports category, and then click OK as needed to return to the document.

d. Zoom in, open the Header area, click the table move handle in the header to select the header, then save the header to the Header Gallery.

e. Name the building block Green Reports header, create a **Green Reports** category, and then click OK as needed to return to the document.

f. Close the Header area, save your changes, then close the file without exiting Word.

8. Insert building blocks.

a. Open the file WD G-7.docx from the drive and folder where you store your Data Files, save it as **Green Work**, read the document, then apply the Earth theme.

b. Scroll to page 2, then insert the Green Reports header from the Green Reports category in the Header gallery.

c. Replace the information in the Author control with your name if necessary.

d. Insert the Sideline footer in the document, then close headers and footers.

e. Click the title on page 2, open the Text Box gallery, then insert the Intro Sidebar from the Green Reports category.

f. Select the second body paragraph in the document, cut it, select all the text in the sidebar except for the final period, paste the text, click the Paste Options button, click Match Destination Formatting, then press [Backspace] twice to delete the extra line and period

g. Scroll to page 3, click On the Road, then open Building Blocks Organizer.

h. Click the Category heading to sort the items by category, scroll to locate the items in the Green Reports category, click the Measure Your Impact Sidebar, then click Insert.

i. Save your changes, then print your document. Pages 2 and 3 of the completed document are shown in Figure G-22.

j. Close the file and exit Word, not saving changes to the Building Blocks.dotx file if prompted.

FIGURE G-21

FIGURE G-22

▼ INDEPENDENT CHALLENGE 1

You volunteer for an organization that promotes literacy in your community. You have written the text for a literacy fact sheet and now want to format it quickly and attractively. You decide to format the fact sheet using styles, themes, and preformatted building blocks. If you are performing the ACE steps, you will also save some of the formatted content so you can use it again in other documents.

a. Start Word, open the file WD G-8.docx from the drive and folder where you store your Data Files, save it as **Literacy Fact Sheet**, then read the document to get a feel for its contents.

b. Apply the Title style to the title Facts on Literacy.

c. Apply the Heading 2 style to the headings Literacy and Poverty, Literacy and Children, and How Can You Help?

d. Press [Ctrl][Home], then add a Cubicles Sidebar to the document.

e. Select the How Can You Help heading and the paragraphs under it, press [Ctrl][X], click the placeholder text in the sidebar, press [Ctrl][V], then use the Paste Options button to match the destination formatting.

f. Apply the Heading 2 style to How Can You Help? in the sidebar, then set the paragraph spacing before the heading to 0 points and after the heading to 12 points.

g. Add a Puzzle (Even Page) footer to the document. Remove the Company property control, type **For more information contact** followed by your name, then replace Confidential with **555-8799**.

h. Preview several themes applied to the document, then select an appropriate theme.

i. If the text flows onto page two or does not all fit in the sidebar, change the theme fonts to a set of fonts that allows the text to fit on one page and in the sidebar. Delete the blank page 2 if necessary.

j. Change the theme colors applied the document elements as necessary to make the document attractive.

Advanced Challenge Exercise

■ Select the sidebar, then save it as a building block in the Text Boxes gallery in the General category. Be sure to give the building block a meaningful name and description.

■ Open the Footer area, click the Table Move Handle to select the table in the footer, then add the footer to the Footers gallery in the General category. Be sure to give the footer a meaningful name and description.

■ Create a new document, type **Teach a Child to Read**, apply the Title style to the text, then save the document as **Literacy ACE** to the drive and folder where you store your Data Files.

■ Open the Building Blocks Organizer, locate the sidebar building block you created, then insert it in the document.

■ Open the Footer gallery, insert the footer you created, save your changes, print the document, then close the file.

k. Save your changes, print the document, then close the file and exit Word, not saving changes to the Building Blocks.dotx file if prompted.

▼ INDEPENDENT CHALLENGE 2

You work for the Community Relations department at your local hospital. You have written the text for a report on annual giving, and now you need to format the report. You decide to start with a report template and then customize the report with a preformatted text box, a sidebar, a new cover page, and theme elements.

a. Start Word, create a new document using the Oriel Report template, then save it as **Annual Giving Report**.

b. Scroll the document to get a feel for its content and layout, then press [Ctrl][Home].

c. On the cover page, type **Springfield Community Hospital Annual Giving** in the Title property control. (*Note:* Text typed in the Title property control is formatted in small caps.)

d. Type **Invitation to Donors** in the Subtitle property control, remove the Abstract content control, type your name in the Author property control, then select today's date in the Date content control.

e. Scroll to page 2, click the body of the report to select the content control, insert the text file WD G-9.docx, found on the drive and folder where you store your Data Files, then scroll down to view the format and content of the report.

f. Press [Ctrl][Home], then format the following headings in the Heading 1 style: Capital Campaign Exceeds its Goal, Types of Gifts, Planned and Deferred Giving, Named Endowments Leave Lasting Impressions, and Frost Society.

g. Experiment by applying different heading styles to the Annual Fund Gifts subheading: Apply the Heading 2 style to the subheading, apply the Heading 3 style to the subheading, and then apply the Heading 4 style to the subheading.

▼ INDEPENDENT CHALLENGE 2 (CONTINUED)

h. Apply the Heading 4 style to the following subheadings: Memorial or Tribute Gifts, Charitable Bequests, Charitable Gift Annuity, Charitable Remainder Trust, Edna and Franklin Frost Society Members.

i. Click the first body paragraph on page 2, insert a text box using the pull quote style of your choice from the Text Box gallery, then reposition the text box so the page is attractive, if necessary.

j. Select the last paragraph of text under the Capital Campaign Exceeds its Goal heading, cut the paragraph and paste it to the pull quote, then use the Paste Options button to match the destination formatting.

k. Scroll to page 4, click the Frost Society heading, insert a sidebar of your choice, then cut the Edna and Franklin Frost Society Members heading and the list that follows it from the body text and paste it in the sidebar. Use the Paste Options button to match the destination formatting, then apply the Heading 4 style to the heading in the sidebar.

l. Using the Cover Page command, insert a different cover page for the report. Update or remove the content and property controls as necessary.

FIGURE G-23

m. Experiment with different themes, theme colors, theme fonts, and theme effects, and then use these tools to customize the look of the report. Adjust the elements of the report as necessary to make sure each page is attractive and the text fits comfortably on 4 pages. Figure G-23 shows a sample finished report.

n. Save your changes to the document, print a copy, close the document, then exit Word.

▼ INDEPENDENT CHALLENGE 3

You are in charge of publicity for the Sydney Triathlon 2010 World Cup. One of your responsibilities is to create a two-page flyer that captures the spirit of the event and provides the basic details. You format the flyer using styles, themes, and building blocks, keeping in mind that in the end the content needs to fit on two pages. Figure G-24 shows one possible design, but you will create your own design. If you are completing the ACE steps, you will also create a custom theme that can be used for other documents related to the triathlon.

a. Start Word, open the file WD G-10.docx from the drive and folder where you store your Data Files, then save it as Triathlon Flyer, then read the document.

FIGURE G-24

b. Apply the Title style to the title and the Heading 1 style to the following headings: The Triathlon, The Course, Best Views, Public Transport and Road Closures, and The Athletes. Apply other styles to the text as you see fit.

c. Change the Style Set to Modern, apply an appropriate theme, then change the theme colors or theme fonts as necessary to achieve the look you want.

d. Add a continuous section break before The Athletes, then format the second section in two columns using the default column settings.

e. Add a manual page break before the Public Transport and Road Closures heading.

f. Click The Triathlon heading on page 1, insert a sidebar of your choice on page 1, then cut the Best Views heading and paragraphs from the document, including the photo of the Sydney Opera House, and paste it in the sidebar. (*Hint*: Do not cut the page break.) Keep the source formatting for the selection.

g. Click The Athletes heading on page 2, insert a sidebar of your choice on page 2, then cut the Public Transport and Road Closures heading and paragraphs from the document and paste them in the sidebar. Keep the source formatting for the selection.

h. Adjust the size, color, alignment, text wrapping, and position of the sidebar text boxes and the photographs so that the layout of each page is attractive.

i. Adjust the font and paragraph formatting of the document text so that the text is readable and the overall layout of the flyer is harmonious. All the text should now fit on two pages.

Advanced Challenge Exercise

- Customize one or more of the theme colors you used in the flyer, then save the new palette of theme colors with the name Triathlon.
- Adjust the colors of text and other elements in the document as necessary.
- Save the customized theme with the name Triathlon.

j. Add your name to the header, save your changes, print the document, close the file, then exit Word.

▼ REAL LIFE INDEPENDENT CHALLENGE

In this Independent Challenge, you will design and save at least one building block for your work or personal use. Your building block might be the masthead for a newsletter, a cover page for your academic papers or your business reports, a header or footer that includes your company logo, a SmartArt object, a letterhead, a graphic object, a mission statement or disclaimer, or some other item that you use repeatedly in the documents you create.

a. Determine the building block(s) you want to create. If you frequently create documents that include several standard items, such as a newsletter that includes a masthead, a header, a footer, and a text box with the address of your organization, you will want to create several building blocks.

b. Start Word, then save the blank document as **Building Block 1** to the drive and folder where you store your Data Files.

c. Create your first building block. Whenever possible, insert fields and property controls as appropriate. Format the item using themes, styles, fonts, colors, borders, fill effects, shadows, and other effects, as necessary.

d. When you are satisfied with the content and format of the item, select it, including the final paragraph mark, if appropriate, and then save it as a new building block. Make sure to give the item a meaningful name, description, and category, and to save it to the appropriate gallery so you can find it easily.

e. Repeat steps c and d to create as many building blocks as necessary for your documents.

f. Type your name at the top of the document, then save, print, and close the document.

g. Open a blank document, then save it as **Building Block 2** to the drive and folder where you store your Data Files.

h. Create a document in which to use your building block(s). Insert the building block(s) you created, and then format, adjust, and position the building blocks appropriately.

i. Type your name in the document header (or another appropriate location), save the document, print it, and then close the file and exit Word. If you want to save the building blocks you created for future use, save the Building Blocks.dotx file when prompted.

▼ VISUAL WORKSHOP

Create the cover page shown in Figure G-25 using the Exposure cover page design. Replace the photograph with the clip art photograph shown in the figure, replace the placeholder text with the text shown in the figure, increase the font size of the abstract text to 16 points, change the theme colors to Oriel, then delete the second page. Save the document as **Aquarium Cover Page**, then print the document. (*Hints*: Locate the photograph using the keyword **coral**. Choose another photo if the photo shown is not available to you. To delete the second page, delete the page break on the cover page.)

FIGURE G-25

See, touch, and explore the amazing underwater world at the Aquarium of the Atlantic. The Aquarium is open daily 10 a.m. to 5 p.m.

Aquarium of the Atlantic
1538 Commercial Street
Portland, ME 04101
207-555-7445
www.aquariumoftheatlantic.com

Working with Themes and Building Blocks

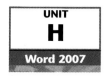

Merging Word Documents

A mail merge operation combines a standard document, such as a form letter, with customized data, such as a set of names and addresses, to create a set of personalized documents. You can perform a mail merge to create letters, labels, and other documents used in mass mailings, or to create standard documents that typically include customized information, such as business cards. In this unit, you learn how to use both the Mail Merge task pane and the commands on the Mailings tab to perform a mail merge. You need to send a letter to people who recently booked a QST tour, confirming their reservation and receipt of their nonrefundable deposit. You also need to send a general information packet to all participants in upcoming QST tours. You use mail merge to create a personalized form letter and mailing labels for the information packet.

OBJECTIVES

Understand mail merge

Create a main document

Design a data source

Enter and edit records

Add merge fields

Merge data

Create labels

Sort and filter records

Understanding Mail Merge

When you perform a **mail merge**, you merge a standard Word document with a file that contains customized information for many individuals or items. The standard document is called the **main document**. The file with the unique data for individual people or items is called the **data source**. Merging the main document with a data source results in a merged document that contains customized versions of the main document, as shown in Figure H-1. The Mail Merge task pane steps you through the process of setting up and performing a mail merge. You can also perform a mail merge using the commands on the Mailings tab. You decide to use the Mail Merge task pane to create your form letters and the commands on the Mailings tab to create your mailing labels. Before beginning, you explore the steps involved in performing a mail merge.

DETAILS

- **Create the main document**

  The main document contains the text—often called **boilerplate text**—that appears in every version of the merged document. The main document also includes the merge fields, which indicate where the customized information is inserted when you perform the merge. You insert the merge fields in the main document after you have created or selected the data source. You can create a main document using either the current document, a template, or an existing document.

- **Create a data source or select an existing data source**

  The data source is a file that contains the unique information for each individual or item. It provides the information that varies in every version of the merged document. A data source is composed of data fields and data records. A **data field** is a category of information, such as last name, first name, street address, city, or postal code. A **data record** is a complete set of related information for an individual or an item, such as one person's name and address. It is easiest to think of a data source file as a table: the header row contains the names of the data fields (the **field names**), and each row in the table is an individual data record. You can create a new data source, or you can merge a main document with an existing data source, such as a data source created in Word, an Outlook contact list, an Access database, or an Excel worksheet.

- **Identify the fields to include in the data source and enter the records**

  When you create a new data source, you must first identify the fields to include. It's important to think of and include all the fields before you begin to enter data. For example, if you are creating a data source that includes addresses, you might need to include fields for a person's middle name, title, department name, or country, even though every address in the data source does not include that information. Once you have identified the fields and set up your data source, you are ready to enter the data for each record.

- **Add merge fields to the main document**

  A **merge field** is a placeholder that you insert in the main document to indicate where the data from each record should be inserted when you perform the merge. For example, in the location you want to insert a zip code, you insert a zip code merge field. The merge fields in a main document must correspond with the field names in the associated data source. Merge fields must be inserted, not typed, in the main document. The Mail Merge task pane and the Mailings tab provide access to the dialog boxes you use to insert merge fields.

- **Merge the data from the data source into the main document**

  Once you have established your data source and inserted the merge fields in the main document, you are ready to perform the merge. You can merge to a new file, which contains a customized version of the main document for each record in the data source, or you can merge directly to a printer or e-mail message.

FIGURE H-1: Mail merge process

Data source document

Field name

Data record

Tour	Title	First Name	Last Name	Address Line 1	City	State	Zip Code	Country
Old Japan	Ms.	Linda	Barker	62 Cloud St.	Bellevue	WA	83459	US
Egypt	Mr.	Bob	Cruz	23 Plum St.	Boston	MA	02483	US
Old Japan	Ms.	Joan	Yatco	456 Elm St.	Chicago	IL	60603	US
Yucatan	Ms.	Anne	Butler	48 East Ave.	Vancouver	BC	V6F 1AH	CANADA
Alaska	Mr.	Fred	Silver	56 Pearl St.	Cambridge	MA	02139	US

Main document

Quest Specialty Travel
340 West Market Street ● San Diego, CA 92101
Tel: (619) 555-1223 ● Fax: (619) 555-0937 ● www.questspecialtytravel.com

June 12, 2010

«AddressBlock»

«GreetingLine»

Thank you for your reservation and $250 deposit to secure your participation in QST's exciting «Tour» tour. You will be joining an exclusive group of fellow QST travelers for an inspiring, adventurous, and memorable experience of a lifetime.

Your reservation and nonrefundable deposit guarantee your place on the tour until 30 days prior to departure. At this point, a 50% nonrefundable advance payment is required to confirm your participation. Payment in full is required one week prior to commencement of the tour. We recommend purchasing a travel insurance policy, as no refunds will be given due to weather or personal circumstances.

Thank you for choosing Quest Specialty Travel. We look forward to travelling with you.

Sincerely,

Ron Dawson
Marketing Manager

Merged document

Quest Specialty Travel
340 West Market Street ● San Diego, CA 92101
Tel: (619) 555-1223 ● Fax: (619) 555-0937 ● www.questspecialtytravel.com

June 12, 2010

Ms. Linda Barker
62 Cloud St.
Bellevue, WA 83459

Dear Ms. Barker:

Thank you for your reservation and $250 deposit to secure your participation in QST's exciting Old Japan tour. You will be joining an exclusive group of fellow QST travelers for an inspiring, adventurous, and memorable experience of a lifetime.

Your reservation and nonrefundable deposit guarantee your place on the tour until 30 days prior to departure. At this point, a 50% nonrefundable advance payment is required to confirm your participation. Payment in full is required one week prior to commencement of the tour. We recommend purchasing a travel insurance policy, as no refunds will be given due to weather or personal circumstances.

Thank you for choosing Quest Specialty Travel. We look forward to travelling with you.

Sincerely,

Ron Dawson
Marketing Manager

Merge fields

Boilerplate text

Customized information

Creating a Main Document

The first step in performing a mail merge is to create the main document—the file that contains the boiler-plate text. You can create a main document from scratch, save an existing document as a main document, or use a mail merge template to create a main document. The Mail Merge task pane walks you through the process of selecting the type of main document to create. You use an existing form letter for your main document. You begin by opening the Mail Merge task pane.

STEPS

1. **Start** Word, **click the** Mailings tab, **click the** Start Mail Merge button **in the Start Mail Merge group, then click** Step by Step Mail Merge Wizard

   The Mail Merge task pane opens, as shown in Figure H-2, and displays information for the first step in the mail merge process: selecting the type of merge document to create.

2. **Make sure the** Letters option button **is selected, then click** Next: Starting document **to continue with the next step**

   The task pane displays the options for the second step: selecting the starting document (the main docu-ment). You can use the current document, start with a mail merge template, or use an existing file.

3. **Select the** Start from existing document option button, **make sure** (More files...) **is selected in the Start from existing list box, then click** Open

   The Open dialog box opens.

4. **Navigate to the location where you store your Data Files, select the file** WD H-1.docx, **then click** Open

   The letter that opens contains the boilerplate text for the main document. Notice the filename in the title bar is Document1. When you create a main document that is based on an existing document, Word gives the main document a default temporary filename.

5. **Click the** Save button 🖫 **on the Quick Access toolbar, then save the main document with the filename** Client Deposit Letter Main **to the drive and folder where you store your Data Files**

   It's a good idea to include "main" in the filename so that you can easily recognize the file as a main document.

6. **Click the** Zoom level button **on the status bar, click the** Text width option button, **click** OK, **select** April 19, 2010 **in the letter, type today's date, scroll down, select** Ron Dawson, **type your name, press** [Ctrl][Home], **then save your changes**

   The edited main document is shown in Figure H-3.

7. **Click** Next: Select recipients **to continue with the next step**

   You continue with Step 3 of 6 in the next lesson.

Using a mail merge template

If you are creating letters or faxes, you can use a mail merge tem-plate to start your main document. Each template includes boiler-plate text, which you can customize, and merge fields, which you can match to the field names in your data source. To create a main document that is based on a mail merge template, click the Start from a template option button in the Step 2 of 6 Mail Merge task pane, and then click Select template. In the Select Template dialog box, select a template from the Letters or Faxes tab that includes the word "Merge" in its name, and then click OK to create the docu-ment. Once you have created the main document, you can cus-tomize it with your own information: edit the boilerplate text,

change the document format, or add, remove, or modify the merge fields.

Before performing the merge, make sure to match the names of the merge fields used in the template with the field names used in your data source. To match the field names, click the Match Fields button in the Write & Insert Fields group on the Mailings tab, and then use the list arrows in the Match Fields dialog box to select the field name in your data source that corresponds to each address field component in the main document. You can also create a main document that is based on a template by using a template to create the main document and then adding merge fields to it.

FIGURE H-2: Step 1 of 6 Mail Merge task pane

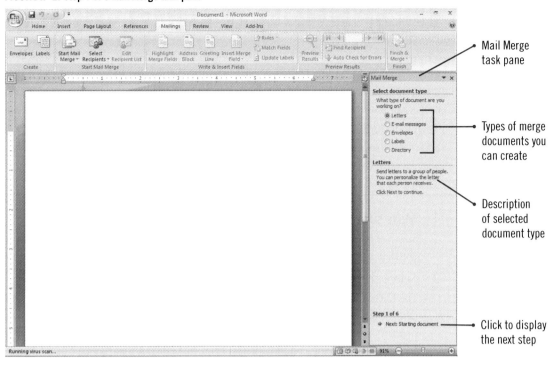

Mail Merge task pane

Types of merge documents you can create

Description of selected document type

Click to display the next step

FIGURE H-3: Main document with Step 2 of 6 Mail Merge task pane

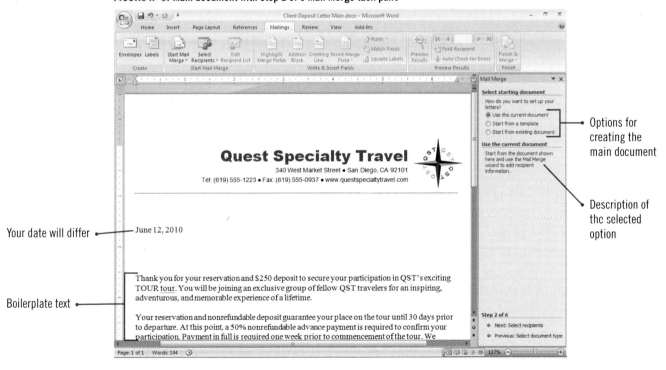

Your date will differ

Boilerplate text

Options for creating the main document

Description of the selected option

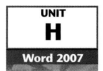

Designing a Data Source

Once you have identified the main document, the next step in the mail merge process is to identify the data source, the file that contains the information that is used to customize each version of the merge document. You can use an existing data source that already contains the records you want to include in your merge, or you can create a new data source. When you create a new data source you must determine the fields to include—the categories of information, such as a first name, last name, city, or zip code—and then add the records. You create a new data source that includes fields for the client name, client address, and tour booked by the client.

STEPS

1. **Make sure Step 3 of 6 is displayed at the bottom of the Mail Merge task pane**

   Step 3 of 6 involves selecting a data source to use for the merge. You can use an existing data source, a list of contacts created in Microsoft Outlook, or a new data source.

2. **Select the Type a new list option button, then click Create**

   The New Address List dialog box opens, as shown in Figure H-4. You use this dialog box both to design your data source and to enter records. The column headings in the Type recipient information... section of the dialog box are fields that are commonly used in form letters, but you can customize your data source by adding and removing columns (fields) from this table. A data source can be merged with more than one main document, so it's important to design a data source to be flexible. The more fields you include in a data source, the more flexible it is. For example, if you include separate fields for a person's title, first name, middle name, and last name, you can use the same data source to create an envelope addressed to "Mr. John Montgomery Smith" and a form letter with the greeting "Dear John."

3. **Click Customize Columns**

   The Customize Address List dialog box opens. You use this dialog box to add, delete, rename, and reorder the fields in the data source.

4. **Click Company Name in the list of field names, click Delete, then click Yes in the warning dialog box that opens**

   Company Name is removed from the list of field names. The Company Name field is no longer a part of the data source.

5. **Repeat Step 4 to delete the Address Line 2, Home Phone, Work Phone, and E-mail Address fields**

   The fields are removed from the data source.

6. **Click Add, type Tour in the Add Field dialog box, then click OK**

   A field called "Tour," which you will use to indicate the name of the tour booked by the client, is added to the data source.

7. **Make sure Tour is selected in the list of field names, then click Move Up eight times or until Tour is at the top of the list**

   The field name "Tour" is moved to the top of the list, as shown in Figure H-5. Although the order of field names does not matter in a data source, it's convenient to arrange the field names logically to make it easier to enter and edit records.

8. **Click OK**

   The New Address List dialog box shows the customized list of fields, with the Tour field first in the list. The next step is to enter each record you want to include in the data source. You add records to the data source in the next lesson.

Merging Word Documents

FIGURE H-4: New Address List dialog box

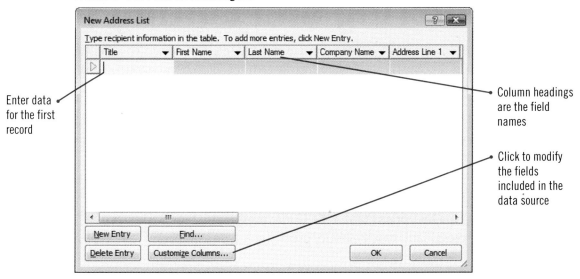

Enter data for the first record

Column headings are the field names

Click to modify the fields included in the data source

FIGURE H-5: Customize Address List dialog box

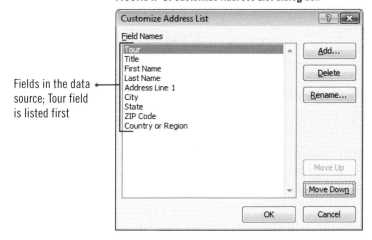

Fields in the data source; Tour field is listed first

Merging with an Outlook data source

If you maintain lists of contacts in Microsoft Outlook, you can use one of your Outlook contact lists as a data source for a merge. To merge with an Outlook data source, click the Select from Outlook contacts option button in the Step 3 of 6 Mail Merge task pane, then click Choose Contacts Folder to open the Choose Profile dialog box. In this dialog box, use the Profile Name list arrow to select the profile you want to use, then click OK to open the Select Contacts dialog box. In this dialog box, select the contact list you want to use as the data source, and then click OK. All the contacts included in the selected folder appear in the Mail Merge Recipients dialog box. Here you can refine the list of recipients to include in the merge by sorting and filtering the records. When you are satisfied, click OK in the Mail Merge Recipients dialog box.

Entering and Editing Records

Once you have established the structure of a data source, the next step is to enter the records. Each record includes the complete set of information for each individual or item you include in the data source. You create a record for each new QST client.

STEPS

QUICK TIP

Be careful not to add spaces or extra punctuation after an entry in a field, or these will appear when the data is merged.

1. **Verify the insertion point is in the Tour text box in the New Address List dialog box, type Old Japan, then press [Tab]**

   "Old Japan" appears in the Tour field and the insertion point moves to the next column in the table, the Title field.

2. **Type Ms., press [Tab], type Linda, press [Tab], type Barker, press [Tab], type 62 Cloud St., press [Tab], type Bellevue, press [Tab], type WA, press [Tab], type 83459, press [Tab], then type US**

   Data is entered in all the fields for the first record.

QUICK TIP

You can also press [Tab] at the end of the last field to start a new record.

3. **Click New Entry**

   The record for Linda Barker is added to the data source and the dialog box displays empty fields for the next record, as shown in Figure H-6. It's okay to leave a field blank if you do not need it for a record.

4. **Enter the following four records, pressing [Tab] to move from field to field, and clicking New Entry at the end of each record except the last:**

Tour	Title	First Name	Last Name	Address Line 1	City	State	ZIP Code	Country
Egypt	Mr.	Bob	Cruz	23 Plum St.	Boston	MA	02483	US
Old Japan	Ms.	Joan	Yatco	456 Elm St.	Chicago	IL	60603	US
Yucatan	Ms.	Anne	Butler	48 East Ave.	Vancouver	BC	V6F 1AH	CANADA
Alaska	Mr.	Fred	Silver	56 Pearl St.	Cambridge	MA	02139	US

5. **Click OK**

   The Save Address List dialog box opens. Data sources are saved by default in the My Data Sources folder so that you can easily locate them to use in other merge operations. Data sources you create in Word are saved in Microsoft Office Address Lists (*.mdb) format.

TROUBLE

If a check mark appears in the blank record under Fred Silver, click the check mark to eliminate the record from the merge.

6. **Type QST Client Data in the File name text box, navigate to the drive and folder where you store your Data Files, then click Save**

   The data source is saved, and the Mail Merge Recipients dialog box opens, as shown in Figure H-7. The dialog box shows the records in the data source in table format. You can use the dialog box to sort and filter records, and to select the recipients to include in the mail merge. You will learn more about sorting and filtering in a later lesson. The check marks in the second column indicate the records that will be included in the merge.

7. **Click QST Client Data.mdb in the Data Source list box at the bottom of the dialog box, then click Edit**

   The Edit Data Source dialog box opens, as shown in Figure H-8. You use this dialog box to edit a data source, including adding and removing fields, editing field names, adding and removing records, and editing existing records.

8. **Click Ms. in the Title field of the Joan Yatco record to select it, type Dr., click OK, then click Yes**

   The data in the Title field for Joan Yatco changes from "Ms." to "Dr." and the Edit Data Source dialog box closes.

QUICK TIP

If you want to add new records or modify existing records, click Edit recipient list in the task pane.

9. **Click OK in the Mail Merge Recipients dialog box**

   The dialog box closes. The file type and filename of the data source attached to the main document now appear under Use an existing list in the Mail Merge task pane.

FIGURE H-6: Record in New Address List dialog box

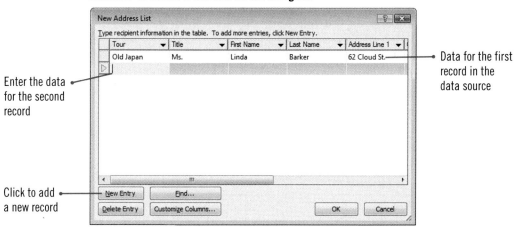

Enter the data for the second record

Click to add a new record

Data for the first record in the data source

FIGURE H-7: Mail Merge Recipients dialog box

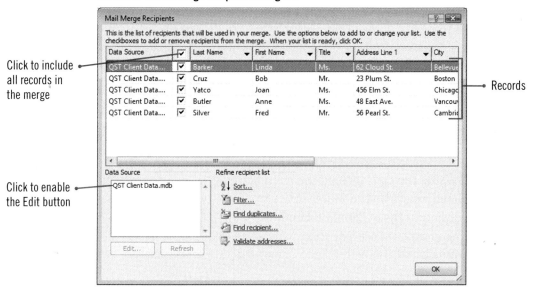

Click to include all records in the merge

Click to enable the Edit button

Records

FIGURE H-8: Edit Data Source dialog box

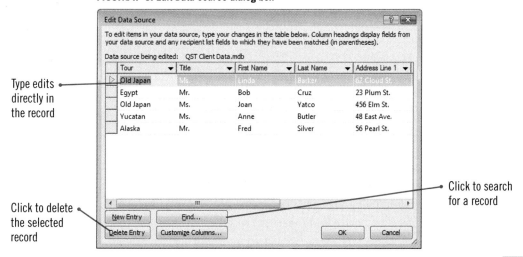

Type edits directly in the record

Click to delete the selected record

Click to search for a record

Adding Merge Fields

After you have created and identified the data source, the next step is to insert the merge fields in the main document. Merge fields serve as placeholders for text that is inserted when the main document and the data source are merged. The names of merge fields correspond to the field names in the data source. You can insert merge fields using the Mail Merge task pane or the Address Block, Greeting Line, and Insert Merge Field buttons in the Write & Insert Fields group on the Mailings tab. You cannot type merge fields into the main document. You use the Mail Merge task pane to insert merge fields for the inside address and greeting of the letter. You also insert a merge field for the tour destination in the body of the letter.

STEPS

1. **Click Next: Write your letter in the Mail Merge task pane**

   The Mail Merge task pane shows the options for Step 4 of 6, writing the letter and inserting the merge fields in the main document. Since your form letter is already written, you are ready to add the merge fields to it.

2. **Place the insertion point in the blank line above the first body paragraph, then click Address block in the Mail Merge task pane**

   The Insert Address Block dialog box opens, as shown in Figure H-9. You use this dialog box to specify the fields you want to include in an address block. In this merge, the address block is the inside address of the form letter. An address block automatically includes fields for the street, city, state, and postal code, but you can select the format for the recipient's name and indicate whether to include a company name or country in the address.

3. **Scroll the list of formats for a recipient's name to get a feel for the kinds of formats you can use, then click Mr. Joshua Randall Jr. if it is not already selected**

   The selected format uses the recipient's title, first name, and last name.

4. **Make sure the Only include the country/region if different than: option button is selected, select United States in the text box, type US, then deselect the Format address according to the destination country/region check box**

   You only need to include the country in the address block if the country is different than the United States, so you indicate that all entries in the Country field except "US" should be included in the printed address.

5. **Click OK, then press [Enter] twice**

   The merge field AddressBlock is added to the main document. Chevrons (<< and >>) surround a merge field to distinguish it from the boilerplate text.

6. **Click Greeting line in the Mail Merge task pane**

   The Insert Greeting Line dialog box opens. You want to use the format "Dear Mr. Randall:" (the recipient's title and last name, followed by a colon) for a greeting. The default format uses a comma, so you have to change the comma to a colon.

7. **Click the , list arrow, click :, click OK, then press [Enter]**

   The merge field GreetingLine is added to the main document.

8. **In the body of the letter select TOUR, then click More items in the Mail Merge task pane**

   The Insert Merge Field dialog box opens and displays the list of field names included in the data source.

9. **Make sure Tour is selected, click Insert, click Close, press [Spacebar] to add a space between the merge field and "tour" if there is no space, then save your changes**

   The merge field Tour is inserted in the main document, as shown in Figure H-10. You must type spaces and punctuation after a merge field if you want spaces and punctuation to appear in that location in the merged documents. You preview the merged data and perform the merge in the next lesson.

FIGURE H-9: Insert Address Block dialog box

Formats for the recipient's name

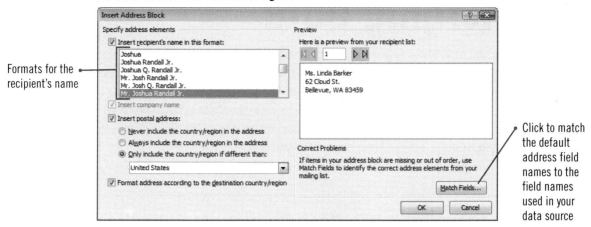

Click to match the default address field names to the field names used in your data source

FIGURE H-10: Merge fields in the main document

Merge fields

Matching fields

The merge fields you insert in a main document must correspond with the field names in the associated data source. If you are using the Address Block merge field, you must make sure that the default address field names correspond with the field names used in your data source. If the default address field names do not match the field names in your data source, click Match Fields in the Insert Address Block dialog box, then use the list arrows in the Match Fields dialog box to select the field name in the data source that corresponds to each default address field name. You can also click the Match Fields button in the Write & Insert Fields group on the Mailings tab to open the Match Fields dialog box.

Merging Data

Once you have added records to your data source and inserted merge fields in the main document, you are ready to perform the merge. Before merging, it's a good idea to preview the merged data to make sure the printed documents will appear as you want them to. You can preview the merge using the task pane or the Preview Results button in the Preview Results group on the Mailings tab. When you merge the main document with the data source, you must choose between merging to a new file or directly to a printer. ▄▄▄▄▄ Before merging the form letter with the data source, you preview the merge to make sure the data appears in the letter as you intended. You then merge the two files to a new document.

STEPS

1. **Click Next: Preview your letters in the Mail Merge task pane, then scroll down as necessary to see the tour name in the document**

   The data from the first record in the data source appears in place of the merge fields in the main document, as shown in Figure H-11. Always preview a document to verify that the merge fields, punctuation, page breaks, and spacing all appear as you intend before you perform the merge.

2. **Click the Next Recipient button ⏩ in the Mail Merge task pane**

   The data from the second record in the data source appears in place of the merge fields.

3. **Click the Go to Record text box in the Preview Results group on the Mailings tab, type 4, then press [Enter]**

   The data for the fourth record appears in the document window. The non-US country name, in this case Canada, is included in the address block, just as you specified. You can also use the First Record ⏮, Previous Record ◀, Next Record ▶, and Last Record ⏭ buttons in the Preview Results group to preview the merged data. Table H-1 describes other commands on the Mailings tab.

4. **Click Next: Complete the merge in the Mail Merge task pane**

   The options for Step 6 of 6 appear in the Mail Merge task pane. Merging to a new file creates a document with one letter for each record in the data source. This allows you to edit the individual letters.

5. **Click Edit individual letters to merge the data to a new document**

   The Merge to New Document dialog box opens. You can use this dialog box to specify the records to include in the merge.

6. **Make sure the All option button is selected, then click OK**

   The main document and the data source are merged to a new document called Letters1, which contains a customized form letter for each record in the data source. You can now further personalize the letters without affecting the main document or the data source.

7. **Click the Zoom level button on the status bar, click the Page width option button, click OK, scroll to the fourth letter (addressed to Ms. Anne Butler), place the insertion point before V6F in the address block, then press [Enter]**

   The postal code is now consistent with the proper format for a Canadian address.

8. **Click the Save button 💾 on the Quick Access toolbar to open the Save As dialog box, then save the merged document as Client Deposit Letter Merge to the drive and folder where you store your Data Files**

   You may decide not to save a merged file if your data source is large. Once you have created the main document and the data source, you can create the letters by performing the merge again.

9. **Click the Office button 🏢, click Print, click the Current page option button in the Page range section of the Print dialog box, click OK, then close all open Word files, saving changes if prompted**

   The letter to Anne Butler prints.

FIGURE H-11: Preview of merged data

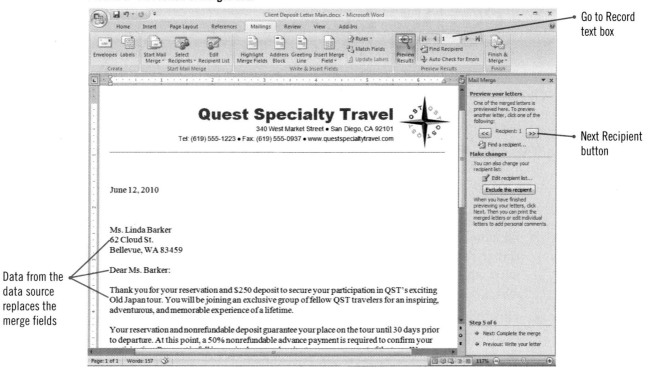

Go to Record text box

Next Recipient button

Data from the data source replaces the merge fields

TABLE H-1: Commands on the Mailings tab

command	use to
Envelopes	Create and print an individual envelope
Labels	Create and print an individual label
Start Mail Merge	Select the type of mail merge document to create and start the mail merge process
Select Recipients	Attach an existing data source to a main document or create a new data source
Edit Recipient List	Edit, sort, and filter the associated data source
Highlight Merge Fields	Highlight the merge fields in the main document
Address Block	Insert an Address Block merge field in the main document
Greeting Line	Insert a Greeting Line merge field in the main document
Insert Merge Field	Insert a merge field from the data source in the main document
Rules	Set rules to control how Word merges the data in the data source with the main document
Match Fields	Match the names of address or greeting fields with the field names used in the data source
Update Labels	Update all the labels in a label main document to match the content and formatting of the first label
Preview Results	Switch between viewing the main document with merge fields or with merged data
Find Recipient	Search for a specific record in the merged document
Auto Check for Errors	Check for and report errors in the merge
Finish & Merge	Specify whether to merge to a new document or directly to a printer or e-mail, and then complete the merge

Creating Labels

You can also use the Mail Merge task pane or the commands on the Mailings tab to create mailing labels or print envelopes for a mailing. When you create labels or envelopes, you must select a standard label or envelope size to use as the main document, select a data source, and then insert the merge fields in the main document before performing the merge. In addition to mailing labels, you can use mail merge to create labels for CDs, videos, and other items, and to create documents that are based on standard or custom label sizes, such as business cards, name tags, and postcards. You decide to use the commands on the Mailings tab to create mailing labels for the information packet you need to send to participants in upcoming QST tours. You create a new label main document and attach an existing data source.

1. **Click the Office button , click New, make sure Blank document is selected, click Create, click the Zoom level button on the status bar, click the Page width option button if necessary, click OK, then click the Mailings tab**

   A blank document must be open for the commands on the Mailings tab to be available.

QUICK TIP

To create an envelope mail merge, click Envelopes to open the Envelope Options dialog box, select an envelope size on the Envelope Options tab, click a Feed method on the Printing Options tab, and then click OK.

2. **Click the Start Mail Merge button in the Start Mail Merge group, click Labels, click the Label vendors list arrow, then click Microsoft if necessary**

   The Label Options dialog box opens, as shown in Figure H-12. You use this dialog box to select a label size for your labels and to specify the type of printer you plan to use. The name Microsoft appears in the Label vendors list box. You can use the Label vendors list arrow to select other brand name label vendors, such as Avery or Office Depot. The many standard-size labels for mailings, CD/DVD faces, business cards, postcards, and other types of labels are listed in the Product number list box. The type, height, width, and page size for the selected product are displayed in the Label information section.

TROUBLE

If your labels do not match Figure H-13, click the Undo button on the Quick Access toolbar, then repeat step 3, making sure to click the second instance of 30 Per Page.

3. **Click the second instance of 30 Per Page in the Product number list, click OK, click the Table Tools Layout tab, click View Gridlines in the Table group to turn on the display of gridlines if necessary, then click the Mailings tab**

   A table with gridlines appears in the main document, as shown in Figure H-13. Each table cell is the size of a label for the label product you selected.

4. **Save the label main document with the filename Client Labels Main to the drive and folder where you store your Data Files**

   Next, you need to select a data source for the labels.

5. **Click the Select Recipients button in the Start Mail Merge group, then click Use Existing List**

   The Select Data Source dialog box opens.

QUICK TIP

To create or change the return address for an envelope mail merge, click the Office button, click Word Options, click Advanced in the left pane of the Word Options dialog box, then enter the return address in the Mailing address text box in the General section in the right pane.

6. **Navigate to the drive and folder where you store your Data Files, open the file WD H-2.mdb, then save your changes**

   The data source file is attached to the label main document and <<Next Record>> appears in every cell in the table except the first cell, which is blank. In the next lesson you sort and filter the records before performing the mail merge.

FIGURE H-12: Label Options dialog box

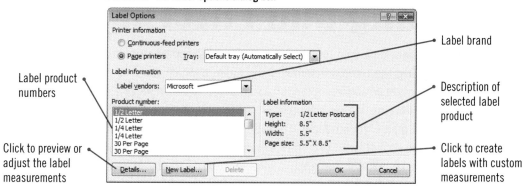

Label brand

Label product numbers

Description of selected label product

Click to preview or adjust the label measurements

Click to create labels with custom measurements

FIGURE H-13: Label main document

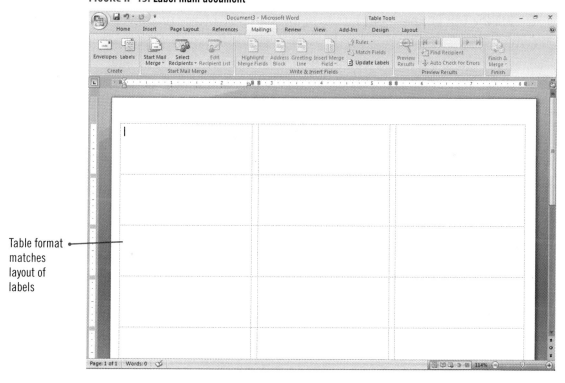

Table format matches layout of labels

Printing individual envelopes and labels

The Mail Merge feature enables you to easily print envelopes and labels for mass mailings, but you can also quickly format and print individual envelopes and labels using the Envelopes or Labels commands in the Create group on the Mailings tab. Simply click the Envelopes button or Labels button to open the Envelopes and Labels dialog box. On the Envelopes tab, shown in Figure H-14, type the recipient's address in the Delivery address box and the return address in the Return address box. Click Options to open the Envelope Options dialog box, which you can use to select the envelope size, change the font and font size of the delivery and return addresses, and change the printing options. When you are ready to print the envelope, click Print in the Envelopes and Labels dialog box. The procedure for printing an individual label is similar to printing an individual envelope: enter the recipient's address in the Address box on the Labels tab, click Options to select a label product number, click OK, and then click Print.

FIGURE H-14: Envelopes and Labels dialog box

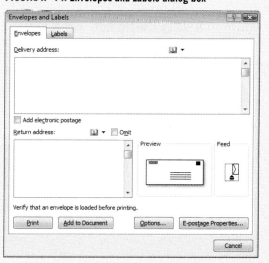

Word 2007

Sorting and Filtering Records

If you are using a large data source, you might want to sort and/or filter the records before performing a merge. **Sorting** the records determines the order in which the records are merged. For example, you might want to sort an address data source so that records are merged alphabetically by last name or in zip code order. **Filtering** the records pulls out the records that meet specific criteria and includes only those records in the merge. For instance, you might want to filter a data source to send a mailing only to people who live in the state of New York. You can use the Mail Merge Recipients dialog box both to sort and to filter a data source. You apply a filter to the data source so that only United States addresses are included in the merge. You then sort those records so that they merge in zip code order.

STEPS

1. **Click the Edit Recipient List button in the Start Mail Merge group**

   The Mail Merge Recipients dialog box opens and displays all the records in the data source.

2. **Scroll right to display the Country field, then click the Country column heading**

   The records are sorted in ascending alphabetical order by country, with Canadian records listed first. If you want to reverse the sort order, you can click the column heading again.

3. **Click the Country column heading list arrow, then click US on the menu that opens**

   A filter is applied to the data source so that only the records with "US" in the Country field will be merged. The grayish-blue arrow in the Country column heading indicates that a filter has been applied to the column. You can filter a data source by as many criteria as you like. To remove a filter, click a column heading list arrow, then click "All."

   > **QUICK TIP**
   > Use the options on the Filter tab to apply more than one filter to the data source.

4. **Click Sort in the Refine recipient list section of the dialog box**

   The Filter and Sort dialog box opens with the Sort Records tab displayed. You can use this dialog box to apply more advanced sort and filter options to the data source.

5. **Click the Sort by list arrow, click ZIP Code, click the first Then by list arrow, click Last Name, then click OK**

   The Mail Merge Recipients dialog box now displays only the records with a US address sorted first in zip code order, and then alphabetically by last name, as shown in Figure H-15.

   > **QUICK TIP**
   > Sorting and filtering a data source does not alter the records in a data source; it simply reorganizes the records for the current merge only.

6. **Click OK**

   The sort and filter criteria you set are saved for the current merge.

7. **Click the Address Block button in the Write & Insert Fields group, then click OK in the Insert Address Block dialog box**

   The Address Block merge field is added to the first label.

8. **Click the Update Labels button in the Write & Insert Fields group**

   The merge field is copied from the first label to every label in the main document.

   > **QUICK TIP**
   > To change the font or paragraph formatting of merged data, format the merge fields before performing a merge, including the chevrons.

9. **Click the Preview Results button in the Preview Results group**

   A preview of the merged label data appears in the main document, as shown in Figure H-16. Only U.S. addresses are included, and the labels are organized in zip code order, with recipients with the same zip code listed in alphabetical order.

10. **Click the Finish & Merge button in the Finish group, click Edit Individual Documents, click OK in the Merge to New Document dialog box, replace Ms. Carmen Landfair with your name in the first label, save the document as Client Labels US Only Zip Code Merge to the drive and folder where you store your Data Files, print the labels, save and close all open files, then exit Word**

FIGURE H-15: US records sorted in zip code order

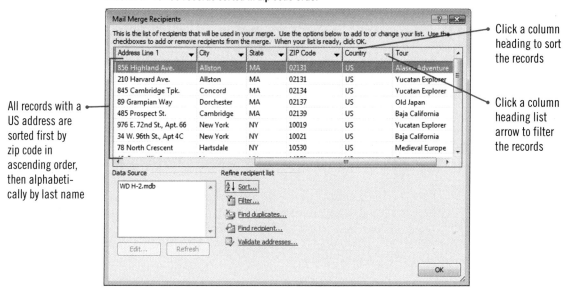

Click a column heading to sort the records

All records with a US address are sorted first by zip code in ascending order, then alphabetically by last name

Click a column heading list arrow to filter the records

FIGURE H-16: Merged labels

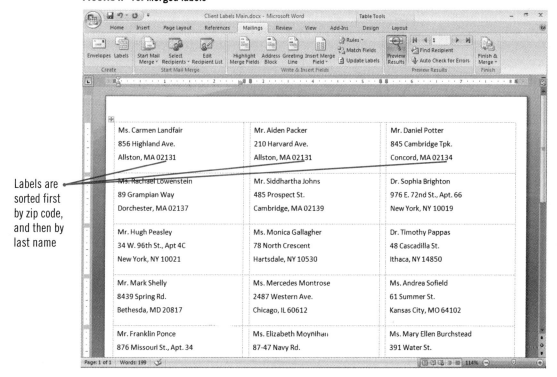

Labels are sorted first by zip code, and then by last name

Inserting individual merge fields

You must include proper punctuation, spacing, and blank lines between the merge fields in a main document if you want punctuation, spaces, and blank lines to appear between the data in the merge documents. For example, to create an address line with a city, state, and zip code, you insert the City merge field, type a comma and a space, insert the State merge field, type a space, and then insert the ZIP Code merge field: <<City>>, <<State>> <<ZIP Code>>.

You can insert an individual merge field by clicking the Insert Merge Field list arrow in the Write & Insert Fields group and then selecting the field name from the menu that opens. Alternatively, you can click the Insert Merge Field button to open the Insert Merge Field dialog box, which you can use to insert several merge fields at once by clicking a field name in the dialog box, clicking Insert, clicking another field name, clicking Insert, and so on. When you have finished inserting the merge fields, click Close to close the dialog box. You can then add spaces, punctuation, and lines between the merge fields you inserted in the main document.

Practice

▼ CONCEPTS REVIEW

Describe the function of each button shown in Figure H-17.

FIGURE H-17

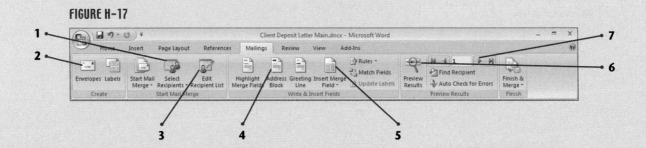

Match each term with the statement that best describes it.

8. Data field
9. Main document
10. Data source
11. Data record
12. Boilerplate text
13. Merge field
14. Sort
15. Filter

a. A file that contains customized information for each item or individual
b. A category of information in a data source
c. A complete set of information for one item or individual
d. A placeholder for merged data in the main document
e. To organize records in a sequence
f. To pull out records that meet certain criteria
g. The standard text that appears in every version of a merged document
h. A file that contains boilerplate text and merge fields

Select the best answer from the list of choices.

16. **In a mail merge, which type of file contains the information that varies for each individual or item?**
    a. Main document
    b. Data source
    c. Filtered document
    d. Sorted document

17. **To change the font of merged data, which element should you format?**
    a. Merge field
    b. Data record
    c. Field name
    d. Boilerplate text

18. **Which command is used to synchronize the field names in a data source with the merge fields in a document?**
    a. Update Labels
    b. Rules
    c. Highlight Merge Fields
    d. Match Fields

19. **Which action do you perform on a data source in order to merge only certain records?**
    a. Sort records
    b. Edit records
    c. Delete records
    d. Filter records

20. **Which action do you perform on a data source to reorganize the order of the records for a merge?**
    a. Sort records
    b. Edit records
    c. Delete records
    d. Filter records

▼ SKILLS REVIEW

1. Create a main document.

a. Start Word, change the style of the document to No Spacing, then open the Mail Merge task pane.

b. Use the Mail Merge task pane to create a letter main document, click Next, then select the current (blank) document.

c. At the top of the blank document, type New England Humanities Council, press [Enter], then type 1375 Harbor Street, Portsmouth, NH 03828; Tel: 603-555-8457; www.nehumanities.org

d. Press [Enter] five times, type today's date, press [Enter] five times, then type We are delighted to receive your generous contribution of AMOUNT to the New England Humanities Council (NEHC).

e. Press [Enter] twice, then type Whether we are helping adult new readers learn to read or bringing humanities programs into our public schools, senior centers, and prisons, NEHC depends upon private contributions to ensure that free public humanities programs continue to flourish in CITY and throughout the REGION region.

f. Press [Enter] twice, type Sincerely, press [Enter] four times, type your name, press [Enter], then type Executive Director.

g. Center the first two lines of text, change the font of New England Humanities Council to 28 point Bernard MT Condensed, then remove the hyperlink. (*Hint*: Right-click the hyperlink.)

h. Save the main document as Donor Thank You Main to the drive and folder where you store your Data Files.

2. Design a data source.

a. Click Next, select the Type a new list option button in the Step 3 of 6 Mail Merge task pane, then click Create.

b. Click Customize Columns in the New Address List dialog box, then remove these fields from the data source: Company Name, Address Line 2, Country or Region, Home Phone, Work Phone, and E-mail Address.

c. Add an Amount field and a Region field to the data source. Be sure these fields follow the ZIP Code field.

d. Rename the Address Line 1 field Street, then click OK to close the Customize Address List dialog box.

3. Enter and edit records.

a. Add the following records to the data source:

Title	First Name	Last Name	Street	City	State	Zip Code	Amount	Region
Mr.	John	Conlin	34 Mill St.	Exeter	NH	03833	$250	Seacoast
Mr.	Bill	Webster	289 Sugar Hill Rd.	Franconia	NH	03632	$1000	Seacoast
Ms.	Susan	Janak	742 Main St.	Derby	VT	04634	$25	North Country
Mr.	Derek	Gray	987 Ocean Rd.	Portsmouth	NH	03828	$50	Seacoast
Ms.	Rita	Murphy	73 Bay Rd.	Durham	NH	03814	$500	Seacoast
Ms.	Amy	Hunt	67 Apple St.	Northfield	MA	01360	$75	Pioneer Valley
Ms.	Eliza	Pope	287 Mountain Rd.	Dublin	NH	03436	$100	Monadnock

b. Save the data source as Donor Data to the drive and folder where you store your Data Files.

c. Change the region for record 2 (Bill Webster) from Seacoast to White Mountain.

d. Click OK to close the Mail Merge Recipients dialog box.

4. Add merge fields.

a. Click Next, then in the blank line above the first body paragraph, insert an Address Block merge field.

b. In the Insert Address Block dialog box, click Match Fields.

c. Click the list arrow next to Address 1 in the Match Fields dialog box, click Street, then click OK.

d. In the Insert Address Block dialog box, select the Never include the country/region in the address option button, then click OK.

e. Press [Enter] twice, insert a Greeting Line merge field using the default greeting line format, then press [Enter].

f. In the first body paragraph, replace AMOUNT with the Amount merge field.

g. In the second body paragraph, replace CITY with the City merge field and REGION with the Region merge field. (*Note*: Make sure to insert a space before or after each merge field as needed.) Save your changes to the main document.

5. Merge data.

a. Click Next to preview the merged data, then scroll through each letter, examining it carefully for errors.

b. Click the Preview Results button on the Mailings tab, make any necessary adjustments to the letter, save your changes, then click the Preview Results button to return to the preview of the document.

c. Click Next, click Edit individual letters, then merge all the records to a new file.

d. Save the merged document as Donor Thank You Merge to the drive and folder where you store your Data Files, print a copy of the last letter, shown in Figure H-18, then save and close all open files.

6. Create labels.

a. Open a new blank document, click the Start Mail Merge button on the Mailings tab, then create a label main document.

b. In the Label Options dialog box, select Avery US Letter 5160 labels, then click OK.

c. Click the Select Recipients button, then open the Donor Data.mdb file you created.

d. Save the label main document as Donor Labels Main to the drive and folder where you store your Data Files.

7. Sort and filter records.

a. Click the Edit Recipient List button, filter the records so that only the records with NH in the State field are included in the merge, sort the records in zip code order, then click OK.

b. Insert an Address Block merge field using the default settings, click the Preview Results button, then notice that the street address is missing and the address block includes the region.

c. Click the Preview Results button, then click the Match Fields button to open the Match Fields dialog box.

d. Click the list arrow next to Address 1, click Street, scroll down, click the list arrow next to Country or Region, click (not matched), then click OK.

e. Click the Preview Results button to preview the merged data, and notice that the address block now includes the street address and the region name is missing.

f. Click the Update Labels button, examine the merged data for errors, then correct any mistakes.

g. Merge all the records to an individual document, shown in Figure H-19, then save the merged file as Donor Labels NH Only Merge to the drive and folder where you store your Data Files.

h. In the first label, change Ms. Eliza Pope to your name, print the document, save and close all open Word files, then exit Word.

FIGURE H-18

New England Humanities Council
1375 Harbor Street, Portsmouth, NH 03828; Tel: 603-555-8457; www.nehumanities.org

March 4, 2010

Ms. Eliza Pope
287 Mountain Rd.
Dublin, NH 03436

Dear Ms. Pope,

We are delighted to receive your generous contribution of $100 to the New England Humanities Council (NEHC).

Whether we are helping adult new readers learn to read or bringing humanities programs into our public schools, senior centers, and prisons, NEHC depends upon private contributions to ensure that free public humanities programs continue to flourish in Dublin and throughout the Monadnock region.

Sincerely,

Your Name
Executive Director

FIGURE H-19

Ms. Eliza Pope	Mr. Bill Webster	Ms. Rita Murphy
287 Mountain Rd.	289 Sugar Hill Rd.	73 Bay Rd.
Dublin, NH 03436	Franconia, NH 03632	Durham, NH 03814
Mr. Derek Gray	Mr. John Conlin	
987 Ocean Rd.	34 Mill St.	
Portsmouth, NH 03828	Exeter, NH 03833	

▼ INDEPENDENT CHALLENGE 1

You are the director of the Eliot Arts Center (EAC). The EAC is hosting an exhibit of ceramic art in the city of Cambridge, Massachusetts, and you want to send a letter advertising the exhibit to all EAC members with a Cambridge address. You'll use Mail Merge to create the letter. If you are performing the ACE steps and are able to print envelopes on your printer, you will also use Word to print an envelope for one letter.

a. Start Word, then using either the Mailings tab or the Mail Merge task pane, create a letter main document using the file WD H-3.docx, found in the drive and folder where you store your Data Files.

b. Replace Your Name with your name in the signature block, then save the main document as EAC Member Letter Main.

c. Use the file WD H-4.mdb, found in the location where you store your Data Files, as the data source.

d. Sort the data source by last name, then filter the data so that only records with Cambridge as the city are included in the merge.

e. Insert an Address Block and a Greeting Line merge field in the main document, then preview the merged letters.

f. Merge all the records to a new document, then save it as EAC Member Letter Merge.

Advanced Challenge Exercise

■ If you can print envelopes, select the inside address in the first merge letter, then click the Envelopes button in the Create group on the Mailings tab.

■ On the Envelopes tab, verify that the Omit check box is not selected, then type your name in the Return address text box along with the address 60 Crandall Street, Concord, MA 01742.

■ Click Options. On the Envelope Options tab, make sure the Envelope size is set to Size 10, then change the font of the Delivery address and the Return address to Times New Roman.

■ On the Printing Options tab, select the appropriate Feed method for your printer, then click OK.

■ Click Add to Document, click No if a message box opens asking if you want to save the new return address as the default return address, then print the envelope.

g. Print the first merge letter, close all open Word files, saving changes, and then exit Word.

▼ INDEPENDENT CHALLENGE 2

One of your responsibilities at Green Mountain Forestry, a growing forestry services company, is to create business cards for the staff. You use mail merge to create the cards so that you can easily produce standard business cards for future employees.

a. Start Word, then use the Mailings tab or the Mail Merge task pane to create labels using the current blank document.

b. Select Microsoft Business Card 2" high x 3.5" wide labels. (*Hint*: Select the seventh instance of Business Card in the Product number list box.)

c. Create a new data source that includes the fields and records shown below:

Title	First Name	Last Name	Phone	Fax	E-mail	Hire Date
President	Sandra	Bryson	(541) 555-3982	(541) 555-6654	sbryson@gmf.com	1/12/07
Vice President	Philip	Holm	(541) 555-2323	(541) 555-4956	pholm@gmf.com	3/18/09

d. Add six more records to the data source, including one with your name as the Administrative Assistant.

e. Save the data source with the filename GMF Employee Data to the drive and folder where you store your Data Files, then sort the data by Title.

▼ INDEPENDENT CHALLENGE 2 (CONTINUED)

f. In the first table cell, create the Green Mountain
Forestry business card. Figure H-20 shows a sample
business card, but you should create your own
design. Include the company name, a street address,
and the Web site address www.gmforestry.com. Also
include First Name, Last Name, Title, Phone, Fax,
and E-mail merge fields. (*Hint*: If your design
includes a graphic, insert the graphic before inserting the merge fields. Insert each merge field individually, adjusting the spacing between merge fields as
necessary.)

FIGURE H-20

g. Format the business card with fonts, colors, and
other formatting features. (*Hint*: Make sure to select
the entire merge field, including the chevrons, before formatting.)

h. Update all the labels, preview the data, make any necessary adjustments, then merge all the records to a new document.

i. Save the merge document as **GMF Business Cards Merge** to the drive and folder where you store your Data Files,
print a copy, then close the file.

j. Save the main document as **GMF Business Cards Main** to the drive and folder where you store your Data Files,
close the file, then exit Word.

▼ INDEPENDENT CHALLENGE 3

You need to create a team roster for the children's softball team you coach. You decide to use mail merge to create the team
roster. If you are completing the ACE steps, you will also use mail merge to create mailing labels.

a. Start Word, then use the Mailings tab or the Mail Merge task pane to create a directory using the current blank document.

b. Create a new data source that includes the following fields: First Name, Last Name, Age, Position, Parent First Name,
Parent Last Name, Address, City, State, Zip Code, and Home Phone.

c. Enter the following records in the data source:

First Name	Last Name	Age	Position	Parent First Name	Parent Last Name	Address	City	State	Zip Code	Home Phone
Sophie	Wright	8	Shortstop	Kerry	Wright	58 Main St.	Camillus	NY	13031	555-2345
Will	Jacob	7	Catcher	Bob	Jacob	32 North Way	Camillus	NY	13031	555-9827
Brett	Eliot	8	First base	Olivia	Eliot	289 Sylvan Way	Marcellus	NY	13032	555-9724
Abby	Herman	7	Pitcher	Sarah	Thomas	438 Lariat St.	Marcellus	NY	13032	555-8347

d. Add five additional records to the data source using the following last names and positions:
O'Keefe, Second base
George, Third base
Goleman, Left field
Siebert, Center field
Choy, Right field
Make up the remaining information for these five records.

e. Save the data source as **Softball Team Data** to the drive and folder where you store your Data Files, then sort the
records by last name.

f. Insert a table that includes five columns and one row in the main document.

g. In the first table cell, insert the First Name and Last Name merge fields, separated by a space.

h. In the second cell, insert the Position merge field.

i. In the third cell, insert the Address and City merge fields, separated by a comma and a space.

j. In the fourth cell, insert the Home Phone merge field.

k. In the fifth cell, insert the Parent First Name and Parent Last Name merge fields, separated by a space.

l. Preview the merged data and make any necessary adjustments. (*Hint*: Only one record is displayed at a time when you preview the data.)

m. Merge all the records to a new document, then save the document as **Softball Roster Merge** to the drive and folder where you store your Data Files.

n. Press [Ctrl][Home], press [Enter], type **Wildcats Team Roster 2010** at the top of the document, press [Enter], type **Coach:** followed by your name, press [Enter], then center the two lines.

o. Insert a new row at the top of the table, then type the following column headings in the new row: **Name, Position, Address, Phone, Parent Name.**

p. Format the roster to make it attractive and readable, save your changes, print a copy, then close the file.

q. Close the main document without saving changes.

Advanced Challenge Exercise

- Open a new blank document, then use Mail Merge to create mailing labels using Avery US Letter 5162 address labels.
- Use the Softball Team Data data source you created, and sort the records first in zip code order, and then alphabetically by parent last name.
- In the first table cell, create your own address block using the Parent First Name, Parent Last Name, Address, City, State, and Zip Code merge fields. Be sure to include proper spacing and punctuation.
- Update all the labels, preview the merged data, merge all the records to a new document, then type your name centered in the document header.
- Save the document as **Softball Labels Merge ACE** to the drive and folder where you store your Data Files, print a copy, close the file, then close the main document without saving changes.

r. Exit Word.

▼ REAL LIFE INDEPENDENT CHALLENGE

Mail merge can be used not only for mailings, but to create CD/DVD labels, labels for file folders, phone directories, business cards, and many other types of documents. In this independent challenge, you design and create a data source that you can use at work or in your personal life, and then you merge the data source with a main document that you create. Your data source might include contact information for your friends and associates, inventory for your business, data on one of your collections (such as music or photos), or some other type of information.

a. Determine the content of your data source, list the fields you want to include, and then determine the logical order of the fields. Be sure to select your fields carefully so that your data source is flexible and can be merged with many types of documents. Generally it is better to include more fields, even if you don't enter data in them for each record.

b. Start Word, start a mail merge for the type of document you want to create (such as a directory or a label), then create a new data source.

c. Customize the columns in the data source to include the fields and organization you determined in step a.

d. Add at least 5 records to the data source, then save it as **Your Name Data** to the location where you store your Data Files.

e. Write and format the main document, insert the merge fields, preview the merge, make any necessary adjustments, then merge the files to a document.

f. Adjust the formatting of the merge document as necessary, add your name to the header, print a copy, save the merge document as **Your Name Merge Document**, save the main document as **Your Name Main Document**, both to the drive and folder where you store your Data Files, then close all open files and exit Word.

▼ VISUAL WORKSHOP

Using mail merge, create the postcards shown in Figure H-21. Use Avery US Letter 3263 wide postcard labels for the main document and create a data source that contains at least four records, including your name. Save the data source as Patient Data, save the merge document as Patient Appointment Card Merge, and save the main document as Patient Appointment Card Main, all to the drive and folder where you store your Data Files. (*Hints*: Notice that the postcard label main document is formatted as a table. To layout the postcard, insert a nested table with two columns and one row in the upper-left postcard; add the text, graphic, and merge field to the nested table; and then remove the outside borders on the nested table. The clip art graphic uses the keyword "tooth" and the font is Comic Sans MS.) Print a copy of the postcards.

FIGURE H-21

Sylvia T. Ramirez, D.D.S.

425 East 72nd Street, New York, NY 10021
Telephone: 212-555-0890

Mr. Francisco Cortez
874 East 86th Street
Apt. 3B
New York, NY 10028

Our records indicate it is time for your dental cleaning and exam. Please call our office now to schedule your appointment.

Sylvia T. Ramirez, D.D.S.

425 East 72nd Street, New York, NY 10021
Telephone: 212-555-0890

Mr. Thomas Parker
756 Lexington Avenue
Apt. 6C
New York, NY 10024

Our records indicate it is time for your dental cleaning and exam. Please call our office now to schedule your appointment.

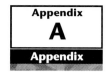

Restoring Defaults in Windows Vista and Disabling and Enabling Windows Aero

Files You Will Need:

No files needed.

Windows Vista is the most recent version of the Windows operating system. An operating system controls the way you work with your computer, supervises running programs, and provides tools for completing your computing tasks. After surveying millions of computer users, Microsoft incorporated their suggestions to make Windows Vista secure, reliable, and easy to use. In fact, Windows Vista is considered the most secure version of Windows yet. Other improvements include a powerful new search feature that lets you quickly search for files and programs from the Start menu and most windows, tools that simplify accessing the Internet, especially with a wireless connection, and multimedia programs that let you enjoy, share, and organize music, photos, and recorded TV. Finally, Windows Vista offers lots of visual appeal with its transparent, three-dimensional design in the Aero experience. This appendix explains how to make sure you are using the Windows Vista default settings for appearance, personalization, security, hardware, and sound and to enable and disable Windows Aero. For more information on Windows Aero, go to *www.microsoft.com/windowsvista/experiences/aero.mspx*.

OBJECTIVES

Restore the defaults in the Appearance and Personalization section

Restore the defaults in the Security section

Restore the defaults in the Hardware and Sound section

Disable Windows Aero

Enable Windows Aero

Restoring the Defaults in the Appearance and Personalization Section

The following instructions require a default Windows Vista Ultimate installation and the student logged in with an Administrator account. All of the following settings can be changed by accessing the Control Panel.

STEPS

- To restore the defaults in the Personalization section

    1. Click Start, and then click Control Panel. Click Appearance and Personalization, click Personalization, and then compare your screen to Figure A-1

    2. In the Personalization window, click Windows Color and Appearance, select the Default color, and then click OK

    3. In the Personalization window, click Mouse Pointers. In the Mouse Properties dialog box, on the Pointers tab, select Windows Aero (system scheme) in the Scheme drop-down list, and then click OK

    4. In the Personalization window, click Theme. Select Windows Vista from the Theme drop-down list, and then click OK

    5. In the Personalization window, click Display Settings. In the Display Settings dialog box, drag the Resolution bar to 1024 by 768 pixels, and then click OK

FIGURE A-1

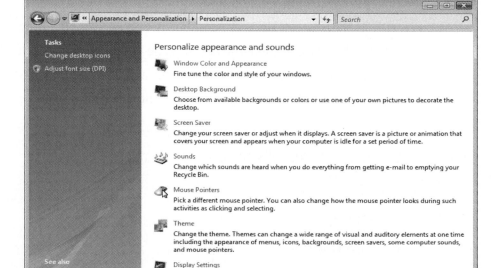

- To restore the defaults in the Taskbar and Start Menu section

  1. Click Start, and then click Control Panel. Click Appearance and Personalization, click Taskbar and Start Menu, and then compare your screen to Figure A-2

  2. In the Taskbar and Start Menu Properties dialog box, on the Taskbar tab, click to select all checkboxes except for "Auto-hide the taskbar"

  3. On the Start Menu tab, click to select the Start menu radio button and check all items in the Privacy section

  4. In the System icons section on the Notification Area tab, click to select all of the checkboxes except for "Power"

  5. On the Toolbars tab, click to select Quick Launch, none of the other items should be checked

  6. Click OK to close the Taskbar and Start Menu Properties dialog box

- To restore the defaults in the Folder Options section

  1. Click Start, and then click Control Panel. Click Appearance and Personalization, click Folder Options, and then compare your screen to Figure A-3

  2. In the Folder Options dialog box, on the General tab, click to select Show preview and filters in the Tasks section, click to select Open each folder in the same window in the Browse folders section, and click to select Double-click to open an item (single-click to select) in the Click items as follows section

  3. On the View tab, click the Reset Folders button, and then click Yes in the Folder views dialog box. Then click the Restore Defaults button

  4. On the Search tab, click the Restore Defaults button

  5. Click OK to close the Folder Options dialog box

- To restore the defaults in the Windows Sidebar Properties section

  1. Click Start, and then click Control Panel. Click Appearance and Personalization, click Windows Sidebar Properties, and then compare your screen to Figure A-4

  2. In the Windows Sidebar Properties dialog box, on the Sidebar tab, click to select Start Sidebar when Windows starts. In the Arrangement section, click to select Right, and then click to select 1 in the Display Sidebar on monitor drop-down list

  3. Click OK to close the Windows Sidebar Properties dialog box

FIGURE A-2 FIGURE A-3 FIGURE A-4

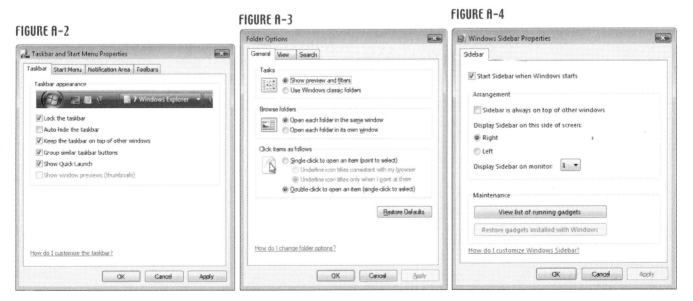

Restoring the Defaults in the Security Section

The following instructions require a default Windows Vista Ultimate installation and the student logged in with an Administrator account. All of the following settings can be changed by accessing the Control Panel.

STEPS

- To restore the defaults in the Windows Firewall section

    1. Click Start, and then click Control Panel. Click Security, click Windows Firewall, and then compare your screen to Figure A-5

    2. In the Windows Firewall dialog box, click Change settings. If the User Account Control dialog box appears, click Continue

    3. In the Windows Firewall Settings dialog box, click the Advanced tab. Click Restore Defaults, then click Yes in the Restore Defaults Confirmation dialog box

    4. Click OK to close the Windows Firewall Settings dialog box, and then close the Windows Firewall window

- To restore the defaults in the Internet Options section

    1. Click Start, and then click Control Panel. Click Security, click Internet Options, and then compare your screen to Figure A-6

    2. In the Internet Properties dialog box, on the General tab, click the Use default button. Click the Settings button in the Tabs section, and then click the Restore defaults button in the Tabbed Browsing Settings dialog box. Click OK to close the Tabbed Browsing Settings dialog box

    3. On the Security tab of the Internet Properties dialog box, click to uncheck the Enable Protected Mode checkbox, if necessary. Click the Default level button in the Security level for this zone section. If possible, click the Reset all zones to default level button

    4. On the Programs tab, click the Make default button in the Default web browser button for Internet Explorer, if possible. If Office is installed, Microsoft Office Word should be selected in the HTML editor drop-down list

    5. On the Advanced tab, click the Restore advanced settings button in the Settings section. Click the Reset button in the Reset Internet Explorer settings section, and then click Reset in the Reset Internet Explorer Settings dialog box

    6. Click Close to close the Reset Internet Explorer Settings dialog box, and then click OK to close the Internet Properties dialog box

FIGURE A-5

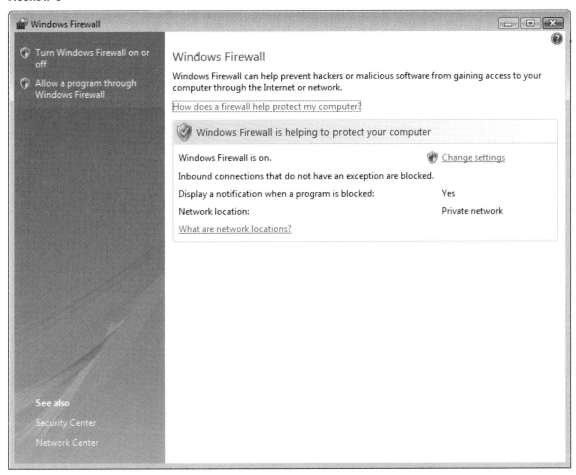

FIGURE A-6

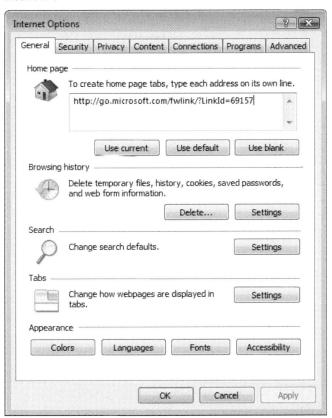

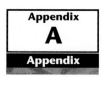

Restoring the Defaults in the Hardware and Sound Section

The following instructions require a default Windows Vista Ultimate installation and the student logged in with an Administrator account. All of the following settings can be changed by accessing the Control Panel.

STEPS

- To restore the defaults in the Autoplay section

  1. Click Start, and then click Control Panel. Click Hardware and Sound, click Autoplay, and then compare your screen to Figure A-7. Scroll down and click the Reset all defaults button in the Devices section at the bottom of the window, and then click Save

- To restore the defaults in the Sound section

  1. Click Start, and then click Control Panel. Click Hardware and Sound, click Sound, and then compare your screen to Figure A-8

  2. In the Sound dialog box, on the Sounds tab, select Windows Default from the Sound Scheme drop-down list, and then click OK

- To restore the defaults in the Mouse section

  1. Click Start, and then click Control Panel. Click Hardware and Sound, click Mouse, and then compare your screen to Figure A-9

  2. In the Mouse Properties dialog box, on the Pointers tab, select Windows Aero (system scheme) from the Scheme drop-down list

  3. Click OK to close the Mouse Properties dialog box

FIGURE A-7

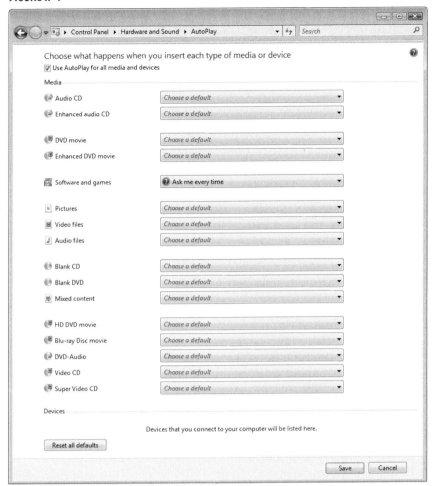

FIGURE A-8

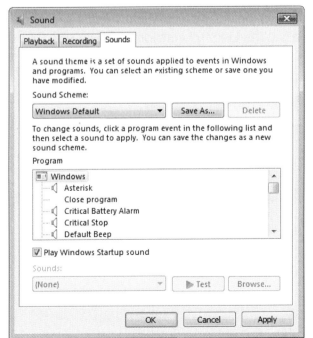

FIGURE A-9

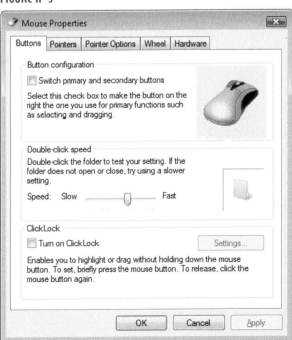

Disabling and Enabling Windows Aero

Unlike prior versions of Windows, Windows Vista provides two distinct user interface experiences: a "basic" experience for entry-level systems and more visually dynamic experience called Windows Aero. Both offer a new and intuitive navigation experience that helps you more easily find and organize your applications and files, but Aero goes further by delivering a truly next-generation desktop experience.

Windows Aero builds on the basic Windows Vista user experience and offers Microsoft's best-designed, highest-performing desktop experience. Using Aero requires a PC with compatible graphics adapter and running a Premium or Business edition of Windows Vista.

The following instructions require a computer capable of running Windows Aero, with a default Windows Vista Ultimate installation and student logged in with an Administrator account.

STEPS

- **To Disable Windows Aero**

We recommend that students using this book disable Windows Aero and restore their operating systems default settings (instructions to follow).

1. **Right-click the desktop, select** Personalize, **and then compare your screen in Figure A-10. Select** Window Color and Appearance, **and then select** Open classic appeareance properties for more color options. **In Appearance Settings dialog box, on the Appearance tab, select any non-Aero scheme (such as** Windows Vista Basic **or** Windows Vista Standard**) in the Color Scheme list, and then click OK. Figure A-11 compares Windows Aero to other color schemes. Note that this book uses Windows Vista Basic as the color scheme**

- **To Enable Windows Aero**

1. **Right-click the desktop, and then select** Personalize. **Select** Window Color and Appearance, **then select** Windows Aero **in the Color scheme list, and then click OK in the Appearance Settings dialog box**

FIGURE A-10

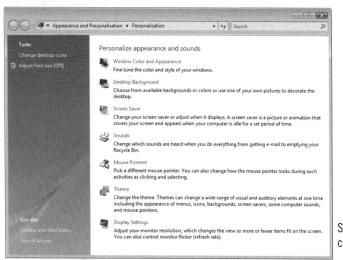

Select other
color schemes

FIGURE A-11

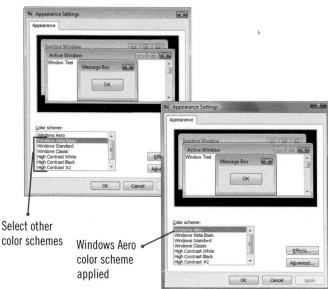

Windows Aero
color scheme
applied

Glossary

Active The state of being of the document or program currently in use so that any action performed is performed on that document; on the taskbar, the button of the active document is darker than the buttons of other open documents.

Adjustment handle The yellow diamond that appears when certain shapes are selected; used to change the shape, but not the size, of a shape.

Alignment The position of text in a document relative to the margins.

Anchored The state of a floating graphic that moves with a paragraph or other item if the item is moved; an anchor symbol appears next to the paragraph or item when the floating graphic is selected and formatting marks are displayed.

Ascending order Lists data alphabetically or sequentially (from A to Z, 0 to 9, or earliest to latest).

AutoComplete A feature that automatically suggests text to insert.

AutoCorrect A feature that automatically detects and corrects typing errors, minor spelling errors, and capitalization, and inserts certain typographical symbols as you type.

Automatic page break A page break that is inserted automatically at the bottom of a page.

AutoText A feature that stores frequently used text and graphics so they can be easily inserted into a document.

Backward-compatible A software feature that enables documents saved in an older version of a program to be opened in a newer version of the program.

Bibliography A list of sources that you consulted or cited while creating a document.

Bitmap graphic A graphic that is composed of a series of small dots called "pixels" and often saved with a .bmp, .png, .jpg, .tif, or .gif file extension.

Blog An informal journal that is created by an individual or a group and available to the public on the Internet; short for weblog.

Blogger The person who creates and maintains a blog.

Boilerplate text Text that appears in every version of a merged document.

Bold Formatting applied to text to make it thicker and darker.

Border A line that can be added above, below, or to the sides of a paragraph, text, or table cell; a line that divides the columns and rows of a table.

Brightness The relative lightness of a photograph.

Building block A reusable piece of formatted content or document part that is stored in a gallery.

Bullet A small graphic symbol used to identify an item in a list.

Cell The box formed by the intersection of a table row and table column.

Cell reference A code that identifies a cell's position in a table. Each cell reference contains a letter (A, B, C, and so on) to identify its column and a number (1, 2, 3, and so on) to identify its row.

Center Alignment in which an item is centered between the margins.

Character spacing Formatting that changes the width or scale of characters, expands or condenses the amount of space between characters, raises or lowers characters relative to the line of text, and adjusts kerning (the space between standard combinations of letters).

Chart A visual representation of numerical data, usually used to illustrate trends, patterns, or relationships.

Click and Type A feature that allows you to automatically apply the necessary paragraph formatting to a table, graphic, or text when you insert the item in a blank area of a document in Print Layout or Web Layout view.

Click and type pointer A pointer used to move the insertion point and automatically apply the paragraph formatting necessary to insert text at that location in the document.

Clip A media file, such as a graphic, photograph, sound, movie, or animation, that can be inserted into a document.

Clip art A collection of graphic images that can be inserted into documents, presentations, Web pages, spreadsheets, and other Office files.

Clip Organizer A library of the clips that come with Word.

Clipboard A temporary storage area for items that are cut or copied from any Office file and are available for pasting. *See also* Office Clipboard and System Clipboard.

Column break A break that forces text following the break to begin at the top of the next column.

Compatible The capability of different programs to work together and exchange data.

Content control An interactive object that is embedded in a document and that expedites your ability to customize the document with your own information.

Contextual tab Tab on the Ribbon that appears when needed to complete a specific task; for example, if you select a chart object in a document, three contextual Chart Tool tabs (Design, Layout, and Format) appear.

Contrast The difference in brightness between the darkest and the lightest areas of a photograph.

Copy To place a copy of an item on the Clipboard without removing it from a document.

Crop To trim away part of a graphic.

Cut To remove an item from a document and place it on the Clipboard.

Cut and paste To move text or graphics using the Cut and Paste commands.

Data field A category of information, such as last name, first name, street address, city, or postal code.

Data record A complete set of related information for a person or an item, such as a person's contact information, including name, address, phone number, e-mail address, and so on.

Data source In a mail merge, the file with the unique data for individual people or items.

Delete To permanently remove an item from a document.

Descending order Lists data in reverse alphabetical or sequential order (from Z to A, 9 to 0, or latest to earliest).

Dialog box launcher An icon available in many groups on the Ribbon that you can click to open a dialog box or task pane related to the current group.

Document The electronic file you create using Word.

Document properties Details about a file, such as author name or the date the file was created, that are used to describe, organize, and search for files.

Document window The workspace in the program window that displays the current document.

Draft view A view that shows a document without margins, headers and footers, or graphics.

Drag and drop To move text or a graphic by dragging it to a new location using the mouse.

Drawing canvas A workspace for creating graphics.

Drawing gridlines A grid of nonprinting lines that appears within the margins in Print Layout view to help you size, align, and position graphics.

Drop cap A large dropped initial capital letter that is often used to set off the first paragraph of an article.

Endnote Text that provides additional information or acknowledges sources for text in a document and that appears at the end of a document.

Field A code that serves as a placeholder for data that changes in a document, such as a page number.

Field name The name of a data field.

File An electronic collection of stored data that has a unique name, distinguishing it from other files.

Filename The name given to a document when it is saved.

Filter In a mail merge, to pull out records that meet specific criteria and include only those records in the merge.

First line indent A type of indent in which the first line of a paragraph is indented more than the subsequent lines.

Floating graphic A graphic to which a text wrapping style has been applied, making the graphic independent of text and able to be moved anywhere on a page.

Font The typeface or design of a set of characters (letters, numbers, symbols, and punctuation marks).

Font effect Font formatting that applies a special effect to text, such as a shadow, an outline, small caps, or superscript.

Font size The size of characters, measured in points (pts).

Footer Information, such as text, a page number, or a graphic, that appears at the bottom of every page in a document or a section.

Footnote Text that provides additional information or acknowledges sources for text in a document and that appears at the bottom of the page on which the note reference mark appears.

Format Painter A feature used to copy the format settings applied to the selected text to other text you want to format the same way.

Formatting marks Nonprinting characters that appear on screen to indicate the ends of paragraphs, tabs, and other formatting elements.

Full Screen Reading view A view that shows only the document text on screen, making it easier to read and annotate.

Gallery A location where styles, themes, or building blocks, such as headers, footers, and text boxes, are stored.

Gridlines Nonprinting blue dotted lines that show the boundaries of table cells.

Group A collection of related commands on a tab on the Ribbon.

Gutter Extra space left for a binding at the top, left, or inside margin of a document.

Hanging indent A type of indent in which the second and subsequent lines of a paragraph are indented more than the first.

Hard page break *See* Manual page break.

Header Information, such as text, a page number, or a graphic, that appears at the top of every page in a document or a section.

Header row The first row of a table that usually contains the column headings.

Highlighting Transparent color that can be applied to text to call attention to it.

Horizontal ruler A ruler that appears at the top of the document window in Print Layout, Draft, and Web Layout view.

Horizontal scroll bar *See* Scroll bar.

Hyperlink Text or a graphic that opens a file, Web page, or other item when clicked. Also known as a link.

I-beam pointer The pointer used to move the insertion point and select text.

Indent The space between the edge of a line of text or a paragraph and the margin.

Indent marker A marker on the horizontal ruler that shows the indent settings for the active paragraph.

Inline graphic A graphic that is part of a line of text.

Insertion point The blinking vertical line that shows where text will appear when you type in a document.

Integrate To incorporate a file or part of a file created in one program into a file created in another program; for example, to insert an Excel chart into a PowerPoint slide or an Access table into a Word document.

Interface *See* User Interface.

Italic Formatting applied to text to make the characters slant to the right.

Justify Alignment in which an item is flush with both the left and right margins.

Keyboard shortcut A combination of keys or a function key that can be pressed to perform a command.

Landscape orientation Page orientation in which the page is wider than it is tall.

Launch To open or start a program on a computer.

Left-align Alignment in which the item is flush with the left margin.

Left indent A type of indent in which the left edge of a paragraph is moved in from the left margin.

Line spacing The amount of space between lines of text.

Link A connection between two or more text boxes so that the text flows automatically from one text box to another. *See also* Hyperlink.

Live Preview A feature that lets you point to a choice in a gallery or palette and preview the choice applied to the document without actually applying the choice.

Mail merge To merge a main document that contains standard text with a file that contains customized information for many individual items to create customized versions of the main document.

Main document In a mail merge, the document with the standard text.

Manual page break A page break inserted to force the text following the break to begin at the top of the next page.

Margin The blank area between the edge of the text and the edge of a page.

Merge To combine adjacent cells into a single larger cell. *See also* mail merge.

Merge field A placeholder that you insert in the main document to indicate where the data from each record should be inserted when you perform a mail merge.

Microsoft Office Word Help button A button used to access the Word Help system.

Mini toolbar A toolbar that appears faintly above text when you first select it and includes the most commonly used text and paragraph formatting commands.

Mirror margins Margins used in documents with facing pages, where the inside and outside margins are mirror images of each other.

Multilevel list A list with a hierarchical structure; an outline.

Negative indent A type of indent in which the left edge of a paragraph is moved to the left of the left margin.

Nested table A table inserted in a cell of another table.

Nudge To move a graphic a small amount in one direction using the arrow keys.

Office button An element of the Word program window that provides access to commands for creating, opening, saving, printing, and sharing documents, and to options for personalizing Word.

Office Clipboard A temporary storage area shared by all Office programs that can be used to cut, copy, and paste multiple items within and between Office programs. The Office Clipboard can hold up to 24 items collected from any Office program. *See also* Clipboard and System Clipboard.

Online collaboration The ability to incorporate feedback or share information across the Internet or an intranet.

Open To use one of the methods for opening a document to retrieve it and display it in the document window.

Orphan The first line of a paragraph when it appears alone at the bottom of a page.

Outdent *See* Negative indent.

Outline view A view that shows the headings of a document organized as an outline.

Paragraph spacing The amount of space between paragraphs.

Paste To insert items stored on the Clipboard into a document.

Point (pt) The unit of measurement for text characters and the space between paragraphs and characters; 1/72 of an inch.

Portrait orientation Page orientation in which the page is taller than it is wide.

Preview *See* Print Preview.

Print Layout view A view that shows a document as it will look on a printed page.

Print Preview A view of a file as it will appear when printed.

Program tab A single tab on the Ribbon specific to a particular view, such as Print Preview.

Property control A control that contains document property information or a placeholder, and that can be used to assign or update the document property directly from the document.

Pull quote A text box that contains a quote or excerpt from an article, formatted in a larger font size and placed on the same page.

Quick Access toolbar A customizable toolbar that contains buttons you can click to perform frequently used commands.

Quick Part A reusable piece of content that can be inserted into a document, including a field, document property, or a preformatted building block.

Quick Style set A group of related styles that share common fonts, colors, and formats, and that can be used together in a document to give it a polished look.

Ribbon An area that displays Word commands, organized into tabs and groups.

Right-align Alignment in which an item is flush with the right margin.

Right indent A type of indent in which the right edge of a paragraph is moved in from the right margin.

Rotate handle A green circle that appears above a graphic when the graphic is selected; drag the rotate handle to rotate the graphic.

Sans serif font A font (such as Calibri) whose characters do not include serifs, which are small strokes at the ends of letters.

Save To store a file permanently on a disk or to overwrite the copy of a file that is stored on a disk with the changes made to the file.

Save As A command used to save a file for the first time or to create a new file with a different filename, leaving the original file intact.

Scale To resize a graphic so that its height to width ratio remains the same.

Screen capture A snapshot of your screen, as if you took a picture of it with a camera, which you can paste into a document.

Scroll To use the scroll bars or the arrow keys to display different parts of a document in the document window.

Scroll arrow The arrow at the end of a scroll bar that is clicked either to scroll a document one line at a time or to scroll a document left and right in the document window.

Scroll bar The bar on the right edge (vertical scroll bar) or bottom edge (horizontal scroll bar) of the document window that is used to display different parts of the document in the document window.

Scroll box The box in a scroll bar that can be dragged to scroll a document.

Section A portion of a document that is separated from the rest of the document by section breaks.

Section break A formatting mark that divides a document into sections.

Select To click or highlight an item in order to perform some action on it.

Serif font A font (such as Times New Roman) whose characters include serifs, which are small strokes at the ends of letters.

Shading A background color or pattern that can be applied to text, tables, or graphics.

Shape A drawing object, such as a rectangle, oval, triangle, line, block arrow, or other shape that you create using the Shapes command.

Shortcut key *See* Keyboard shortcut.

Sidebar A text box that is positioned adjacent to the body of a document and contains auxiliary information.

Sizing handles The white circles that appear around a graphic when it is selected; used to change the size or shape of a graphic.

SmartArt A diagram, list, organizational chart, or other graphic created using the SmartArt command.

Soft page break *See* Automatic page break.

Sort To organize data, such as table rows, items in a list, or records in a mail merge, in ascending or descending order.

Split To divide a cell into two or more cells.

Status bar The bar at the bottom of the Word program window that shows information about the document, including the current page number, the total number of pages in a document, the document word count, and the on/off status of spelling and grammar checking; also contains the view buttons, the Zoom level button, and the Zoom slider.

Style A named collection of character and/or paragraph formats that are stored together and can be applied to text to format it quickly.

Subscript A font effect in which text is formatted in a smaller font size and placed below the line of text.

Suite A group of programs that are bundled together and share a similar interface, making it easy to transfer skills and program content among them.

Superscript A font effect in which text is formatted in a smaller font size and placed above the line of text.

Symbol A special character that can be inserted into a document using the Symbol command.

System Clipboard A clipboard that stores only the last item cut or copied from a document. *See also* Clipboard and Office Clipboard.

Tab A part of the Ribbon that includes groups of buttons for related commands. *See also* Tab stop.

Tab leader A line that appears in front of tabbed text.

Tab stop A location on the horizontal ruler that indicates where to align text.

Table A grid made up of rows and columns of cells that you can fill with text and graphics.

Table style A named set of table format settings that can be applied to a table to format it all at once.

Template A formatted document that contains placeholder text you can replace with your own text.

Text box A container that you can fill with text and graphics.

Theme A set of unified design elements, including theme colors, theme fonts for body text and headings, and theme effects for graphics that can be applied to a document all at once.

Title bar The bar at the top of the program window that indicates the program name and the name of the current file.

Toggle button A button that turns a feature on and off.

User interface A collective term for all the ways you interact with a software program.

Vertical alignment The position of text in a document relative to the top and bottom margins.

Vertical ruler A ruler that appears on the left side of the document window in Print Layout view.

Vertical scroll bar *See* Scroll bar.

View A way of displaying a document in the document window; each view provides features useful for editing and formatting different types of documents.

View buttons Buttons on the status bar that are used to change document views.

Web Layout view A view that shows a document as it will look when viewed with a Web browser.

Widow The last line of a paragraph when it is carried over to the top of the following page, separate from the rest of the paragraph.

WordArt A drawing object that contains text formatted with special shapes, patterns, and orientations.

Word processing program A software program that includes tools for entering, editing, and formatting text and graphics.

Word program window The window that contains the Word program elements, including the document window, Quick Access toolbar, Ribbon, and status bar.

Word-wrap A feature that automatically moves the insertion point to the next line as you type.

XML Acronym that stands for eXtensible Markup Language, which is a language used to structure, store, and send information.

XML format The Word 2007 file format.

Zoom level button A button on the status bar that is used to change the zoom level of the document in the document window.

Zoom slider An adjustment on the status bar that is used to enlarge or decrease the display size of the document in the document window.

Zoom in To enlarge the display size of a document in the document window so that less of the document shows on screen.

Zoom out To reduce the display size of a document in the document window so that more of the document shows on screen.

Index

viewing, WD 16, WD 17
viewing and modifying properties, WD 41
Document Information panel, WD 41
document properties, updating, WD 162
Document Recovery task pane, OFF 15
document window
program windows, OFF 6, OFF 7
splitting, WD 28
Word program window, WD 4, WD 5
.docx file extension, OFF 8, WD 8
dot symbol (·), WD 10
Draft view, WD 17
drag and drop operation, WD 26
dragging
moving graphics, WD 134, WD 135
resizing graphics, WD 132, WD 133
Draw Table command, WD 106
drawing
shapes, WD 140–141
tables, WD 121
text boxes, WD 136
drawing canvas, WD 141
drop cap(s), WD 51
Drop Cap dialog box, WD 51

▶**E**
Edit Data Source dialog box, WD 184, WD 185
Edit Recipients List command, WD 189
editing
building block content, WD 168
building blocks, WD 167
chart data, WD 142
data source records, WD 184–185
documents. *See* editing documents
footers, WD 90, WD 91
headers, WD 90, WD 91
editing documents, WD 25–41
copying and pasting text, WD 28–29
cutting and pasting text, WD 26–27
finding and replacing text, WD 32–33
hyperlinks, WD 38–39
Office Clipboard, WD 30–31
preparing documents for distribution, WD 40–41
researching information, WD 36–37
Spelling and Grammar checker, WD 34–35
ellipsis, OFF 10
e-mailing documents directly from Word, WD 39
Encrypt Document option, Prepare command, WD 40
endnotes, WD 66, WD 67
envelope(s), printing, WD 191
envelope mail merges, WD 190
Envelopes and labels dialog box, WD 191
Envelopes command, WD 189
error correction. *See* correcting errors
Excel, OFF 2, OFF 3
Excel Spreadsheet command, WD 106
exiting programs, OFF 4, OFF 5

▶**F**
F4 key, repeating actions, WD 54
faxing documents directly from Word, WD 39
fields
data, data sources, WD 178
matching, mail merge, WD 186
matching in mail merge, WD 186
merge. *See* merge fields
page number, WD 86, WD 87
file(s)
creating, OFF 8, OFF 9

opening, OFF 10, OFF 11
recovering, OFF 15
saving, OFF 8, OFF 9, OFF 10, OFF 11
file extensions
Office programs, OFF 8
Word documents, OFF 8
filename(s), WD 8, WD 9
data sources, WD 178
Office programs, OFF 8
filtering records in data source, WD 192, WD 193
Find and Replace dialog box, WD 32, WD 33
Find recipient command, WD 189
finding and replacing text, WD 32–33
finding synonyms, WD 36–37
Finish & Merge command, WD 189
first line indent, WD 60
First Line Indent marker, WD 60, WD 61
floating graphics, WD 130, WD 131, WD 134
font(s), WD 50–51
color, WD 50, WD 51
limiting number in document, WD 50
Quick Style sets, WD 154
sans serif, WD 50
serif, WD 50
Font dialog box, WD 52, WD 53
font size, WD 12, WD 13, WD 50
Fonts list, WD 50, WD 51
footers
adding, WD 88, WD 89
custom, adding to gallery, WD 89
deleting, WD 90
editing, WD 90, WD 91
positioning, WD 88
footnotes, WD 66, WD 67
converting to endnotes, WD 66
format, dates, WD 88
Format Painter, WD 52–53
Format Picture dialog box, WD 131
formatting
chart elements, WD 142
columns, WD 84–85
custom formats for tables, WD 120–121
documents. *See* formatting documents
text. *See* formatting text
formatting documents, WD 77–95
AutoText, WD 91
columns, WD 84–85
dividing documents into sections, WD 80–81
footers, WD 88–91
headers, WD 88–91
inserting clip art, WD 94–95
inserting tables, WD 92–93
margins, WD 78–79
page breaks, WD 82–83
page numbering, WD 86–87
text. *See* formatting text
formatting marks, WD 10
formatting text, WD 49–67
aligning paragraphs, WD 56–57
bibliographies, WD 67
borders, WD 64, WD 65
bullets, WD 62, WD 63
clearing formatting, WD 61
copying formats using Format Painter, WD 52–53
endnotes, WD 66, WD 67
fonts, WD 50–51
footnotes, WD 66, WD 67
indents, WD 60–61
line spacing, WD 54, WD 55
Mini toolbar, WD 12–13

numbering, WD 62, WD 63
paragraph spacing, WD 54, WD 55
Quick Styles, WD 55
shading, WD 64, WD 65
tabs, WD 58–59
themes, WD 57
formulas in tables, WD 116, WD 117
Full Screen reading view, WD 17

▶**G**
Go To command, WD 32
grammar errors, correcting, WD 34–35
graphics, WD 129–145
bitmap, WD 130
brightness, WD 131
changing proportions, WD 132
changing shape, WD 135
charts, WD 142–143
clip art, WD 94–95
color, WD 131
contrast, WD 131
cropping, WD 94, WD 132
drawing shapes, WD 140–141
floating, WD 130, WD 131, WD 134
inline, WD 130, WD 131
inserting, WD 130–131
page layout, WD 144–145
positioning, WD 130, WD 134–135
rotating, WD 140, WD 141
scaling, WD 132, WD 133
shadows, WD 139
shifting order of layers in stack, WD 140
sizing, WD 132, WD 133
SmartArt, WD 143
text boxes, WD 136–137
3-D effects, WD 139
visual effects, WD 135
WordArt, WD 138–139
Greeting Line command, WD 189
gridline(s), tables, WD 119, WD 162
groups
commands, OFF 6
Word program window, WD 4, WD 5
gutter, WD 79

▶**H**
hand pointer, WD 5
hanging indent, WD 60
Hanging Indent marker, WD 60, WD 61
hard page breaks, WD 82, WD 83
header(s)
adding, WD 88, WD 89
custom, adding to Header gallery, WD 89
dates, WD 88
deleting, WD 90
editing, WD 90, WD 91
positioning, WD 88
Header gallery, WD 89
header row, repeating on every page of table, WD 112
Help system, OFF 14–15
hide white space pointer, WD 5
Highlight Merge Fields command, WD 189
highlighting
all instances of specific text, WD 32
text in documents, WD 65
horizontal ruler, Word program window, WD 4, WD 5
horizontal scroll bar, Word program window, WD 4, WD 5